Assessment of Couples and Families

THE FAMILY THERAPY AND COUNSELING SERIES

Consulting Editor

Jon Carlson, Psy.D., Ed.D.

Assessment of Couples and Families

Contemporary and Cutting-Edge Strategies

Edited By

LEN SPERRY

Brunner-Routledge
New York and Hove

2004

Cover image: ©Racioppa/Getty Images
Cover design: Elise Weinger

Published in 2004 by
Brunner-Routledge
270 Madison Avenue
New York, NY 10016
www.brunner-routledge.com

Published in Great Britain by
Brunner-Routledge
27 Church Road
Hove, East Sussex
BN3 2FA
www.brunner-routledge.com

Library of Congress Cataloging-in-Publication Data

Assessment of Couples and Families: Contemporary and Cutting-Edge
strategies / Len Sperry, Editor.
   p. cm.
ISBN 0–415–94657–3 (hardcover)
1. Family assessment. 2. Marital Psychotherapy. 3. Family Psychotherapy.
4. Couples-Psychology.
[DNLM: 1.Couples Therapy–methods. 2. Family Relations. 3. Family Therapy–methods. 4. Models, Psychological. 5. Spouses–psychology. WM 430.5.M3
A846 2004] I. Sperry, Len. II. Title. III. Series.
   RC488.53.A875 2004
   616.89'156—dc22

                                                            2003027250

THIS BOOK IS DEDICATED TO THE MEMORY OF THE LATE KENNETH I. HOWARD, PH.D., A CHERISHED MENTOR, COLLEAGUE, AND FRIEND TO ME, AND A MAJOR FIGURE IN THE FIELD OF PSYCHOLOGICAL MEASUREMENT, EVALUATION, AND OUTCOMES RESEARCH.

Contents

Contributors

Editor

Len Sperry, M.D., Ph.D. Professor of mental health counseling at Florida Atlantic University and clinical professor of psychiatry and behavioral medicine at the Medical College of Wisconsin; he is coauthor of *The Disordered Couple; The Intimate Couple; Marital Therapy: Integrating Theory and Technique; Family Therapy: Ensuring Treatment Efficacy, Brief Therapy With Individuals and Couples;* and the forthcoming, *Family Therapy Techniques: Integrating and Tailoring Treatment.* He has also edited *Integrative and Biopsychosocial Therapy: Maximizing Treatment Outcomes With Individuals and Couples.* Dr. Sperry serves on several editorial boards, including *The Family Journal* and the *American Journal of Family Therapy.*

Chapter Authors

Dennis A. Bagarozzi, Ph.D. President of Human Resources Consultants. He is the author of *Enhancing Intimacy in Marriage: A Clinician's Guide* and editor of the Family Measurement Techniques section of the *American Journal of Family Therapy.*

W. Robert Beavers, M.D. Director of the Family Studies Center in Dallas and clinical professor of psychiatry at the University of Texas Southwestern Medical School; his approach to family assessment is described in *Successful Families: Assessment and Intervention.*

James H. Bray, Ph.D. Associate professor of family and community medicine and director of the Family Counseling Clinic at Baylor College of Medicine; he has published in the areas of divorce, remarriage, and family assessment.

Ronald J. Chenail, Ph.D. Professor of family therapy at Nova Southeastern University in Ft. Lauderdale, Florida; he serves on the editorial boards of *the Journal of Systemic Therapies, Qualitative Research in Psychology,* and is the editor-elect of *the Journal of Marital and Family Therapy.*

Lisa Connelly, M.A. Clinical research coordinator at the Mayerson Center for Safe and Healthy Children and The Childhood Trust at Cincinnati Children's Hospital Medical Center; she is also project coordinator for the Trauma Treatment Replication Center.

Maureen Duffy, Ph.D. Associate professor and chairperson of the counseling program at Barry University in Miami Shores, Florida; her areas of clinical and research interest are qualitative approaches and neuroscience application in systemic family therapy.

M. Sylvia Fernandez, Ph.D. Associate professor of counseling at Barry University in Miami Shores, Florida; she is a licensed professional counselor, national certified counselor, an approved clinical supervisor, and a national certified school counselor.

William N. Friedrich, Ph.D., ABPP Professor and consultant in the Department of Psychiatry and Psychology at the Mayo Clinic, Rochester, Minnesota, and a diplomate in clinical and family psychology; he has published widely on the assessment and treatment of child abuse.

Robert B. Hampson, Ph.D. Associate professor of psychology at Southern Methodist University and research coordinator of the Family Studies Center in Dallas, Texas; with Robert Beavers, he is the coauthor of *Successful Families: Assessment and Intervention.*

Luciano L'Abate, Ph.D. Professor emeritus of psychology, Georgia State University and president, Workbooks for Better Living; he is the editor of *Family Psychology and Therapy,* vols. I and II, and author of *Family Evaluation.*

A. Rodney Nurse, Ph.D., ABPP Director of family psychological services, Boyer Foundation, and codirector of Collaborative Divorce Associates; he is the author of *Family Assessment: Effective Use of Personality Tests with Couples and Families.*

Erna Olafson, Ph.D., Psy.D. Associate professor of clinical psychiatry and pediatrics at Cincinnati Children's Hospital Medical Center and the University of Cincinnati School of Medicine; she has published widely on assessment and treatment of child abuse.

Sloane E. Veshinski, M.S. Instructor and the director of the Barry Family Enrichment Center at Barry University, where she is currently a doctoral student; she is a licensed marriage and family therapist and certified addictions professional.

Lynelle C. Yingling, Ph.D., LMFT President of J&L Human Systems Development and coauthor of *GARF Assessment Sourcebook: Using the DSM-IV Global Assessment of Relational Functioning.*

Series Foreword

For one who is free from views

There are no trees,

For one who is delivered by understanding

There are no follies,

But those who grasp after views and philosophical opinions,

They wander around the world annoying people.

Sutta Nipata

Whether it is mental or physical, accountability is mandated in today's world of health care. We once *practiced* therapy. As therapy has evolved, we no longer can practice but must instead *perform* at acceptable professional levels. We can no longer do something because we feel that it is the right thing to do. We are held accountable by our clients, professional licensing boards, insurance companies, and even the legal system.

I am frequently asked to provide objective data about the effectiveness of my clinical practice. I once used statements like "they returned for treatment"; "paid their bill"; "referred others"; "didn't divorce"; or "seemed happy." This no longer works.

This helpful book shows how to create assessment-based couple and family therapy. Readers are provided with the strategies and inventories needed to document their work; specifically, the assessment strategies focus on child custody; child abuse and family violence; divorce; couple conflict; and intimacy. The 100+ assessment devices can be easily compared by reviewing the matrix provided at the end of chapter 3 through chapter 10. This book can quickly assist the practitioner in assessing and documenting family factors and dynamics.

I thank Len Sperry and his collaborators for providing information that most of us did not have available in our professional training.

Jon Carlson
Lake Geneva, Wisconsin

REFERENCE

Nipata, S. (1924). *Sacred Books of the East, Vol. 10*. E. Max Miller, (Ed.), London: Oxford University Press.

Foreword

by Jay Lebow

The field of couple and family therapy began with two broad foci: building a systemic theory applicable to families and creating innovative family-centered methods of intervention. This earliest era in family therapy was a time of "big" ideas (e.g., epistemology, systems theory, and cybernetics) that challenged the prevailing individual-centered paradigm. In this context, the systemic paradigm was presented as *the* explanation for all psychopathology (for that matter, for most human behavior) and family intervention was seen as the antidote for all human problems.

Although the positive impact of the systemic revolution cannot be overstated (it changed the fundamental way most mental health professionals view the social context in relation to individual behavior), it is striking that this early work in family systems theory and family intervention occurred without development of a technology for measuring couple or family process. Without such a technology, those interested in understanding the processes within couples and families were left to rely completely on their own observational skills and those of their colleagues when they needed data testing their hypotheses. Given this, it is not surprising that, despite the considerable time and energy devoted to efforts to observe families in that era, family process remained very much in the eye of the beholder, subject to the idiosyncrasies of individual observation and construction. Many alternative strong arguments emerged about how these "data" from families provided evidence in support of various theoretical vantage points about what was essential to "healthy" family process, leading to widely disparate viewpoints about what was crucial in the lives of these families. Using these "data," proponents of each approach could look at families through their particular lens and present convincing arguments for the accuracy of their particular vantage points.

The hindsight of history indicates that this state of affairs allowed the emergence and development of many vital core insights, such as the importance of the social system on individual functioning and of circular arcs of causality, but also led to the promulgation and wide dissemination of several regrettable errors, such as claims that double binds by mothers caused schizophrenia and the vision of a mutually shared co-creation of family violence. For all of the dramatic and important insights of the first generation of family therapists, the emergence of a true science of family relationships required development of a body of methods for assessing couples and families.

Such instruments number among the core elements for building a science as well as methods of clinical practice. Science fully depends on instrumentation; without measures, we are left without the means to operationalize key independent and dependent variables in research and thus to test hypotheses. This leaves the field mired in the prescientific state of early family therapy. Clinical practice is no less limited in the absence of instrumentation and remains deficient in methods of assessment to enable case formulation and to track treatment progress.

Unfortunately, the technology of instrumentation evolves slowly. Instruments not only need to be developed in relation to the core constructs within a domain, but also need to be shown to be reliable; to be tested for their content and construct validity; to establish norms on a large enough and sufficiently diverse sample; and to be marketed in a form that allows for dissemination. A good instrument often takes years to develop; some of the best instruments described in this volume have evolved over decades. Furthermore, the technology of instrumentation requires a diversity of instruments. Self-report measures and those completed by raters serve different purposes and typically show less than perfect convergence, so both types of measures are needed. There also are needs for brief measures and longer ones to serve different purposes; measures of general couple and family functioning; measures targeted to more specific aspects of family life (e.g., domestic violence); and measures that easily translate into scale scores. Other measures that provide a wider range of qualitative information in the way of open ended responses are also needed.

Assessment of Couples and Families: Contemporary and Cutting-Edge Strategies marks the progress made in instrumentation to assess couples and families and also delineates that progress. Its publication heralds the emergence of a body of validated measures that are now available for use in assessing couples and families. Bringing together a number of experts in specific kinds of instrumentation, this volume covers the breadth of methods for assessing couples and families. A number of chapters cover measures specifically constructed for assessing couples and families; others provide a guide to the applicability of measures developed to assessing individual functioning in children and adults in the context of looking at couple and family functioning. Each chapter provides considerable depth within the specific domain covered. The succinct format for descriptions of the measures makes access to and comparison of their most salient properties easy and very reader friendly.

The large number of sophisticated and well-constructed measures described in this volume speaks to the advance of measurement assessing couples and families. This advance runs parallel to and merges with the greater sophistication of the newest generation of couple and family therapies and of the most recent research on couple and family process. The measures surveyed in this volume now can serve admirably to anchor research focused on couples and families and in the clinical assessment and in the tracking of progress in treatment. These measures can also be used as the foundation for sophisticated assessment that can provide the basis for developing relational diagnoses of the future.

This important book will surely become a core resource for students, practicing clinicians, and family researchers. However, as indicated in the concluding chapter, instrumentation in couple and family therapy remains a work in progress. *Assessment of Couples and Families: Contemporary and Cutting-Edge Strategies* marks the state of the art in the continuously evolving field of instrumentation for assessing couples and families.

Jay Lebow, Ph,D., ABPP
The Family Institute at Northwestern University
Evanston, Illinois

Preface

Assessment of couples and families today is quite different than it was 10 years ago. Then, traditional assessment tended to be informal and theory driven. Today, contemporary assessment is likely to be more formal and accountability driven. Not surprisingly, couples and family therapy is facing the same pressures of cost-effectiveness and outcomes-oriented accountability as individual therapy is.

Of the various reasons for this change, not the least is the tumultuous changes in health care, including managed care. In addition to financial and accountability demands, there have been major social changes in the family and scientific advances and research developments that affect the assessment process, resulting in demand for more cutting-edge assessment strategies. One indication of how social changes have affected couple and family assessment is that in the past, assessment tended to focus largely on premarital and marital issues; however, formal assessment now focuses on—and is even court ordered for—child custody and family violence issues. Finally, recent research has led to development of cutting-edge strategies that have considerable clinical value and utility for those who practice couples and family therapy as well as for those who are training to practice this type of therapy.

This book briefly reviews the impact of various changes and research developments on the assessment process and their implications for couple and family therapy today as well as future couple and family assessment. Then, it provides an in-depth description of the many increasingly sophisticated assessment tools available to clinicians today, including issue-specific, self-report inventories, standardized inventories, and observational methods. More important, it provides readers with strategies for systematically utilizing these various inventories and observational methods as well as collateral information to address critical clinical treatment issues and legal questions involving premarital decisions; separation; divorce; mediation; family violence; child custody; and so on.

This book brings together in a single publication the major contemporary and cutting-edge assessment tools and strategies relevant to clinical and legal issues encountered in working with couples and families. It identifies and describes assessment strategies for specific issues and applications: child custody; child abuse and family violence; divorce; couple conflict; and intimacy. Each chapter in part II and part III ends with a matrix summarizing pertinent information on all instruments reviewed in that chapter. This feature allows readers to compare over 100 assessment devices (interview, observational, clinician-rated, or self-report inventories) across eight chapters. Finally, it provides extensive case material to illustrate the clinical use of these various assessment tools and strategies

Assessment of Couples and Families: Contemporary and Cutting-Edge Strategies is intended for use by students and clinicians. Besides serving as a textbook, it can serve as an indispensable resource for practicing clinicians who need a ready reference to assessment measures and strategies that can be invaluable in addressing critical clinical treatment issues such as separation; divorce; mediation; family violence; child custody; and others.

Acknowledgments

This book would not have been possible without the cooperation of the distinguished researchers–clinicians–authors who contributed so much to it. I want to express my heartfelt gratitude not only for their excellent chapters but also for their willingness to "dialogue" with Dr. Luciano L'Abate in the final chapter. Dr. L'Abate, the acknowledged father of family assessment, reviewed early versions of the chapters, provided specific feedback, and invited their response. This dialogue reflects the best of academic discourse and I am pleased to include it in the book.

I also want to acknowledge the editorial staff at Taylor & Francis, New York with whom I had the good fortune to work on this project. I am most grateful to George Zimmar, Emily Epstein Loeb, Shannon Vargo, Dana Ward Bliss, and to production project editor, Joette Lynch, Taylor & Francis, Boca Raton. Thanks, everyone.

PART I

Basic Considerations and Models

CHAPTER 1

Assessment of Couples and Families
An Introduction and Overview

LEN SPERRY

THE REALITY OF CLINICAL PRACTICE TODAY

Today, many clinicians are increasingly being referred for or called upon to deal with critical clinical treatment issues that require a working knowledge of couple and family assessment resources. These referrals may involve various challenges such as suitability for marriage; marital separation; divorce; mediation; family violence; and child custody for which couple and family assessment data and/or methods and strategies would be useful or essential. Unfortunately, graduate education in clinical psychology and counseling primarily trains clinicians to work with individual clients and conceptualize cases in terms of individual personality dynamics rather than in terms of systemic or couple and family dynamics. Accordingly, many have not had formal coursework, training, or supervised experience in couple and family assessment. Even those who have completed degrees in marital and family therapy may not have received much in the way of formal training and supervised experience in formally assessing couples and families. Thus, the discussion in this and subsequent chapters can be helpful in addressing such clinical considerations as marital issues, family violence, or child custody.

This book provides a general framework for couple and family assessment and an overview of various types of general and specific strategies for systematically and effectively collecting and coordinating interview data; self-report inventories; observational methods; collateral information; and so forth into the process of treatment planning and intervention. This chapter introduces the topic of couple and family assessment as an extension of individual assessment. It notes the diversity of views about assessment among the various family therapy approaches and considers whether formal family assessment is basically incompatible with such contemporary family approaches as narrative therapy and related social constructionist systems. It then provides a map of subsequent chapters by providing an overview of the issues and assessment methods and strategies that clinicians need to work effectively with individuals, couples, and families, emphasizing the psychometric properties of reliability and validity.

FROM INDIVIDUAL ASSESSMENT TO FAMILY ASSESSMENT

Why should a clinician be concerned with assessing family factors and dynamics, particularly if he or she is working primarily or entirely with individuals? A related question is whether family assessment (and, for that matter, couples assessment) is only of value to those conducting family therapy. This book endeavors to describe and illustrate the value of utilizing couple and family assessment for those who practice individual therapy as well as those who work therapeutically with couples and families.

The past few decades have witnessed a major shift in clinical assessment—from an exclusive focus on assessing personal attributes and individual pathology (i.e., symptoms and impaired functioning) to a greater awareness of the value of considering how family attributes, relationship patterns, systemic distress, and impaired functioning affect an individual's attitudes, behaviors, distress, and level of functioning. The reasons for this shift in thinking are many, although a principal reason is the recognition that an individual is inseparable from the system, which is the site of pathology.

> Diagnosis means "to know," and understanding a problems situation can be called diagnosing. The process of diagnosing starts with observing data, forming concepts to the situation, and finally arranging the information in a particular way. All therapists have an epistemological base, and clinicians will diagnose differently according to this base.
>
> (L'Abate, Ganahl, & Hansen, 1986, p. 34)

A traditional, nonsystemic epistemology, which is the basis of the medical model, focuses on combining discrete clinician observations and individual dynamics; a systemic epistemology, which is the basis of family systems thinking, focuses on the whole system, including relational dynamics. In systemic assessment, diagnosis depends on the clinician's observation and elicitation of relational functioning, patterns, and styles rather than simply on the diagnostic criteria and individual symptoms and impairment characteristic of DSM-IV diagnostic thinking. "By bringing more people into therapy who are involved in the relational field of the identified patient, family therapy and diagnosis has moved more to the idea that the person within the system is part of the relationship system" (L'Abate, Ganahl, & Hansen, 1986, p. 34). In short, from a systemic perspective, an adequate assessment and diagnosis of an individual must necessarily involve the entire family system.

Differing Views of Couple and Family Assessment in the Family Training Program

Even though a systemic epistemology informs assessment and diagnosis in family therapy, it cannot be concluded that those who practice family therapy have reached a consensus about what constitutes appropriate and effective couple and family assessment. Nor does a consensus exist on training therapists in family assessment. Although some training programs in marital and family therapy provide students and trainees with formal instruction and supervision in using formal assessment methods with couples and families, others do not. This is not to say that assessment is less important in some approaches, but rather that it is different. Why is this?

Some insight into this query comes about by examining and comparing the place of assessment in the major approaches to family therapy. In a comparison of seven such approaches (behavioral; structural; strategic; Bowenian; experiential; solution-focused; and collaborative), Yingling et al. (1998) noted that each of these diverse approaches adopts a uniquely different theoretical perspective that "determines" which factors and variables are indicative of functionality or dysfunctionality; therefore, it should not be too surprising that what is assessed and how and when it is assessed in the course of treatment varies considerably from approach to approach.

For example, formal assessment and history taking are essential in behavioral family therapy, but neither is typically a part of experiential family therapy. Nevertheless, assessment "is a natural part of the (experiential family) therapy process. It is accomplished through information given by the family as the therapist becomes acquainted with them as a group and individually" (L'Abate, Ganahl, & Hansen, 1986, p. 38). Furthermore, although goals and clinical outcomes are specified in terms of changes in family structure and boundaries in structural family therapy, outcomes that evaluate the efficacy of the relationship of family and therapists are more important in collaborative approaches. The question becomes: Is an integrative approach to couple and family assessment possible? Many believe that such an approach will be possible to the extent that a set of common factors and dynamics involved in relational functioning is forthcoming.

Two encouraging developments in this regard are efforts to create a uniform system of relational diagnosis, the so-called Classification of Relational Disorders (CORD) that originated in the GAP Committee on the Family

(Kaslow, 1996), and the introduction of the Global Assessment of Relational Functioning (GARF) into DSM-IV and DSM-IV-TR (American Psychiatric Association, 2000).

Family Assessment and Narrative and Social Constructionist Therapies

Striking at the very heart of family assessment is the concern that formal family assessment is incompatible with narrative and social constructionist therapies. Some would agree, claiming that formal assessment is a modernist convention focused on objective "truth" and as such is incompatible with a social constructivist, postmodern view. Some family assessment models, that is, the Beavers family systems model and its assessment methods; the Beavers Interactional Scales; and the Self-Report Family Inventory (SFI), have much in common with structural family therapy and related approaches; however, the traditional use of these models and related assessment methods appear to have little in common with narrative and other constructivists approaches.

Nevertheless, Carr (2000) would contend that family assessment models like the Beavers model can easily be viewed as social constructions. Assessment models and methods that "have been found to be useful for solving problems, the hallmark of a valid social construction" (Carr, 2000, p. 127), can be compatible with social constructivism, depending on how they are utilized. For example, scores on the SFI can be utilized, not as global knowledge of a family's or family member's cohesiveness or conflict, but rather as specific, local knowledge and insights that a particular client might consider. Thus, it is one thing for a therapist to share assessment feedback and indicate that coaching, problem-solving, and communication skills might reduce the sense of distress and help solve presenting concerns more efficiently. It is another to imply or state the "truth" that the client is a poor communicator or poor problem solver. Finally, Carr notes that a commitment to social constructionism as a framework for clinical practice does not preclude a commitment to quantitative research grounded in empirical models of family functioning.

THE CONTENT AND STRUCTURE OF SUBSEQUENT CHAPTERS

Chapter 2 is the other chapter in part I, Basic Considerations and Models. It continues the introduction to family and couple assessment by focusing on applied issues and methods for evaluating couples and families. It addresses such issues as who is assessed; characteristics of family functioning to be assessed; and factors that influence a clinician's observations of family functioning.

Part II, General Strategies, contains chapter 3 through chapter 6, while part III, Specific Applications, contains chapter 7 through chapter 10. The reader will recognize that a common outline structures these chapters. The purpose of this outline is to increase ease of reading as well as to facilitate a comparison of instruments from section to section and chapter to chapter. For the most part, in their chapters, the authors follow the following specified five-point structure (I through V).

I. *Issues and Challenges of Assessment.* This section describes and briefly illustrates the specific clinical, legal, and ethical (if relevant) issues and challenges associated with the chapter focus. Typically, the need for assessment of couple and/or family dynamics and functioning is described along with various technical and practical issues relevant to the topic.

II. *Instruments.* This section provides a brief, clinically relevant description of a number of common inventories used by clinicians and family researchers. These instruments have been chosen because of their psychometric characteristics (i.e., reliability and validity), availability, and ease of administration. For the most part, each instrument or assessment method follows a common format. Table 1.1 summarizes this format.

III. *Strategy for Utilizing Assessment Results.* This section provides a step-by-step strategy for assessing a particular issue such as marital conflict, child custody, and so forth. For example, the assessment strategy might be (a) Interview the clients; (b) administer specific inventories; (c) collect collateral data (school records, other interview data); (d) review and analyze the assessment data and various reports; (e) conceptualize the case based on the review and analysis; and (f) plan treatment and interventions based on these data and the conceptualization.

IV. *Case Example.* This section illustrates the use of specific instruments as well as the assessment strategy. The case material demonstrates how one or more of the specific inventories are incorporated as part of the preceding step.

V. *Inventory Matrix.* Finally, this very brief section summarizes pertinent information on all the instruments, inventories or methods in the chapter in the form of a matrix or chart. The matrix provides the reader with a concise side-by-side comparison of each instrument.

Finally, part IV, Postscript and Future Prospects, which contains chapter 11, provides comments on the previous chapters as well as a perspective on the future of assessment involving couples and families. In an effort to be interactive, the author of chapter 11 has invited other chapter authors to respond to his commentary and critique.

TABLE 1.1 Format for Instrument Description

Name of assessment instrument or method	Indicates the authors or developers and date of publication and revisions, if any, of the instrument or method.
Type of instrument	Indicates type and form of the instrument or method, e.g., self-report, observational, clinician-rated, standard psychological instrument, outcome measure, etc.
Use–target audience	Specifies main use and targeted client, i.e., couple, family, parent–child, child custody, etc.
Multicultural	Indicates cultural applicability of the method; specifies other available language versions besides English that are available.
Ease and time of administration	Characterize the ease of administration for the instrument of method, i.e., easy, complicated, etc.; provides number of items and average time needed to complete the instrument; indicates if a manual is available.
Scoring procedure	Specifies the (a) method, i.e., paper and pencil, etc.; and (2) average time to score the instrument; indicates if electronic or alternative form of administration or a computer scoring option is available, that information is indicated.
Reliability	Specifies types of reported reliability coefficients, such as test–retest, internal consistency, i.e., Cronbach's alpha, and inter-rater (or scorer) reliability if applicable; also gives overall assessment: high, moderate, average, or below average reliability; if none reported, say: "no published or reported reliability data."
Validity	Specifies the types of reported validity, i.e., construct related, criterion related, if none reported, say: "no published or reported validity data."
Availability and source	Provides information on availability and source of the instrument or method; if journal article provides assessment device, then journal reference is indicated; when only commercially available, name and/or address/phone number of supplier is indicated.
Comment	Provides chapter authors with opportunity to share professional evaluations of clinical utility and value of this instrument or method.

RELIABILITY AND VALIDITY: A BRIEF OVERVIEW

As just noted, the technical description of each assessment instrument or method includes data on two key psychometric properties: reliability and validity. Because major clinical recommendations such as child custody are often based on clinical assessment, it is essential that the assessment instruments and methods on which these recommended courses of action are made are highly reliable and valid. It is also necessary that the clinician be sufficiently apprised of the appropriate use and limitations of such devices.

Even though this is a text on assessment, it cannot be assumed that all readers will be sufficiently familiar with these two key psychometric properties to appreciate the technical discussion on the various inventories and assessment methods adequately. Graduate training programs in clinical psychology, counseling psychology, and family psychology are likely to require formal instruction and experience in assessment that addresses psychometric issues. However, other graduate programs, such as marital and family therapy training programs, are less likely to emphasize these concepts. Accordingly, a brief overview of the concepts of reliability will be given as well as descriptions and illustrations of various types of each.

Reliability

Reliability is the extent to which a test or any assessment procedure yields the same result when repeated. In other words, reliability is the consistency of a measurement or the degree to which an instrument or assessment device measures the same way each time it is used under the same condition with the same individual. A measure is considered reliable if an individual's scores on the same test given twice are similar. Technically speaking, reliability is not measured, but is estimated and represented as a correlation coefficient. The higher the reliability coefficient is, the more confidence one can have in the score. Reliability coefficients at or above .70 are considered adequate; those at or above .80 are considered good; those at .90 or above are considered excellent (Hambleton & Zaal, 1991). Three types of reliability can be described: test–retest, internal consistency, and interrater reliability.

- *Test–retest reliability*—the agreement of assessment measures over time. To determine it, a measure or test is repeated on the same individuals at a future date. Results are compared and correlated with the initial test to give a measure of stability. The *Spearman–Brown formula* is used for calculating this estimate of reliability.
- *Internal consistency*—the extent to which tests or procedures assess the same characteristic, skill, or quality. It is a measure of the precision between the observers or of the measuring instruments used in a study. This type of reliability often helps clinicians and researchers interpret data and predict the value of scores and the limits of the relationship among variables. For example, the Family Adaptation Scale (FAD) is a questionnaire to evaluate families in terms of seven functions including communication patterns. Analyzing the internal consistency of the FAD items on the Communications subscale reveals the extent to which items on this family assessment device actually reflect communication patterns among family members. The internal consistency of a test can be computed in different ways.
- *Split-halves reliability*—a measure of internal consistency derived by correlating responses on half the test with responses to the other half.
- *Cronbach's alpha*—another, more sophisticated method. This method divides items on an instrument or measure and computes correlation

values for them. Cronbach's alpha is a correlation coefficient, and the closer it is to one, the higher the reliability estimate of the assessment device.

- *Kuder-Richardson coefficient*—another means of estimating internal consistency. It is used for instruments or measures that involve dichotomous responses or items, such as "yes"/"no," while Cronbach's alpha is used with Likert-Scale types of responses or items. Finally, it should be noted that the primary difference between test–retest and internal consistency estimates of reliability is that test–retest involves two administrations of the measure or instrument, whereas internal consistency methods involve only a single administration of the instrument.

- *Inter-rater reliability*—the extent to which two or more individuals (raters) agree. Inter-rater reliability addresses the consistency of the implementation of a rating system. For example, inter-rater reliability can be established in following scenario: Two clinical supervisors are observing the same family being treated by a counseling intern through a two-way mirror. As part of the observation, each supervisor independently rates the family's functioning on the GARF Scale. One supervisor rates the family at 62 and the other at 64 (on the 1- to 100-point scale). Because inter-rater reliability is dependent upon the ability of two or more observers to be consistent, it could be said that inter-rater reliability is very high in this instance.

Validity

Validity refers to the ability of an assessment device or method to measure what it is intended to measure. Whereas reliability is concerned with the accuracy of the assessment device or procedure, validity is concerned with the study's success at measuring what the researchers set out to measure. Four types of validity can be described:

- *Face validity*—concerned with how a measure or procedure appears. Does it seem like a reasonable way to gain the information? Does it seem to be well designed? Does it seem as though it will work reliably? Unlike content validity, face validity does not depend on established theories for support (Fink, 1995).

- *Criterion-related validity*, or criterion-referenced validity—used to demonstrate the accuracy of a measure or procedure by comparing it with another measure or procedure previously demonstrated to be valid. For example, a paper-and-pencil test of family functioning, the SFI, appears to measure the same family dynamics and functioning as does a related observational assessment, the Beavers Interactional Scales. By comparing the scores of family members' self-report of family functioning with the therapist's observational ratings of family functioning, the SFI was validated by using a criterion-related strategy in which self-report scores were compared to the Beavers Interactional Scales ratings.

- *Construct validity*—seeks agreement between a theoretical concept and a specific measuring device or procedure. For example, a family researcher developing a new inventory for assessing marital intimacy might spend considerable time specifying the theoretical boundaries of the term intimacy and then operationally defining it with specific test items or a rating schema in order to achieve an acceptable level of construct validity.
- *Convergent validity* and *discriminate validity*—two subcategories of construct validity. Convergent validity is the actual general agreement among ratings, gathered independently of one another, where measures should be theoretically related. Discriminate validity is the lack of a relationship among measures that theoretically should not be related. To understand whether an assessment device has construct validity, three steps are followed. First, the theoretical relationships are specified. Next, the empirical relationships between the measures of the concepts are examined. Finally, the empirical evidence is interpreted in terms of how it clarifies the construct validity of the particular measure being tested (Carmines & Zeller, 1991, p. 23).
- *Content validity*—based on the extent to which a measurement reflects the specific intended domain of content (Carmines & Zeller, 1991, p. 20). Content validity can be illustrated using the following example: Family researchers attempting to measure a family structural dimension such as adaptability must decide what constitutes a relevant domain of content for that dimension. They may look for commonalities among several definitions of adaptability or utilize the Delphi technique or a similar strategy so that a consensus opinion or conceptualization of family adaptability from a group of recognized experts on the topic can be reached.

Correlation coefficients can be derived for criterion-related and construct validity. Validity coefficients for assessment devices tend to be much lower than reliability coefficients. For example, validity coefficients for the MMPI-2 are about .30.

CONCLUDING NOTE

This chapter has begun the discussion of couple and family assessment. We have described the shift that has occurred, and is still occurring, from individual assessment to family assessment. We have also noted that, owing to the diversity of viewpoints on the content and process of assessment, no single or integrative approach to family assessment currently exists. In addition, a basic incompatibility appears to exist between formal family assessment and the newer social constructivist approaches; however, assessment methods are actually quite compatible with such approaches, depending on the manner in which assessment information is framed with clients and families. Finally, the common structure of subsequent chapters was briefly introduced and because of the diversity of graduate training in assessment theory, two key psychometric properties, reliability and validity, were described and illustrated. An extended discussion of some of these and other theoretical and technical issues involving family assessment is continued in chapter 2.

REFERENCES

Carr, A. (2000). Editorial: Empirical approaches to family assessment. *Journal of Family Therapy*, 22: 121–127.
L'Abate, L., Ganahl, G., & Hansen, J. (1986). *Methods of family therapy*. Englewood Cliffs, NJ: Prentice Hall.
Kaslow, F. (Ed.). (1996). *Handbook of relational diagnosis and dysfunctional family patterns*. New York: Wiley.
Yingling, L., Miller, W., McDonald, A., & Galwaler, S. (1998). *GARF assessment sourcebook: Using the DSM-IV Global Assessment of Relational Functioning*. Washington, D.C.: Brunner/Mazel.

ANNOTATED BIBLIOGRAPHY

American Psychological Association (1985). *Standards for educational and psychological testing*. Washington, D.C.: Author. This work on focuses on reliability, validity, and the standards that clinicians and researchers need to achieve in order to ensure accuracy.
Carmines, E. G., & Zeller, R. A. (1991). *Reliability and validity assessment*. Newbury Park: Sage Publications. An introduction to research methodology that includes classical test theory, validity, and methods of assessing reliability.
Hambleton, R. K., & Zaal, J. N. (Eds.). (1991). *Advances in educational and psychological testing*. Boston: Kluwer Academic. Information on the concepts of reliability and validity in psychology and education and techniques in statistical analysis for social scientists are addressed.

CHAPTER 2

Models and Issues in Couple and Family Assessment[1]

JAMES H. BRAY

Roger and Karen scheduled an appointment at the family counseling clinic for help with their marriage and children. Their primary concern was the increase in conflict between all of the family members; an inability to communicate effectively; and the increasing tendency to attack each other when addressing family concerns. Karen feels that Roger does not understand the stress and demands in caring for their daughter, who was recently diagnosed with a chronic health problem. In addition, Karen's parents are about to live with them for a while to help care for the daughter. After several sessions, Karen states that she feels that Roger understands the family problems and everyone is getting along better. She wants to stop therapy. Although conflict is less frequent, the couple does not yet have effective problem-solving skills to resolve problems on their own. The therapist is concerned that when Karen's parents arrive, the couple will not be able to handle the added stress of the in-laws and their relationships may deteriorate even further.

Karen's stated needs are somewhat different from the therapist's assessment of the problems confronting the couple and family. The therapist, who perceives the issues of empathy and support that brought the family into treatment, also believes that the couple's conflict resolution skills are ineffective. In addition, the therapist is concerned because an external stressor will soon challenge the couple's problem-solving skills: Karen's parents' intrusions into

1. This chapter is an updated version of Bray, J. H. (1995). Family assessment: Current issues in evaluating families. *Family Relations, 44,* 469–477. Reprinted with permission of the National Council on Family Relations. Preparation of this chapter was partially supported by National Institute of Alcohol Abuse and Alcoholism grant RO1 AA 08864.

the family's relationships. The discrepancies between individual self-reports and observed behaviors represent important considerations in couple and family assessment (Bray & Frugé, 2000).

Accurate assessment of family relationships and functioning is an important issue in evaluating and treating couples, families and children (Bray & Frugé, 2000; Spirito et al., 2003). Formal assessment is always a challenge because of the press of time to develop and execute a treatment plan. However, in family interventions, just as in individual psychotherapy, the success of a treatment plan often depends on accurate assessment of the nature of the problem and the potential for solutions (Szapocznik & Kurtines, 1989).

This chapter reviews and discusses applied issues and methods for evaluating couples and families. This chapter is organized along the following topics: (a) what a family is; strategies for identifying the family; and who should be included in the assessment; (b) the important characteristics of family functioning; (c) important factors that influence observations of family functioning; (d) issues in assessing families; and (e) clinical application of family assessment.

WHAT IS A FAMILY? WHAT IS A HEALTHY FAMILY?

The composition of modern American families is quite diverse and includes traditional two-parent families with children; single-parent families; stepfamilies; extended kin families; quasi-kin families; and a host of other configurations (Bray, 1993, 1999; Levine, 1994). In addition, cohabitating or gay and lesbian families may include nonbiological relationships as their functional core. Networks of gay men and women have developed families of choice, in addition to their families of origin (Lovejoy, 1989). In recognition of this fact, the National Institute of Mental Health (NIMH) defined family as "a network of mutual commitment" (Pequegnat & Bray, 1997). Thus, persons who fulfill relationship roles heretofore traditionally specified by biological or legal relationships are now considered family members for the purpose of supporting each other and understanding their social contexts (Mellins, Ehrhardt, Newman, & Conrad, 1996).

Which type of family member performs which type of role can change with time and circumstances, particularly with the high rate of marital transitions and divorce, and due to illness. The diversity of family compositions presents unique challenges for assessment. Some of the challenges include (a) how to define families and how to determine the individuals who should be included in services; (b) where to draw the boundaries that define "the family" in any particular case; and (c) how to handle the fluidity of families in which family composition changes over time (e.g., beginning or ending of romantic involvements; due to divorce; or as a result of interventions that change the boundaries of families to include additional supports or to separate disruptive or detrimental influences such as drug-abusing family members; Bray & Frugé, 2000).

There are as many definitions of healthy and dysfunctional families as there are theories of family functioning and family relationships (Bray, 1995a, b; Walsh, 2003). Although many of these theories overlap in their perspectives, unique aspects are important to consider in describing healthy family processes. A complete review of theories of healthy families is beyond the scope of this chapter. However, a brief discussion of common aspects of systems approaches to couples and families is provided to orient the reader to basic assumptions of this approach.

Healthy couples and families promote the well-being and functioning of each individual family member through the maintenance of clear and effective communication; mutually beneficial interactional patterns; clear boundaries between the generations and between family subsystems; and expectations that change over time according to the internal demands of family members and external demands of the environment (Bray, 1995a, b; Walsh, 2003). A balance is maintained between the needs for family stability and change that promotes the health of individual family members. All families have problems as they go through transitions across the life cycle; dysfunctional families have an inability to make these transitions without experiencing problems (Carter & McGoldrick, 1988; Watzlawick, Weakland, & Fisch, 1974).

> ...an ordinary family; that is, the couple has many problems of relating to one another, bringing up children, dealing with in-laws, and coping with the outside world. Like all normal families, they are constantly struggling with these problems and negotiating the compromises that make a life in common possible. (Minuchin, 1974, p. 6)

Although it is argued that family assessment should flow from solid family theory, a major problem in the family assessment area is the lack of a unified theory of family functioning (Grotevant, 1989). Agreement has not been reached concerning a family diagnostic system, as with the DSM-IV for individual psychopathology, and many in the field disagree about which constructs or processes are essential to assess (Bray, 1995b). Some family-oriented theorists argue that formal assessment is unnecessary for clinical practice.

The NIMH definition of family as a "network of mutual commitment" is a good example of the complexity of evaluating couples and families (Pequegnat & Bray, 1997). This definition may certainly facilitate a more realistic picture of the context of modern families. However, the basic definition includes such a broad spectrum of potential family members that consistent definitions of family may be difficult. One possible guideline is to relate the definition of family makeup to the goals of the treatment plan. For example, if the outcome of interest is developing a competent and happy marital relationship in a stepfamily, then the members of the family invited to treatment sessions might include only those directly related or involved in the marriage. On the other hand, if the treatment goals include the children in the stepfamily, the boundaries of the family could be extended to those involved in the care of the children as well as those who can facilitate or impede this important family function (Bray & Frugé, 2000).

Regardless of the particular definition, the constellation of family membership is dynamic and changes over time. Changes in composition of families are a common finding in providing treatment for modern families. In addition, some prevention and treatment programs may result in changes in family composition, such as when an abusive or drug-abusing family member is removed from the family (Pequegnat & Szapocznik, 2000).

CHARACTERISTICS OF FAMILY FUNCTIONING

Efforts to capture the complexity and subtlety of family relationships, their natural processes, and the influences on family members on family life over time have led to a variety of assessment strategies (Bray & Frugé, 2000; Grotevant & Carlson, 1989; Jacob & Tennenbaum, 1988). Such diversity of perspectives is useful in reflecting the uniqueness of each family and the rich tapestry of family dynamics. However, five types of family characteristics are frequently assessed in research and evaluation of families. These characteristics have been frequently measured in family research and are useful in treatment as well (Bray, 1995a; Fisher, 1976; Grotevant, 1989). These characteristics include (a) Family Composition; (b) Family Process; (c) Patterned Relationships; (d) Family Affect; and (e) Family Organization. Family Complexity and Diversity interact among all of these factors.

Family Composition includes family membership (e.g., couple only, couple with children, single-parent family); structure of the family (e.g., cohabitating couple, first-marriage family, divorced family, stepfamily); and factors such as Ethnic Group (e.g., African–American, Hispanic) and Sexual Orientation (heterosexual, homosexual, bisexual). Family Composition is a key marker for other aspects of family functioning. For example, children in single-parent families and stepfamilies often have more behavior problems than do children in first-marriage families; parenting practices often differ as well.

Family Process Factors include interactions and transactions among family members that characterize patterns of behavioral exchanges between family members and the function or outcomes associated with these interactions. Process measures reflect core features of transactional behavior such as conflict, communication, and problem solving. Family Process, which is the transactions between family members without regard to content, is distinguished from content. For example, when Karen said to Roger, "You never help me give our daughter medicine," the content is medicine and chores. However, the process, "you never help me," could easily apply to any content area other than medicine. In this regard, process also refers to the message or metacommunication, "I do not feel supported by you."

Process can also refer to the nature of the transactional patterns. For instance, if Roger says to Karen, "I would like to make love with you now," and Karen responds by saying, "When I am finished taking care of our daughter," the function of "taking care of our daughter" may be to avoid discussion or action on Roger's request to make love. Consequently, depending on their context, exactly the same words (content) could have very different functions (process). In this case, what is reflected may be part of a *pattern* in which an emotionally laden request receives a response that changes the topic of conversation.

Patterned Relationships refer to sequences of couple or family interactions that develop over time and are related to positive or negative outcomes. For example, Gottman (1993, 1994) has identified a sequence of interactions in marital relationships that are highly predictive of divorce. These include couples' criticism, contempt, defensiveness, stonewalling. Couples start with being overly critical of each other. In happy couples, the rate of positive to negative statements is five positive statement to every negative one. In unhappy couples, there is one positive to every one negative statement. This pattern is followed by couples feeling and exhibiting contempt for each other, often exhibited by nonverbal facial expressions and reactions between the two. Next, couples become defensive and do not hear each other. More focus is on how a spouse is going to respond to the partner, rather than listening to what the partner is saying. Finally, couples stonewall and basically shut down their interactions with each other. At this point, many couples recast their relationship as totally negative, which is highly predictive of eventual divorce. These types of patterned relationships may develop over time or may be present in the early stages of a relationship. Gottman and colleagues are able to identify these patterns through observational and self-reported assessments.

Family Affect relates to the nature of the emotional expression among family members. The emotional tone and volume of interactions are important aspects of the context of family processes and greatly affect how family members experience or interpret communications. Measures of expressed emotion between family members, particularly negative emotion, offer some of the most reliable predictors of outcome in studies of chronic problems such as schizophrenia, mood disorders, and alcoholism (O'Farrell, Hooley, Fals–Stewart, & Cutter, 1998). Similarly, considerable research has found that negative affect is foremost in families with acting-out and antisocial adolescents (Robbins, Hervis, Mitrani, & Szapocznik, 2001). As noted before, Gottman (1994) found that happy couples give five positive statements to every negative statement.

A broad range of affective qualities must be considered in determining the character of family relations; expression of affect is often related to culture and ethnicity. These range from loving, supportive, and nurturing to negative, hostile, and sarcastic. In addition, the level or volume of affective tone is also important and may range from families in which there is little affect, or affect is overcontrolled, to families in which the volume of positive or negative affect is very high. Negative affect at high volume is usually disruptive of family life. Thus, the widespread acceptance is that negative affect is undesirable and interventions to correct it are needed. In addition, very high levels of affectivity in general can be problematic in some families, but need not be problematic in every case.

Family Organization factors are the roles and rules (spoken and unspoken) within the family. This also refers to expectations for behavior that contribute to family functioning. These factors include aspects such as (a) boundaries, (b) decision hierarchy, and (c) the distribution of labor and emotional support functions. Boundaries refer to the emotional and psychological closeness or distance between family members and between the family and the external world (Carter & McGoldrick, 1988; Szapocznik & Kurtines, 1989). Functional boundaries need to be permeable to permit interaction across them, but the nature of which boundaries are appropriate may differ according to the developmental stage of the family (see the discussion on context). Families with an infant, for example, naturally have strong boundaries around the mother and infant. As the infant grows, the boundary between mother and infant becomes more flexible and eventually, when the child and siblings are developmentally in a similar stage, the boundaries among siblings may be stronger than the boundary around the mother and child.

Another interesting boundary issue occurs in the relation of nuclear and extended family/kin networks. In some cultures, boundaries around the nuclear family are quite inflexible, whereas in others boundaries between the nuclear family and their extended or kinship network are quite fluid. As indicated next (under context), culture is an important defining feature of families that will prescribe the nature of acceptable family interactions. What is acceptable may change considerably from family to family and from culture to culture.

Family Diversity and Complexity are responsible for important variations within and across the factors presented previously. For example, Family process may be quite different for various family compositions in diverse ethnic groups at different developmental stages; these differences may result in important disparities in individual functioning for family members in different family roles (cf. Bray, 1995a; Fine, 1993; Kaslow, Celano, & Dreelin, 1995; Szapocznik & Kurtines, 1993). For example, hypothesized relationships among these factors may not hold in different family structures, such as single-parent families or stepfamilies (Bray, 1999; Hetherington & Clingempeel, 1992). Families are also dynamic rather than static systems. Relationships between factors noted at one point may change in form over time. Thus, as families develop and family members move into different family roles (e.g., infant grows and begins school; children leave the home), the natures of family composition, process, affect, and organization will be affected by these important developmental transitions.

FACTORS THAT INFLUENCE OBSERVATIONS OF FAMILY FUNCTIONING

Context, which plays a critical role in influencing families (Bray & Frugé, 2000), includes the observable interactions and settings for family interactions as well as the meanings and interpretations of those interactions by individual family members. The contexts in which families are observed may have an impact on how families behave. Therefore, different family relationships and interactions may be on view depending on the context in which the family is observed and what the family is asked to do (i.e., discussing a family problem versus planning a family vacation). For example, in a clinic, a family may be on their best behavior, but in their own dining room, they may interact in a more typical way that includes more negative interactions and affect.

Another example of the context of family is consideration of how the stage of a family's life cycle may influence its behavior. Family life cycle theory teaches that most families progress through a definable set of stages, each of which is characterized by an interrelated set of developmental tasks and dynamics (e.g., caring for young children). Life cycle theory suggests that the ways in which families adapt to predictable and unpredictable challenges and changes are greatly influenced by the life cycle stage of the family (Carter & McGoldrick, 1988).

Yet a third example of context is the consideration of broader cultural and ethnic attributes that may specifically define and influence family life cycle stages and the characteristic behaviors of certain groups of families. Thus, the appraisal of family functioning and, in particular, the definition of "normality" should be considered in the context of the specific life cycle stages as well as in context of cultural/ethnic dimensions (Walsh, 2003). Furthermore, environmental context in terms of community and interactions between family and community may provide a wider framework for assessing the needs and conditions of children and adolescents (cf. Gray, 2001).

Most of the current models of family relationships and functioning are based on Caucasian, middle-class families that do not necessarily reflect variations typical of families from different cultural and ethnic backgrounds (Bray, 1995a). Indeed, most family measures, with a few exceptions (e.g., Friedmann, Astedt–Kurki, & Paavilainen, 2003; Shek, 1998, 2002; Szapocznik & Kurtines, 1993; Szapocznik, Rio, Hervis, et al., 1991), are based on these models and have not been validated with families from diverse ethnic backgrounds (Baer & Bray, 1999; Bray, 1995b; Hampson, Beavers, & Hulgus, 1990; Kaslow et al., 1995; Morris, 1990). Researchers and clinicians are cautioned to keep this limitation in mind when using measures and instruments developed on one ethnic group to assess the health and dysfunction of families from other ethnic and cultural backgrounds (Fine, 1993).

However, standardized family measures can still be useful in providing information about the family at several different points, using the same assessment ruler. So-called objective measures can then be interpreted in the broader context of what is known about the life and culture of the family. Thus, although many measures have not been used with a particular cultural group, the practitioner can nevertheless use the measure across a sample of ethnically specific families and establish his own sense of how families compare with each other on a particular measure. This "don't throw the baby out with the bath water" approach is intended to encourage practitioners not to discount fully family measures used with their populations. Rather, learn how these measures can be helpful in a practice setting and what they indicate about the specific cultural group served in the practice setting.

ISSUES IN ASSESSING FAMILIES

In choosing a family assessment strategy, clinicians should first determine which aspects of family functioning are most likely to be relevant to the goals of prevention and treatment of most interest (Floyd, Weinand, & Cimmarusti, 1989). This consideration involves several dimensions: (a) the members of the family who are being evaluated; (b) the methods of the assessment that have been selected; and (c) the methods of examining the family system by using all these sources of information (Dakof, 1996; Davidson, Quinn, & Josephson, 2001). It is also important in assessing interpersonal interactions to distinguish properties of the relationship (e.g., conflict, cohesion) from feelings or attitudes (e.g., anger, positivity–negativity) that individuals have about the relationship (Thompson & Walker, 1982). As previously stated, deciding whom to include in the assessment of the family system is a major issue in conducting a family assessment.

Insights have emerged from family research that can be very useful for clinical applications (e.g., Pequegnat & Szapocznik, 2000). For example, family research measures are often based on self-report data from individual family members describing their own perceptions of the family, rather than reports from multiple family members or direct observations of families in interaction (Bray, 1995a, b; Fisher, Kokes, Ransom, Phillips, & Rudd, 1985). Most surveys and assessments of individual family members utilize this type of information, with the assumption that self-report information represents valid and complete information on family functioning.

Family research reveals that information obtained from an individual may or may not accurately reflect the functioning of the entire couple or family (Fisher et al., 1985; Hayden et al., 1998; Jacob & Windle, 1999; Ransom, Fisher, Phillips, Kokes, & Weiss, 1990). Several studies have found statistically significant and clinically important differences among family members' reports of family functioning (Cole & McPherson, 1993; Cook & Goldstein, 1993; Stevenson–Hinde & Akister, 1995). For instance, research on the breakup of relationships indicates that partners frequently report significant differences in satisfaction with the relationship and why it is ending (Gottman, 1994; Hetherington, 1993). The examination of the differences in perceptions between individual family members can be useful for prevention and treatment efforts; logic and clinical practice suggest that bridging these differences in perception can have therapeutic value for improving the quality of relationships (Bray, 1995a).

Although the assessment of an individual's perceptions is suitable for evaluating certain aspects of the family system (e.g., differentiation within the family of origin), these assessments are not truly measures of the family system as a whole. Information obtained from individuals within a family can be transformed into relational measures by various means that are beyond the scope of this chapter (Bray, 1995a, c; Cole & McPherson, 1993; Fisher et al., 1985; Kolevzon, Green, Fortune, & Vosler, 1988; Ransom et al., 1990). Suffice it to say that family-level measures can be developed from averaged or weighted responses of individual family members. This provides an overall evaluation of the family that may be helpful if it provides information about how distressed this family is in comparison to other families with whom the practitioner has successfully worked (Olson, 1977). As mentioned earlier, self-reports of individual family members can also simply be compared to those of other members of the family to see how much agreement exists on issues likely to be important in prevention or treatment programs.

An alternative approach would be to observe directly how family members interact and try to solve a problem in which several diverse points of view are likely to be present. The interactions that occur around a task may reveal the typical positive and negative patterns of family interaction. Fisher et al. (1985) termed this category of measurement *transactional assessment*. Transactional assessment involves some type of direct observation of family members in a predefined standard task or structured interaction. These assessments reflect interactions at a system level, rather than a simple sum or averaging of individual points of view. These assessments can measure the interactions of all the participating members of the family or focus on several individuals who seem to dominate the discussion and decision-making process within the family.

In contrast to self-report measures, these directly observed transactional assessments also represent an outsider's view of the family. These assessments involve a trained professional's making judgments about family interactions. However, family members can also make ratings and observations about family interactions, as exemplified by Gottman's work on marital relationships (Gottman, 1993, 1994; Gottman & Levenson, 1992).

Controversy about the necessity to assess the entire family is unresolved in the research and the clinical literatures (Bray, 1995b; Carlson, 1989). Occasionally, examining the interactions of various family dyads (e.g., a couple within the family) and triads (e.g., two parents and a child) may be more useful than examining the family as a whole (Bray, 1995a; Cole & Jordan, 1989; Dickstein et al., 1998; Gable, Belsky, & Crnic, 1992; Hetherington & Clingempeel, 1992; Hetherington et al., 1999; Kashy & Kenny, 1990; Kenny & LaVoie, 1984). Sometimes, information from smaller family subgroups can lead to more focused treatment plans. Changing the behavior of a few members of a family will ultimately lead to shifts in the entire family (Szapocznik & Kurtines, 1989). This marks a shift from viewing and discussing the family exclusively as a coherent whole. In recognizing that many critical aspects of family functioning are reflected in specific processes and interactions between particular family members (e.g., the couple), the arena of family assessment and intervention has become more differentiated. It recognizes that sometimes individual perceptions are most useful, while at other times contrast in individual perceptions; measures of full family functioning; or the functioning of family subsystems may be most useful. More recent efforts include assessments of the entire family, important subsets, and individual characteristics (Gaughan, 1995; Hayden et al., 1998; Heffer & Snyder, 1998; Miller, Ryan, Keitner, Bishop, & Epstein, 2000; Skinner, Steinhauer, & Sitarenios, 2000; Watson & McDaniel, 1998; Wilkinson, 2000).

Without a consensus on what constitutes a "gold standard" in family measurement (Bray, 1995a), researchers and clinicians usually rely on more than one method for assessing family process (how the family behaves when it is together) and outcomes (whether the family successfully achieves the goals that it has articulated). The two most common measurement methods in family assessment are the use of self-report instruments and behavioral observations of family interactions (Bray, 1995b). It is important to understand that the information obtained by these methods does not always agree (Cole & McPherson, 1993; Cook & Goldstein, 1993; Kolevzon et al., 1988; Markman & Notarius, 1987), but may be combined to provide significant overlap and consensus (Jacob & Windle, 1999).

Self-Report Methods

Self-reports of family functioning are probably the most common means of assessing family relations and processes in research contexts (Bray, 1995b); hundreds of published self-report measures of family functioning have been published. Self-report measures include perceptions of the family by individual family members; ratings by family members of other family members' behavior or relationships; and self-reports of affect and emotions while engaging in certain behaviors (Bray, 1995b). It is beyond the scope of this chapter to review them in any detail, so the reader is referred to excellent books by Fredman and Sherman (1987), Grotevant and Carlson (1989), and Touliatos, Perlmutter, and Straus (1990) for reviews of many of the family measures.

Self-report instruments of family functioning (Bray, 1995b) have many benefits. Foremost, self-reports are usually economical; they are easy to collect in a clinic setting and can be administered in repeated sessions to document changes within the family. Self-report measures thus can be a convenient gauge for changes in outcomes as a result of a preventive or treatment intervention. To measure changes over time, however, the clinician must be careful to select measures that reflect the kinds of changes likely to occur in the prevention or treatment program rather than a measure of stable family or individual characteristics (Jacob, 1995). It is also wise to select more specific measures of family functioning with reasonable theoretical or empirical linkages to the prevention or treatment interventions evaluated, in addition to global reports on family functioning. For example, an intervention trying to restore a woman to a responsible role in the family should assess not only her individual perceptions, but also actual behaviors within the family to determine if the woman, in fact, has been restored to a responsible role in the family.

Observational Methods

Observations of families can range from qualitative measures, such as narrative descriptions of family relations, to very quantitative approaches such as the specific coding of interactional sequences (e.g., microanalytic coding; Carlson & Grotevant, 1987; Gottman, 1994; Ransom et al., 1990). Qualitative approaches may include experiential activities that help engage the family and serve as the beginning of the change process (Deacon & Piercy, 2001). Coding of observational measures attempts to assess the real-time patterning of family interactions of interest to family clinicians.

The three dimensions of standardized observations are (a) what is observed (i.e., the tasks that family members are asked to perform); (b) where it is observed (i.e., home, office); and (c) how it is observed (i.e., the coding system employed; Bray, 1995b; Bray & Frugé, 2000). To facilitate comparisons between families, it is desirable to establish a specific task to be performed by each family (e.g., plan a menu). The form of the task chosen often reflects common problematic situations in average family life (e.g., discussing how to solve a discipline problem with a child). Alternatively, the specific task may be carefully designed to stimulate dimensions of interaction thought to be particularly relevant to the problem being investigated (e.g., discussing who is going to have custody of a child after a divorce).

- *What is observed?* Problem-solving tasks, in which family members are asked to identify a common problem, discuss it, and attempt to develop a solution to it (Markman & Notarius, 1987), are widely used. These tasks are engaging and often revealing of typical patterns of family interactions. This type of task can elicit discord, creativity, and a family's usual style or pattern of conflict resolution. Problems selected may be identified as internal to the family or couple versus external. Also, standardized games, such as the Simulated Family Activity Measurement (SIMFAM; Straus & Tallman, 1971), can be used as the catalyst for a problem-solving task. Other types of tasks include providing emotional support or encouragement for a family member; planning pleasant events (e.g., a family trip or vacation); describing qualities of the family; making up stories to standardized pictures (e.g., the Thematic Apperception Test); putting together puzzles or games; and talking about what happened during the day (Grotevant & Carlson, 1989).

  Each type of task tends to elicit different types of family interactions. For instance, the task of discussing differences in individual views asks family members to defend their positions on certain ideas and values and can reflect issues of power, group pressure, and autonomy; the planning tasks may be more likely to elicit positive interactions and role relationships. In all family assessments, it is important to sample various content domains to ensure obtaining a picture of how the family functions across a variety of meaningful domains.

- *Where does the observation take place?* Direct observation of family interaction is often set in a clinic due to financial and logistical constraints. Direct observations, however, can also be set in more natural settings such as the home (e.g., dinner table conversations) or school (e.g., classroom). Research indicates that families show little reactivity to observation per se (Jacob, Tennenbaum, Seilhamer, Bargiel, & Sharon, 1994) and to exposure to standardized tasks (Szapocznik, Santisteban, Rio, et al., 1989), although different types of behavior may be exhibited in different settings. Thus, the setting used for observation should be selected for the purpose of the assessment and chosen to maximize the chances for a relevant sample of behavior. For example, if parent management strategies for child behavior problems is the target, a home observation setting may be particularly useful. The use of more naturalistic and longer term observational approaches may also be required in the case of behavior that occurs rarely, such as temper tantrums or abusive behaviors.

- *How are families observed?* Family interactions can be used to obtain global ratings (e.g., positive to negative quality of interaction) on the one hand, or highly specific frequency counts of a particular behavior (e.g., how many times a parent criticized a child) on the other (Bray, 1995b). The latter type of observation can be very useful for identifying linked patterns of behaviors (Gottman, 1993; Markman & Notarius, 1987). For example, what follows a parental criticism of a child? Is a critical parental behavior followed by an adolescent-compliant or -rebellious behavior? Actually, it may vary by family. In some families, parental criticism of an adolescent may result in adolescent-compliant response, while in another it may result in adolescent-rebellious response. See Grotevant and Carlson (1989) and Markman and Notarius (1987) for reviews of various behavioral observation systems, and other examples (Pequegnat et al., 2001; Robbins et al., 2001; Szapocznik et al., 1991).

CONCLUDING NOTE: CLINICAL APPLICATION OF FAMILY ASSESSMENTS

Even though good family measures are available, family-oriented practitioners frequently do not use standardized or formal family assessments in their practices (Boughner, Hayes, Bubenzer, & West, 1994; Bray, 1995b; Floyd, Weinand, & Cimmarusti, 1989). Yet, clinicians have many reasons to use formal, standardized methods for assessing families (Bray, 1995b). Evaluations conducted before prevention or treatment intervention begins can provide a rich source of information about the family and can be used to develop initial hypotheses about problem areas, causes of problems, and potential areas of strengths. Assessment also ensures that a broad range of routine information is collected to make certain that important areas are not overlooked. By using a battery of self-report methods, a substantial amount of information can be ascertained with minimal clinician time. In addition, because most clients and family members initially view the presenting problem as within an individual, completing family assessment instruments begins to redefine the problem as a family systems issue, which can start the therapeutic process.

Many of the available family measures and methods have been developed for research contexts and have not been specifically applied to clinical practice. Consequently, many instruments do not provide the instructions or clinically relevant norms and comparisons necessary for use in practice settings. However, more recent work in couple and family assessment has integrated research findings into clinically relevant and useful methods (Gottman 1994, 1996; Hayden et al., 1998; Heffer & Snyder, 1998; Miller et al., 2000; Skinner et al., 2000; Szapocznik & Kurtines, 1989; Watson & McDaniel, 1998; Wilkinson, 2000).

Using a standard battery of instruments also facilitates comparisons between a family's current functioning and published normative data. Given the limitations of family assessment, it is probably wise to view the normative data as suggestive, rather than as defining pathology. Likewise, clinicians and researchers need to be cognizant of different norms for various family structures (e.g., nuclear, single-parent, step-parent) and ethnic backgrounds (Bray,

1995b). In addition, initial assessments can be compared to posttreatment assessments to document intervention-related changes. With changes in health care reimbursement and the demand for demonstration of treatment efficacy, formal assessments that document positive change are becoming a central part of the therapeutic process. Clinicians who are able to demonstrate treatment effectiveness empirically are likely to be in greater demand in the near future. The use of measures will make it easier for clinicians to compare families and gain insights that may be applicable to future client families.

It is clear that more attention is needed to develop methods that can capture the complex phenomena of family relationships found in this arena. A number of new and promising methods are currently being developed in other areas of family research that may provide clinicians with innovative ways of assessing family relationships and outcomes. These types of innovations will facilitate further development of effective family prevention and treatment interventions.

REFERENCES

Baer, P. E., & Bray, J. H. (1999). Adolescent individuation and alcohol usage. *Journal of Studies on Alcohol, 13*, 52–62.

Boughner, S. R., Hayes, S. F., Bubenzer, D. L., & West, J. D. (1994). Use of standardized assessment instruments by marital and family therapists: A survey. *Journal of Marital and Family Therapy, 20*, 69–75.

Bray, J. H. (1993). Families in demographic perspective: Implications for family counseling. *The Family Journal, 1*, 94–96.

Bray, J. H. (1995a). Assessment of family health and distress: An intergenerational systems perspective. In J. C. Conoley & E. Werth (Eds.), *Family assessment* (pp. 67–102), Lincoln, NE: Buros Institute of Mental Measurement.

Bray, J. H. (1995b). Family assessment: Current issues in evaluating families. *Family Relations, 44*, 469–477.

Bray, J. H. (1995c). Methodological advances in family psychology. *Journal of Family Psychology, 9*, 107–109.

Bray, J. H. (1999). From marriage to remarriage and beyond: Findings from the Developmental Issues in Stepfamilies Research Project. In E. M. Hetherington (Ed.), *Coping with divorce, single-parenting and remarriage: A risk and resiliency perspective* (pp. 253–271). Hillsdale, NJ: Lawrence Erlbaum Associates Publishers.

Bray, J. H., & Frugé, E. F. (2000). Assessment and evaluation of families with HIV/AIDS: Application to prevention and care. In W. Pequegnat & J. Szapocznik (Eds.), *Working with families in the era of HIV/AIDS* (pp. 27–43), Thousand Oaks, CA: Sage.

Carlson, C. I. (1989). Criteria for family assessment in research and intervention contexts. *Journal of Family Psychology, 3*, 158–176.

Carlson, C. I., & Grotevant, H. D. (1987). A comparative review of family rating scales: Guidelines for clinicians and researchers. *Journal of Family Psychology, 1*, 23–47.

Carter, E. A., & McGoldrick, M. (Eds.). (1988). *The changing family life cycle* (2nd ed.). New York: Gardner Press.

Cole, D. A., & Jordan, A. E. (1989). Assessment of cohesion and adaptability in component family dyads: A question of convergent and discriminant validity. *Journal of Counseling Psychology, 36*, 456–463.

Cole, D. A., & McPherson, A. E. (1993). Relation of family subsystems to adolescent depression: Implementing a new family assessment strategy. *Journal of Family Psychology, 7,* 119–133.

Cook, W. L., & Goldstein, M. J. (1993). Multiple perspectives on family relationships: A latent variables model. *Child Development, 64,* 1377–1388.

Dakof, G. A. (1996). Meaning and measurement of family: Comment on Gorman–Smith et al. (1996). *Journal of Family Psychology, 10,* 142–146.

Davidson, B., Quinn, W. H., & Josephson, A. M. (2001). Assessment of the family: Systemic and developmental perspectives. *Child & Adolescent Psychiatric Clinics of North America, 10,* 415–429.

Deacon, S. A., & Piercy, F. (2001). Qualitative methods in family evaluation: Creative assessment techniques. *American Journal of Family Therapy, 29,* 355–373.

Dickstein, S., Seifer, R., Hayden, L. C., Schiller, M., Sameroff, A. J., Keitner, G., Miller, I., Rasmussen, S., Matzko, M., & Magee, K. D. (1998). Levels of family assessment: II. Impact of maternal psychopathology on family functioning. *Journal of Family Psychology, 12,* 23–40.

Fine, M. A. (Ed.) (1993). Family diversity (special issue). *Family Relations, 42*(3).

Fisher, L. (1976). Dimensions of family assessment: A critical review. *Journal of Marriage and Family Counseling, 2,* 367–382.

Fisher, L., Kokes, R. F., Ransom, D. C., Phillips, S. L., & Rudd, P. (1985). Alternative strategies for creating "relational" family data. *Family Process, 24,* 213–224.

Floyd, F. J., Weinand, J. W., & Cimmarusti, R. A. (1989). Clinical family assessment: Applying structured measurement procedures in treatment settings. *Journal of Marital and Family Therapy, 15,* 271–288.

Fredman, N., & Sherman, R. (1987). *Handbook of measurements for marriage and family therapy.* New York: Brunner/Mazel.

Friedmann, M. L., Astedt–Kurki P., & Paavilainen, E. (2003). Development of a family assessment instrument for transcultural use. *Journal of Transcultural Nursing, 14,* 90–99.

Gable, S., Belsky, J., & Crnic, K. (1992). Marriage, parenting, and child development: Progress and prospects. *Journal of Family Psychology, 5,* 276–294.

Gaughan, E. (1995). Family assessment in psychoeducational evaluations: Case studies with the Family Adaptability and Cohesion Evaluation Scales. *Journal of School Psychology, 33,* 7–28.

Gottman, J. M. (1993). A theory of marital dissolution and stability. *Journal of Family Psychology, 7,* 57–75.

Gottman, J. M. (1994). *What predicts divorce? The relationship between marital processes and marital outcomes.* Hillsdale, NJ: Erlbaum.

Gottman, J. M. (1996). *What predicts divorce? The measures.* New York: Erlbaum.

Gottman, J. M., & Levenson, R. W. (1992). Marital processes predictive of later dissolution: Behavior, physiology, and health. *Journal of Personality and Social Psychology, 63,* 221–233.

Gray, J. (2001). The Framework for the assessment of children in need and their families. *Child Psychology & Psychiatry Review, 6,* 4–10.

Grotevant, H. D. (1989). The role of theory in guiding family assessment. *Journal of Family Psychology, 3,* 104–117.

Grotevant, H. D., & Carlson, C. I. (1989). *Family assessment: A guide to methods and measures.* New York: Guilford Press.

Hampson, R. B., Beavers, W. R., & Hulgus, Y. (1990). Cross-ethnic family differences: Interactional assessment of White, Black, and Mexican–American families. *Journal of Marital and Family Therapy, 16,* 307–319.

Hayden, L.C., Schiller, M., Dickstein, S., Seifer, R., Sameroff, S., Miller, I., Keitner, G., & Rasmussen, S. (1998). Levels of family assessment: I. Family marital and parent–child interaction. *Journal of Family Psychology, 12,* 7–22.

Heffer, R. W., & Snyder, D. K., (1998). Comprehensive assessment of family functioning. In L. L'Abate (Ed.), *Family psychopathology: The relational roots of dysfunctional behavior* (pp. 207–233). New York: Guilford Press.

Hetherington, E. M. (1993). An overview of the Virginia longitudinal study of divorce and remarriage. *Journal of Family Psychology, 7,* 39–56.

Hetherington, E. M., & Clingempeel, W. G. (1992). Coping with marital transitions: A family systems perspective. *Monographs of the Society for Research in Child Development, 57,* Nos. 2–3, Serial No. 227.

Hetherington, E.M., Henderson, S., & Reiss, D. (1999). *Adolscent siblings in stepfamilies. Family functioning and adolescent adjustment.* Malden, MA: Blackwell.

Jacob, T. (1995). The role of time frame in the assessment of family functioning. *Journal of Marital & Family Therapy, 21,* 281–288.

Jacob, T., & Tennenbaum, D. L. (1988). *Family assessment: Rationale, methods, and future directions.* New York: Plenum.

Jacob, T., & Windle, M., (1999). Family assessment: Instrument dimensionality and correspondence across family reporters. *Journal of Family Psychology, 13,* 339–354.

Jacob, T., Tennenbaum, D., Seilhamer, R. A., Bargiel, K., & Sharon, T. (1994). Reactivity effects during naturalistic observation of distressed and nondistressed families. *Journal of Family Psychology, 8,* 354–363.

Kashy, D. A., & Kenny, D. A. (1990). Analysis of family research designs: A model of interdependence. *Communication Research, 17,* 462–482.

Kaslow, N., Celano, M., & Dreelin, E. D. (1995). A cultural perspective on family theory and therapy. *Psychiatric Clinics of North America, 18,* 621–633.

Kenny, D. A., & LaVoie, L. (1984). The social relations model. In L. Berkowitz (Ed.), *Advances in experimental social psychology* (Vol. 18, pp. 141–182). Orlando, FL: Academic Press.

Kolevzon, M. S., Green, R. G., Fortune, A. E., & Vosler, N. R. (1988). Evaluating family therapy: Divergent methods, divergent findings. *Journal of Marital and Family Therapy, 14,* 277–286.

Levine, C. (1994). AIDS and the changing concept of the family. In R. Bor & J. Elford (Eds.), *The family and HIV* (pp. 3–22). London: Cassell.

Lovejoy, N. C. (1989). AIDS: Impact on the gay man's homosexual and heterosexual families. *Marriage and Family Review, 14,* 285–316.

Markman, H. J., & Notarius, C. I. (1987). Coding marital and family interaction: Current status. In T. Jacob (Ed.), *Family interaction and psychopathology: Theories, methods, and findings* (pp. 329–390). New York: Plenum Press.

Mellins, C. A., Ehrhardt, A. A., Newman, L., & Conard, M. (1996). Selective kin: Defining the caregivers and families of children with HIV disease. In L. Sweet Jemmott & A. O'Leary (Eds.), *Women and AIDS: Coping and care* (pp. 123–149). New York: Plenum.

Miller, I. W., Ryan, C. E., Keitner, G. I., Bishop, D. S., & Epstein, N. B. (2000). The McMaster approach to families: Theory, assessment, treatment and research. *Journal of Family Therapy, 22,* 168–189.

Minuchin, S. (1974). *Families and family therapy.* Cambridge: Harvard University Press.

Morris, T. M. (1990). Culturally sensitive family assessment: An evaluation of the Family Assessment Device used with Hawaiian–American and Japanese–American families. *Family Process, 29,* 105–116.

O'Farrell, T. J., Hooley, J., Fals–Stewart, W., & Cutter, H. S. G. (1998). Expressed emotion and relapse in alcoholic patients. *Journal of Consulting and Clinical Psychology, 66,* 744–752.

Olson, D. H. (1977). Insiders' and outsiders' view of relationships: Research strategies. In G. Levinger & H. Raush (Eds.), *Close relationships* (pp. 115–135). Amherst: University of Massachusetts Press.

Pequegnat, W., & Bray, J. H. (1997). Families and HIV/AIDS: Introduction to the special section. *Journal of Family Psychology, 11,* 3–10.

Pequegnat, W., & Szapocznik, J. (2000). *Working with families in the era of HIV/AIDS,* Thousand Oaks, CA: Sage.

Pequegnat, W., Bauman, L. J., Bray, J. H., DiClemente, R., DiIorio, C., Hoppe, S. K., Jemmott, L. W., Krauss, B., Miles, M., Paikoff, R., Rapkin, B., Rotheram–Borus, M. J., & Szapocznik, J. (2001). Measurement of the role of families in prevention and adaptation to HIV/AIDS. *AIDS and Behavior, 5,* 1–19.

Ransom, D. C., Fisher, L., Phillips, S., Kokes, R. F., & Weiss, R. (1990). The logic of measurement in family research. In T. W. Draper & A. C. Marcus (Eds.), *Family variables: Conceptualization, measurement, and use* (pp. 48–66). Newbury Park: CA: Sage.

Robbins, M. S., Hervis, O., Mitrani, V. B., & Szapocznik, J. (2001). Assessing changes in family interaction: The Structural Family Systems Ratings. In P. K. Kerig and K. M. Lindahl (Eds.), *Family observational coding systems: Resources for systemic research* (pp. 207–224. Hillsdale, NJ: Lawrence Erlbaum Associates.

Shek, D. T. L. (1998). The Chinese version of the Self-Report Family Inventory: Does culture make a difference? *Research on Social Work Practice, 8,* 315–329.

Shek, D. T. L. (2002). Assessment of family functioning in Chinese adolescents: The Chinese version of the Family Assessment Device. *Research on Social Work Practice, 12,* 502–524.

Skinner, H., Steinhauer, P., & Sitarenios, G. (2000). Family Assessment measure (FAM) and process model of family functioning. *Journal of Family Therapy, 22,* 190–210.

Spirito, A., Brown, R. T., D'Angelo, E., Delamater, A., Rodrigue, J., & Siegel, L. (2003). Society of Pediatric Psychology task force report: Recommendations for the training of pediatric psychologists. *Journal of Pediatric Psychology, 28,* 85–98.

Stevenson–Hinde, J., & Akister, J. (1995). The McMaster model of family functioning: Observer and parental ratings in a nonclinical sample. *Family Process, 34,* 337–347.

Straus, M. A., & Tallman, I. (1971). SIMFAM: A technique for observational measurement and experimental study of families. In J. Aldous (Ed.), *Family problem solving* (pp. 381–438). Hinsdale, IL: Dryden Press.

Szapocznik, J. & Kurtines, W. M. (1989). *Breakthroughs in family therapy with drug abusing and problem youth.* New York: Springer Publishing Company.

Szapocznik, J. & Kurtines, W. M. (1993). Family psychology and cultural diversity: Opportunities for the theory, research and application. *American Psychologist, 48,* 400–407.

Szapocznik, J., Hervis, O., Rio, A. T., Mitrani, V. B., et al. (1991). Assessing change in family functioning as a result of treatment: The Structural Family Systems Rating Scale (SFSR). *Journal of Marital & Family Therapy, 17,* 295–310.

Szapocznik, J., Santisteban, D., Rio, A., Perez–Vidal, A., et al. (1989). Family effectiveness training: An intervention to prevent drug abuse and problem behaviors in Hispanic adolescents. *Hispanic Journal of Behavioral Sciences, 11,* 4–27.

Thompson, L., & Walker, A. (1982). The dyad as the unit of analysis: Conceptual and methodological issues. *Journal of Marriage and the Family, 44,* 889–900.

Touliatos, J., Perlmutter, B. F., & Straus, M. A. (Eds.). (1990). *Handbook of family measurement techniques.* Newbury Park, CA: Sage Publications.

Walsh, F. (2003). *Normal family processes: Growing diversity and complexity* (3rd ed.). New York: Guilford Press.

Watson, W. H., & McDaniel, S. H. (1998). Assessment in transitional family therapy: The importance of context. In J. W. Barron (Ed.), *Making diagnosis meaningful: enhancing evaluation and treatment of psychological disorders* (pp. 161–195). Washington, D.C., U.S.: American Psychological Association.

Watzlawick, P., Weakland, J., & Fisch, R. (1974). *Change: Principles of problem formation and problem resolution.* New York: Norton.

Wilkinson, I. (2000). The Darlington Family Assessment System: Clinical guidelines for practitioners. *Journal of Family Therapy, 22,* 211–224.

PART II

General Strategies

CHAPTER 3

Qualitative Strategies in Couple and Family Assessment

MAUREEN DUFFY AND RONALD J. CHENAIL

Use of qualitative assessments in couples and family therapy provides many of the same advantages that qualitative research provides in human science inquiry. Qualitative strategies are flexible and nonreductionist, focused on meaning and on understanding and interpretation of experience and relationships. The complexity and multiple perspectives present in couples and family therapy provide rich opportunities for the clinician interested in qualitative assessment to represent family members' thoughts; actions; interactions; conversations; realities; motivations; beliefs; and lives in terms of words; figures; pictures; diagrams; matrices; drawings; observations; and stories. Qualitative assessment strategies span the continuum from noninterventive, observational strategies to interventive, prescribed activities and tasks. Additionally, the clinician as expert diagnostician can make qualitative assessments or, more commonly, can include the couple or family in a collaborative process of assessment (Franklin & Jordan, 1995; Gilbert & Franklin, 2003; Jordan & Franklin, 2003).

Qualitative assessment approaches are well suited for use in couples and family counseling. According to Goldman (1990, 1992), qualitative assessment methods tend to encourage an active role for clients; emphasize their holistic perspectives; encourage self-learning on their part from a developmental point of view; work well in group settings; reduce the difference between assessment and counseling; and work well when exploring the individualist aspects of the particular couple or family (e.g., culture, ethnicity, sexual identities, and socioeconomic levels; Ponterotto, Gretchen, & Chauhan, 2001).

Deacon and Piercy (2001) add that qualitative approaches to assessment are advantageous for the therapist because

- They encourage clients' active self-reflection.
- They create a complementary relationship between therapy and assessment.
- They can be selected according to the therapist's particular theory or model of therapy.
- They can be utilized to create a shared, participatory, and/or collaborative relationship.
- They foster clients' empowerment.
- They can increase clients' commitment to the assessment and therapy process.
- They can support couples' and families' communication and understanding in therapy.
- They can generate a contextually rich view of the clients.
- They can be flexible in their use with diverse populations.
- They can be sensitive to the couples' or families' personal worldviews.

Like all assessment, qualitative assessment is linked to a particular view of the world. The clinician can use qualitative assessments from a normative or a nonnormative clinical standpoint. Thus, qualitative assessments in couples and family therapy can be situated along the following three dimensions: (a) the noninterventive–observational, interventive–prescriptive continuum; (b) the expert–collaborative continuum; and (c) the normative or nonnormative clinical standpoint continuum.

This chapter will present a number of clinically useful qualitative assessment strategies and provide detailed descriptions of each method and clear procedures for its use, interpretation, and evaluation. Each method will be discussed within the framework of the three dimensions discussed in the previous paragraph (see Table 3.1).

OBSERVATIONAL STRATEGIES

Observing Structure, Hierarchy, and Interactions

Qualitative assessment name. Observing structure, hierarchy, and interactions is grounded in the work of Salvador Minuchin, who developed the structural model of family therapy, and Jay Haley, who developed the strategic model of family therapy. Minuchin and Haley are considered founders of family therapy and began to publish their work in the 1960s and 1970s.

Type of assessment. This is an observational assessment of family structure and organization; hierarchy; family subsystems; boundaries; coalitions; and alliances.

Use–target audience. This strategy is particularly suitable for family groups, including multigenerational families; it may also be used with couples and parts or subsystems of families.

Multicultural. Observation of structural, hierarchical, and interactional patterns of particular couples and families encourages therapist attention to the culturally specific and unique aspects of each couple and family.

Ease and time of administration. This strategy requires therapist understanding of the theoretical concepts underlying the observation; observation is continuous over the course of treatment. The therapist need not identify primarily as a structural or strategic family therapist to find these observations useful.

Scoring procedure. Scoring comprises clinical judgment and decisions based on observations.

Reliability/validity. Trustworthiness of structural/strategic model-based observations has been established by use over time. Outcome effectiveness has been scientifically validated by National Institute on Drug Abuse (NIDA) grant-supported work of Jose Szapocznik (Szapocznik & Coatsworth, 1999) and Howard Liddle (Liddle & Dakoff, 1995) at the University of Miami with drug-abusing adolescents.

Availability and source. For detailed information, see the works of Salvador Minuchin, Jay Haley, Charles Fishman, Harry Aponte, Cloe Madanes, and James Keim. Selected references include Aponte, 1994; Haley, 1991; Madanes, Keim, and Smessler, 1995; Minuchin, 1974; Minuchin and Fishman, 1981; Minuchin, Lee, and Simon, 1996.

Comment. One of the significant contributions of the structural/strategic models is the emphasis on observation and assessment of truly interactional sequences and phenomena as opposed to the observation and assessment of individual affect and behavior. Assessments, interventions, and outcomes based on the structural/strategic models are among the most widely researched of the systemic approaches.

Conducting and Utilizing Observational Assessment of Structure, Hierarchy, and Interactions

Assessment of family or couple structure, hierarchy, and interactions is begun at the initial clinical interview and continues throughout therapy. This form of assessment is used to conceptualize the case, to develop appropriate interventions, and, during the termination phase of therapy, to evaluate clinical outcome and effectiveness. Assessment of structure, hierarchy, and interactions is integrated within the therapeutic process. No formal and separate assessment phase is used in this method. Much of the structure, hierarchy, and interactional patterns can be observed from how family members respond to clinical questions and interact together during the session. The therapist may also need to ask the couple or family particular questions related to the following indicators if additional information is required to make a fuller assessment.

The structure of a family refers to the members of the couple or family, including extended family members, and their patterns of interaction, closeness, distance, conflict, conflict management, expressions of affect, problem-solving style, and rules and regulations (whether covert or overt) that govern their ways of relating to one another. The therapist assesses the family's structure by observing and assessing the following indicators:

- who sits close to whom and who sits furthest away from whom
- who initiates conversation about key family issues and who remains quiet
- who speaks spontaneously and who speaks only when spoken to
- who identifies the problem or goals for the therapy
- who agrees and who disagrees with the identified problem or goals
- what topics are permitted to be spoken about and who is allowed to talk about or comment on them; what topics seem to be off-limits for family members to discuss
- who can interrupt or disagree and who cannot
- how emotion is expressed and responded to by various family members
- whose opinion counts most and whose does not; who attempts to solve problems and who is less involved
- who is effective and competent at handling particular family tasks and who seems less effective
- who teams up with whom to get something done or to take a position

Carefully observing and assessing these indicators will provide the couple and family therapist with a wealth of interactional information about the family's structure and boundaries between individual members as well as sub-systems within the family. This information can then be utilized to develop appropriate systemic interventions and treatment plans.

Hierarchy is a concept related to the concept of family structure, but is important to consider and observe specifically because of its connection to issues of power, decision making, and roles within a couple or family. The therapist assesses hierarchy and other interactional patterns within the family by carefully attending to the following:

- who is in charge of which activities and functions within the couple or family
- who is in charge of discipline and who is in charge of fun
- who can make independent decisions and who must be consulted
- who has veto power over important decisions
- how family roles are tied to traditional gender roles
- who gets nurtured and by whom; who gets less nurturing from other family members

Case Example

Janice and Tom were parents of two small children, a 4-year-old boy, Billy, and an 8-month-old girl who had just started sleeping through the night. Janice and Tom complained of being chronically exhausted and frazzled. They were up most nights because Billy would not stay in his bedroom at night and routinely came into their room, fidgeting and crying, shortly after they attempted to go to bed. During the initial family therapy session, the therapist observed the parents' weak and ineffectual attempts to manage Billy's demands for attention. Billy repeatedly interrupted conversation between the therapist and Billy's parents by whining or by persistently asking them to play with the toys he had brought with him to the session. Billy's parents tried to pacify him without clearly telling him to be quiet and entertain himself. In the same way, Billy's parents felt powerless and expressed disagreement over how to handle the increasingly intolerable nighttime situation. Their only point of agreement was that they disagreed with their pediatrician's suggestion to lock Billy in his room at night.

The therapist was able to support Billy's parents in their efforts to take charge of the situation and clearly enforce the "must stay in your own bed rule." The therapist also encouraged Janice and Tom to develop a variety of ways of taking charge—learning how to take charge by being firm and consistent and also learning how to take charge by being playful and comforting.

Summary

Since the development of the structural and strategic models of family therapy, multiple new theories and models of couple and family therapy have been developed. However, the relational assessment of a couple or family's structure, hierarchy, and patterns of interaction remains a cornerstone of sound systemic work and can enhance case conceptualization and treatment planning by therapists practicing from many different systemic models. It is significant that clinical research has established the success of structural/strategic assessment and intervention with adolescent drug abusers—a large population that is difficult to treat.

INTERVIEWING

Diagnostic Interviewing

Qualitative assessment name. Diagnostic interviewing refers to the general method of interviewing clients within a framework of preexisting criteria that will then be used to make clinical assessments. In individual therapy, interviewing from within the framework of the DSM-IV to arrive at a clinical diagnosis is an example of diagnostic interviewing. In couples and family therapy, diagnostic interviewing is used to identify areas that couples or family members experience as problematic and as sources of strength. Identifying psychopathology of an individual member of the couple or family may be a part of the diagnostic interviewing process, if, in the judgment of the clinician, the presence of individual psychopathology is compounding the relational problems.

Type of assessment. This interview format is open ended. In diagnostic interviewing for couples, the following interpersonal domains are explored in order to arrive at a clinical diagnosis of the relational problems: Commitment to the Relationship; Emotional Expressiveness; Sexual Functioning; Development of Shared Goals and Aspirations; Gender Roles and/or Role Functioning; Communication Skills and Styles; Perceptions of Intimacy; and Conflict Management. In diagnostic interviewing for families, these domains are explored: Goal Setting; Hierarchy and Distribution of Power; Boundaries; Problem-Solving Skills; Role Functioning; Emotional Expressiveness and Responsiveness; Communications Skills and Styles; Social Support; and Conflict Management. It is important to remember that diagnostic interviewing should focus on process and not content areas. The specific questions chosen are inevitably tied to the theory and/or model that the therapist is utilizing.

Use–target audience. Couples and families are the target audience.

Multicultural. The therapist bears the responsibility for ensuring that the interview is conducted in a multiculturally sensitive way. Diagnostic interviewing should specifically take into account and include a focus on cultural factors unique to the couple or family.

Ease and time of administration. In most couples and family therapy, initial diagnostic interviews take between 1 and 2 hours. Additional sessions are scheduled as needed. Keep in mind that many family therapists purposefully do not make a clear distinction between "diagnosis" and "intervention."

Scoring procedure. Responses to the interview questions are compared to the criteria used by the therapist and a qualitative clinical assessment is then made. The assessment may be in the form of a problem description, a resource or strength description, and/or a score on the Global Assessment of Relational Functioning (GARF) Scale (American Psychiatric Association, 2000).

Reliability/validity. The particular diagnostic framework used by the clinician determines these. The diagnostic interviewing work with couples of John Gottman (1994a, b, 1999a, b), for example, is based on rigorous empirical study and has resulted in a reliable model identifying couple behaviors predictive of marriages that fail or those that succeed.

Availability and source. Resources for diagnostic interviewing are ordinarily found in the theoretical literature describing a particular family therapy approach. Additional excellent resources to enhance diagnostic interviewing are also available, among them the work of Atkinson (1999); Carlson and Sperry (1997); Gottman (1994a, b, 1999a, b); Karpel (1994); and Kaslow (1996).

Comment. Diagnostic interviewing requires the therapist to clearly think through and articulate the theoretical framework within which he or she is working.

Utilizing Diagnostic Interviewing with Couples

The sample interview questions included here are based on the work of Gottman (1999a) and Atkinson (1999). The first set of questions is designed to assess the commitment of each partner to the marriage and the strength of the marital bond. The second set is designed to assess the couple's management of conflict and the presence of behaviors predictive of marital failure. These samples are broad-based general questions that, in practice, would need to be broken down into smaller questions focusing on particular aspects of the general theme. These questions should be asked in a conjoint session.

Commitment and Strength of Marital Bond questions:

- Does your partner know what your hopes and dreams are for your marriage?
- Do you have a shared set of hopes and dreams that you can talk about or do you think that your hopes and dreams for your relationship are different from one another?
- Do you know your partner's pet peeves, current interests and hobbies, likes and dislikes?
- Does your partner know what you are most worried about now?
- Does your partner know how things are going for you at work and what challenges you experience there?
- What memories from the past and experiences from the present do you have that are closest to your image of what being together in a good way is like?
- When your partner wants to make you happy or laugh, what kinds of things is he or she likely to do?

These questions are important because they provide information about the commitment to the relationship, each partner's level of awareness of the other's internal world, and whether the couple has a shared vision for who they are together and for their future. Shared vision, friendship and reliance upon the other, and awareness of the other's thoughts and feelings are predictive of marital success.

Conflict Management questions:

- Can you describe what happens (what you say and do and how you feel) when you get into a disagreement?
- What do you see your partner saying and doing and how do you imagine he or she is feeling?
- How do you try to resolve arguments or problems once they have come up?

- What behaviors (include verbal and physical behaviors) of your partner hurt or upset you most?
- Do both of you try to resolve problems once they have come up or does one of you wind up doing more than the other to fix things?
- Do you feel that your partner values your opinions about things?
- If you have an idea about solving a problem or doing something differently in your relationship, is your partner open to hearing and trying out your suggestion or advice?

These questions are also important because they reveal how a couple fights and makes efforts to repair the relationship after the fight. They also reveal the presence of what Gottman (1994a, b, 1999a, b) calls the "four horsemen of the apocalypse," namely, criticism, defensiveness, contempt, and stonewalling. Contempt is the behavior in marriage most definitively predictive of marital failure and Gottman clearly identifies it as a form of abuse that must not be empathized with but that must be named as abusive and stopped. Contempt takes the form of belittling, mocking, put-downs (especially in front of others), and other forms of scorn and derision that come from one person assuming a superior position in relationship to the other.

Case Example

Wanda wanted the racy new Infiniti FX 35 that she was crazy about. Craig was very uncomfortable with the idea, complaining that they did not have $40,000 to spend on a car and repeatedly asked her in a mocking kind of way who she was trying to impress and attract. Wanda countered that "you only live once" and they would manage to pay for the car somehow. She was outgoing, a little flamboyant, and loved beautiful clothes, furnishings, and cars that were a little out of reach financially. Craig grew up with the injunction not to "make a show of yourself or stand out." Wanda's desire for the car was highly symbolic for Craig in terms of their sexual functioning, financial goals, and as a challenge to the values of his family of origin.

In this case, the therapist could actively help each partner to understand the internal world of the other around the issue of the car by asking each to reflect upon and share what meanings buying that car would hold for each, including exploring Craig's fears and insecurities and Wanda's needs and desires that she was seeing the car as fulfilling. This kind of therapeutic conversation would address what is at stake for each partner in the marriage in this situation and help unfold the maps of each one's internal world, thus making these maps more available to the other. Additionally, the therapist would directly address Craig's derisive behavior by naming it as contempt; explain the research findings on contempt; and strongly suggest that Craig discontinue any practices of contempt. The therapist would point out that Craig had already expressed his admiration for Wanda in many ways to which he could reconnect and also help Craig learn ways of expressing a different point of view clearly without resorting to insults.

Summary

Diagnostic interviewing is a theoretically driven method of obtaining information from client couples and families in order to arrive at a clinical description of the client's problems and strengths. This information forms the basis for developing targeted interventions that utilize the client's resources to manage problems differently in a more effective and satisfying way.

Interventive Interviewing

Qualitative assessment name. Interventive interviewing is based on the idea that any relationship or involvement is interventive in that it changes the system. Interventive interviewing refers to the use of a variety of categories of questions designed not only to obtain information for assessment but also to initiate therapeutic change simultaneously. The categories of questions include: circular questions (Fleuridas, Nelson, & Rosenthal, 1986; Penn, 1985; Selvini–Palazzoli, Boscolo, Cecchin, & Prata, 1980); reflexive questions (Tomm, 1987a, b, 1988); solution-focused questions (Berg & De Jong, 1996; de Shazer, 1988) and narrative questions (White & Epston, 1990). The Milan Group introduced the idea of circular questioning and Tomm introduced the phrase "interventive interviewing."

Type of assessment. The interview format is open ended.

Use–target audience. Individuals, couples, and families are the target audience.

Multicultural. Interventive interviewing is multiculturally respectful because it elicits information unique to the client's culture and worldview and makes no normative presuppositions.

Ease and time of administration. This interviewing method requires theoretical understanding of interventive interviewing and skill in question construction.

Scoring procedure. No formal scoring is done; "scores" are clients' responses to interventive questions that trigger changes in perception and/or behavior.

Reliability/validity. These are determined by trustworthiness demonstrated pragmatically through clinical effectiveness of technique over time.

Availability and source. An excellent "primer" on the use of circular questioning is the article by Fleuridas, Nelson, and Rosenthal (1986). Tomm's (1987a, b, 1988) *Family Process* series on interventive interviewing is the landmark articulation of the method and rationale.

Comment. Interventive interviewing has changed the landscape of family therapy by operationalizing the second-order cybernetics view (von Foerster, 1981), namely, that one is part of the system that one observes or "assesses" and changes the system by virtue of doing so.

Utilizing Interventive Interviewing with Couples and Families

Interventive interviewing with couples and families is marked by the therapist's reliance on the question rather than on the statement, on the interrogative form rather than on the declarative form. Statements communicate the worldview and preferences of the therapist, but questions invite clients to reflect on their experiences and to communicate their worldviews. Questions are seen as having the potential for triggering client change by inviting clients to see things differently within the context of the interaction between therapist and client. Interventive questions are nonblaming questions that invite clients to reflect on their beliefs, feelings, and behaviors, thus freeing them to think about themselves and their relationships with others in less defensive, more exploratory ways. Interventive questions avoid or remove the negative connotations usually associated with conversations about problems and stuck patterns of living.

Questions, framed nonjudgmentally, also have the potential for increasing clients' awareness of and concern for the other. Thus, questions are not considered neutral tools for obtaining information and assessment, but rather are interventive by their very nature, inviting change that can occur rapidly. The major categories of interventive questions are circular questions, reflexive questions, solution-focused questions, and narrative questions. To facilitate demonstration of the variety of interventive questions, examples of each will be included within the description for clinical use and not as a separate "case example" category.

Circular questions. In contrast to linear questions, circular questions focus on the relationships among persons and among the beliefs and views held by an individual person. Linear questions assume a sequence of action, such as cause and effect. The question "Why are you so angry?" is a good example of a linear question because it presumes that there is a knowable cause for the anger that precedes the anger in time. Examples of circular questions are: "How does your partner begin to reconnect with you when you have been arguing with each other?" or "When you get upset and raise your voice, which of your children seems to be most concerned and which seems to be least concerned?" or "How do they know that you have cooled down?" Circular questions invite clients to reflect on the relational effects of their thinking and acting. Such questions shift the client's view from that of actor to that of observer, from first or second person ("I" or "you") to third person ("he," "she," or "they"), bringing the presence of the other into much greater focus.

Reflexive questions. Reflexivity refers to a blurring between subject and object, self and other. It is the presence of the observer in all description. For example, assigning a DSM-IV diagnosis results in a particular description of a client, but it also reveals that the diagnostician has some alignment with the assumptions and theories supporting the DSM-IV. Likewise, the nightly news presents information about current events, but the order of the news items reveals editorial values about what is most significant. Reflexive questions invite clients to think about how they experience and describe themselves; how they present themselves to others; how others perceive them; what a change would mean to their lives and relationships; and how that change might be accomplished. Because reflexive questions are relational, they are also circular, but Tomm (1987b) distinguishes reflexive questions from circular questions by suggesting that "reflexive questioning focuses more heavily on an explicit recognition of the autonomy of the family in determining the outcome" (p. 182).

Examples of reflexive questions are: "In the midst of the monumental job of caring for your dying adult son, how are you maintaining your own sense of balance so that you can continue to be there for him?" and "In that so much of what you are saying to your son is said by your being there for him now, what things would upset you if you did not get to say them to him in words before he died?" and "Even if it never happens, what conversation do you imagine would be most helpful for your son's father to have now so that after your son's death his father would be less angry and less hurt?" These questions are gently suggestive of possible alternatives for action and reflection for the family to consider.

Solution-focused questions. Solution-focused questions play to the strength and resilience side of the court and are grounded in the postmodern constructivist view of knowledge. This view holds that individuals bring forth knowledge by their language practices and that western language practices are predominantly problem focused. As a result of problem-saturated talk, the strengths and solutions to problems that people utilize in their daily lives go unnoticed and are not brought forth in language to the same extent that problems are. Solution-focused questions are designed to bring forth exceptions to problem saturation and to emphasize competence, resilience, and strength. To help a therapist get in the appropriate mind-set for asking solution-focused questions, Insoo Kim Berg (n.d.) suggests that the therapist keep in mind that there must be good reasons for why a client has acted in a particular way.

Several categories of solution-focused questions exist:

- *Pre-session change questions*—ask what differences occurred between the time the appointment was set and the first session, capitalizing on the hope and positive change that often occur before the first session.
- *Exception questions*—ask about when the problem is less intense or less of a concern for the client or when it could have occurred but did not.
- *Miracle questions*—ask clients to describe how they would know the problem was not there anymore if they went to sleep and a miracle happened, and the problem went away—but they did not know that the miracle had happened because they were sleeping. This question encourages clients to focus, in a detailed and specific way, on how life would be different in the absence of the problem and how they would be feeling and living differently.

- *Scaling questions*—ask clients to consider how they would know they had made some progress from baseline toward their goals and what they would need to do to move another point or half point forward. The scaling question breaks goals down into manageable, realistic steps.
- *Coping questions*—ask how clients have been able to do what they have done, emphasizing the strength and dignity in surviving and managing life's hardships and obstacles.

Examples of solution-focused questions are, "When were there times that your toddler son might have had a tantrum but did not?" "Instead of having a tantrum, what did he do?" "What was different about how you were responding to him?"

Narrative questions. Narrative questions are rooted in the metaphor of the story and are designed to help clients represent their lives, relationships, and life experiences as part of an expanding and richer narrative or storyline. The work of White and Epston (1990) has been pivotal in providing family therapists with a theoretical framework and question construction guidelines from which to develop narrative practices. White and Epston drew from French philosopher Michel Foucault's analysis of knowledge in which persons were seen as being recruited into particular ways of thinking about the world and themselves and then measuring themselves and their lives against this dominant view. An example of a dominant discourse is the contemporary western representation of female beauty as young, thin, and unblemished. This dominant discourse provides an unyielding and agonizing standard against which young girls and women measure themselves and find themselves wanting.

Narrative questions help clients to reflect on their unwitting participation in this dominant discourse and to separate themselves from it. Clients are encouraged, through narrative questions, to think about their lives and relationships differently and to develop their own preferred stories and accounts of their life and relationships. Dominant narratives box people in. Narrative questions can be seen as a form of protest against the anonymous but powerful requirements of collective social knowledge and as an opportunity for clients to free themselves from the restrictions of such knowledge. Examples of narrative questions are: "What does being a 'good enough' mother as opposed to a 'perfect' mother mean for you?" "How would a 'good enough' mother think about the problems your teenage daughter is having?" "What would a 'good enough' mother tell a 'perfect mother' about being gentler on oneself?"

Summary

Understanding the systemic and nonnormative, nonpathologizing nature of circular, reflexive, solution-focused, and narrative questions and practice at question construction are the key skills required for effective interventive interviewing. Interventive interviewing involves therapist and client in a process of ongoing collaborative assessment and change.

Adult Attachment Interview

Qualitative assessment name. The Adult Attachment Interview (AAI) was developed by George, Kaplan, and Main through the Department of Psychology at the University of California, Berkeley, in 1985; the third edition was developed in 1996 (George, Kaplan, & Main, 1985, 1996). Both are unpublished manuscripts.

Type of assessment. The AAI is a semistructured interview designed to identify attachment representations in adults by examining narrative accounts of adults' early childhood experiences with parents or other primary caregivers for coherence, quality of presentation, and level of remembered detail.

Use–target audience. The AAI is intended for use with adults. Because early key attachment experiences are conceptualized as influencing emotion and behavior in later significant relationships, the AAI is particularly useful in couples work.

Multicultural. Emerging research (Rodrigues, Wais, Zevallos, & Rodrigues, 2001) is suggesting the universality of attachment scripts across cultures and therefore supports the use of the AAI with diverse populations.

Ease and time of administration. The AAI takes between 45 minutes and an hour and a half to complete. It consists of 20 open-ended questions, many requiring clarifying and/or probing follow-up questions. Administering the AAI requires specific training in the method and general skill in interviewing.

Scoring procedure. Scoring of the AAI is a complex process and requires completion of a 2-week intensive training course in the scoring and coding procedures developed by Main and Goldwyn. Each interview is transcribed verbatim and is rated on 14 nine-point scales. Certification in the administration and scoring of the AAI requires an additional 18 months, consisting of three tests taken at 6-month intervals. Each test requires the trainee to code a set of approximately 10 AAI transcripts.

Reliability/validity. Test–retest reliabilities of 78% (Bakermans–Kranenburg & Van IJzendoorn, 1993) and 90% (Benoit & Parker, 1994) have been reported.

Availability and source. The AAI protocol is available on the Web at: www.psychology.sunysb.edu/attachment/measures/content/aai_interview.pdf. It is made available on the Web only to provide context and access to the interview questions for those interested in the AAI and research surrounding it. The scoring manual is only available to those who have completed the specialized AAI training.

Comment. Data from this assessment interview is now being linked to developments in neuroscience (Cozolino, 2002; Siegel, 1999). The quality of brain integration of neural networks is hypothesized to be linked to the quality of early attachment relationships with parents or primary caregivers—the more secure the attachment, the better the integration of neural networks. This is a fascinating frontier at the intersection of neuroscience, attachment theory, and clinical family therapy practice.

Utilizing the Adult Attachment Interview in Couples and Family Therapy

The AAI is a semistructured interview in which the interviewer asks the respondent a series of questions primarily focused on recollections of the relationship with his mother and father. The bulk of the interview concentrates on the respondent's memories of early childhood and adolescent experiences and whether he experienced a parent as threatening or coercive. The interview includes specific questions about whether the respondent feels that any early childhood experience was negative or served as an impediment in life. The interview shifts to the present when the interviewer asks how the respondent thinks his childhood experiences have affected the development of his personality in general; what the quality of the respondent's current relationship with his parents is like; and how the respondent feels when he is separated from his children now. The interview also includes questions about loss of a loved one or other traumas and invites the respondent to speculate on why his parents acted as they did when the respondent was a child. The interview ends with a future focus in which the respondent is asked questions about his hopes and wishes for his children. The interview is taped and a verbatim transcript is made.

The respondent's answers to the questions compose a narrative of understanding and meaning or lack of it and of coherence or confusion about childhood experiences. Persons specifically trained in the coding of the AAI code the transcript according to the conventions of qualitative discourse analysis. The results of the coding are classified into one of four categories:

- (F) Secure—freely autonomous when the transcript narratives are internally coherent and consistent. Those with traumatic childhoods as well as those with stable, loving childhoods may be classified as secure because the criteria for classification are narrative coherence not the nature of the childhood experiences.
- (D) Insecure—dismissing when the narratives give evidence of minimization or denial of the significance of early childhood experiences and of relationships with parents or show idealization of parents.
- (E) Insecure—preoccupied when the narratives show confusion and inconsistency about early childhood relationships, experiences, and their meaning. The transcripts also give evidence of preoccupation with parents and/or current relationships with parents characterized by anger or by efforts to please.
- (U) Unresolved—narrative disorganization about a loss or trauma within the context of a narrative that meets the criteria for one of the three

preceding categories and would be so classified if it were not for the evidence of intense mourning, guilt, or irrational beliefs surrounding a loss or trauma.

The quality of early attachment experiences is increasingly being linked to brain development and neural integration (Schore, 2003). Narrative coherence and therefore secure attachment as scored on the AAI are hypothesized as reflecting better integration of neural networks in the brain (Cozolino, 2002; Siegel, 1999).

Case Example

A mother whose AAI score is (E) insecure–preoccupied may oscillate between anger at her parents and attempts to please them, thus preoccupying her so that she has difficulty identifying and responding to the emotional needs of her young child. Her attachment template oscillates between overvaluation and derogation of her parents, negatively affecting her ability to think clearly and making her vulnerable to emotional overreactions to her child's behavior.

Summary

The AAI is an instrument that has been widely used and researched by developmental psychologists and is gaining wider attention as neuroscience links early attachment experiences to brain development and integration. For family therapists, the attachment profiles obtained from the AAI provide information about the primary attachment pattern influencing a parent or spouse. For those who are insecurely attached, interventions can be appropriately targeted to help dismissive clients identify and respond to the emotional needs of others; to help preoccupied clients individuate and react less intensely to the behaviors of others; and to help those with unresolved trauma make sense and construct meaning around their experience of loss or abuse.

GRAPHIC METHODS

Genogram

Qualitative assessment name. The conceptual foundation for the use of genograms was advanced by Murray Bowen. The graphic and interpretive techniques for constructing and using genograms were refined and promoted by McGoldrick and colleagues at the Multicultural Family Institute of New Jersey.

Type of assessment. A genogram is a graphic representation of a person's family, interpersonal relationships among family members, and family history over multiple generations. The genogram is typically coconstructed by the therapist and client and represents key life-cycle events (e.g., birth, marriage, divorce, death) as well as the nature and intensity of relationships among family members. For example, it can be used in family assessment from a normative and a nonnormative clinical standpoint. Used by Bowenian therapists, the genogram can be used to track family patterns of enmeshment and disengagement—concepts that are normative within Bowen family systems theory. On the other hand, the genogram can also be used in a nonnormative way by solution-focused therapists to identify family patterns of strength, resilience, and problem-solving skill.

Use–target audience. The genogram can be used in couples and family therapy to represent family relationships visually and to identify or construct patterns of relationship, feeling, and behaving across a number of generations. In couples therapy, genograms can be constructed for each partner; major family patterns and themes can then be compared and discussed. For therapists working with individual clients who wish to introduce a family perspective, the use of a genogram can be particularly helpful in invoking the wider influence of family and context.

Multicultural. The genogram is a culturally sensitive and culturally specific assessment tool. The cultural context of the family and of individual family members is considered a fundamental part of using and interpreting the genogram. Hardy (Hardy & Laszloffy, 1995) has proposed the cultural genogram for use in training culturally competent family therapists.

Ease and time of administration. This is a simple method requiring that the therapist use pencil and paper and have a basic knowledge of the symbols and conventions used in genogram construction. A basic genogram can be developed in only several minutes; adding detail and complexity may require that the therapist encourage the client to gather more information about family history. The genogram can be enlarged and refined over time as more information about family history becomes available.

Scoring procedure. Representing and interpreting family history and family patterns of feeling and behaving is a process of coconstruction between the client and therapist. Factual information about marriages, significant relationships, births, divorces, deaths, and so forth is obtained from the client and represented graphically. As information about individual members of the client's extended family is gathered, patterns of feeling and behaving may become evident and may be identified or suggested by the client or the therapist. The process of interpretation is akin to thematic analysis in qualitative research in which recurring and dominant themes are identified.

Reliability/validity. The trustworthiness of the genogram is demonstrated by its consistent use over time by family therapists to identify family patterns and themes and the consistent perceived usefulness of the tool by therapists and clients. The use of the genogram has expanded to include a focus on strengths, resilience, culture, spirituality, and problem-solving skills, as well as its traditional use to identify pathology and family emotional themes.

Reliability and validity issues do emerge with respect to the role of memory and the accuracy of retrieved family history data.

Availability and source. McGoldrick's books on genograms (McGoldrick & Gerson, 1985; McGoldrick, Gerson, & Shellenberger, 1999) are basic references for developing skills in the construction and use of the genogram in therapy. Foster, Jurkovic, Ferdinand, and Meadows (2002) describe a manualized, research-focused approach for using the genogram with couples. Magnuson and Shaw (2003) provide an excellent review of the state of clinical practice and clinical training involving the use of the genogram. Various computer software programs to facilitate production of professional quality genograms are available.

Comment. Irrespective of preferred family therapy modality, a focus on a client's family history through the use of the genogram immediately expands the frame to include larger cultural themes and context.

Utilizing the Genogram in Couples and Family Therapy

Constructing a genogram is similar to building a family tree. The first step in developing a genogram is to identify the index person. The index person is typically the identified patient in family therapy or each partner in couples therapy, in which two genograms are constructed, one for each partner. Squares are used to identify males and circles to identify females. Birth and death dates are written above the symbol on the left and right, respectively. An "X" inside the symbol indicates the family member is dead. Marriage is indicated by a solid horizontal line connecting the symbols for male and female; living together is indicated by a dotted horizontal line connecting the symbols for the partners. Lesbian couples are indicated by two circles with inverted triangles inside them connected by a solid horizontal line. Gay couples are indicated by two squares with inverted triangles inside them connected by a solid horizontal line. Divorce is indicated by a double hash mark on the horizontal line connecting the couple, with the date of divorce next to it. Children are listed from oldest to the youngest, from left to right, with the symbols for male or female on vertical lines descending from the horizontal line between the couple. A solid vertical line indicates a biological child; a dotted line indicates a foster child; and a dual solid and dotted line indicates an adopted child. Other symbols indicate pregnancy, miscarriage, stillbirth, and identical or fraternal twins. Substance abuse is indicated by a horizontal line bisecting the symbol for male or female with the bottom half of the symbol shaded in. A significant mental or physical problem is indicated by a vertical line bisecting the symbol for male or female and the left side of the symbol shaded in.

In the genogram, the index person is indicated by a double circle or square and marriage or living together is then indicated as described earlier, with any children also symbolized. Parents and siblings of the index person are then symbolized, as are grandparents, aunts, uncles, and cousins as the family history becomes known. Each generation occupies its own line or latitude on the genogram, similar to a family tree, with the older generations (great grandparents, grandparents) on the upper part of the genogram and the children and subsequent generations on the lower part.

Relationships within a generation (for example, between siblings) or across generations, (for example, between a grandmother and granddaughter) are also indicated by specific symbols. Two solid lines between two people on the genogram indicate a close relationship; a dotted line indicates a distant relationship; a zigzag line indicates a conflicted or hostile relationship; and two solid lines with a zigzag line between them indicate a close, conflicted relationship.

A basic genogram can be constructed within a single therapy session using the knowledge of family history that the client brings with him or her. The therapist may ask the client to interview various family members in order to find out more information about family members, particularly in preceding generations. As the client brings in more information about his or her family, the genogram can be enhanced. A sufficiently detailed genogram will immediately reveal patterns of marriage and divorce, family size, multiple marriages or relationships, separation and divorce, and substance abuse or physical illness. The therapist will then use the genogram to help the client develop an enhanced understanding of larger family patterns. These patterns would include family vulnerabilities like addiction or depression, losses, and traumas, as well as family strengths, resources, and resiliencies, like adapting and prospering as an immigrant family without the support of extended kin. Ideally, this increased awareness will allow the client to see his or her place in the family history with greater emotional distance and increased cognitive understanding.

Case Example

Eric and Joy had been married for 18 months when they sought therapy because of increasing arguments and tension over money and communication. Eric complained that Joy was not as warm and close as she once was and that she did not pay attention to the cost of things; Joy complained that Eric wanted to spend too much time at home and was becoming boring. Eric was building his own spin-off business, with his father's help, from his father's successful insurance agency. Joy had a degree in advertising and was signed up with a professional temp agency. She worked 3 or 4 days most weeks. When she did not feel like working, she turned down the temporary jobs.

Eric's Genogram

Eric was the older of two boys. His mother and father had been married for 31 years; in the early years of their marriage, Eric's mom worked in the insurance agency that her husband had started. Gradually, as the business became more successful, she turned her attention to the children and their school and extracurricular activities. Eric's dad was very focused on doing the right thing, working hard, being a good provider, and living by the book. His father was a career military officer who bred this sense of duty and consistency into him. Eric was protected by his mother and tried very hard to receive approval from his father, who was not emotionally expressive.

Joy's Genogram

Joy was the third child of five, with one older brother and sister and one younger brother and sister. Joy's mother and grandmother worked as professionals—her grandmother as a physician and her mother as a pharmacist. Joy's father was an investigative journalist for the leading newspaper in their city. Family life was rough and tumble with boisterous dinner conversations and a steady stream of friends and her father's talkative newspaper colleagues throughout the house. Joy's mother participated in rock climbing, sailing, and white-water rafting whenever she could. Joy was interested in everything but had a hard time focusing on anything in particular. She worshipped her father and had little time for her mother, whom she saw as self-centered and aloof.

Interpretation and Therapeutic Use

Eric valued the pattern of hard work, commitment, and loyalty that he saw in his family when considering his genogram. He also saw the multigenerational father–son pattern of seeking approval and lack of emotional expressiveness. Joy relished the intellectual vigor that characterized her multigenerational family. In thinking about her genogram, Joy also began to see the women in her family in a new light. Although she had always valued her father's curiosity, love of life, and brashness, she began to appreciate her mother and grandmother as trailblazers and independent spirits in their own, more quiet ways.

In discussing Joy's genogram, Eric was vividly reminded of how Joy's own free-spirited ways were what had attracted him to her in the first place. Eric also recognized that he did not want to spend the rest of his life waiting for his father's approval and began to see himself as a "good enough" son already. In so doing, he moved closer to Joy and began to accept her invitations to have more fun and play in their relationship. For her part, Joy began to see herself as a strong woman in a line of strong women, although not as quiet or solitary as her mother, and started to focus on her career aspirations, which pleased Eric. Joy also began to see Eric's steadiness and loyalty as a reflection of his commitment to her rather than as a boring and plodding personality trait. She saw that, in overvaluing her father's unpredictable hours and activities, she had undervalued Eric's reliable presence and pleasure in the ordinary things of domestic life.

Summary

The genogram is a basic family therapy assessment tool that has numerous applications in clinical practice. The genogram enables therapist and client to identify family patterns of strength and deficit quickly and to locate an individual's life within the multigenerational family and wider community and culture.

CREATIVE AND METAPHOR-BASED METHODS

Zaltman Metaphor Elicitation Technique

Qualitative assessment name. Zaltman Metaphor Elicitation Technique (ZMET), developed by Harvard University's Dr. Gerald Zaltman (2003), is a patented qualitative research tool that enables participants to understand their thinking more fully and to share this thinking with others (Christensen & Olson, 2002, p. 478). ZMET was originally created to help researchers map the knowledge structures of consumers, employees, and managers (see Leary, Zaltman, & Wheeler, 2002) and its strengths have now been applied to working with couples and families.

Type of assessment. In therapy, ZMET uses visual and nonvisual "images" gathered from and/or generated by family members to elicit and probe the metaphors that represent their thoughts and feelings about a topic. The images are explored through a guided interview and the data produced through these interviews lead to the identification of family members' constructs or constructions of meaning. The individual constructs are then grouped together to form a consensus map that charts the relationships between the various constructs (Zaltman, 1996, pp. 16–19).

Use–target audience. ZMET can be used with individuals, couples, families, and groups.

Multicultural. ZMET can be used with couples and families from all cultures.

Ease and time of administration. The successful use of ZMET involves four parts: (a) client preparation (1 half-hour); (b) one-on-one interview with the client (1 to 2 hours); (c) analysis of the interview data and quality control with constructs and consensus maps (1 to 2 weeks); and (d) presentation of results to client (one to two sessions) (Christensen & Olson, 2002; Coulter, Zaltman, & Coulter, 2001; Zaltman, 1996, 2003).

Scoring procedure. The one-on-one interviews are coded in terms of constructs and then relationships between the constructs are constructed to form consensus maps (Christensen & Olson, 2002, p. 486; Leary, Zaltman, & Wheeler, 2002).

Reliability/validity. ZMET employs a number of techniques to increase the rigor of its analysis: (a) varied questioning techniques that build in redundancy and help to create greater levels of confidence in the analysis and the importance of the ideas being expressed; (b) one-on-one interviews recorded and transcribed so that their content can be reviewed throughout the analysis process (Christensen & Olson, 2002, p. 483); (c) incorporation of the constant comparative method of analysis from grounded theory that requires individuals conducting the analysis to return continuously to the transcript to validate the coding process (Glaser & Strauss, 1967); and (d) use of member checking by presenting the consensus maps to clients for their validation of the results (Patton, 2002).

Availability and source. Information on ZMET can be located at the Olson Zaltman Associates Web site (http://www.olsonzaltman.com/)

Comment. Although the application of ZMET to psychotherapy is relatively recent, the approach has been used successfully to assess psychologically the thoughts and feelings of customers, employees, and managers (e.g., Leary, Zaltman, & Wheeler, 2002).

Conducting and Utilizing ZMET with Families

To initiate the ZMET process, the therapist identifies a subject area upon which to focus the exercise (e.g., going to school, parenting children, managing finances, maintaining intimacy, etc.). This step can also be done collaboratively with the client. Family members are asked to gather 8 to 10 pictures that reflect their thoughts and feeling about the subject over the next week and to bring the images with them to the next therapy session.

In the next session, the therapist asks the family members to share their feelings and thoughts about the images they have collected. The pictures serve as visual clues or metaphors as the interviewer explores and probes the family members' deeper meanings regarding the pictures. The therapist can use a variety of techniques to elicit thoughts and feelings, such as asking family members to (Coulter, Zaltman, & Coulter, 2001, pp. 4–5; Zaltman, 1996, pp. 14–16)

- Tell stories about pictures to elicit metaphors
- Speak about the pictures not found and to say what they would have said if such an image had been located or created
- Go into more detail or to elaborate more on their feelings and thoughts
- Speak about the color, taste, smell, touch, and sound that the images suggest to them
- Create a play or movie that expresses significant emotions and ideas about a certain picture or pictures
- Create a summary collage from the images and give a verbal description of the image

Recorded interviews are transcribed and the transcripts are coded in terms of constructs that the therapist identifies. Constructs are constructions made by the therapist that represent important thoughts and feelings of the family members. The constructs are given summary names (e.g., metaphors) intended to represent the key features of clients' "mental terrain" (i.e., their concepts, ideas, emotions, values, thoughts, and feelings; Zaltman, 1996, p. 16). As each construct or metaphor is constructed, the therapist can begin to create consensus maps that represent the mental terrain of the family member or members (Christensen & Olson, 2002, pp. 485–487).

After the maps are constructed and validated through constant comparative method, the therapist presents the findings to the family members. These sessions can serve as openings to new areas of discussion in the counseling. In addition, the findings from the ZMET approach can be compared and contrasted with other information generated during the intake and counseling process. This gives the therapist opportunity to triangulate findings and to increase the rigor of the assessments (Patton, 2002). Last, as therapy progresses, the therapist can direct family members to revisit the topic and select new images. The therapist can interview family members again and note what change, if any, has occurred in their thoughts and feelings regarding the topic in question. The therapist can also revisit the consensus maps with the family members to see what changes, if any, have occurred in their reactions to the previously elicited metaphors and consensus maps.

Summary

ZMET, a tool initially developed to explore customers' thoughts and feelings regarding products and advertising campaigns, has evolved into a rigorous assessment method for counselors and therapists.

PROTOCOL FOR USING QUALITATIVE ASSESSMENT STRATEGIES WITH COUPLES AND FAMILIES

The following protocol provides summative guidelines for using the preceding qualitative assessment strategies with couples and families.

1. Select qualitative assessment strategies appropriate for the couple or family and their presenting problem(s). Considerations: Are the strategies selected compatible with the therapist's theoretical framework and clinical operating assumptions?
2. Determine whether the assessment strategies to be used will be diagnostic only or iterative (diagnostic and interventive). Considerations: Will the selected strategies be used at intake only or throughout therapy on an ongoing basis? Diagnostic interviewing and the AAI should be used primarily during intake and as part of a formal assessment process. Observing structure, hierarchy, and interactions; interventive interviewing, genograms; and ZMET should typically be used diagnostically as well as iteratively.

3.   Implement the selected qualitative strategy.

   1. Collect data. (Observe, and/or interview, and/or develop the genogram, and/or construct the consensus map and collaborative activity.)

   2. Analyze and interpret the data. (Ensure that data analysis and interpretation methods are appropriate for the selected strategy.)

4.   Collect additional collateral information about the couple or family, as needed. Possible collateral information could include review of clinical records; interviews with significant others in the client's relational system (e.g., teacher, physician, probation officer, family member, or friend); and results of other clinical or psychological assessments (e.g., inventories of personality, family, self-report, family violence or child abuse, or divorce or child custody). Collecting data from several sources (e.g., multiple family members, other assessments, clinical records, etc.) is a process called *triangulation* in qualitative research and is a method of confirming and verifying results.

5.   Review the preceding information and develop an initial qualitative report for the couple or family assessed. The report may summarize the couple or family system from a relational perspective only or it may additionally provide assessment information about each individual member of the couple or family. Individual family member reports should be akin to "within-case" analyses in qualitative research and relational or systemic reports akin to "cross-case" analyses. Some reports include within-case and cross-case analyses, whereas others include the cross-case or relational perspective only. The clinician determines the most appropriate report form based on the clinical purpose for the report.

   Reports can be oral, written, graphic, or artistic in format. Reports based on observing structure, hierarchy, and interactions are often oral. Reports based on diagnostic interviewing and the AAI are typically written. Reports based on interventive interviewing may be oral or written; if written, such reports may be in the form of letters to the client and may include reflections of the therapist about the client's new understandings or positive life changes. Reports based on the genogram should include a graphic component and reports using the ZMET may include a graphic or artistic component.

6.   Present preliminary assessment results/report to the couple or family before revising the qualitative report. Use of qualitative assessment strategies involves a collaborative process of verification of results. What this means is that the clinician presents preliminary results and interpretations to the couple or family for their comments and feedback prior to revising or summarizing the results. In qualitative research, this process

is called member checking. The revised report incorporates the results of this member checking process.

For the preliminary and the revised reports, qualitative assessments about parental or couple functioning should never be provided to parents in the presence of children. Qualitative reports about children's functioning should be provided to parents and may be provided to the children in an age-appropriate way, as deemed therapeutic by the clinician. Qualitative assessments of adolescent functioning should be given to an adolescent and to the adolescent's parents within a context of respect and sensitivity for the adolescent's growing autonomy.

7. Review preliminary report and feedback from member checking and develop a revised report. This can be an iterative report reflecting the interactional effect between the therapist's use of the qualitative strategies and movement in the couple or family since the beginning of the clinical assessment process or it can be a summative report more reflective of the clinician's diagnostic impressions.

EXTENDED CASE EXAMPLE

Background Information and Presenting Problem

Elaine, a 43-year-old paralegal, and her 45-year-old husband Sam, the owner–operator of a small house-repairs business, came to therapy requesting help for their 14-year-old son, Brian, who expressed fear and resentment about transferring to a new middle school. The family had recently moved to a new neighborhood because they wanted Brian and his 10-year-old sister, Danielle, to benefit from the better schools in this new location. The parents described Brian as quiet and "into himself," but they said they had never thought much of it and were happy that he had not been a behavioral problem at school or home. Brian's academic performance at his previous middle school was average. The family moved to their new neighborhood about 6 weeks before the start of the school year. During the first 3 weeks of school, Brian attended school for only 7 full days. On the other days, Brian came home sick or did not go to school in the first place because of stomach pain and headaches. The school's attendance office had contacted the parents about Brian's situation; his parents had taken him to their primary care doctor who could not find anything wrong with him and referred him for therapy.

Based on the presenting problem, and on the therapist's systemic theoretical framework, the therapist decided to utilize the following qualitative assessment

TABLE 3.1 Matrix: Qualitative Assessment Strategies With Couples and Families

Assessment instrument	Specific couple and family applications	Cultural/ language	Instructions/use: T = time to take; S = time to score; I = items	Computerized: a = scoring; b = report	Reliability/ validity	Availability
Observing structure, hierarchy, and interactions	Parents, partners, or children; provides visual and language-based profile of relational patterns	Administer in any language	T = 60–120 min; S = 60–120 min; I = n/a	a = no; b = no	Triangulation	Books; journal articles
Diagnostic interviewing	Parents, partners, or children; provides visual and language-based profile of relational patterns	Administer in any language	T = 60–120 min; S = 60–120 min; I = responses to questions	a = no; b = no	Triangulation; member checks	Books; journal articles
Adult Attachment Inventory (AAI)	Parents or partners; provides narrative accounts of relational patterns	Administer in any language	T = 45–90 min; S = several hours; I = 20	a = no; b = no	Test-retest reliability: .70–.90	AAI workshops; AAI Web sites
Interventive interviewing Circular Reflexive; Solution-Focused Narrative	Parents, partners, or children; language-based; used to identify and change relational patterns	Administer in any language	T = 60–120 min; S = 60–120 min; I = responses to questions	a = no; b = no	Triangulation; member checks	Books; journal articles
Genogram	Parents, partners, or children; provides graphic of multigenerational relationships and family themes	Administer in any language	T = 10–30 min; S = 20–60 min; I = n/a	a = no; b = yes	Triangulation; member checks	Books; journal articles; computer software
Zaltman Metaphor Elicitation Technique (ZMET)	Parents, partners, or children; visual and language-based construction of image and consensus maps	Administer in any language	T = 60–120 min; S = several hours; I = n/a	a = no; b = no	Triangulation; member checks; constant-comparative method	Journal articles; www.olsonzaltman.com

strategies: observation of structure, hierarchy, and family interactions; interventive interviewing; construction of a genogram; and the ZMET (Step 1). She elected to use the strategies iteratively (diagnostically and interventively) with the goal of facilitating rapid change (Step 2).

During the initial 90-minute session, the therapist observed the family's structure, hierarchy, and interactions. Although the parents expressed concern for Brian and his obvious difficulty in going to school, they were not emotionally expressive with each other or towards Brian; they easily lapsed into a pattern of bewildered silence, shrugging their shoulders and waiting for the therapist to say something. When Brian's parents asked him if there were any problems at school, Brian said that he did not know and the family lapsed into silence again. The therapist quickly concluded that the parents had limited skill in providing emotional support to each other or to their introverted 14-year-old son and that the family was floundering and leaderless in the domain of emotional expressiveness. Family members were insufficiently involved with one another. The therapist utilized interventive interviewing in order to help the family members give voice to their unexpressed feelings and worries and lived experiences within their family. Each family member was asked to describe what he or she imagined the other family members were most worried about as they sat in the room finding it hard to say anything (Step 3).

In addition, the therapist asked the parents about their fondest hopes for Brian and what they imagined he had been going through since the move and transfer to the new middle school. The therapist asked the parents to think back to their early teenage years and to describe a time when an older person had given them some encouragement or helped out and what that had meant to them. She also asked the parents to share their perspectives on how being a teenager today is different from being a teenager when they were growing up. The data collected from the family through the process of interventive interviewing provided the basis for further assessment of Brian's and his parents' worries and fears and also began to open up space for connection between them through sharing of meanings and reflections about adolescence and getting support from adults (Step 4).

Building upon the emerging themes of isolation versus mutual support, and bewilderment versus active encouragement and emotional expressiveness, the therapist helped the family to construct their genogram and locate themselves within the wider context of their larger family and cultural history, at least as much of it as they were able to pull together. Brian's parents were second-generation Irish immigrants and were part of the Irish Diaspora, with close relatives whom they had never met in Australia, England, and other parts of the U.S. As they constructed their genogram, the family began to see that their enduring work ethic and "suffer in silence" style made sense given the challenges and lack of support that their grandparents and great-grandparents contended with as immigrants to the southern U.S. without extended family or an Irish exile community to depend upon. Brian began to express an interest in his cultural history and his parents began to reflect on how difficult it had been for their families without active support from other relatives or a community.

The qualitative assessments that the therapist had selected worked synergistically and helped the family to reflect on themes of isolation, support, encouragement, and expressiveness. Brian's parents were thinking about and commenting upon their cultural heritage of "suffer in silence" and were questioning how they could change that history for Brian and Danielle. A fuller assessment of Brian's particular fears about school and his relationships was critical. The therapist decided to involve the family fully in that assessment because the context had now been set for greater reflection and sharing with one another through use of the other qualitative assessments described. The therapist built upon Brian's interest in art and symbols and used the ZMET for this purpose.

Brian was asked to collect 8 to 10 pictures that represented school to him; his mother and father were asked to help him with the assignment. The family used their computer and scanner to collect digital images and printed off the results for the therapist. In the next two therapy sessions, the therapist interviewed Brian about the images he had collected (e.g., pictures of a prison, a jungle scene, teenagers dressed in "Goth" attire, and some weapons). The therapist engaged the child in a conversation and explored the preliminary analysis of each image as a metaphor for school (e.g., school as a prison). Each picture-to-metaphor connection was analyzed and the therapist began to construct a consensus map of Brian's feelings, thoughts, and concepts of school. This helped to identify Brian's central constructs (e.g., fear of the unknown and isolation); overall desired end state (e.g., feeling safe, connected, and comfortable at school); and missing constructs (e.g., the roles of friends at school). Brian and his family made a summary collage of the digital images that served as a baseline assessment of Brian's experience of school throughout the course of therapy. As he became more comfortable with his new school, Brian and his family removed certain images from the collage that no longer represented a feature of his mental map and added new images that represented his changed map of the school.

The therapist used oral and written reports to Brian and his family in an iterative process throughout therapy and worked collaboratively with the family to develop graphic assessments through the use of the genogram and ZMET (Step 5 and Step 6). The oral reports consisted of summarizing and commenting upon the themes derived from the qualitative assessment data—namely, isolation versus mutual support and bewilderment versus active encouragement and emotional expressiveness. The therapist invited Brian and his parents to reflect on these themes and to add their own comments and meanings to them in an ongoing collaborative and iterative process.

The therapist developed written reports in the form of letters to Brian and his parents after each session. In the letters, the therapist would reflect on the most recent therapy session by posing interventive questions to each family member related to the major theme discussed in the session. In this way, more data for ongoing iterative assessment and intervention were collected. Through building a genogram, the family created a more coherent and articulated history than they had constructed previously and they were able to stand back from that history and see themselves and their own challenges within it. The collage and consensus map of Brian's fears and hopes developed through the ZMET provided the family and the therapist with a baseline assessment that the family manipulated and modified as Brian's relationship to school, friends, and family changed (Step 7).

CONCLUDING COMMENTS

The qualitative assessment methods included in this chapter consist of classic assessments like the genogram and structural and strategic observations and novel methods like the ZMET. The postmodern perspective on interpersonal assessment is represented in the section on interventive interviewing. Additionally, an overlooked resource, the AAI has been included for family therapists interested in using this assessment to guide therapy toward repair of insecure attachments in the service of brain integration, consistent with the latest findings in neuroscience. The ZMET, also based in part on findings from neuroscience, can help the therapist and family create coherent narratives and mental maps that also enhance brain integration and development.

The role of theory in assessment selection has been emphasized and assessment techniques representing multiple philosophical paradigms have been presented. Qualitative assessments in couples and family therapy are the cornerstone of the work of practicing family therapists; in fact, some therapists also suggest that the use of qualitative approaches can have therapeutic benefits for clients (e.g., Gale, 1992). It is hoped that this chapter has been a review of methods with which the reader is already familiar as well as an invitation to explore some new ones.

REFERENCES

American Psychiatric Association. (2000). *The diagnostic and statistical manual of mental disorders,* (4th ed., text revision). Washington, D.C.: Author.

Aponte, H. J. (1994). Bread and spirit: Therapy with the new poor: Diversity of race, culture, and values. New York: Norton.

Atkinson, B. (1999). Brainstorms: Rewiring the neural circuitry of family conflict. *Family Therapy Networker, July/August,* 23–33.

Bakermans–Kranenburg, M. J., & Van IJzendoorn, M. H. (1993). A psychometric study of the adult attachment interview: Reliability and discriminant validity. *Developmental Psychology, 29,* 870–880.

Benoit, D., & Parker, K. C. H. (1994). Stability and transmission of attachment across three generations. *Child Development, 65,* 1444–1456.

Berg, I. K. (n.d.). *Hot tips.* Retrieved July 16, 2003, from http://www.brief-therapy.org/insoo_essays.htm

Berg, I. K., & De Jong, P. (1996). Solution-building conversations: Coconstructing a sense of competence with clients, *Families in Society, 77,* 376–391.

Carlson, J., & Sperry, L. (Eds.) (1997). *The disordered couple.* New York: Taylor & Francis.

Christensen, G. L., & Olson, J. C. (2002). Mapping consumers' mental models with ZMET. *Psychology & Marketing, 19*(6), 477–501.

Coulter, R. A., Zaltman, G., & Coulter, K. S. (2001). Interpreting consumer perceptions of advertising: An application of the Zaltman Metaphor Elicitation Technique. *Journal of Advertising, 30*(4), 1–20.

Cozolino, L. (2002). *The neuroscience of psychiatry: Building and rebuilding the human brain.* New York: Norton.

Deacon, S. A., & Piercy, F. P. (2001). Qualitative methods in family evaluation: Creative assessment techniques. *The American Journal of Family Therapy, 29*(5), 355–373.

de Shazer, S. (1988). *Clues: Investigating solutions in brief therapy.* New York: Norton.

Fleuridas, C., Nelson, T. S., & Rosenthal, D. M. (1986). The evolution of circular questions: Training family therapists. *Journal of Marital and Family Therapy, 12,* 113–127.

Foster, M. A., Jurkovic, G. J., Ferdinand, L. G., & Meadows, L. A. (2002). The impact of the genogram on couples: A manualized approach. *The Family Journal: Counseling and Therapy for Couples and Families, 10,* 34–40.

Franklin, C., & Jordan, C. (1995). Qualitative assessment: A methodological review. *Families in Society, 16*(5), 281–295.

Gale, J. (1992). When research interviews are more therapeutic than therapy interviews. *The Qualitative Report, 1*(4). Retrieved September 7, 2003, from http://www.nova.edu/ssss/QR/QR1-4/gale.html

George, C., Kaplan, N., & Main, M. (1985). The attachment interview for adults. Unpublished manuscript, University of California, Berkeley.

George, C., Kaplan, N., & Main, M. (1996). Adult attachment interview. Unpublished manuscript (3rd ed.), Department of Psychology, University of California, Berkeley.

Gilbert, D. J., & Franklin, C. (2003). Qualitative assessment methods. In C. Jordan & C. Franklin (Eds.), *Clinical assessment for social workers: Quantitative and qualitative methods* (2nd ed., pp. 139–178). Chicago: Lyceum Books.

Glaser, B. G., & Strauss, A. L. (1967). *The discovery of grounded theories: Strategies for qualitative research.* Chicago: Aldine.

Goldman, L. (1990). Qualitative assessment. *Counseling Psychologist, 18*(2), 205–213.

Goldman, L. (1992). Qualitative assessment: An approach for counselors. *Journal of Counseling and Development, 70*(5), 616–621.

Gottman, J. M. (1994a). *Why marriages succeed or fail.* New York: Simon & Schuster.

Gottman, J. M. (1994b). *What predicts divorce?* Hillsdale, NJ: Lawrence Erlbaum.

Gottman. J. M. (1999a). *The marriage clinic: A scientifically based marital therapy.* New York: Norton.

Gottman, J. M. (1999b). *The seven principles for making marriage work.* New York: Crown Publishers.

Haley, J. (1991). *Problem-solving therapy* (2nd ed.). San Francisco: Jossey–Bass.

Hardy, K. V., & Laszloffy, T. A. (1995). The cultural genogram: Key to training culturally competent family therapists. *Journal of Marital and Family Therapy, 21,* 227–237.

Jordan, C., & Franklin, C. (2003). *Clinical assessment: Quantitative and qualitative methods* (2nd ed.). Chicago: Lyceum Books.

Karpel, M. A. (1994). *Evaluating couples: A handbook for practitioners.* New York: Norton.

Kaslow, F. W. (Ed.). (1996). *Handbook of relational diagnosis and dysfunctional family patterns.* Wiley Interscience.

Leary, K., Zaltman, G., & Wheeler, M. (2002). Thoughts and feelings about anticipating negotiation. Retrieved August 25, 2003, from Harvard University, The Mind of the Market Laboratory Web Site: http://www.hbs.edu/mml/negotiation/index.html

Liddle, H. A., & Dakoff, G. A. (1995). Family-based treatment for adolescent drug use: State of the science. In E. Rahdert & D. Czechowicz (Eds.), *Adolescent drug abuse: Clinical assessment and therapeutic interventions* (pp. 218–254). National Institute on Drug Abuse Research monograph 156. NIH Pub. No. 95-3908. Rockville, MD: National Institute on Drug Abuse.

Madanes, C., Keim, J., & Smessler, D. (1995). *The violence of men: A therapy of social action.* San Francisco: Jossey–Bass.

Magnuson, S., & Shaw, H. E. (2003). Adaptations of the multifaceted genogram in counseling, training, and supervision. *The Family Journal: Counseling and Therapy for Couples and Families, 11,* 45–54.

McGoldrick, M., & Gerson, R. (1985). *Genograms in family assessment.* New York: Norton.

McGoldrick, M., Gerson, R., & Shellenberger, S. (1999). *Genograms: Assessment and intervention* (2nd ed.). New York: Norton.

Minuchin, S. (1974). *Families and family therapy.* Cambridge: Harvard University Press.

Minuchin, S., & Fishman, H. C. (1981). *Family therapy techniques.* Cambridge, MA: Harvard University Press.

Minuchin, S., Lee, W-Y., & Simon, G. M. (1996). *Mastering family therapy: Journeys of growth and transformation.* New York: Wiley.

Patton, M. Q. (2002). *Qualitative research & evaluation methods* (3rd ed.). Thousand Oaks, CA: Sage.

Penn, P. (1985). Feed forward: Future questions, future maps. *Family Process, 24,* 299–311.

Ponterotto, J. G., Gretchen, D., & Chauhan, R. V. (2001). Cultural identity and multicultural assessment: Quantitative and qualitative tools for the clinician. In L. A. Suzuki, J. G. Ponterotto, & P. J. Mellor (Eds.), *Handbook of multicultural assessment: Clinical, psychological, and educational applications* (2nd ed., pp. 67–99). San Francisco: Jossey–Bass.

Rodrigues, L. M., Wais, D. P., Zevallos, A., & Rodrigues, R. R. (2001, April). Attachment scripts across cultures: Evidence for a universal script. Poster session presented at Society for Research in Child Development, Minneapolis, MN.

Schore, A. N. (2003). *Affect dysregulation and disorders of the self.* New York: Norton.

Selvini–Palazzoli, M., Boscolo, L., Cecchin, G., & Prata, G. (1980). Hypothesizing–circularity–neutrality: Three guidelines for the conductor of the session. *Family Process, 19,* 3–12.

Siegel, D. J. (1999). *Developing mind: Toward a neurobiology of interpersonal experience.* New York: Guilford.

Szapocznik, J., & Coatsworth, J. D. (1999). An ecodevelopmental framework for organizing risk and protection for drug abuse: A developmental model of risk and protection. In M. Glantz & C. R. Hartel (Eds.), *Drug abuse: Origins and interventions* (pp. 331–366). Washington, D.C.: American Psychological Association.

Tomm, K. (1987a). Interventive interviewing: Part I. Strategizing as a fourth guideline for the therapist. *Family Process, 26,* 3–13.

Tomm, K. (1987b). Interventive interviewing: Part II. Reflexive questioning as a means to enable self-healing. *Family Process, 26,* 167–183.

Tomm, K. (1988). Interventive interviewing: Part III. Intending to ask lineal, circular, strategic, or reflexive questions? *Family Process, 27,* 1–15.

von Foerster, H. (1981). *Observing systems.* Seaside, CA: Intersystems.

White, M., & Epston, D. (1990). *Narrative means to therapeutic ends.* New York: Norton.

Zaltman, G. (1996). Metaphorically speaking. *Marketing Research, 8*(2), 13–21.

Zaltman, G. (2003). *How customers think: Essential insights into the mind of the market.* Boston: Harvard Business School Press.

CHAPTER 4

Effective Use of Psychological Tests with Couples and Families

A. RODNEY NURSE AND LEN SPERRY

When it includes a standard test battery, family assessment involves applying to couples and families scientifically sound psychological and personality tests that have stood the test of time with practicing clinicians. Although most of these tests were originally developed to evaluate individuals, the instruments discussed in this chapter have considerable value with couples and families. This chapter will describe four well-known and highly regarded instruments for the process of couple and family evaluation. These tests are the Minnesota Multiphasic Personality Inventory-2; the Millon Clinical Multiaxial Inventory-III; the Rorschach Ink Blot Method; and the Kinetic Family Drawing Test. It will also describe a seven-step clinical protocol for effectively utilizing these instruments in the process of assessing couples and families. Finally, it provides a detailed case example that illustrates the tests and the clinical protocol. This chapter reflects the basic orientation of A. Rodney Nurse's *Family Assessment: Effective Use of Personality Tests With Couples and Families* (1999).

MMPI-2: ASSESSING SYMPTOMS, MOODS, AND COUPLE TYPES

Instrument name. The Minnesota Multiphasic Personality Inventory (MMPI) is the most widely used clinical testing instrument in the United States. It was developed by Starke Hathaway and Charnley McKinley, named after the University of Minnesota, and first published in 1943. A revised version, MMPI-2, was published in 1989. For clinical pattern interpretation purposes both versions of the test are sufficiently similar to justify applying the couple pattern research drawn from the original MMPI to MMPI-2 clinical patterns. This application is particularly appropriate with well-defined, high two-point clinical scores above T of 70, or close (Greene, 2000; Butcher, 1990, 2002).

Type of instrument. MMPI-2 is a standardized personality inventory providing a quantitative measure of psychological symptoms, emotional adjustment and psychopathology (e.g., hypochondriasis, depression, etc.)

Use–target audience. The MMPI-2 is intended as a personality screening tool for individuals 18 and older. A related instrument, the Minnesota Multiphasic Personality Inventory–Adolescent (MMPI-A), is designed for use with 14 to 18 year olds and is useful with parents or partners for a variety of purposes. Five common couple clusters have been articulated and are described in this chapter.

Multicultural. The MMPI-2 is available in English, Spanish, Hmong, and French versions; however, computer-generated interpretive reports are available only in English.

Ease and time of administration. An easy-to-administer inventory, the MMPI-2 calls for the client to respond "true" or "false" to 567 items and takes 60 to 90 minutes to complete. The MMPI-2 may be taken in paper-and-pencil format, audiocassette, or in a computer format and requires a sixth- to eighth-grade reading level.

Scoring procedure. The MMPI-2 is always scored on at least 10 scales measuring various clinical or personality dimensions and 3 scales related to validity and test-taking attitude. Ordinarily, 4 additional validity scales are scored together with more than 80 additional clinical scales, including 2 germane to marital and family issues. It may take 15 to 20 minutes to hand score and chart the basic clinical profile. Computerized scoring, however, is typically the standard, not only because it easily scores the large number of additional scales, but also because accuracy is guaranteed, additional hypotheses are generated, and basic research-grounded interpretive statements may be provided.

Reliability. As indicated in the MMPI-2 manual, moderate test–retest reliabilities are reported, ranging from .67 to .92. Split half reliabilities are also moderate median correlations of .70 (Groth–Marnat, 1999).

Validity. An unweighted mean validity coefficient of .30 is reported (Weiner, Spielberger, & Abeles, 2002).

Availability and sources. Several scoring and interpretive computer programs are available, including the version generated by the developers of the MMPI-2 distributed by Pearson Assessments (formerly National Computer Systems) to qualified professionals. Pearson sells the test manual (Butcher et al., 2001). Although basic interpretive hypotheses are provided in addition to scoring, clinicians interested in an in-depth, research-grounded dynamic interpretive report may utilize the Alex Caldwell report system (2001).

Comment. This is the most widely used standardized psychological test and has considerable value with couples and families as noted in the following sections.

Using the MMPI-2 With Couples

Because work with couples typically focuses first on dysfunctional relationships, the MMPI-2, which measures behavioral symptoms and mood states that may have an impact on a partner and/or stem from a partner's impact, has considerable usefulness as an initial assessment device. Two new scales have been developed that have particular relevance to family and couple assessment:

- Family Problems Scale (FAM). Families with high scores on this content scale are described as lacking in love and being quarrelsome and unpleasant. Their childhoods may be portrayed as abusive and their marriages seen as unhappy and lacking in intimacy and affection. FAM is a gross measure reflecting problems, past and present, in the family as a whole. It is useful in initial screening to ascertain the degree of seriousness of family problems.
- Marital Distress Scale (MDS). This scale has the advantage of focusing on measuring distress or discord in close relationships, rather than measuring more global family problems as with the FAM. The MDS is described as an efficient discrimination of maladjustment in marriages at a *T* score of 60 or above.

Five-Cluster Classification of Couples Seeking Therapy

Research on the original MMPI cited by Nurse (1999) suggests that as many as 50% of couples with marital problems fall into one of five recognized MMPI clusters. Renaming them slightly from the original research, Nurse labels these clusters as openly warring couples; unhappy problem-focused couples; husband-blaming couples; psychologically disordered couples; and distant, calm couples. Each of these couples and MMPI codes is briefly described in terms of interactional dynamics and unique treatment issues.

Openly warring couples (4-3/4-9 codes). Warring wives present with poorly controlled anger and hostility that is expressed in a cyclical fashion, as reflected in their 4-3 high-point code. Following a submissive, suppressive phase, a build-up of tension can result in a loss of control seen in angry, aggressive acting-out. This may be triggered as much by internal stimuli as by externally based stress. Between stormy bouts of anger expressions, they are models of (culturally stereotyped) "femininity," displaying passivity and submissiveness (although periodically complaining behavior) as they defer to their husbands. Not surprisingly, this submissive behavior adds to suppressed resentment that, in time, erupts.

Warring husbands act on their impulses and are frequently rebellious against the restraints of authority and usual socially accepted standards. This reflects their high Scale 4. Accompanying this is a high level of energy, indicated by Scale 9, which serves to provide fuel to the acting-out. Because of their freedom from anxiety, worry, and guilt, these husbands often make a comfortable, smoother, and socially facile appearance initially. At the same time, they are impatient with anything beyond a superficial relationship given their craving for excitement. A seemingly submissive wife, who follows the husband's lead uncritically and without question, as well as satisfied needs for attention and sex, fits the husband's needs for someone to cater to his impulses and action orientation.

Therapy with this couple tends to be volatile, and the therapist's challenge is to join with their fighting style and help them learn to fight fairly. This is not a couple that excels at communicating verbally or reasons well with problems. Instead, this is an action-oriented couple that, if they can fight fairly to resolve conflicts, may be able to reach solutions to their problems and stay together satisfactorily.

Unhappy, problem-focused couples (2-1-3/2-7 codes). This couple is quite common in couples therapy, often presenting with unhappiness or depressive features and high levels of marital dissatisfaction. They typically present with a problem-solving orientation and an openness to self-appraisal. Unhappy, problem-focused husbands tend to have 2-7 codes and present with unhappiness, worry, and tension. They blame themselves; easily feel inadequate despite their achievements; and, interestingly, have the capacity for satisfying and rewarding interpersonal relationships because they are turned in on themselves. They seek advice and help from therapists and are likely to follow therapeutic suggestions.

Unhappy, problem-focused wives tend to have major symptoms of depression. Their overall code is often 2-1-3, which is known as the neurotic triad configuration. Like their husbands, they are anxious and self-doubting and tend to be dependent and immature. They seem capable of maintaining a long-suffering, unhappy role in the relationship; consequently, their motivation for change may be less than optimal. Not only will a worsening of the relationship present a crisis, but positive change can also upset the couple or family homoeostatic balance.

In couples therapy, therapists may find that intimacy is the core issue for these couples and that they deal with intimacy issues by maintaining some degree of disengagement. Thus, efforts to increase their interaction and intimacy may increase conflict and their perception that therapy "makes things worse." Accordingly, the strategy is to focus gently on the dynamics of interaction, without blaming, and concentrate on the couple's ability to work on practical solutions to identified problems. Such couples do maintain long-standing marriages, solving problems somehow with avoidance and yet resolving them nevertheless. If therapy goes even reasonably well, this couple has the potential to move past their avoidant pattern, interact more directly, and evolve into a positive, growing marriage relationship.

Husband-blaming couples (4-6/2-4 scales). In these couples, angry husband blaming (4-6) by the wives is linked to apologetic, although sometimes resentful, acceptance of blame by the husbands (2-4). These women attempt to present themselves as psychologically healthy, yet are guarded as reflected in L and K scores elevated above the F score. They tend to see the world in right–wrong, black–white terms and are reluctant to engage in self-criticism, which is consistent with the 4-6 code. When Scale 1 is also elevated, "whining somatization" can be noted. A blaming woman is also wary and suspicious; if there is verified reason for this suspiciousness and no history of delinquency or past major difficulty in social relations, it may well be that she is reacting to the present couple dispute instead of being a characterological problem.

The striking feature of the husbands' typical profile (2-4) is depression; these men are suffering from a generally unhappy, dysphoric mood accompanied by feelings of inadequacy, lack of self-confidence, self-depreciation, and strong guilt feelings. For the husbands, their wives' blaming and perceived nagging may provide justification for their resentfulness and self-destructive behavior (e.g., alcohol abuse and suicidal ideation).

Therapy needs to focus on both partners learning to take responsibility for themselves, avoiding blaming, and understanding more of their own psychological make-up. Therapy can help them learn to be more empathic with their partners. To this end, a couples group could prove useful. If the husband's depression continues, a medication evaluation should be considered. For wives, a group separate from their husbands could also provide a place to learn to modify the extreme black-and-white thinking and to learn how to shoulder more responsibility without blaming.

Psychologically disordered couples (1-2-3/2-4-6-8 codes). These couples have the greatest conflict potential of all five couple clusters. Psychologically disordered husbands are clearly seeking help and may even be exaggerating symptoms to attract attention. However, they appear to be seeking help for good psychological reasons. Their clinical scale profile is a saw-toothed pattern in which Scales 2, 4, 6, and 8 are significantly elevated above the other scales. These husbands are depressed, angry, and distrustful as well as feeling alienated from others; others view them as moody and unpredictable. They are likely to be ruminative, preoccupied, and inflexible in problem solving.

In contrast to the overly acute nature of their husbands' presentation, psychologically disordered wives are attempting to avoid, deny, and generally not deal with unacceptable feelings and impulses. However, despite this effort, they appear to have a chronic neurotic condition and are usually diagnosed with somatoform disorders, anxiety disorders, and/or depressive disorders. They are unsure, rather inept females who may have grown accustomed to a high level of unhappiness and considerable discomfort.

When in therapy, these wives are seldom highly motivated for treatment because of their melancholy adjustment to a chronic condition and their pattern of denial. In contrast, their husbands are actively seeking help. However, because of the unstableness of their conditions, the husbands may have difficulty in persevering in treatment. Unlike the four other clusters, these couples may need intensive individual psychological evaluation and probably collateral psychiatric evaluation to plan treatment effectively. Both spouses may need medication. When therapy is undertaken, the therapeutic plan, including goals, objectives, and intermediate tactics, must be thoroughly delineated with as much collateral help as appropriate (e.g., medication, support groups, and availability for emergencies). If these couples make changes, they will be even more threatening than for many couples with other dysfunctional patterns. If the disordered husband behaves in a more sane way, he must take more responsibility for his actions. At the same time, the disordered wife must tolerate the anxiety of looking at herself psychologically and assuming more responsibility for herself without focusing as much on her husband. Not surprisingly, psychophysiological stress reactions are to be expected.

Distant, calm couples (within normal limits 4-8/8 spike codes). Typically, the MMPI profiles for these couples fall within normal limits. Compared to other couple clusters, these couples are relatively satisfied with their marriages. They tend to be older and have been married longer than other couple clusters.

These distant, calm husbands are likely to think somewhat differently from others (mild 8). This may reflect their creativity, avant-garde attitude, or schizoid or avoidant personality structure. They tend to avoid reality through daydreaming and fantasy. Their distant, calm wives also have some sense of differentness and avoidance, yet they may be more genuinely concerned about social problems and issues. The couple's distancing pattern may reflect their response to situational conflicts, or it may reflect their habitual level of social and interpersonal relatedness.

Their apparent lack of acute distress does not mean that they are not silently suffering the angst of emptiness, separation, deprivation, and lack of meaning associated with their high Scale 8 scores. Nevertheless, therapists who come across such seemingly normal MMPI profiles suggesting the couple is without symptoms and is not demonstrating any obvious psychopathology might look to other instruments such as the MCMI-III or the Millon Index of Personality Styles (MIPS; Millon, 1994) for further clues. Among MMPI-2 interpreters, such "normal" profiles can mean that the couple has become adjusted to their chronically ingrained problems and issues.

Interpreting Couple MMPI-2s not in the Five Clusters

Some of the MMPI-2 couple patterns falling outside the five groupings will have one partner who does fit a pattern in one of the five groups. The reader is referred to descriptions of other code types in Greene (2000) and Groth–Marnat (1999). The evaluating therapist should also be cognizant of certain red flag warnings about potentially dangerous problems. These include high elevations on Scale 9 (Mania), which can indicate narcissistic, grandiose, and overly active (hypomanic) behavior, and high elevations on Scale 6 (Paranoid) that could indicate suspicious hostility, blaming, or projection of negative feelings onto others. See Nurse (1999) for a discussion of other red flags and interview suggestions related to following up on them. Nurse (1999) also discusses gender issues related to two MMPI-2 scales, as well as scale indicators of spousal dominance and submission issues.

Summary

This section presented an approach for interpreting couple MMPI-2s based on an elaboration of probable interactional dynamics of an MMPI-2 typology of five types of couples originally identified in MMPI research. Because up to 50% of couples with marital problems fall into this typology, therapists would do well to become familiar with these types and their therapeutic implications for couples treatment. Suggestions were also made for considering other patterns and the clinical utility of other specialized and content scales relevant in working with couples.

MCMI-III: ASSESSING PERSONALITY STYLES OR DISORDERS OF MARITAL PARTNERS

Instrument name. The Millon Clinical Multiaxial Inventory (MCMI-III), in its third edition, was developed by Theodore Millon (1977, 1996, 1997a, b).

Type of instrument. The MCMI-III is a standardized personality inventory that includes 24 clinical scales and 4 scales concerning reliability and validity. Eleven clinical scales measure clinical personality patterns and three indicate severe personality patterns, with very high scores similar to DSM-IV-TR personality disorders. Moderate clinical personality pattern scores reflect personality traits, while a slightly elevated score represents personality features. Seven scales assess DSM-IV-TR, Axis I, clinical syndromes (i.e., anxiety; somatoform; bipolar; dysthymia; alcohol dependence; drug dependence; and posttraumatic stress disorder) and three reflect serious clinical syndromes (i.e., thought disorder, major depression, and delusional disorder).

Use–target audience. This instrument is used for assessing and making treatment decisions in adults (18 years and older), focusing on personality style and disorders, unique among tests. An adolescent version, the Millon Adolescent Clinical Inventory (MACI), is available and has been normed on 13 to 19 year olds.

Multicultural. English and Spanish versions are available. Computer-generated interpretive reports are available only in English.

Ease and time of administration. The inventory consists of 175 statements about personality and behavior to which the individual responds "true" or "false" as applied to him or her. It can be completed in 20 to 30 minutes and may be taken directly on a computer or in paper format. An eighth-grade reading level is specified.

Scoring procedure. Computer scoring of the 28 scales takes only a few minutes to provide a simple profile with minimal interpretive comments or a full interpretive report.

Reliability. Moderate levels of reliability have been noted. Test–retest reliabilities have been reported in a range from .67–.91 to .67–.69 for 1 year as well as an internal consistency of .80 (Groth–Marnat, 1999).

Validity. Although the positive predictive power of the MCMI-II ranged between .30 and .80, predictive values for the MCMI-III were not reported in the test manual (Millon, 1997a).

Availability and source. This inventory can be obtained from Pearson Assessments (formerly National Computer Systems, Inc.).

Comment. The MCMI-III, developed empirically from a theoretical base, has accrued over 600 references, including a number of books. Over the course of a quarter of a century it has reached an established place among clinicians, including those working with couples in whom DSM-IV Axis I and II issues are suspected in one or both partners.

Using the MCMI-III With Couples

At the present time, the MCMI-III is the only major and widely used psychological inventory that assesses qualities of personality styles and personality disorders within the context of an empirically derived theory consistent with DSM-IV-TR. This makes it a core instrument for a comprehensive assessment battery. Even used alone for screening, the inventory is extremely useful in arriving at hypotheses about the personality structure and interactive pattern of the underlying the immediate conflicts, overt anxiety, and depressive, or acting-out, features that partners present with in couples therapy.

The Process of Couple MCMI-III Analysis

1. Check for satisfactory validity and response style scores.
2. Next, note significant scores on the profile of each spouse so that indications of personality styles/disorders and any clinical syndromes are compared with other information collected, such as the clinical interview and previous records or collateral data. Beyond comparing family history of psychiatric and substance dependence, information on the partners' family-of-origin histories, attraction to each other, and courting history can be usefully compared with their scores on the 14 personality style/ disorders scales.
3. After completing this overall analysis, an in-depth analysis of the personalities and interaction patterns needs to be undertaken. This can be done with the help of Millon's *MCMI-III Manual* (1997a) or Millon's *Disorders*

of Personality (1996). With couple interpretations, it is particularly important to look at the behavioral level, that is, expressive behavior and interpersonal behavior. From this level, inferences can be systematically drawn about linkages with features or domains falling at other levels. These levels include the polarities of *pleasure–pain, active–passive,* and *self–other.* Identifying where couples fall with reference to these polarities (especially self–other) and their personality styles/disorders can be most clinically useful in understanding the homeostatic function of these balances. This is because the couple or family system tends to make adjustments to maintain the status quo, thereby preserving the relationships between individuals that meet some individual needs. This analysis permits a more detailed description of the interactive pattern of the personality expressions of the couple, and provides the basis for planning and therapeutic treatment, which can be sharpened by reference to personality-guided therapy (Millon, 1999). A detailed example of this analysis process applied to the dependent/narcissistic couple may be found in Nurse's (1997) chapter in *The Disordered Couple.* See also Nurse's chapter in *The Millon Inventories* (Millon, 1997b), which provides illustrations of the process.

Prototypic MCMI-III Couple Relational Patterns

This section briefly describes six MCMI-III couple relationship patterns commonly seen in outpatient treatment settings.

Narcissistic Male/Histrionic Female

Males with a very high score on the Narcissistic scale (5) may act in an arrogant fashion with a tendency irresponsibly to ignore social norms and standards. They may show little empathy and act in an interpersonally exploitive manner, seemingly unaware of the negative impact on others. These males may have self-glorifying fantasies of success, yet may move from job to job always looking for employment that meets how they think they should be treated. Yet, narcissistic males maintain a cool aura, seemingly not shaken by anything. However, it is particularly important on this scale to determine whether a high score represents a style or a disorder (Craig, 1999). With a narcissistic style, subtle attitudes may be reflective in a moderate way of these characteristics, except under pressure when the attitudes and behaviors can become significantly more pronounced.

Females in this relational pattern often show a marked peak on the Histrionic scale (4). They convey an engaging, fleeting, and often theatrical attitude, conveying a high level of excitement and activity. Histrionics seek to be the center of attention, developing ways of being socially stimulating, but they avoid reflecting on even fleeting unwanted emotions, seeking to deny contradictory feelings as they are constantly in action. At a level of style they may be dramatic and energetic but can enter more into relationships. Given the frequent lack of any symptoms evident on the MCMI clinical syndrome scale scores, some with slight scale elevations appear to have simply histrionic features and are up-beat and free from indications of maladjustment. If an elevation on the Compulsive scale (7) occurs, their general emotional style is likely to be balanced by some capacity to be organized, thorough, and conscientious, while remaining expressive and outgoing as reflected in a moderately elevated histrionic scale score. This pattern suggests a person functioning relatively effectively.

In the couple relationship, the truly histrionic female will likely be attracted to the narcissistic male because of his sureness, command, and interest in her. He is likely to be attracted to her because of her apparent attraction to him and his own fantasies of how enhanced his life would be and how others will see him with her on his arm. They are likely to become disillusioned, periodically fight, and sometimes even triangulate a child or other individual in a struggle to gain power and make up for what they do not have with each other.

Because these patterns represent some gender stereotypes, it may be useful for the couple to be seen by a male/female cotherapy team. Each therapist in individual sessions prior to some of the couple sessions could prepare his or her same-gendered client by acknowledging strengths and achievements coupled with setting structured goals. For the female, these sessions could include practicing on channeling/controlling feeling expressions; for the male, they could focus on empathy practice (with the therapist avoiding mirroring, which serves to reinforce narcissism). For the more moderate, normal-appearing histrionic/narcissistic couple, it may be that that couple difficulties lie in relationship problems more than in the personality structure of either.

Compulsive Female/Dependent–Avoidant Male

Females with a high elevation on the Compulsive scale (7) appear excessively disciplined and maintain a highly structured, organized life. They see themselves as conscientious, devoted to thoroughness, and fearful of not doing things in the best possible way. They maintain an inner world that is cognitively constricted (i.e., narrow and rule bound, anticipating that others will behave similarly). Sometimes using reaction formation as a major defense, they appear super-reasonable, not dealing with contrary feelings, and fearful of underlying feelings such as anger. Although their lives may be full of tension and tight control of emotions, research suggests that an elevated compulsive score may indicate more conscientiousness than compulsivity (Craig, 1999), an effective and rewarded style in many environments.

Males with an elevation on the Dependent (3) and Avoidant (2A) scales have a need for close relationships but hesitate about approaching others out of a fear of rejection. Their style is interpersonally submissive but not expressive. They may be seen as cognitively naive, avoiding confrontation; sometimes they experience themselves as weak and alienated. They may feel a need to become involved with, if not devoted to, others; they introject others' views and maintain relationships through the use of fantasy in order to avoid significant anxiety. At a level of personality style, moderate level scores point to a person with a significant emotional neediness who, because of the importance of relationships, is hesitant to take action without being sure of acceptance.

Couples therapy with couples demonstrating more pronounced score patterns such as these needs to proceed slowly and often needs to be accompanied with individual sessions. Conjoint sessions must appeal to the female's need to do the right thing and the male's need for a close relationship with reassurance of acceptance. In couple sessions the goal is for the male to become more assertive and capitalize on his abilities developed outside the home and to become more active in the home. The goal for the female is modify her sometimes too conscientious pattern so as to be in more control of it, thus turning it to positive use and being less constricted by it, and to move from being passive and only (restrictively) nurturing others to paying increased attention to her own needs as well as those of others.

Narcissistic Male/Narcissistic Female

As noted earlier, males with a marked peak on the Narcissistic scale (5) may act in an arrogant, condescending fashion with a tendency irresponsibly to ignore social norms and standards. They may show little empathy and act in an interpersonally exploitive manner, seemingly unaware of the negative impact on others. They view themselves as special and have fantasies of love and success that drive them to high levels of achievement, yet they may repress and/or reshape affect and distort facts to maintain their self-illusions in the face of failures. Typically, they maintain a cool aura of self-possessed optimism unless their confidence is shaken.

Females with very high elevations on the Narcissistic scale (5) may present much as narcissistic males. They are interested in others in large part for what they can gain from them in terms of their own self-esteem, and thus they can behave amorously. Nevertheless, they tend to be self-deceptive, self-centered, and rationalize; until their confidence is shaken, they present with a cool, imperturbable demeanor.

As a couple, narcissistic males and females tend to have similar blind spots: repressing and denying the same negative aspects of their personalities. This means that they cannot easily confront each other without being aware of similar self-aggrandizing traits in themselves. Although they believed earlier in their relationship that they were "made for each other" because they reflected each other, with the arrival of a child or other shifts in their interpersonal balance, each misses the other's focused attention. Their intense attachment can switch from positive to negative, blaming each other and pointing out the negative parts of the other's personality, and thereby warding off confronting themselves with their own experiences of deprivation and recognition of their short-comings. By recognizing the couple's interlocking narcissistic styles, a couple therapist can more easily avoid responding negatively to these individuals' self-focused approaches to life and instead can support their effectiveness while gently helping them gain more actual empathy with each other. A couple demonstrating narcissistic styles (rather than disorders) may have developed a broader base and a better interpersonal connection, giving the therapist a platform to assist them in building a sounder marriage relationship despite the arrival of a child, loss of a job, illness, or other unbalancing occurrence.

Histrionic–Narcissistic Female/Compulsive Male

In this profile, the Histrionic pattern (Scale 4), mixed with Narcissistic features (Scale 5) of superiority and entitlement, increases the possibility of irresponsible, acting-out behavior considerably beyond that of the prototypical histrionic personality disorder in females. These individuals tend to be attracted to Compulsive (Scale 7), that is, conscientious, males whom they view as stable, goal oriented, and secure. However, with time they experience such men as boring and rigid. These females may have sought out other types of relationships, but after being wounded, may have retreated to safe kinds of husband–father relationships with a compulsive male in order to lick their wounds.

Males with a compulsive or conscientious personality (Scale 7) are likely to have been excited and attracted to these affectively dominated females whom they typically view as intriguing, colorful, and vivacious. Yet, with the passage of time and relational demands, these males become disconcerted with their partners, whom they now view as flighty, irresponsible, and supremely selfish and vain.

Relationally, these females will be the source of feeling expressiveness in the relationship, while these males will be the voice of reason. Couple therapy stressing improved communication could focus on having these couples get to know each other as specific, unique individuals. Unfortunately, without the benefit of couples therapy or other corrective experiences, neither partner is likely to move beyond these limiting roles without expressing his or her humanity.

Antisocial Female/Antisocial–Narcissistic Male

Clinicians inexperienced with the MCMI-III may improperly conclude that both partners are antisocial or psychopathic personalities because of elevated

6A Scales. In keeping with Millon's clinical formulation of this scale as primarily a measure of aggression, such scale elevations (particularly at a moderate level) reflect the competitive, aggressive attitude and style associated with successful entrepreneurs. These are the "antisocial" style individuals who are likely to come in for couple therapy. It would be surprising if true psychopaths, who comprise only a minority of antisocial personality disorders, came for therapy.

Couples with this pattern who show up for therapy typically take risks, exploit (usually within the limits of the law), and shade the truth to meet their own needs. Yet, they view themselves as law-abiding individuals. When they become involved in close romantic relationships, they can carry some of these antisocial qualities into that relationship. Thus, they can be competitive and can view their relationship as a game in which they match wits with each other. They may admire each other's ability to succeed in business; however, they can be tough, argumentative, and insensitive to each other's feelings.

With this couple, an imbalance can be anticipated because of the male's narcissistic (Scale 5) entitlement. His partner will become incensed at his self-centeredness. When she finds ways to puncture his confident front, he may respond with hurt, rage, and vindictiveness. Their motivation for coming for couples therapy is probably so that each can gain an advantage over the other. When the therapist does not express judgment of who is right, they can impatiently join in turning on the therapist, only to seek a new one. Therapists need to be aware that this therapy could be the first stage in a long divorce battle in which neither gives because winning is everything for them.

Dependent Male/Dependent Female

Dependent partners (Scale 3) tend to be so "nice" to each other that they inevitably tread lightly in their relationship. Unfortunately, treading lightly allows little opportunity for openly dealing with their problems. Consequently, problem solving only appears to occur when one partner quickly acquiesces in order to avoid being criticized. At some level, each partner may be looking for a good parent and thus may develop considerable resentment, although he tends to squelch this; if irritation comes out unexpectedly, he may hurriedly apologize. Each partner has the capacity to be kind, loving, and caring with each other. If they begin to develop personally outside the relationship—through work experiences, for instance—and maintain their same way of couple relating, this dissonance in their lives may bring them to couples therapy. By helping each recognize his growing resentment and assisting each in learning to communicate his feelings, the therapist can help these needy people experience developing together. When dependent style couples seek help, the therapist needs to discover what has unbalanced their relationship, for example, the growth of one, a new child, a promotion, a relationship external to the marriage, and so forth.

Summary

The MCMI-III uniquely provides informational, descriptive hypotheses about personality structure as well as syndromal indications. The MCMI-III profile helps the couples therapist draw understandable hypotheses about the couple relationship and interactive pattern in guiding planning for interventions.

THE RORSCHACH: APPLICATION TO FAMILIES

Format of the Rorschach

Instrument name. The Rorschach Ink Blot Test, usually called the Rorschach, was named after the Swiss psychiatrist who developed and first published it in 1921,

Type of instrument. It is a projective tests consisting of 10 inkblots.

Use–target audience. This test is used with all ages except the youngest of children for gathering information describing personality as reflected in the perceptual processes of the person and the associational dynamics related to content. It is particularly valuable for in-depth personality evaluations of parents or partners with issues involving child custody, child abuse, and divorce, as well as in planning psychotherapy with adults, adolescents, and children.

Multicultural. This instrument can be administered in any language. A Spanish language manual is available from the publisher of Exner's *Comprehensive System for the Rorschach*; however, computer-generated interpretive reports based on Exner's system are available only in English.

Ease and time of administration. In administering the Rorschach using Exner's *Comprehensive System* (Exner, 1993, 2001; the most extensively used system), the examiner sits side by side with the examinee, thus avoiding distractions or unconscious shaping of responses caused by an examiner's inadvertent changes of facial expression or body posture. The examiner presents each blot with the instructions to respond to the question: "What might this be?" A follow-up inquiry using carefully delineated questioning helps the examiner to be clear about the location of the response, what went into making the response, and a sense of the nature of the content of the response.

Scoring procedure. Using the *Comprehensive System*, responses are categorized by using scoring procedures painstakingly developed to maximize consistency of assessor scoring. Entered into a computer, these resulting scores are combined based on research-derived procedures. A computer program provides not only the combinations of scores but also a lengthy narrative of research and clinically based hypotheses for the assessor to use as an interpretive base (Exner et al., 2003).

Reliability. Test–retest reliabilities are reported in the range of .75 to .85, while intercoder agreement is in the range of .79 to .88 (Groth–Marnat, 1999).

Validity. An unweighted mean validity coefficient of .29 is reported in over 2,200 Rorschach protocols. This suggests that the Rorschach "is generally as valid as the MMPI" (Weiner, Spielberger, & Abeles, 2002, p. 9).

Availability and source. Materials for the comprehensive system are distributed by Psychological Assessment Resources, Inc. to qualified professionals.

Comment. Despite this empirically based comprehensive system protocol, crafting a clinical report requires intensive instruction and supervision. It requires as well extensive experience with the Rorschach, coupled with interview data about the examinee, typically complemented by the results of other psychological tests and inventories.

Using the Rorschach With Families

The Rorschach has a unique, significant, and often essential place in family treatment situations in which a thorough, in-depth understanding of personality is required on which to base decisions with far-reaching effects on the lives of family members, particularly children. For example, when an appraisal is sought about the mental state of parents and children in a heated, drawn-out, child custody dispute, the Rorschach can be a crucial source of uniquely salient information. It can also be helpful in complicated family situations when a puzzling child problem presents. Notably, the Rorschach findings in these situations may uncover processes not readily apparent, such as a thought disorder; the discovery of depression and its depth; and the dynamics of acting-out problem behavior.

Response styles (Exner, 1993) have particular relevance for understanding family behavior because they consistently influence or provide direction for various and sometimes diverse personality features manifest in family interaction. As such, they form major anchoring points for the therapist in searching for family system patterns. At the same time, the therapist must pay attention to consistent, pervasive behaviors on the part of each individual. These dominant Rorschach features are the Lambda Index; Experience Balance; Reflections; the Passive/Active Relationship; and the Hypervigilance Index. Nurse (1999) provides a cogent description of each of these dominant Rorschach features and suggests how each may have an impact on the family process and the strategy of the family therapist.

In considering the interpersonal, family-related implications of Rorschach findings, Exner's recent handbook on interpretation can serve as a primary reference (2001). Research has resulted in identifying 11 key variable or clusters that provide substantial core information on the individual's personality and point the way toward organizing the remaining Rorschach data. Nurse (1999) offers a clinically useful discussion of these key variables.

Summary

The Rorschach is particularly applicable in situations requiring in-depth personality evaluations because a family is facing situations that have far-reaching effects on its members, especially those involving children. In addition to diagnostic assessment and treatment planning, these issues include separation, divorce, abuse, and identifying psychosis and clinical depression. This section focused on the dominant interpersonal style and key characteristics of the Rorschach and their implications for understanding family interaction and for developing targets for therapeutic change.

THE KINETIC FAMILY DRAWING TEST: CLUES TO FAMILY RELATIONSHIPS

Instrument name. The Kinetic Family Drawing Test (KFD) follows in the tradition of other family drawing tests described since 1950. Robert Burns and S. Harvard Kaufman are credited with adding the "kinetic" conception to the family drawing test.

Type of instrument. This test is a projective drawing measure of family dynamics.

Use–target audience. The KFD is utilized with children or adolescents and is also sometimes used with the entire family to assess family relationships and interaction patterns.

Multicultural. Owing to the unique instructions for administration, this test can be administered in any language

Ease and time of administration. The KFD is easy to administer: simply provide the child with a plain sheet of white paper and a number-2 pencil and say, "Draw a picture of everyone in your family, including you, doing something. Try to draw whole people, not cartoons or stick people. Remember, make everyone doing something—some kind of action" (Burns & Kaufman, 1970, pp. 19–30). The instruction to have everyone "doing something" added to instructions to draw a family has turned out to be a very important contribution. The testing procedure usually takes 20 minutes or less.

Scoring procedure. There is no generally accepted scoring procedure even though a formal scoring system that focuses on actions, styles, and symbols has been proposed (Burns & Kaufman, 1972; Handler & Habenicht, 1994). Some contend that the proposed scoring system has not proven particularly useful and a more integrative, holistic approach has been offered instead (Thompson & Nurse, 1999). One holistic approach is for the therapist/ evaluator, after the drawing system, to try to duplicate physically the actual postures and imagine the actions indicated on the KFD. These kinesthetic experiences can trigger feelings and thoughts for the therapist/evaluator that may be akin to the client's. For instance, acting out a child's smile with arms out toward family members, compared with duplicating a scowling, hiding child crouching in a corner, would certainly elicit different feelings and thoughts for the clinicians.

Reliability. Test–retest reliabilities have been low, which is not surprising because this instrument is often scored/interpreted qualitatively. However, when quantitative scoring was used, interscorer agreement is reported in the range of .87 to .95 (Groth–Marnat, 1999).

Validity. Overall validity has been rather low and variable (Groth–Marnat, 1999).

Availability and source. The KFD and the Kinetic School Drawing (KSD) (Knoff, 1985), comprising the Kinetic Drawing Systems (KDS) (Knoff & Prout, 1985), are distributed by Western Psychological Services, Inc.

Comment. Although it lacks the extensive empirical and experimental data that would provide it the validity of such clinical instruments as the MMPI-2, the MCMI-III, or the Rorschach, the KFD is included in this chapter because it is the only widely used drawing method that attempts to elicit responses pertaining directly to understanding the family system from the perception of the person drawing. It has been noted that the KFD is considered a pictorial analog of "family sculpting" as described by Satir (1967).

Using the KFD With Families

The KFD can be utilized with families in various ways. The standard way is to collect and analyze the KFD from the child or children at the onset of treatment and use it in conceptualization of and treatment planning for the case. Thompson and Nurse (1999) suggest some other uses of this assessment tool. One is to have everyone in a family session do a KFD by themselves, then have the family discuss the different drawing perceptions of the family members with the guidance of the therapists. Such discussion of similarities and differences can stimulate talk about affectionate family bonds and significant differences among family members.

Alternatively, the therapist may have family members work together to draw one KFD on a large sheet of art paper with crayons rather than on a regular sheet of paper with a pencil. The instructions are the same except that family members are asked to decide together what each member is to draw and where on the large sheet of paper each member will accomplish the drawing task. This step is particularly important because it gives the observer examples of family interaction. The therapist–observer pays attention to such questions as who leads, who has the final say, and how the actual drawing is executed by those involved. These observations can be shared in subsequent discussions with the family to ascertain if these family patterns are representative outside the consulting room and, if they are, what the implications of these patterns might be. An additional approach is for the family to act out the actions depicted in the family KFD. Finally, the KFD can serve as a starting point for a general family discussion, with the drawer or drawers of the picture alone or involving the entire family.

TABLE 4.1 Matrix: Four Standard Psychological Tests With Families and Couples

Assessment instrument	Specific couple and family applications	Cultural/ language	Instructions/use: T = time to take; S = time to score; I = items	Computerized: a = scoring; b = report	Reliability(R); validity (V)	Availability
Minnesota Multiphasic Personality Inventory (MMPI-2)	Parents or partners/adolescent version; provides symptoms and mood states; five common couple clusters are described	English; Spanish; Hmong; French	T = 60–90 min; S = 2–3 min for computer scoring; I = 567	a = yes; b = yes	R = .70 split half; R = .67–.92 test–retest; V = .30	National Computer Systems, Inc.
Millon Clinical Multiaxial Inventory (MCMI-III)	Parents or partners; provides personality style/syndromal data; six common couple relational patterns	English; Spanish (interpretive reports only in English)	T = 20–30 min; S = a few minutes for computer scoring; I = 175	a = yes; b = yes	R = .67–.91 test–retest; R = .80 internal Consistency; V = low to .30	National Computer Systems, Inc.
Rorschach (Comprehensive System Version)	Parents or partners; for in-depth personality evaluations, e.g., child custody, abuse, divorce, etc.	Administer in any language (interpretive reports only in English)	T = 45–60 min, including inquiry; S = variable; I = 10 inkblots	a = yes, with clinician input; b = yes	R = .75–.85 test–retest; R = .79–.88 intercoder agreement; V = .29	Psychological Assessment Resources, Inc.
Kinetic Family Drawing (KFD) Test	Children and/or adolescents, or whole family to assess family relationships and interaction	Administer in any language	T = 20 min; S = variable time to score/interpret; I = n/a	a = no; b = no	R = .87–.95 interscorer agreement; V = low and variable	Journal article; Western Psychological Services, Inc.

Summary

KDF is a useful method for family therapists. Although it currently lacks the impressive psychometric properties of other standard assessment measures, the KFD is the only drawing method that seems to tap consistently into family interrelationships. Because it can provide clues about family relationships, it is particularly helpful as one instrument in a battery of tests, although it can be used by itself. Given its simplicity of administration, it will probably continue to be used worldwide.

PROTOCOL FOR USING TESTS WITH COUPLES AND FAMILIES

The following protocol can be useful when utilizing the MMPI/MMPI-2, MCMI-III, KFD, and the Rorschach with couples and families.

1. Select psychological tests that are appropriate to the questions raised, call for the psychological assessment, and are appropriate for the couple or family.
2. Administer and score the tests.
3. Collect additional information on the couple or family through interview, observation, clinical records, collateral information, or other self-report measures.
4. Review and develop an initial test report for each partner or each family member tested.
5. Review and develop a final test report on the couple or the entire family.
6. Feed data back to the couple or family as appropriate.

It is useful to keep in mind that, when developing an initial test report (Step 4) involving the MMPI/MMPI-2, MCMI-III, KFD, and Rorschach, that a concurrence of results on these instruments may or may not occur. Differences may reflect the need to over-report symptoms to gain some advantage or to underreport symptoms to put the best foot forward (e.g., the parent seeking child custody in a divorce proceeding). Finn (1996) and Nurse (1999) have offered some clinically useful guidelines for reviewing such test results. A modified version of these guidelines is presented here.

When disturbance is present on the MMPI/MMPI-2 and the Rorschach, most probably the client is aware of difficulties in coping on a day-to-day basis and ordinarily has a history of confirming that difficultly.

When the MMPI/MMPI-2 clinical scale scores fall within the normal range while the Rorschach shows significant disturbances, the clinician needs to consider the possible uses of the test as viewed by the client carefully. For example, if the client has something to gain by appearing "normal," his MMPI scores may simply mean underreporting. If it appears that nothing is to be gained for underreporting, it is likely that psychological disturbances appear under stressful, unfamiliar circumstances despite ordinarily maintaining an adequate adjustment in familiar surroundings, or there may be a conscious denial of disturbance by the family member.

When the disturbance is high on the MMPI/MMPI-2 and low on the Rorschach, two possibilities exist. The client may be over-reporting on the MMPI/MMPI-2, which may reflect malingering or a call for help, probably for assistance with an immediate situation. Alternatively, if the Rorschach is defensive, constricted, and generally shut down, it may be that the client can respond accurately on the impersonal MMPI/MMPI-2, while needing to be protective in the interpersonal, emotionally arousing context of the Rorschach. In this instance, high MMPI/MMPI-2 scores do not necessarily represent over-reporting, particularly if the situation involves no anticipated gain for expressing psychopathology.

Very rarely, low disturbances are noted on the MMPI/MMPI-2 and on the Rorschach. Although this is not common in clinical settings, it does occur occasionally in marital evaluations. For example, both partners may have little in the way of psychological disturbance, yet may need to enhance their relationship, or they may be so ill-matched that they need to find a more effective way of relating, coexisting, or divorcing.

When data on the MMPI/MMPI-2 and the Rorschach diverge, a review of the MCMI-III may clarify matters. For example, the narcissistic person may have great difficulty consciously describing himself in other than self-aggrandizing terms on the MMPI/MMPI-2 with accompanying minimizing awareness of psychological problems. In contrast to this underreporting, the Rorschach may pick up considerable psychological disturbance. Similarly, the identification of a dependent personality on the MCMI-III may indicate a propensity to over-report symptoms on the MMPI/MMPI-2 to establish a therapeutic relationship. The anticipation of the dependent personality may be that appearing needy is necessary to be cared for and loved; however, the Rorschach may indicate relatively little disturbance.

In the process of developing a final test report on the couple or the family (Step 5), individual test reports are reviewed along with interview, observational, and other sources of data. This information is then synthesized and integrated and forms the basis for feedback and possible modification of the original treatment plan.

Providing feedback to the couple or family is an important part of the assessment process (Step 6). Under the ethics code of the American Psychological Association, a clinician/evaluator who is a psychologist would have an obligation to discuss test findings with clients. Typically, the clinician/evaluator meets with individual partners or parents to discuss their own results. Reviewing results individually with the clinician and without the presence of the other partner or parent provides an environment more conducive to exploratory discussion, including considering the implications for the couple relationship or family. A joint meeting with both partners or parents and the clinician follows. At that meeting, each partner or parent is encouraged to share as much about his own test feedback, as he is willing. The clinician then focuses on key couple or family dynamics that have emerged from the evaluation and discusses relevant treatment or decisional implications and recommendations.

If a family evaluation is involved and the child tested is below the age of 13, feedback on the child's testing would be provided primarily to the parents. However, if the individual is an adolescent, feedback would be provided first through discussing with him or her privately. Then the adolescent would be helped in a joint session with the therapist and parents to tell the parents what he or she considered most important about the test results. The therapist would support the adolescent and fill in important gaps in feedback for the parents.

CASE EXAMPLE

The follow case report delineates the use of traditional psychological assessment methods with a family that involves issues of divorce and child custody. The case illustrates the protocol for using tests with couples and families wherein each step is noted in brackets.

Background Information and Reason for Testing

Jack S., a 31-year-old engineering technician, and Jill S., his 30-year-old wife who works in a clerical managing position, are separated and have initiated divorce proceedings. Both have begun new live-in relationships. Their 9-year-old daughter, Mary, has witnessed many of the couple's fights over the years. Her teacher notes that she is functioning below her intellectual potential and does not relate well to her classmates and has raised concern. As part of the child custody evaluation, each family member is given a battery of tests (Step 1 and Step 2) and additional information is gathered from a number of sources, including their new partners; interviews; home visits; discussions with collaterals; letters; legal documents; and other data sources (Step 3). Jack is requesting primary custody of Mary, and is open to liberal visitation by the child's mother.

Individual and Family Testing Summary

MMPI-2 and Rorschach results for Jack suggest a test pattern (Step 4) of low disturbance levels on both, while his MCMI-III profile indicates little if any disturbance and is consistent with an overall controlled, organized, and possibly constricted person. His style is to sidestep dealing with his feelings by pushing them away or avoiding any awareness of them. Complementing this repressive style is a perceptual processing style in which he narrows and simplifies information as it comes to him; thus he can maintain an appearance of composure, work efficiency, and conventionality in his behaviors. Nevertheless, this repressive/suppressive defensive process feeds underlying resentment that can periodically break through. There is also some indication that he is ruminating about some self-perceived negative features in his personality and behavior. The testing also suggests that he has some positive parenting skills and attitudes.

MMPI-2 results for Jill indicate low disturbance while the Rorschach points to a significant level of disturbance. Her MCMI-III also indicates psychological disturbance characteristic of individuals with anxiety disorders in the context of a histrionic personality disorder. Despite the appearance of putting up a good front, indications are that she is grief stricken about an emotional loss. Testing reveals a personality style that has important implications for her parenting (Step 4). She behaves socially in an often charming and effective way consistent with her histrionic and (mildly) narcissistic style. Unfortunately, this appearance of focusing on others seems motivated less by her interests in them than in what they can do for her. She is fearful of rejection and needs constant reassurance that she is the superior, effective person she strives to be. This self-focus may be so strong that it can interfere with her ability to extend herself toward her daughter as her daughter evolves into an increasingly independent person.

Furthermore, her readiness for underlying hostility to break through the actual breakthrough is expected to upset other household members. The potential violence of her verbal and, sometimes, physical outbursts is at a level to be potentially damaging for a child. The ubiquity of her underlying hostility means that her relationships with adults and children are likely to be more superficial, and she is likely to put others off. Finally, she has not developed a workable problem-solving style in that she vacillates and is unsure about which way is better for herself. She reverses decisions, thus having a hard time depending on herself.

On the KFD Mary identifies her family as her father, stepmother (father's new partner), her aunt and uncle (who are temporarily staying with her father), and their son. Strikingly, Mary does not include her mother in her drawing. Based on all information gathered, Mary is a very angry girl. As reflected by her anger, her distress is marked. Its power and its pervasiveness are such that it impairs her ability to think things through without internal disruptions. Her inconsistent decision-making patterns create an unsettled state, and she suffers from poor reality testing accompanied by distortions in her ways of thinking about the world. Perhaps it is this internal disorganization that makes her feels so vulnerable, resulting in hypervigilance. Mary clearly needs help in dealing with her anger and to alleviate negative feelings about herself. Testing reveals that her sense of personal worth is very poor and her need for safety is significant.

A concern that needs to be addressed is that her mother views Mary as very disturbed, seeing her as acting-out and acting-in, with depression and probably high anxiety. This relationship between mother and daughter is reinforced by the fact that Mary does not include her mother in her family drawing. Interestingly, her father does not see a disturbance in Mary. Their different views of Mary may reflect their different relationships with her. That is, mother–daughter relationships may reflect conflict and difficulty, whereas the relationship with her father may be relatively free of problems.

Based on these test interpretations, which primarily reflect individual dynamics, an integrative, synthesis interpretation of family dynamics and relationships can be articulated (Step 5). The overriding feature of this family grouping is that of angry expression. Mother, Jill, has not only a temper, but also a ubiquitous angry quality underlying her relationships, despite an overt orientation to charming others. This readiness to break through her social, other-oriented exterior is made worse by her inadequate controls over expression of feelings, particularly anger. Her anger seems matched by her daughter's marked hostility, also characterized by lack of adequate controls, even in comparison with other 9 year olds. Collateral information confirms a long history of flare-ups between mother and daughter that have become increasingly frequent since the parental breakup.

It is likely that Mary's fear of abandonment, stimulated when the mother left, significantly fuels these flare-ups, even though the mother has returned to visit regularly. Despite Jill's action in leaving the family home, her sense of loss and accompanying loneliness are probably related to her frayed connection to her daughter. She cannot acknowledge her ambivalence at not having more contact with her daughter and thus fights in a custody "battle" for her, precipitating this evaluation. Were she not to fight so strongly, she would need to confront her ambivalence about her daughter, manage her anxiety, and deal with the guilt for, in many ways, rejecting her daughter.

Jack, as father, does not have the same problem of ubiquitous anger that his wife displays. Rather, he holds in all feelings, including anger, until, rarely, the provocation is strong enough that he can explode. He can pick Jill's most extreme behavior to righteously express his own and thereby not need to look at his own role in the family conflict. The mix of anger between them has developed and serves to maintain a cyclical fight dynamic.

Mary was traumatized and responded with her fearfulness by identifying with her aggressive mother even while being very angry with her. Mary's anger overwhelms her, disrupting her thinking process, particularly when confronted with her mother's anger or in the wake of it. Mary's reaction generalizes to others. She is hyperalert, wary, and mistrustful, and does not easily mix with other children. This standoffish attitude means that she cannot benefit from the day-to-day feedback from peers so necessary for adequate development. Thus, her personality development is faltering at the present time.

Treatment and Custody Recommendations

Based on these findings, Mary needs some individual play therapy to handle her built-up trauma. Jill, her mother, likewise needs individual therapy to learn to manage her anger and find more constructive ways to respond under pressure. The two of them need sessions with a family therapist to work on their relationship. A final healing process is for mother, daughter, and father to meet with the family therapist to rework the child's trauma with them and establish a working coparenting relationship. In the meantime, the recommendation is for the father to continue to have primary physical custody and the parents to have joint legal custody. Relatively short, 2- to 4-hour mother–daughter visits are recommended, perhaps three times per week. Jill can utilize long-term therapy to help her modify her histrionic style and narcissistic traits.

Feedback of Results

The clinician/assessor provided feedback to the parents (Step 7). The evaluator first met individually with Jack, and then with Jill, to review their individual results, but each parent's individual results were not discussed with the other parent. However, in a joint session with the evaluator, each parent was encouraged to share as much as he or she was willing with the other. With the parents together, the circular problem of the anger dynamic with the three of them and the mother–daughter conflict was discussed, and feedback to the parents about Mary's testing was provided. Mary's results were not discussed with her because of her age.

CONCLUDING COMMENTS

This chapter has described the use of standard psychological tests in the process of evaluating couples and families. Four such tests were discussed: MMPI-2, MCMI-III, Rorschach, and KFD, as well as a protocol for utilizing these instruments in clinical practice. The instruments and the protocol were illustrated in a detailed case example, suggesting how therapists might use such instruments, as long as their use is within their scope of practice, or the alternative of referring to a family-oriented psychologist for such an evaluation. Finally, a matrix (Table 4.1) summarizes key attributes of these instruments.

REFERENCES

Burns, R., & Kaufman, S. (1970). *Kinetic family drawing (KFD)*. New York: Brunner/Mazel.

Burns, R., & Kaufman, S. (1972). *Actions, styles, and symbols in kinetic family drawings (KFD)*. New York: Brunner/Mazel.

Butcher, J. (1990). *MMPI-2 in psychological treatment*. New York: Oxford University Press.

Butcher, J. (2002). *Clinical personality assessment*, 2nd ed. New York: Oxford University Press.

Butcher, J., Dahlstrom, G., Graham, J., Tellegen, A., & Kaemmer, B. (2001). *MMPI-2: Manual for administration and scoring*. Minneapolis: University of Minnesota Press.

Caldwell, A. (2001). *Caldwell MMPI-2 report*. Los Angeles: Caldwell.

Craig, R. (1999). Overview and current status of the Millon Clinical Axial Inventory. *Journal of Personality Assessment, 72*(3), 390–406.

Exner, J. (1993). *The Rorschach: A comprehensive system. Basic foundations*. (Vol. 1, 3rd ed.). New York: Wiley.

Exner, J. (2000). *A primer for Rorschach interpretation*. Asheville, NC: Rorschach Workshops.

Exner, J. (2001). *A Rorschach workbook for the comprehensive system*. Asheville, NC: Rorschach Workshops.

Exner, J. et al. (2003). *Rorschach interpretation assistance program: Version 4 plus for Windows*. Odessa FL: Psychological Assessment Resources.

Finn, S. (1996). Assessment feedback integrating MMPI-2 and Rorschach findings. *Journal of Personality Assessment, 67*(3), 543–557.

Graham, J. (1990). *MMPI-2: Assessing personality and psychopathology*. New York: Oxford University Press.

Greene, R. (2000). *The MMPI/MMPI-2: An interpretive manual*, 2nd ed. Boston: Allyn & Bacon.

Groth-Marnat, G. (1999). *Handbook of psychological assessment*, 3rd ed. New York: Wiley.

Handler, L., & Habenicht, D. (1994). The kinetic family drawing technique: A review of the literature. *Journal of Personality Assessment, 63*(3), 440–464.

Knoff, H. (1985). *Kinetic drawing system for family and school: Scoring booklet*. Los Angeles: Western Psychological Services.

Knoff, H., & Prout, T. (1985). *Kinetic drawing system for family and school: A handbook*. Los Angeles: Western Psychological Services.

Millon, T. (1977). *Manual for the Millon Multiaxial Inventory (MCMI)*. Minneapolis: National Computers Services.

Millon, T. (1994) *Millon index of personality styles*. New York: Psychological Corporation.

Millon, T. (1996). *Disorders of personality: DSM-IV and beyond*. New York: Wiley.

Millon, T. (1997a). *Manual for the Millon Multiaxial Inventory-III (MCMI-III)*. Minneapolis: National Computers Services.

Millon, T. (1997b). *The Millon instruments*. New York: Guilford.

Millon, T. (1999). *Personality-guided couple therapy*. New York: Wiley.

Nurse, A. (1997). The dependent/narcissistic couple. In J. Carlson & L. Sperry (Eds.), *The disordered couple*. New York: Burnner/Mazel.

Nurse, A. (1999). *Family assessment: Effective use of personality tests with couples and families*. New York: Wiley.

Rorschach, H. (1921/1942). *Psychodiagnostics*. Bern, Switzerland: Verlag Hans Huber.

Satir, V. (1967). *Peoplemaking*. Palo Alto, CA: Science and Behavior Books.

Thompson, P., & Nurse, R. (1999). The KFD Test: Clues to family relationships. In A. Nurse, *Family assessment: Effective use of personality tests with couples and families* (pp. 124–134), New York: Wiley.

Weiner, I., Spielberger, C., & Ableles, N. (2002). Scientific psychology and the Rorschach inkblot method. *The Clinical Psychologist, 55*(4), 7–12.

CHAPTER 5

Observational Assessment of Couples and Families

ROBERT B. HAMPSON AND W. ROBERT BEAVERS

Not wrung from speculations and subtleties, but from common sense and observation...

—Sir Thomas Browne

He is a great observer, and he looks quite through the deeds of men.

—Shakespeare

Learning about people by watching them behave is perhaps the oldest assessment tool in evaluating human behavior. Direct observation of humans in context allows an undiluted behavior sample untainted by verbiage, self-report social desirability, or purposeful distortions. However, as will be demonstrated, the behavior must be interpreted and rated within a context and within the theoretical bounds of an assessment model. The observer is provided a conceptual framework and specific behaviors to observe and rate. Thus, the observational rating is a product of the tool, so understanding the model and tool is a necessary step in choosing and using an assessment model.

This chapter will describe several well-known and frequently used clinical rating scales and observational assessment tools designed for the overall evaluation of couples and families. It will not cover observational assessment tools designed to measure highly specific individual or interactional behavior in research studies (Barton, Alexander, & Turner, 1993; Bell & Bell, 1989). The instruments and models include the Beavers Interactional Competence and Style Scales; the Circumplex Model Clinical Rating Scale; the McMaster Model Clinical Rating Scale; and the Global Assessment of Relational Functioning (GARF). The instruments and underlying models will be discussed, and then a detailed case example will be provided to illustrate how assessment can be used as a guide in planning intervention in family therapy.

BEAVERS INTERACTIONAL SCALES: COMPETENCE AND STYLE

Instrument name. The Beavers Interactional Competence Scale and Interactional Style Scale were derived originally from the Beavers–Timberlawn Scale (Beavers, 1977). These scales were refined and standardized by Beavers and Hampson (1990).

Type of instrument. These scales are presented as Likert-type ratings. Subscales are rated from 1 to 5, and the global competence rating is a 1 to 10 scale. The ratings are based on family interaction observed over a 10-minute period.

Use–target audience. The intended target group is a two (or more)-generational family system, usually parents and children. The scales can and have been used for couples, but several of the subscales do not apply to single-generational systems.

Multicultural. The scales have been used (and norms published) on various ethnic groups in the United States (Hampson, Beavers, & Hulgus, 1990). The scales have also been used in Finland, Sweden, Denmark, Italy, Germany, Mexico, and Japan. The accompanying self-report scale (Self-Report Family Inventory; SFI) is also available in several foreign languages. This instrument has been studied and used with clinical and nonclinical families.

Ease and time of administration. Once a rater has been trained to reliability, the actual time of administration is 10 minutes. Prior to an initial session, the family is instructed to "discuss together what you would like to see changed in your family," while the interviewer leaves the room. Usually 10-minute segments are videotaped. Rater teams (for research) or the therapist views the tape, or the live interaction, and the ratings are done immediately following the 10-minute interaction.

Scoring procedure. The interactional scales are hand scored immediately after the 10-minute observation.

Reliability. Inter-rater reliability coefficients of .85 or above have been noted for global ratings of competence and style. Reliability of individual Likert subscales ranges from .74 to .93.

Validity. The Beavers Interactional Competence Scale correlates +.72 (canonical correlation) with the self-report scale (SFI). The competence scale also correlates favorably with other measures of family functioning (McMaster) (Beavers & Hampson, 1990).

Availability and source. These rating scales have been made readily available through the authors' book, *Successful Families. Assessment and Intervention* (1990). They can also be ordered from the Family Studies Center, 6343 Forest Park Road, 7th floor, Dallas, Texas, 75235-9121 (www.familystudiescenter.org). The observational scales cost $15.00, and the accompanying SFI is $15.00.

Comment. The Beavers Interactional Scales have evolved over 30 years of observation of clinic and nonclinic families of a wide variety of structure, ethnicity, and nationality. The scales are based on the Beavers systems model, which has studied family competence as well as dysfunction. The model also can identify family system lacks and needs at different levels of disturbance, as well as suggested strength-building procedures and guidelines for therapy at different levels. The Style scale, unique to this model, provides a rating of centripetal (internalizing) and centrifugal (externalizing) forces, also useful in therapy planning.

The Beavers Systems Model

The dimensions of Competence and Style provide a useful map for identifying levels of family health and dysfunction. Figure 5.1 illustrates this model. Family Competence ranges from *optimal* to *severely dysfunctional,* and is plotted along the horizontal axis. From left to right, the continuum of family competence ranges from *extreme rigidity* (chaotic, noninteractive) through marked dominance–submission patterns to *greater capacity for egalitarian and more successful transactions.*

The vertical axis represents Family Style, a dimension unique to the Beavers model. It ranges from *highly centripetal* (internalizing, lower end) to *highly centrifugal* (externalizing, upper end). The representation is intended to depict more rigid and extreme styles to be found in more dysfunctional families, and a more blended and flexible style in the more competent families. The resultant arrow shape shows the clinical and empirical findings that healthy families show a flexible and blended family style so that they can adapt stylistic behavior as developmental, individual, and family needs change over time. At the most dysfunctional end of the competence dimension are the most rigid and extreme family styles; these families' extreme rigidity and limited coping skills disallow variation in interactional behavior. The V-shaped "notch" on the left represents the finding that severely disturbed families show more extreme and rigid styles, with no moderation or blending of stylistic behavior.

The Rating Scales

The Competence scale has a global rating based on the ratings on 12 subscales. These are (with inter-rater reliabilities in parentheses):

- Structure of the Family:
  - Overt Power: *chaotic* to *egalitarian* (.83)
  - Parental Coalition: *parent–child* to *strong parental* bond (.85)
  - Closeness: *indistinct boundaries* to *close, distinct boundaries* (.72)
- Mythology: Reality Perception: *incongruent* to *congruent/realistic* (.86)
- Goal-Directed Negotiation: *inefficient* to *efficient* problem solving (.83)

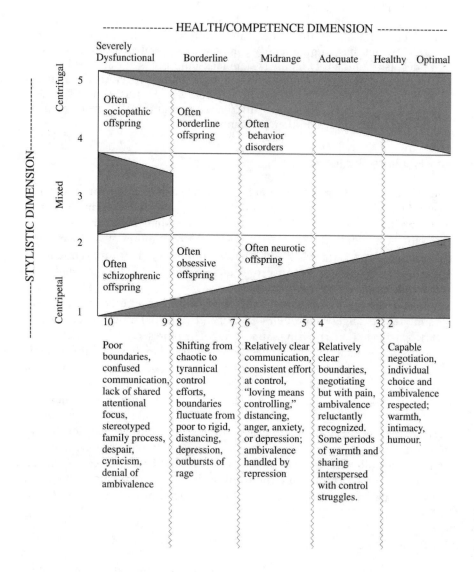

FIGURE 5.1. Beavers systems model.

- Autonomy:
    - Clarity of Expression: *indirect* to *direct* expression of feelings/thoughts (.82)
    - ⟶ Responsibility: *disowning* versus *owning* responsibility for personal issues (.86)
    - Permeability: *open* versus *unreceptive* to other members (.86)

- Family Affect:
  - Range of Feelings: *taboos* to *wide range of feeling expressed* (.84)
  - Mood and Tone: *open/optimistic* to *cynical/pessimistic* (.89)
  - ✓• Unresolvable Conflict: *chronic unresolved* to *ability to resolve* (.77)
  - Empathy: *empathic* versus *inappropriate* responses (.88)
- Global Health/Pathology: *optimal* to *dysfunctional* (.85)

The Beavers Interactional Style Scale has a global rating, as well as seven subscales. Middle ratings on each scale are representative of mixed/blended style in more competent families; extremes of style are more characteristic of the rigid (either–or) styles found in more dysfunctional families:

1. Dependency Needs: *encouraged* (CP) to *discouraged* (CF) (.81)
2. Adult Conflict: *covert/hidden* (CP) to *open/direct* (CF) (.74)
3. Physical Proximity: *very closely spaced* (CP) to *distant* (CF) (.83)
4. Social Presentation: *overly concerned* (CP) versus *unconcerned* (CF) about their impression (.74)
5. Expression of Closeness: *high* (CP) versus *denial* (CF) of closeness (.77)
6. Aggressive/Hostile Expression: *discouraging* (CP) versus *solicitation/encouragement* (CF) (.81)
7. Types of Feelings: *warm/positive* (CP) versus *angry/hostile* (CF) (.83)
8. Global CP/CF rating: *extreme* CP to *mixed–extreme* CF (.80)

Using the Beavers Scales With Families and Couples

The 10-minute observation usually precedes the first therapy session, after which the therapist trained in the use of the Beavers system begins to work with the family. The Beavers model offers specific guidance for developing a therapy plan for the family, based on the observational assessment. The assessment of family competence and style provides for seven different clinically useful groupings of families, which have been described in detail elsewhere (Beavers & Hampson, 2003); each requires a somewhat different therapeutic stance (Hampson & Beavers, 1996a, b). A brief summary of family types typically encountered in a clinic setting follows:

- *Midrange* families are the most frequently occurring families in the general population and represent a substantial number of clinic families. They are of quite traditional structure and are invested in maintaining a consistent rule structure ("loving means controlling"). Cultural stereotyping of sex roles is predominant in these families.
- *Midrange centripetal* families are characterized by concern for rules and authority; no overt defiance is expected. Family members keep their anger and dissension in check; no allowance is made for expression of overt disagreement or hostility. Thus, internalizing and repression will manifest as

anxiety and depression. These families need therapists who will join them; model straightforward expression and negotiation of differences; encourage clarity and honesty; and promote nonverbal awareness of affect. Paradoxical techniques often backfire because trust is so vital to these families.

- *Midrange mixed* and *midrange centrifugal* families also attempt to control by authority, but that control is less effective in producing consistent and internalized behavior control. To deal with behavioral transgressions, these families use criticism, blame, and anger expressed overtly. Adults spend little time together and satisfaction is sought outside the family. Individual manifestations of psychiatric disturbance are manifest as acting-out disorders. Centrifugal families rarely present voluntarily for treatment because they have more reliance on action than words as a means of dealing with human distress. They require a therapist who can maintain some control over conflict situations and helps the family verbalize conflict issues. Eventually, the therapist helps the family redefine bad behavior as needy, and conflict as desire for nurturance. The therapist cannot "join" the family as "warm and fuzzy"; he or she needs to exert more structuring and control.

- *Borderline level* families are more concerned about control than are midrange families—to the near exclusion of concerns for happiness, intimacy, or satisfaction. Individual family members find little emotional support in these rigid systems, yet separation and individuation issues are often unresolved.

- *Borderline centripetal* families are rigid, control-oriented systems that are often rigidly organized. They alternate between rigid control efforts and chaotic interaction. Offspring are typically compulsive (including anorexia), which mimics the family pattern of little joy and an illusory level of control over self and the world. Thus, therapists for this family group need to maintain a power differential with the family and physically set boundaries for intrusions. They need to focus on satisfaction and possibilities and with the possibility of satisfaction and enjoyment in relating. Paradoxical procedures can be useful in interrupting vicious cycles of behavior (this is perhaps the only clinical group in which this is effective).

- *Borderline centrifugal* families are much more open in the direct expression of anger and hostility; there is frequent leave-taking. Control themes are overt blaming and direct emotional assaults; the cyclical chaos is more overt than covert. Nurturance is not available to parents or children; satisfaction is sought outside the family. Psychiatric disorders typically include externalizing disorders (conduct, substance abuse) and cyclical disorders that reflect the rigid-to-chaos fluctuations (members of these families often have borderline personality disorders). They need therapists who can maintain effective control; limit the number of members attending; focus on the basic; help the family organize simple actions and activities; organize generational boundaries; and help members take risks with neediness and emotional pain.

- *Severely dysfunctional* families are the most limited in making adjustments for developmental needs of offspring, in negotiation and basic communication skills, and in clarity and contextual coherence. Boundaries are vague and amorphous, and parent–child coalitions may supplant adult coalitions in these families. Expressions of coherent affective tone are missing, and family members typically look bewildered and feel considerable despair.
- *Severely dysfunctional centripetal* families are vague and indistinct structures in which verbal incoherence and chaos predominate. Members have little, if any, sense of individuation and frequently speak for each other; children do not progress through normal patterns of separation and autonomy. Crises and losses are not handled through sharing; emotional isolation and taboos about dealing with crisis issues are firmly felt. Children in these families are inhibited and overcontrolled; some families have schizophrenic offspring (obviously with strong biological loadings). Therapists who work with these families must structure and organize; promoting contextual and communicational clarity is the first job. Throughout every session, the therapist must facilitate encounters; demand coherence; promote clarity; block intrusions; and reinforce collaboration among family members.
- *Severely dysfunctional centrifugal* families are characterized by chaos of a different sort; their boundary with the outside world is diffuse (the definition of who constitutes the family is often ambiguous), and the internal chaos is more behavioral than verbal. Family interaction is characterized by negative exchanges: teasing, name-calling, put-downs, and overt hostility. Leave-taking is frequent, and when satisfaction (which is sought away from home) is not attained, family members may return home even more cynical than when they left. No nurturance is provided for offspring, and they develop a hostile attitude toward others, often manifest as sociopathy or extreme aggression. These families seldom come to therapy on their own; for those that do, or are court ordered to attend therapy, they need a therapist who can keep firm control of the session, including seating arrangements and determining who shall attend. Eventually, the therapist must help family members pair words with behavior; coordinate basic activities; and emphasize risk taking with positive feelings.

Using the Beavers model, observational rating scales can provide a useful roadmap, not only for the classification of families, but in anticipating a given family's basic lacks and needs. An appropriate match of therapist orientation with the competence and style level of the family (Hampson, 1996a) or couple (Hampson, Prince, & Beavers, 1999) can facilitate greater gains in therapy than an apparent mismatch. Family competence is a much stronger predictor of therapy outcome (Hampson & Beavers, 1996b) or dropout status (a study currently in progress) than any other factor, including family structure, income and SES, and ethnicity.

The observational scales can be used in conjunction with the self-report instrument from the Beavers model, the SFI. This is a brief (36 items) and reliable instrument that measures family Competence, Style (Cohesion), and three additional scales: Conflict, Leadership, and Emotional Expressiveness. It is often informative to see which family members view the family as more or less competent when planning therapeutic goals and strategies. The SFI also shows a high level of convergence with the observational scales in a clinical sample (Hampson, Beavers, & Hulgus, 1989).

THE MCMASTER MODEL CLINICAL RATING SCALE

Instrument name. The McMaster Clinical Rating Scale is an observational rating scale based on the McMaster model of family functioning (Epstein et al., 2003). The original model was developed by Epstein while at McMaster University. More recently, the clinical rating scale, its sibling self-report scale (FAD: family assessment device), and structured interview (McSIFF: McMaster structured interview for family functioning; Bishop et al., 2000) have been studied by the Brown University group (Miller, Ryan, Keitner, Bishop, & Epstein, 2000).

Type of instrument. The McMaster CRS is a Likert-type rating scale designed to measure overall family function (a global rating). There are also six subscales, each rated from 1 (*very disturbed*) to 7 (*superior*): Problem Solving; Communication; Roles; Affective Responsiveness; Affective Involvement; and Behavior Control. The rating is based on observing (or conducting) a detailed family interview.

Use–target audience. The McMaster CRS is designed to be used on entire families following a detailed clinical interview.

Multicultural. The self-report FAD has been translated into 14 different languages and has been used on a wide variety of ethnic and socioeconomic groups in this country. The CRS, however, has been studied primarily with clinical and nonclinical families, mostly of middle-class status (Miller et al., 2000).

Ease and time of administration. The CRS can be completed by trained raters in a matter of minutes. However, because it is based on observation of a detailed clinical interview, that time must be factored into the total administration. The McSIFF and its precursor, the McMaster model structured interview (Bishop et al., 1987) can take 90 minutes to administer. The authors indicate that individuals at various levels of training can become reliable on the CRS, but the interview needs to be conducted by an experienced clinician.

Scoring procedure. Each scale is rated from 1 (*very disturbed*) to 7 (*superior*). A manual describes concise anchor descriptions for Points 1, 5 (nonclinical range), and 7 on each scale.

Reliability. Miller et al. (1994) report acceptable test–retest reliabilities (.81 to .87) across subscales and good inter-rater reliabilities (.68 to .87).

Validity. The CRS has shown adequate correspondence with the self-report FAD scales for a variety of clinical groups (Miller et al., 1994). In one study of discriminative validity, the CRS scale scores were significantly more disturbed for patents' families during the acute phase of depression than at postacute follow-up.

Availability and source. The McMaster CRS is $15.00 and the McSIFF interview protocol is $40.00. The scales are available from Christine Ryan, Ph.D., or Ivan Miller, Ph.D., Brown University Family Research Program, Rhode Island Hospital — Potter 3, 593 Eddy Street, Providence, RI 02903 (phone: (401) 444-3534; FAX: (401) 444-3298).

Comment. The McMaster CRS is based upon 30 years of clinical observation and research. Descriptors of disturbed families are based firmly upon collective observations in clinical settings. The scale does not attempt to measure all aspects of family life, but rather the dimensions deemed to be most predictive of disturbance versus competence in families in clinic settings.

Using the McMaster Clinical Rating Scale

Following the detailed clinical interview (McSIFF), the McMaster CRS ratings quantify and summarize the major findings probed during the interview. The questions in the interview deal with family functioning, by asking the family members directly a question about how they operate. For example, under the domain of Family Roles, the interviewer asks directly who is involved in grocery shopping, laundry, repairs, and so forth. The clinical interview takes from 90 to 120 minutes. The CRS has six family functioning domains and a summary, "overall family functioning." By providing summary ratings from 1 (*very disturbed*) to 7 (*superior*), a profile of family strengths and needs is constructed, which then allows the therapist to construct goals.

- *Problem Solving* is the first dimension rated. Effective problem solving refers to family behavior that resolves problems to a degree that the family can move along effectively. The most effective families do not have fewer problems, but rather are able to solve them readily. The McMaster model offers seven steps in effective problem solving (Epstein et al., 2003). More disturbed families are less able to resolve differences and solve problems effectively, so more problems are unresolved.
- *Communication* refers to the exchange of verbal information within the family. Communication within families is subdivided into instrumental (task) and affective areas. More competent families utilize clear (coherent) and direct (spoken to the intended recipient) verbal messages. At lower levels of competence, the communication becomes more masked (unclear) and indirect (deflected or diverted to/through someone else).
- *Role Functioning* has to do with consistent role maintenance within the family. This dimension addresses the assignment of roles in the family (allocation) and the ability to maintain stable role performance over time

(accountability). More competent families have more stable, predictable performance and maintenance of key family functions, while more disturbed families show more fluctuation and less accountability in performance of key family functions.

- *Affective Responsiveness* concerns the range and appropriateness of family members' emotional interaction. Healthy families are able to experience and respond to a full range of human emotions, in a context appropriate to that emotion; more disturbed families show limitation on the ranges and types of feelings expressed, as well as some inappropriate emotional responses (laughing at someone's sorrow).

- *Affective Involvement* refers to the level and type of dyadic relationships within the family structure. This addresses the manner in which family members show interest and investment in each other. The model presents six types of involvement, ranging from *lack of involvement* to *symbiotic involvement*, with "empathic involvement" in the middle as a descriptor of the more competent families. The extremes of involvement represent the relationships in more disturbed families.

- *Behavior Control* refers to the family's means of shaping and directing members' behavior in three major domains: dangerous situations, development of socialization skills, and satisfying/regulating biological needs and drives. Families differ in the way in which they are consistent, direct, and fair. More competent families employ "flexible behavior control," which represents reasonable and negotiable methods of discipline. More disturbed families are of two extremes: *rigid behavior control* (narrow, rigid, non-negotiable) and *laissez-faire behavior control* (lax, no standards, no a priori rules).

Identifying a family's strengths and weaknesses can alert a therapist to the most pressing problem areas as therapy begins. Therapists derive a family profile of strengths and needs, and then follow the McMaster model's treatment approach, as described in the problem-centered systems therapy of the family (PCSTF; Epstein & Bishop, 1981). Subsequent evaluations can be used in research studies evaluating the effectiveness of family therapy or individually to monitor the progress of a given case.

CIRCUMPLEX MODEL CLINICAL RATING SCALE

Instrument name. Clinical Rating Scale for the circumplex model of marital and family systems (Olson & Killorin, 1983) is an observational rating scale based on the major theoretical dimensions of the circumplex model (Olson & Gorall, 2003). It was initially developed in 1980 and has evolved over several modifications of the circumplex model, with revisions in 1983, 1985, and 1988.

Type of instrument. The CRS is a checklist-type rating scale, with descriptors for each dimension at each rating point. It is to be used following observation or direction of a semistructured family interview.

Use–target audience. The circumplex CRS is designed to be used by trained raters for observing couples and families.

Multicultural. The scales of the circumplex model, including the self-report Family Adaptability and Cohesion Evaluation Scales (FACES I, II, III, and IV), have been used in many foreign countries and been translated into several languages. The CRS is less widely used than the FACES.

Ease and time of administration. The completion of the rating scale takes only a few minutes for trained raters. The clinical interview on which the ratings are based is an unspecified length. Olson and Killorin (1988) indicate that the clinical interview can be semistructured, yet should cover the basic dimensions of the model (Cohesion, Flexibility, and Communication). It is also important for the family to dialogue with each other, for example, asking them to describe a typical week and how they handle their daily routines.

Scoring procedure. Each of the three major theoretical dimensions of the circumplex model, as well as composite subscales, is rated by the observer following the interview. The scales and their composites will be described later. Cohesion dimensions are rated from 1 to 2 (*disconnected*) through 5 to 6 (connected) to 9 to 10 (*enmeshed*). Flexibility dimensions are rated from 1 to 2 (*inflexible–rigid*) through 5 to 6 (flexible) to 9 to 10 (*overly flexible–chaotic*). Communication dimensions are rated from 1 to 2 (*low*) through 3 to 4 (facilitating) to 5 to 6 (*high*). The first two scales are based on a curvilinear distribution in which Competence is theoretically in the middle; Communication is a unidimensional scale, from low to high.

Reliability. The circumplex CRS has good internal and inter-rater reliability. Alpha coefficients for the three dimensions include: .95 for Cohesion; .94 for adaptability (Flexibility); and .97 for Communication (Thomas & Olson, 1993). Test–retest reliabilities have also been reported: .83 for Cohesion; .75 for adaptability (Flexibility); and .86 for Communication.

Validity. Support for the curvilinear distribution of circumplex rating scale scores has been demonstrated via regression analysis. Cohesion and Flexibility have been curvilinearly related to family communication and family satisfaction (both linear). Thus, the CRS more closely fits the circumplex theory than do the self-report FACES instruments.

Availability and source. The circumplex CRS is available for $30.00 from Life Innovations, P.O. Box 190, Minneapolis, Minnesota, 55440-0190 (www.lifeinnovations.com). A circumplex training package containing a training manual, training video, and the CRS costs $50.00.

Comment. The CRS is a less widely used instrument than the circumplex model self-report scale, the FACES. Challenges in the past have been concerned with the curvilinear nature of some of the scales, especially the Flexibility scale (and its predecessor, "adaptability"). Other models (Lee, 1988; Beavers & Voeller, 1983) state that Chaos and Rigidity are closely related in evolution of system development, rather than polar opposites.

Using the Circumplex CRS with Couples and Families

Following an interview or detailed discussion task, raters (or therapists) rate the family on specific dimensions of each of the subscales of the major dimensions of Cohesion, Flexibility, and Communication. The cohesion subscales, which range from *Disconnected* (1 to 2) to *Overly Connected/Enmeshed* (9 to 10), include dimensions of Emotional Bonding, Family Involvement, Marital Relationship, and Parent–Child Relationships. The Cohesion dimension also provides ratings for Internal Boundaries (Time, Space, Decision Making) and External Boundaries (Friends, Interests, Activities). Descriptive rating points for each level of cohesion are provided.

The Flexibility scales, representing a curvilinear distribution from *inflexible* (*rigid*) through flexible to *overly flexible/chaotic*, provide the following subscales: Leadership (*authoritarian* to *limited leadership*); Discipline (*autocratic* to *laissez-faire*); Negotiation (*imposed decisions* to *impulsive decisions*); Roles (*rigid* to *shifting*); and Rules (*inflexible* to *changing* rule structure).

The Communication scale is a directional, linear rating from low to high levels of communication skills. The dimensions rated include Listeners' Skills (Empathy, Attentive Listening); Speakers' Skills (Speaking for Oneself, Speaking for Others); Self-Disclosure; Clarity; Continuity; and Respect and Regard. Olson's view of Communication is that it is a facilitating dimension within the various family types as described by the Flexibility and Cohesion dimensions. Communication is also an important part of the prepare/enrich assessment for premarital and married couples.

GLOBAL ASSESSMENT OF RELATIONAL FUNCTIONING (GARF) SCALE

Instrument name. The Global Assessment of Relational Functioning (GARF) scale is an appendix in the current DSM-IV and DSM-IV-TR to assist clinicians in their evaluation and diagnosis of individual patients by emphasizing their relational context. The current instrument evolved through multiorganization collaboration. Spearheaded by a critique of the DSM system's lacking a family or relational axis by Lyman Wynne, the GAP Committee on the Family began developing such a rating scale. In 1989, after key DSM-IV chairpersons endorsed the development of such a scale, a multiorganization task force was convened by Robert Beavers (then president of AAMFT, on the GAP Committee, and on the board of AFTA). The result was the Coalition on Family Diagnosis, cochaired by Florence Kaslow and Herta Guttman; that coalition, with participation from 12 different organizations, developed the GARF (Yingling, Miller, McDonald, & Galewater, 1998).

Type of instrument. The GARF is a dimensional rating scale analogous to the Global Assessment of Functioning (GAF) Axis in DSM-IV. Ratings are based on a 1 to 99 rating. The most satisfactory family ratings are 81 to 99; less satisfactory = 61 to 80; predominantly unsatisfactory = 41 to 60; rarely satisfactory = 21 to 40; and chaotic is 1 to 20. These ratings are done for the Global Family/Couple Interaction. Separate subratings of the family/couple's Problem Solving, Organization, and Emotional Climate can also be made using the same number line.

Use–target audience. The GARF is intended to be used for rating the contextual relationship for a given patient/client, regardless of the formal definition of that relationship. This includes couples and families, but can also include life partners, key friendships, and support networks for single/unattached people.

Multicultural. Most of the published reports regarding the GARF are set in clinical settings, primarily with English-speaking clients.

Ease and time of administration. The GARF can be completed in a matter of minutes by trained clinicians. The rating most typically follows the completion of a family/couple therapy session, although less formal interactions can be rated. It is even possible to rate a family on the basis of a client's report of the relational system.

Scoring procedure. Following the session or interaction observed, the rater completes a GARF rating scale for Global Functioning, as well as the subscales addressed previously. A single number is assigned to each dimension.

Reliability. Reliability analysis of the GARF has shown a fairly broad spectrum of inter-rater reliability scores. Since the GARF presents a 20-point range within each of the five levels of functioning, exact-number reliability between pairs of raters has ranged from .34 to .75 (Gordon, 1997). However, when the range of ratings was broadened to within 5 rating points within the same level, the reliability estimates (kappa coefficients) were consistently higher: Global = +.79; Problem Solving = +.73; Organization = +.86; and Emotional Climate = +.83 (Gordon, 1997). Some evidence suggests that raters with higher levels of training in family systems theory and therapy have higher agreement ratings with more ability to be generalized (Mottarella, Philpot, & Fritzsche, 2001).

Validity. The relationship between GARF ratings and other ratings of family/couple functioning indicate generally adequate construct and clinical validity. For example, GARF and Beavers Interactional Competence were correlated –.69 (different directions of scores) at the initial session and –.54 with mother's SFI competence (Henney, 1994). GARF change scores (pre–post GARF ratings across therapy) have correlated well with therapists' ratings of change (.47) and clients' report of change (.36). Also, initial GARF ratings have been associated with severity ratings of the client at intake (–.52) (Ross & Doherty, 2001).

Availability and source. The GARF is printed in the DSM-IV and DSM-IV-TR as an axis provided for further study. A good resource is *GARF Assessment Sourcebook: Using the DSM-IV Global Assessment of Relational Functioning* by Yingling and coauthors (1998).

Comment. The GARF is a brief and fairly simple instrument that can be used by therapists and researchers. It can be used on a session-by-session basis to track progress in relational functioning. It addresses only the "competence" dimension of family/couple functioning.

Using the GARF With Couples and Families

GARF ratings may be performed by therapists or nonparticipating raters. Although the particular interaction task or setting is not specified, it is typical that the raters provide global and subscale ratings following the first therapy session, rather than after a specified interaction sequence. Yingling et al. (1998) provide several excellent examples of the use of the GARF to monitor session-by-session progress in family therapy cases. It is important that the rater be the same person every session because between-rater variance for exact-point numerical ratings can be rather large (Henney & Hampson, 1994).

The functioning categories and ranges of scores help classify families from *dysfunctional* to *satisfactory*. Based on the history of the couple/family, it is often useful to classify past relational functioning as well as current relational functioning. The GARF authors recommend rating the highest level of functioning and the lowest level of functioning within the past year, much like the GAF rating in the DSM-IV.

Ratings are performed for the overall level of family functioning. The GARF developers also recommend subscale ratings for more specific behaviors. *Problem Solving* refers to the relational unit's ability to negotiate rules and differences, adapt and cope with stressful events, provide clear and direct communication, and resolve conflict. *Organization* refers to the clarity and ongoing distinctness of roles and interpersonal boundaries; power distribution and hierarchical functioning; behavioral control; and personal responsibility for actions. *Emotional Climate* represents the family's overall mood and tone; quality of caring, attachment, and empathy; respect and valuing; and quality of sexual relating. Although it is true that there are not large differences among the ratings (Beavers & Hampson, 1990), these ratings can be useful in determining specific family/couple lacks and needs.

The highest level of functioning, satisfactory relational functioning (81 to 100), describes a relational context that is structured and predictable, yet flexible in the face of the need to adapt. Conflicts are typically resolved successfully. Each member is unique and the power distribution is shared. These relational units appear satisfied and optimistic and therefore can display a wide range of feelings as the situation dictates.

Somewhat unsatisfactory relational units (61 to 80) demonstrate adequate, mostly normal patterns of relating, but with more pain and struggle than the satisfactory group. Some conflicts are not resolved. Decision making is competent, but control struggles may interfere with egalitarian relationships. Some feelings are masked; warmth and caring are present, but not as

TABLE 5.1 Observational Family Ratings

Assessment instrument	Specific couple and family applications	Cultural/ language	Instruction/use: T = time to take; S = time to score; I = items	Computerized: a = scoring; b = report	Reliability (R)/validity (V)	Availability
Beavers Interactional Competence and Style; SFI	Whole families; classifies family competence and behavioral style; suggestions for appropriate therapy	English; Spanish; Italian; Portuguese; Greek; Chinese; Japanese; German	T = 10 min; S = 10 min; I = 12 competence, 8 style	a = no; b = no	R = 0.85 (inter-rater); R = 0.88 (alpha); V = 0.72 (canonical)	Family Studies Center (Dallas, TX); www.familystudiescenter.org
McMaster Clinical Rating Scale	Whole families; classifies families on general functioning and composite behaviors	English; French; 12 other languages	T = 90 min with interview; S = 10 min; I = 7 scales; McSIFF interview: 35 pages of questions	a = no; b = no	R = 0.68–0.87 (inter-rater); R =0.81–0.87 (test–retest); V = good clinical validity	Brown University Family Research Program
Circumplex Clinical Rating Scale	Whole families; couples; measures cohesion, change (adaptability), and communication	English; Spanish; several other languages	T = 45–60 min; S = 10–15 min; I = 3 global scales, 13 subscales	a = no; b = no	R = 0.95–0.97 (alphas); R =0.75–0.86 (test–retest); V = good support for circumplex theory	Life Innovations, Inc., Minneapolis, MN; www.lifeinnovations.org
GARF	Any relational unit: family, couple, partner, support system	English	T = 15–60 min; S = 10 min; I = 4 global ratings	a = no; b = no	R = 0.73–0.86 (inter-rater); V = 0.69 (with Beavers Competence)	American Psychological Assn. (DSM-IV-TR)

unconditional as in the satisfactory units. Parenting is adequate, but less spontaneous than in the former group.

Predominantly unsatisfactory couples and families (41 to 60) demonstrate more difficulty with clarity, problem solving, and transitory adaptations to change. Control themes predominate and an emphasis on rules is common. Decision making is intermittently effective; these families are rigid or lack sufficient structure to enforce rules (see Beavers style dimension). Different feelings are disallowed; pain and anger are typically not handled well. Although some warmth and support are present, they are often contingent and unequally distributed.

Rarely satisfactory units (21 to 40) provide relatively low levels of support. Expectations for behavior are rigidly and obsessionally followed or are largely ignored. These units do not handle change and transition well. Obvious emotional distancing or physical leave-taking and hostility prevent smooth communication and negotiation. The emotional climate is quite barren or openly hostile. Alternations between attempts at rigid control and chaotic functioning disallow continuity in these families.

Chaotic relational units (1 to 20) lack coherence and continuity. Day-to-day routines are negligible and communication is indirect and incoherent. Relationships are overly dependent (see "centripetal") or overly distant and hostile (see "centrifugal"). Relational boundaries fluctuate, and no one knows where he or she stands with other family members. Despair, cynicism, and lack of hope predominate, so little emotional nurturance is provided.

By rating a family or couple on global functioning and the individual subscales, a profile of family strengths and needs can be mapped (Yingling et al., 1998).

PROTOCOL FOR USING OBSERVATIONAL ASSESSMENTS WITH COUPLES AND FAMILIES

The following protocol can be useful when utilizing any of the whole-family assessment rating scales addressed in this chapter. Some require more time and detail in terms of administration, and some require a videotaped assessment segment.

1. Obtain written consent for the observational procedure as well as consent for videotaping (when used). Assure the family that no one outside the clinic supervisors and direct therapists will be viewing the tape.
2. Select an assessment tool that fits the needs of the clinic or practice that is using the instrument. For example, the Beavers Model Rating Scales can be used within a rather brief time period at the beginning of the first session. The McMaster model provides much more overt detail (McSIFF interview), which is then summarized through the rating scales.

3. An interviewer or therapist introduces the discussion task. For the Beavers scales, it is, "For the next 10 minutes, I would like you to discuss together what you would like to see changed in your family," while the interviewer leaves the room. For the McMaster model, the detailed clinical interview (McSIFF) is conducted by an experienced clinician. For the circumplex model, there is no specific task, but the family is asked to engage in interactive dialogue, such as describing their typical week. No set procedure or task is specified for the GARF.

4. Rate the family, based on the observed interactional sequences. Raters typically are trained and well versed in the particular model they are using. For example, it takes approximately 15 hours of rater training to reach inter-rater reliabilities of +.90 using the Beavers scales.

5. When possible, use the self-report version of the model with individuals, to compare each member's perception of the family with the overall ratings. These are the SFI (Beavers), FAD (McMaster), and FACES III or IV (circumplex).

6. Use the family ratings to help set therapeutic goals. The identification of specific lacks and needs of the family helps provide an operational list of tasks that need to be accomplished. The identification of family competence and style (Beavers) also helps therapists tailor their approach to each family, in terms of control (power differential), partnership, and disclosure of strategy with the family.

7. Rerate the family at several points along the therapy time-line, to monitor progress and check on the therapeutic alliance. In the authors' clinical setting, families are rerated at the sixth session, and every six sessions thereafter. In several studies using the GARF, these ratings are provided after every session (Yingling et al., 1998).

8. Provide feedback to the family about the assessment; where they appear to be having problems; and the fact that certain goals can be established in the initial session.

Whenever rating scales are used, a certain degree of subjectivity may be present, so the decision about who will perform the rating is important. In the authors' studies, the therapist is always one of the family's raters because the rating is done at the outset of the first session. Neutral research rating teams also view the tapes during the week, and these ratings are added to the case files prior to the second session. Interestingly, and much like the findings of Kolevzon, Green, Fortune, & Vosler (1988), the authors have found that, in the beginning, therapists tend to rate the families they are beginning to treat as slightly more dysfunctional than the neutral raters do. Family members' ratings (on the SFI) tend to line up more with the neutral raters. At the close of therapy, the therapists' ratings put the family in a more competent direction than the neutral raters, and line up more with the family members' views.

It is also informative to see which family member's rating on the SFI rates the family as more or less disturbed than the outside raters rate it. The authors' studies have found that adolescents in general, and acting-out adolescents, in particular, rate their families as more disturbed than the raters. However, in certain internalizing (CP) patterns, it is not uncommon for the symptomatic adolescent (e.g., anorexic adolescents) to paint a picture of perfection in their families. These varying perspectives can provide a therapist with some important insights into family dynamics.

CASE EXAMPLES

Case1: A CF Family

The school district referred this family because Jose, age 12, was disruptive in class and was not making adequate progress in any subject. In previous years, Jose had done grade-appropriate work and had not been a behavior problem.

This family, of Hispanic origin, consisted of Jose, his mother Rosa, age 35, and an older sister Lupe, age 17, who was not in school; in addition the father, Miguel, age 37, had lived elsewhere for the last year in a household that included his 22-year-old girlfriend. Jose had had frequent verbal conflicts with Rosa and in one instance was stopped by Lupe from physically hurting his mother. The onset of Jose's defiant behavior coincided with Miguel's departure.

Miguel came frequently into the home; he brought groceries and gave money to Rosa at irregular intervals. He worked as an auto mechanic and was hard pressed to keep two families going. He would not come to evaluation or treatment, so the family that appeared (Step 1: obtain informed consent for evaluation) consisted of Jose, Rosa, and Lupe. The family discussion task ("What would you like to see changed in your family?"), based on the Beavers Interactional Scales (Step 2: choose an appropriate instrument and model; Step 3: introduce the discussion task), was punctuated by uncomfortable silence and distancing. When the family members spoke, it was about blaming Jose for not being more compliant and respectful of his mother. Lupe and Rosa had a tentative coalition, mostly against Jose, but also in their unlikely wish to have Miguel reintegrated into the family. The family fluctuated between chaotic outbursts and attempts at rigid control; they had poor negotiation skills. Each member tended to blame someone else for his or her frustrations. The family affect was rather hopeless and cynical, and unresolved conflict abounded. The family was rated at "borderline" in competence on the Beavers Interactional Competence Scale (Step 4: rate the family's interaction).

In terms of stylistic behavior (also Step 4: rate the family's interaction), there were consistent indicators of centrifugal family behavior: open conflicts, more open hostility, and discouraged dependency needs in the offspring. The family also spaced themselves physically apart, especially Jose, who was all the way across the room from his mother and sister. They appeared unconcerned about their social presentation to outsiders. The family was rated "borderline centrifugal," which, according to the Beavers model, is open in the direct expression of anger and hostility; leave-taking is frequent. Control themes are overt blaming and direct emotional assaults; the cyclical chaos is more overt than covert. Nurturance is not available to parents or children, and satisfaction is sought outside the family. Psychiatric disorders typically include externalizing disorders (conduct, substance abuse), and cyclical disorders that reflect the rigid-to-chaos fluctuations (members of these families often have borderline personality disorders). They need therapists who can maintain effective control; limit the number of members attending; focus on the basic; help the family organize simple actions and activities; organize generational boundaries; and help members take risks with neediness and emotional pain.

On the SFI, taken by all three (Step 5: use self-report scales related to the observational model), the results were similar, except that Jose graded the family somewhat lower in competence than his sister and mother did. All three rated the family style (Cohesion Factor) as disengaged/centrifugal. Jose's lower competence rating is quite characteristic of the "symptom bearer," indicating lower levels of family satisfaction and higher levels of unresolved conflict, as well as greater emotional distance from the rest of the family.

The combined results placed the family in the borderline CF group. In six sessions with this family, it was necessary to focus on reasonable goals (Step 6: set reasonable goals based on the assessment). It was established that Rosa did not expect Miguel ever to return to her home and that Jose's acting out was coincidental with his father's moving out and taking up with another woman. Rosa was unemployed with a sixth grade education and Lupe was poorly equipped for the working world because she had left school after the 10th grade.

Task 1 was to help Rosa to become empowered to become the head of the family. With help, she was able to tell Miguel that she needed and appreciated his help but that he was confusing and damaging his son with his intermittent appearances in which he behaved as the authoritarian father. This confused Jose and undermined Rosa's authority, which was necessary to develop some kind of structure upon which to rely. Rosa was able to tap into Miguel's real love for Jose and he became more clearly an adjunct to Rosa's running the house rather than trying to run her as well.

Task 2 (Task 1 made this goal easier to accomplish) was to reduce or eliminate Jose's disruptive behavior and get him back on track in school. As he was helped to see his mother as a dedicated parent who loved him, he was also allowed to vent his anger and sadness that Miguel was not going to return to the home and be a real father. Less confusion meant less despairing anger and he began to focus on his schoolwork again and accept the loss of this father.

In Task 3, Lupe was encouraged to study for a G.E.D., which would assist her in getting her high school diploma in order to get a job. She was an intelligent young woman who needed some direct encouragement in growing up and being helpful to herself and to her family.

The borderline CF style dictated the necessity for a more directive approach to help the family clear up confusion and focus on the "do-able." The grief over the loss of a father was brought out and reduced the overt hostility always seen in borderline CF families.

Because the authors' Family Studies Center contracts for a six-session family model with its grantors, the SFI is a better instrument for evaluating results than is the GARF. The SFI reflects changes more rapidly (Step 7: re-evaluate the family periodically). Use of the GARF is limited to longer-term treatment. In both of these case histories, significant increase was reported in family competence, although the style did not change with the CP family and only modestly with the CF family. The use of the SFI with school children and school reports of behavior and functioning offer better and quicker evidence of improvement (Step 8: share the results to help the family plan future goals).

Case 2: A CP Family

The Lee family referred themselves to the sliding fee clinic as a result of acting out behavior in their younger daughter, Michelle, who was 18 and a senior in high school. The family consisted of the father, Benny, his wife, Grace, their older daughter, Rosa (22), and Michelle. The family was Filipino; they moved from the Philippines when Rosa was a baby; Michelle was born in the United States. Mr. Lee was an educated professional. Mrs. Lee held a college degree, but did not work outside the home.

Mr. Lee had gotten fed up with Michelle's increasing tendency to defy her parents. His blood pressure was up and tension headaches were common; he had three auto accidents in the past two months. Some of her behaviors involved sneaking out in the middle of the night, taking the car without permission, and running up charge cards to the maximum. Michelle constantly complained that her parents were too strict, and she had to sneak out and defy in order to have a halfway "normal" life. The Lees referred to their expectation of compliance as "the Filipino way", and thought Michelle was entirely "too American".

The entire family presented for the initial family assessment. Mr. Lee had trouble with the fact that a videotape was being made of the family's interaction. He consented (Step 1) to participate only if the therapist remained in the room (she said that would, but she would not talk) and he remained off camera. The family discussion task (again, "What would you like to see changed in your family?", Steps 2 and 3) revealed a number of key interactions. First, Mr. Lee controlled every exchange in the family, from directing who was to talk to correcting the perspective of individuals who had a divergent view. His wife, no patsy, would occasionally redirect or contradict his comments. However, these exchanges were all done with little emotion, in a very mechanical tone. When Michelle disagreed or tried to defend her behavior as "normal", he would lecture on about how she was threatening to blow the family apart by not following the Filipino way. The older daughter, Rosa, was a passive, sad, and ineffectual person who deferred to her parents. She also had a negative relationship with Michelle, who referred to Rosa as "the narc". There was a tone of invasiveness on both parents' part, who labeled the behaviors of their daughters as "American" and "little mama". It was clear, however, that the scapegoat in this system was Michelle. While many CP families have individuals with only internalizing disorders, this "fallen saint" pattern is another variation on the scapegoating theme.

From the observation of the family, and their description of the circular nature of the interaction (act out, ground her, more acting out, etc.), that the control themes in the family were quite rigid, and that rigid control gave way to chaos as the effectiveness of parental control was defied. The family was stuck. The operating themes within the family were expectations for perfect behavior, condemnation for not following the "correct" culture, and dominance/submission. This family was rated as "Borderline" in competence on the Beavers Competence Scale (Step 4), and as Centripetal in Style (Step 4 also), given the emphasis on compliant and "correct" behavior, and the suppression of the expression of negative feelings. Michelle was clearly the "fallen saint" in this system.

The Borderline Centripetal family system, according to the Beavers model, is a control-oriented structure that lacks intimacy and spontaneity. They are stuck in control efforts. When these families seek help, it is to help further control the fallen saint, not to relinquish control. Any effort on the therapists' part to increase the control (shape the offender) or challenge the control of the tyrant is doomed to failure. The former solidifies the cyclical control themes, and the latter will result in the controlling member pulling the family out of treatment. Instead, the therapist needs to go below the control issues, to the underlying feelings of the family members. They are upset, disappointed, and probably very lonely. Hence, getting family members to address what they miss and long for can be a powerful tool.

Second, there will be strong attempts of different factions to pull the therapist into their side of the struggle. The therapist needs to steer clear of judgments and side-taking. As the focus on relationships and lost hopes and dreams progresses, it becomes clear that there is not a specifically-defined villain and victim. They are all hurting. It is a good idea to cater to the emotional needs of the most powerful person in the family initially, so he/she feels understood. This can go a long way to preventing the powerful member from pulling the family out of therapy. The SFI (Step 5) was not administered to the Lees.

For the Lee family, the therapeutic goals were several (step 6). One was to develop a focus on the feeling level, especially with family members asking for more of what they liked, rather than rigid rule structures. A second was to shift the "blame" for behavior from the clash of cultures to the individual level. A third was for the parents to learn cooperation and negotiation skills, so they could share parenting roles and duties. A related theme had to do with helping Rosa develop some sense of autonomy, in that the parents would view her strivings to be more independent as a sign of individual competence and not defiance. Finally, Michelle would learn that as control themes softened, she needed to rely less on rebellious tactics to get what she wanted.

When the family began dealing with Task 1, it became clear that each member was feeling isolated and lonely. The guilt-inducing and controlling exchanges that characterized the family began to be interspersed with questions such as "Well, what would you like to see more of?" It was much harder for Mr. Lee than the others to address the feeling level. He also had more difficulty with the second task, that of personalizing rather than culturalizing the deviant behavior. However, there was an important breakthrough when the parental dyad began addressing working as a team (task 3). The more Mr. Lee observed that his wife was reasonably competent in talking with the girls, and even soliciting cooperation from them, the more he felt that he could back off. In fact, he soon "allowed" his wife and daughters to continue counseling without him, a major step in altering his rigid control efforts.

Once this step was reached, the three women were able to negotiate on some key matters, including a more modest social schedule for Michelle, and some independent maneuvering for Rosa. Rosa began taking some classes at the Community College, and had begun joining several activity groups at the church. The three women/family subset attended a total of 15 sessions, and reported a much higher degree of satisfaction. From their reports, Mr. Lee was also happier, and was significantly less stressed out at home.

Re-evaluation (Step 7) at the 12th session involved only Mrs. Lee, Rosa, and Michelle. The discussion was productive and respectful. It was clear that there was less testy behavior on Michelle's part, and the respect for each other was higher. However, since Mr. Lee was not present, it was not possible to tell whether this same interaction would have occurred had he been there. By their reports, however, negotiation and overall interaction was much smoother at home, especially since Mr. Lee had decided that he did not need to control everyone and everything. The rating at the 12th session found this family at the higher Midrange level of competence, still with a modestly Centripetal style, so there was a noticeable improvement in their functioning level.

CONCLUSION

The various family observational assessment systems in this chapter focus on the "macro" level of assessment, examining the "big picture" of family functioning. As mentioned earlier, a wide variety of more "micro" assessment procedures measure highly specific behaviors within family interaction sequences, but these may be less amenable to therapy planning and intervention than the models presented here.

The assessment models presented in this chapter probably have more similarities than differences. The Beavers model addresses family competence, which refers to structure, autonomy, communication clarity, and boundaries. In a similar vein, the McMaster model addresses overall family functioning, which is also a linear, more-is-better dimension consisting of important family tasks and communication skills. The GARF is also a linear rating scale, comprising dimensions of emotional climate, problem solving, and organization. The circumplex communication rating is also a linear scale, ranging from low to high. However, the flexibility dimension is a curvilinear scale, ranging from polar opposites of rigid to chaotic; these dimensions are close kin in the Beavers model, representing dysfunctional to borderline levels of competence.

The style dimension of the Beavers model describes the behavioral climate of the family and is highly associated with the nature of behavior disorders in family members. This is more of a curvilinear dimension because middle levels of style are associated with healthy family functioning and extremes are found in more disturbed families. This maps on to the circumplex model Cohesion Factor, in which extremes of disengaged and enmeshed are associated with family disturbance. This dimension is addressed on the affective involvement rating on the McMaster model, where "empathic involvement" is optimal, and the extremes of "lack of involvement" and "symbiotic involvement" are more pathological. This dimension is not addressed directly on the GARF. The major models and their instruments are described in Table 5.1.

REFERENCES

Barton, C., Alexander, J. F. & Turner, C. W. (1993). Coding defensive and supportive communications: Discriminant validity and subcategory convergence. *Journal of Family Psychology, 7,* 197–203.

Beavers, W. R. (1977). *Psychotherapy and growth: A family systems perspective.* New York: Brunner/ Mazel.

Beavers, W. R., & Hampson, R. B. (1990). *Successful families: Assessment and intervention.* New York: W. W. Norton.

Beavers, W. R., & Hampson, R. B. (2003). Measuring family competence: The Beavers systems model. In Walsh, F. (Ed.), *Normal family processes* (3rd ed.). New York: Guilford Press.

Beavers, W. R., & Voeller, M. N. (1983). Family models: Comparing the Olson circumplex model with the Beavers systems Model. *Family Process, 22,* 85–98.

Bell, D. C. & Bell, L. G. (1989). Micro and macro measurement of family systems concepts. *Journal of Family Psychology, 3,* 137–157.

Bishop, D. S., Epstein, N. B., Keitner, G. I, Miller, I. W., & Zlotnick, C. (1987). *McMaster Structured Interview of Family Functioning (McSIFF).* Providence, RI: Brown University Family Research Program.

Bishop, D. S., Epstein, N. B., Keitner, G. I., Miller, I. W., Zlotnick, C., & Ryan, C. E. (2000). *McMaster Structured Interview of Family Functioning (McSIFF).* Providence, RI: Brown University Family Research Program.

Epstein, N. B., & Bishop, D. S. (1981). Problem-centered systems therapy of the family. In A. S. Gurman & D. P. Kniskern (Eds.), *Handbook of Family Therapy.* New York: Brunner/Mazel.

Epstein, N. B., Ryan, C. E., Bishop, D. S., Miller, I. W., & Keitner, G. I. (2003). The McMaster model: A view of healthy family functioning. In Walsh, F. (Ed.), *Normal Family Processes* (3rd ed.). New York: Guilford Press.

Gordon, E. D. (1997). *The Global Assessment of Relational Functioning (GARF): Reliability and validity.* Unpublished masters' thesis, Southern Methodist University, Dallas, TX.

Hampson, R. B. & Beavers, W. R. (1996a). Family therapy and outcome: Relationships between therapist and family styles. *Contemporary Family Therapy, 18,* 345–369.

Hampson, R. B., & Beavers, W. R. (1996b). Measuring family therapy outcome in a clinical setting: Families that do better or worse in therapy. *Family Process, 35,* 347–361.

Hampson, R. B., Beavers, W. R., & Hulgus, Y. F. (1989). Insiders' and outsiders' views of family: The assessment of family competence and style. *Journal of Family Psychology, 3,* 118–136.

Hampson, R. N., Beavers, W. R., & Hulgus, Y. F. (1990). Cross-ethnic family differences: Interactional assessment of White, Black, and Mexican–American families. *Journal of Marital and Family Therapy, 16,* 307–319.

Hampson, R. B., Prince, C. C., & Beavers, W. R. (1999). Marital therapy: Qualities of couples who fare better or worse in treatment. *Journal of Marital and Family Therapy, 25,* 411–424.

Henney, S. M. (1994). *Relational diagnosis and assessment in family therapy.* Unpublished masters' thesis, Southern Methodist University, Dallas, TX.

Henney, S. M., & Hampson, R. B. (1994). Social desirability effects on family self-report ratings. Presented at American Psychological Association Convention, Los Angeles.

Kolevzon, M. S., Green, R. G., Fortune, A. E., & Vosler, N. R. (1988). Evaluating family therapy: Divergent methods, divergent findings. *Journal of Marital and Family Therapy, 14,* 277–286.

Lee, C. (1988). Theories of family adaptability: Toward a synthesis of Olson's circumplex and the Beavers systems models. *Family Process, 27,* 73–85.

Miller, I. W., Kabacoff, R. I., Epstein, N. B., Bishop, D. S., Keitner, G. I., Baldwin, L. M., & van der Spuy, H. I. J. (1994). The development of a clinical rating scale for the McMaster Model of Family Functioning. *Family Process, 33,* 53–69.

Miller, I. W., Ryan, C. E., Keitner, G. I., Bishop, D. S., & Epstein, N. B. (2000). The McMaster approach to families: Theory, assessment, treatment, research. *Journal of Family Therapy, 22,* 168–189.

Mottarella, K. E., Philpot, C. I., & Fritzsche, B. A. (2001). Don't take out this appendix! Generalizability of the Global Assessment of Relational Functioning Scale. *The American Journal of Family Therapy, 29,* 271–278.

Olson, D. H., & Gorall, D. M. (2003). Circumplex model of marital and family systems. In Walsh, F. (Ed.), *Normal Family Processes* (3rd ed.). New York: Guilford Press.

Olson, D. H., & Killorin, E. (1983). *Clinical rating scale for the circumplex model of marital and family systems.* Family Social Science, University of Minnesota.

Olson, D. H., & Killorin, E. (1988). *Clinical rating scale for the circumplex model of marital and family systems.* Family Social Science, University of Minnesota.

Ross, N. M., & Doherty, W. J. (2001). Validity of the Global Assessment of Relational Functioning (GARF) when used by community-based therapists. *The American Journal of Family Therapy, 29*, 239–253.

Thomas, V. & Olson, D. H. (1993). Problem families and the circumplex model: Observational assessment using the clinical rating scale. *Journal of Marital and Family Therapy, 19*, 159–175.

Yingling, L. C., Miller, W. E., McDonald, A. L., & Galewater, S. T. (1998). *GARF assessment sourcebook: Using the DSM-IV Global Assessment of Relational Functioning handbook.* New York: Brunner/Mazel.

CHAPTER 6

Clinical Outcomes Assessment of Couples and Families

LEN SPERRY

The practice of behavioral health at the onset of the 21st century is increasingly different from practice during most of the 20th century. This is largely due to the paradigm shift in behavioral health practice that has been underway since the late 1980s. This shift involves every facet of behavioral health practice, including the role of the clinician and the nature of the relationship between clinician and client, as well as clinical practice patterns. This shift has already resulted in the demystification of some basic tenets and "sacred cows" of clinical lore. Central to this paradigm shift is the increasing emphasis on quality and accountability of clinical services provided. Accordingly, quality indicators and cost effectiveness have become primary considerations in behavioral health today. Not surprisingly, clinical outcomes data, a key marker of quality and of accountability, has recently become the norm for the provision of behavioral health services.

This chapter introduces the concept of clinical outcomes assessment with couples and families. It begins by describing the emergence of the concept of accountability and the so called "outcomes revolution" and its impact on clinical practice. It then describes the various types and levels of outcomes assessment and its clinical implications, particularly the practice of family therapy. Therapeutic effectiveness, efficacy, and efficiency are defined, and the point is made that outcomes monitoring fosters the most important of the three concepts: therapeutic efficacy. Next, it discusses recent developments in outcomes measurement and monitoring with couples and families, and then describes the use of five specific measurement tools. Finally, a protocol for utilizing these tools in measuring and monitoring outcomes with couples and families is provided and illustrated with a couple therapy case example.

CLINICIANS, FAMILY THERAPY, AND OUTCOMES MEASUREMENT

Clinical outcomes data and the associated outcomes revolution (Sperry, 1997) reflect a norm radically different from that in which most clinicians were trained. In the past, clinical practice was characterized by independence of clinical judgment; practice constraints; emphasis on therapeutic process; and subjective assessment of clinical progress. The recent shift in focus to an emphasis on accountability, that is, outcomes instead of process and objective assessment of clinical progress, has resulted in many clinicians' confusion and concern about the meaning and implications of this paradigm shift imposed on the profession. Some view this emphasis on accountability and quality as an intrusion into their practice style or as actually or potentially unethical. Some have embraced this norm wholeheartedly, while others have come to accept it as inevitable (Sperry, Brill, Grisson, & Marion, 1997). Whatever their perspective, clinicians must contend with the reality that therapeutic account-ability and clinical outcomes assessment in particular have become a core feature of clinical practice today and will be in the future.

In short, clinical outcomes assessment has been regarded as a necessary but unwelcome task by clinicians, particularly those conducting family ther-apy who are process oriented. "A focus on results rather than process has been anathema to family therapists" (Yingling, Miller, McDonald, & Galwaler, 1998, p. 49). Can this process versus outcome dilemma be resolved? Wynne 1988) suggested a potential solution, which is to "recommend that two primary baselines be given priority in family therapy research: (a) the multiple versions of the family members' 'initial' presenting problem, and (b) the prob-lem identified by consensus of family and therapist (p. 253). Yingling and colleagues (1998) contend that using data from self-report measures of family members along with data from therapist ratings or observations (i.e., the Global Assessment of Relationship Functioning [GARF]) can provide data relevant to process and outcome assessment. They also note that "discussing GARF parameters and charting progress with the client can enhance the ther-apeutic process... [and] the GARF can also be used as a process research tool when combined with case notes that include therapeutic interventions and reflections" (Yingling et al., 1998, p. 49).

TYPES OF OUTCOMES SYSTEMS AND THEIR CLINICAL VALUE

Most clinicians are likely to have had some experience with at least one type of outcomes system. The most common, and often the only, assessment of treatment outcomes that may be required is a simple measure of client satisfaction. Usually, client satisfaction is assessed by a short paper-and-pencil questionnaire that includes such items as how well the client thought he was treated by the therapist and how much he thought he improved during therapy. Although client satisfaction is important, it has not been shown to be an accurate assessment of treatment outcomes; in fact, it is actually a poor measure of clinical improvement. For example, Atkisson and Zwick (1982) showed that symptom improvement explains only 10% of the variance in client satisfaction, while the relationship between clinical improvement and reported satisfaction is not statistically significant for clients still in treatment or for those who have completed treatment.

On the other hand, other outcomes measures have shown clinical utility and value. Outcomes measures and outcomes measurement systems can yield three types of benefits, one of which is its capacity to identify effective treatments. This requires pretreatment and posttreatment assessment of a client's status to determine changes that occurred as a result of treatment. Aggregation of these data across all clients who received a specific treatment is the basis for this first benefit. A second benefit is immediate feedback to clinicians and case managers. This feedback will enable clinicians to identify clients who are improving adequately; those who have improved to a point at which treatment may no longer be necessary; and those whose lack of progress or determination suggests that their treatment should be changed. The third benefit is the ability to identify the specific changes most likely to move the unimproved client onto a more positive growth path—that is, to determine whether involvement of a spouse or family in treatment; transfer to a different therapist and different type of therapy; referral for a medication evaluation; or some other alteration in treatment is most likely to get the client well.

By incorporating feedback from an outcomes system into ongoing clinical cases, clinicians effectively supplement or support a clinician's intuition about treatment decisions. Serial data on changes in symptoms and functioning can be utilized in modifying the course and duration of treatment in terms of focus, modality, and intervention strategies with individuals, couples, or families.

Essentially, three levels of outcomes assessment exist (Sperry, 1997):

- *Outcomes measurement*—quantification or measurement of clinical and functional outcomes during a specific time period. Outcomes measures have traditionally been collected at the beginning and end of treatment. However, serial or concurrent assessment is becoming more common. Measures often include change in symptoms, well-being, functioning, and even patient satisfaction.
- *Outcomes monitoring*—serial or concurrent use of outcomes measures during the course of treatment. The goal of outcomes monitoring is comparison against a standard of expected results to monitor progress or lack of progress over the course of treatment. Monitoring can be done after each

session, every third session, or on some other scheduled basis. The data are then used to alter treatment when it is off course or stagnating. They can also be used to follow progress in a single case or summed and adjusted for risk to compare several patients or programs. Outcomes monitoring can only be accomplished with repeated or concurrent measures, and the information must be available during the treatment.

- *Outcomes management*—ultimate utilization of monitored data in a way that allows individuals and health care systems to learn from experience. Usually, this results in reshaping or improving the overall administrative and clinical processes of services provided. Patient profiling, provider profiling, and site profiling are three common aspects of an outcomes management system.

In a sense, these three levels are developmental levels or stages, with each level a prerequisite for the next. Currently, the majority of outcomes assessment activity is occurring at the outcomes measurement and the outcomes monitoring levels. It is useful to distinguish therapeutic effectiveness and efficacy from therapeutic efficiency. *Therapeutic effectiveness* is the determination that a treatment has a beneficial effect and is the expected outcome for a typical client treated in common practice settings by a typical clinician. On the other hand, *therapeutic efficacy* is the expected outcome for clients treated under optimal conditions by highly qualified clinicians. In short, efficacy defines optimal clinical practice, while effectiveness compares actual with optimal practice (Sperry et al., 1996).

In contrast, *therapeutic efficiency* refers to highly beneficial treatment tailored to the unique needs of a specific client (individual, couple, or family) as they are noted—or measured—over the course of treatment. Therapeutic effectiveness and efficacy answer the question "which treatment or approach is better or best?" Therapeutic efficiency answers the question "which is the best treatment for this client and how can it be optimally provided?" Accordingly, ongoing monitoring of clinical treatment outcomes fosters therapeutic efficiency.

CLINICAL OUTCOMES WITH INDIVIDUALS, COUPLES, AND FAMILIES

The earliest outcomes measurement efforts were primarily focused on psychotherapy with individuals, largely because a principal focus of psychotherapy research was on treatment outcomes. In the late 1980s two instruments for outcomes assessment with individuals, COMPASS-OP and the Outcomes Questionnaire (OQ-45), were widely utilized in clinical practice and research settings (Sperry et al., 1996). Both instruments were occasionally utilized to measure and monitor clinical outcomes with couples; however, they did not provide relational data or insights on systemic dynamics.

Several inventories and scales that assess couple and family dynamics and indicators have been available since the 1970s, but these tools were seldom used in clinical practice to measure pre–posttreatment outcomes, much less monitor clinical outcomes on an ongoing basis. It is true that the Dyadic Adjustment Scale (DAS) was utilized as a pre–post-treatment measure of therapeutic effectiveness in a handful of research studies over the years. However, only recently has the use of such inventories and scales as the DAS and the MSI-R (Marital Satisfaction Inventory—Revised) been advocated for monitoring clinical outcomes of couples therapy (Jacobson, 1984; Jacobson & Follette, 1985; Latham, 1990; Prouty, Markowski, & Barnes, 2000; Snyder & Aikman, 1999).

In terms of treatment outcome measures with families, the Self-Report Family Inventory (SFI), GARF Scale, and the Systematic Assessment of Family Environment (SAFE) Scale have all been utilized as pre–posttreatment measures in clinical research studies (Yingling, Miller, McDonald, & Galwaler, 1994a; Hampson & Beavers, 1996a; Hampson, Prince, & Beavers, 1999; Yingling, 1996). As clinicians become more familiar with the GARF, it has tremendous potential for monitoring clinical outcomes on a session-by-session basis with families (Yingling et al., 1998).

The next section of this chapter describes the use of five inventories and scales for clinical outcomes measurement and for the ongoing monitoring of clinical outcomes with couples and families: GARF, SFI, SAFE, DAS, and MSI-R.

FAMILY AND COUPLE MEASURES

Clinical Outcome Measures for Families

Global Assessment of Relationship Functioning (GARF)

Brief description of the GARF. The GARF is a therapist-rated device for indicating functioning or a family or other ongoing relationship on a continuum ranging from a low of 1 to a high of 100. The continuum is divided into five categories: 1 to 20 = chaotic; 21 to 40 = rarely satisfactory; 41 to 60 = predominantly unsatisfactory; 61 to 80 = somewhat unsatisfactory; and 81 to 100 = satisfactory. It is the only family-oriented measure included in the pages of the DSM-IV/DSM-IV-TR, and is located in Appendix B (American Psychiatric Association, 2000). GARF is analogous to GAF (Global Assessment of Functioning Scale), which is a measure of individual symptomatic distress and functioning; both are coded on Axis V. When assessing or rating a relationship, the clinician is asked to consider three dimensions of relational functioning: Problem Solving, Organization, and Emotional Climate.

Yingling and colleagues (1998) have slightly modified the dimensions Interactional/Problem Solving, Organization, and Emotional Climate, making them subscales that are scored separately, along with an overall GARF score. The psychometric properties and additional information about GARF are discussed in chapter 6.

The GARF as an outcomes measure. Considerable published research and clinical reports are available in which GARF is utilized as an outcomes measure. Most of these reports involve GARF in pre- and posttreatment measurement (Yingling, Miller, McDonald, & Galwaler, 1994a, b, 1998; Hampson, Henny, & Beavers, 1996; Ross & Doherty, 2001). With regard to ongoing assessment of outcomes, Yingling and colleagues (1998) discuss five case examples of the use of GARF as a treatment outcomes monitoring measure. These couple and family cases provide session-by-session ratings of overall GARF scores and subscale ratings for therapy lasting from 7 to 10 sessions. These case discussions are particularly valuable because data from the ongoing monitoring are utilized by the therapists to modify treatment focus and interventions.

Systematic Assessment of Family Environment (SAFE)

Brief description of the SAFE. The Systematic Assessment of Family Environment (SAFE) was developed by Yingling in 1991 along with field testing of the GARF (cf. Chapter 8 for a filler discussion of this instrument). It is a 21-item global assessment instrument for measuring three relational subsystem levels of the family system using two functioning factors for each subsystem level. The three subsystems are: dyadic marital–executive subsystem; parent–child subsystem; and extended family subsystem. Organizational Structure and Interactional Processes are the two factors assessed for each subsystem. Scoring yields ranges for four family types: competent, discordant, disoriented, or chaotic (Yingling, 1996). SAFE is user friendly and available in a Spanish version as well as a cartoon version for use with children under the age of 10 (Yingling et al., 1998). Validity is reported as .74 and .82 (Yingling et al., 1998).

The SAFE as an outcomes measure. The SAFE provides information that can easily be incorporated into a treatment plan. Relatively little has been published about using SAFE for pre–posttreatment evaluation of change or ongoing monitoring of family therapy. Nevertheless, Yingling and colleagues (1998) report collecting serial data on GARF and SAFE for monitoring treatment outcomes. The ease of administration makes this instrument a valuable outcomes measure with families.

Self-Report Family Inventory (SFI)

Brief description of the SFI. The Self-Report Family Inventory (SFI) is a 36-item self-report family instrument developed by Beavers and Hampson (1990) and is based on the Beavers systems model of family functioning. It measures five family domains: health/competence; conflict resolution; cohesion; leadership; and emotional expressiveness. The SFI correlates highly with two well-regarded therapist observational rating scales: the Beavers Interactional Competence Scale and the Beavers Interactional Styles Scale. Spanish and Chinese versions are also available. The psychometric properties and additional information about SFI are discussed in chapter 5.

The SFI as an outcomes measure. Some research in which the SFI has been utilized as an outcomes measure has been published. These reports involve the SFI in pre- and posttreatment measurement (Hampson & Beavers, 1996a, b; Hampson et al., 1999). Apparently no research or other published reports describe the use of the SFI as an ongoing measure of clinical outcomes; however, the ease of administration and brevity of the instrument (only 36 items) make it particularly valuable for monitoring session-by-session outcomes.

Clinical Outcome Measures for Couples

This section includes two well-regarded instruments with considerable potential in clinical outcomes measurement and monitoring: the Dyadic Adjustment Scale and the Marital Satisfaction Inventory—Revised.

Dyadic Adjustment Scale (DAS)

Brief description of the DAS. The Dyadic Adjustment Scale (DAS) is a 34-item self-report instrument for assessing dyadic or relationship adjustment. This instrument was developed by Spanier (1976) to measure the quality of adjustment of couples and other dyads. The DAS comprises four scales: Dyadic Satisfaction, Dyadic Cohesion, Dyadic Consensus, and Affectional Expression. It is one of the first and most extensively utilized relational instruments in clinical practice. A shorter, 14-item version is also available. The psychometric properties and additional information about DAS are discussed in chapter 7.

Spanier developed the instrument on the assumption that the quality of relational adjustment was the key indicator of the viability of a relationship. He defined marital quality as "how the marriage functions during its existence and how partners feel about and are influenced by such functioning (Spanier, 1979, p. 290). The DAS has consistently distinguished couples with better adjustment from those who are more dissatisfied with their relationship, including couple with a greater likelihood of divorce (Prouty et al., 2000). Well over 1000 research studies have been published involving the DAS. Although the instrument has evolved over the years, it remains one of the most commonly used measures of couples adjustment by researchers and clinicians.

The DAS as an outcomes measure. The DAS has a long history of use as an outcomes measure. Considerable research has been reported on its use as a pre–posttreatment assessment tool in studies of therapeutic efficacy and effectiveness with couples (Adam & Gingras, 1982; Brock & Joanning, 1983; Jacobson, 1984; Jacobson & Follette, 1985; Latham, 1990; Prouty et al., 2000). Even though neither this research nor other published reports describe the DAS as used as an ongoing measure of clinical outcomes, the brevity of the instrument—particularly the 14-item version—makes it an attractive choice for monitoring session-by-session outcomes.

Marital Satisfaction Inventory—Revised (MSI-R)

Brief description of the MSI-R. The Marital Satisfaction Inventory—Revised (MSI-R) is a 150-item self-report instrument developed by Snyder (1997). The earlier version, MSI (Snyder, 1981), was well regarded and one of the most often used relational inventories in research and clinical practice. The MSI-R has 13 scales:

- Global Distress
- Affective Communication
- Problem-Solving Communication
- Aggression
- Time Together
- Disagreement About Finances
- Sexual Dissatisfaction
- Role Orientation
- Family History of Distress
- Dissatisfaction With Children
- Conflict Over Child Rearing
- Inconsistency (validity scale)
- Conventionalization (validity scale)

The MSI-R is useful as a diagnostic and a therapeutic tool, as well as a screening instrument. Psychometric properties of and additional information about MSI-R are discussed in chapter 7.

The MSI-R as an outcomes measure. The MSI-R is typically used in the initial phase of therapy in discussing the couple's presenting concerns and in formulating treatment goals. However, it can also be utilized before and after therapy, in a pre–posttreatment fashion, to evaluate overall treatment outcomes (Snyder & Berg, 1983; Iverson & Baucom, 1988; Snyder, Wills, & Grady–Fletcher, 1991; Snyder, Mangrum, & Wills, 1993; Frank, Dixon, & Grosz, 1993). Snyder & Aikman (1999) also note the value of using MSI-R serially throughout the course of treatment in the evaluation of change and for revising treatment goals and interventions. The instrument "can be readministered at multiple points during treatment to evaluate and consolidate gains that the couple has made and to identify residual areas of distress for further work. This idiographic approach to outcome evaluation emphasizes within-partner change across time" (Snyder & Aikman, 1999, p. 1198).

Protocol for Utilizing Ongoing Assessment Method

The following six-step protocol can be useful in utilizing the GARF, SFI, SAFE, DAS, and MSI-R when measuring and monitoring clinical outcomes with couples and families.

1. Initially interview the couple or family.
2. Choose and administer specific inventories.
3. Collect collateral data (relevant work, school, medical records, etc.) and other interview data.
4. Review assessment data and plan treatment.
5. Monitor ongoing clinical outcomes and modify treatment accordingly.
6. Evaluate pre- and posttreatment outcomes, if feasible.

Well-executed interviews of the couple and family (Step 1 and Step 3) are essential in providing sufficient data and background information to develop and implement an effective treatment plan and intervention strategies. At the present time, the decision of which inventories and rating scales (Step 2) to use to measure and/or monitor clinical outcomes is much less complex than the protocols suggested by Bagarozzi (chapter 7) or Yingling (chapter 8). For example, Bagarozzi advocates a four-step funneling or filtering process that progresses from choosing global measures to focused measures. Because of the limited number of suitable potential inventories and scales (i.e., ease of administration and reasonable cost), the clinician might decide to utilize the SFI and GARF or the SAFE and GARF with families, and the GARF and DAS or MSI-R with couples.

Step 5 reflects the basic reason for monitoring outcomes, for example, session by session, every third session, and so forth. In this step, outcomes data transform into valuable feedback information that the clinician can utilize to modify the course and duration of treatment in terms of focus, modality, and intervention strategies. As a result of this feedback and subsequent treatment "course correction," couple or family therapy becomes more closely tailored to couple or family need and circumstance. Presumably, this should lead to more effective and efficient treatment. Finally, the clinical value of outcomes measurement can be evaluated in Step 6 by examining overall pre–posttreatment effects on the given outcome measures, inventories, and/or scales.

CASE STUDY

Jack and Nancy, both age 33, were referred to couples therapy by Nancy's gynecologist. During their first conjoint session (Step 1), the therapist learned that the couple had been married for 7 years and had a 2½-year-old daughter, Sybil. Sybil was their "wonder" child because she had been born after several years of unsuccessful efforts to conceive, including 2 years of painful fertility treatment. Jack had been an accountant at a low-tech manufacturing corporation until he was laid off some 3 months previously; Nancy had worked as a nurse at a local hospital for 3 or 4 years before she married Jack. Both had known each other since college but had never really seriously dated until after graduation.

The couple presented with increased argumentativeness, social and emotional withdrawal, and decreased sexual intimacy. These issues were relatively new in their relationship, apparently beginning soon after Sybil's birth. Nancy had been concerned about Jack's rigidity and seeming lack of emotional expressiveness since they had married and on more than one occasion had indicated her desire for them to seek couples therapy, but Jack was not interested in talking to anyone about himself or his marriage. In the time since he had been laid off, Jack had become increasingly sullen and emotionally distant; Nancy, who had been working part time at the hospital, now felt "forced" to go full time to cover their bills. She was particularly distraught about this because it meant she had less time to care for her daughter. During a recent appointment with her gynecologist, Nancy had begun sobbing when asked how she was doing. It was at this point that the gynecologist referred Nancy for conjoint couples therapy. Both partners acknowledged a moderate level of commitment to their marriage and an even deeper commitment to Sybil, who had become, for all practical purposes, the center of their lives.

The plan was to administer the MSI-R to the couple at the end of the first conjoint session and to interview Nancy and Jack individually in the following week. Then, during their second conjoint session, extensive feedback would be provided incorporating MSI-R, GARF, and interview material in order to formulate a tailored treatment plan collaboratively with the couple. GARF would be evaluated at each conjoint session and the MSI-R was to be administered after every third session and after the last session (Step 2).

Individual interviewing provided a fuller understanding of each partner; their attraction to one another; and the nature of their marital relationship. Nancy's description of her family of origin suggested that she had experienced a warm and secure attachment style and that her early life experiences with parents, siblings, and peers were wholesome and supportive. Her parents were described as encouraging and believed in expressing affection openly. She was the oldest of three siblings and enjoyed helping her mother raise her younger sister and brother. Nancy was a very good student and a leader among her peers. Although Nancy's depression did not meet criteria for a major depressive episode, a diagnosis of adjustment disorder with depressed mood was noted. Although her current GAF was 54, her highest level of function in the past 12 months was judged to be about 85.

On the other hand, Jack's family of origin was less warm and less secure. His mother was described as emotionally unavailable and his father was often critical and demanding. He was a second child and, although he was a competent student, he was no match for his older brother, who was an honor student and top athlete. Needless to say, his brother was his father's favorite child. Jack's fearful attachment style seemed to reflect a sense of personal unworthiness along with an expectation that others would be rejecting and untrustworthy. Jack's current GAF was 62, although his highest level in the past year, when he was still working and quite content with his professional and family life, was probably about 72.

Not surprisingly, Jack had been wary of intimacy and tended to be socially distant and even awkward. However, he felt and acted differently when he first met Nancy. Her energetic presence seemed to make him come alive and feel hopeful about himself and the future. For her part, Nancy was attracted to Jack's quiet, patient gentleness as well as his ruggedly handsome features. Nancy described Jack as a caring father who adored Sybil. She noted that he was certainly more patient as a parent than she and that she had no qualms about his ability to care for their daughter while she was working. Nevertheless, she was angry that she had to work full time at a time and could not spend much time nurturing her growing daughter. It appeared that this reasonably healthy couple's GARF might have been in the mid 70s during the best period of their relationship but had slipped considerably in the past several months (Step 3).

An initial MSI-R profile was derived. It was noteworthy that raw scores on Global Distress (GDS) and Affective Communication (AFC) and Problem-Solving Communication (PSC) were extremely high for Jack and Nancy (see CS-1 in Table 6.1). In line with interview data, Jack and Nancy reported considerable marital distress in their relationship (GDS) and acknowledged a high degree of dissatisfaction with the extent of affection shown each other (AFC). This was particularly evident for Nancy, which reflected Jack's emotional distancing and lack of warmth. Similarly, the profile for both suggested their difficulty in intimate sharing, which most likely was exacerbated by their difficulty in resolving problems and conflict (PSC).

A GARF score of 52 was assessed; using Yingling's profiling system for the GARF (1998). Subscores on Interactional (46), Organizational (56), Emotional Climate (42), as well as an overall score of 52 were recorded (see Table 6.2). Similar to the MSI-R, their GARF profile suggested that communication was frequently inhibited by unresolved conflict; that ineffective anger and emotional deadness interfered with their relationship; and that their decision making was intermittently effective at best. In short, ineffective communication was inhibiting intimacy, problem-resolution, and decision-making processes.

Based on these clinical data, a treatment focus, goals, and intervention strategies were planned and implemented. Because this was a reasonably

TABLE 6.1 MSI-R Subscale Score Monitoring per Specified Conjoint Session (CS) for Female (F) and Male (M) Partners

Subscale	Gender	CS-1	CS-3	CS-6	CS-9
Global Distress (GDS)	F	13	11	7	2
	M	12	9	6	3
Affective Communication (AFC)	F	12	8	5	2
	M	13	10	4	0
Problem-Solving Communication (PSC)	F	13	13	6	3
	M	12	11	5	2
Aggression (AGG)	F	2	1	0	0
	M	1	0	0	0
Time Together (TTO)	F	5	4	3	1
	M	4	4	3	2
Disagreement About Finances (FIN)	F	0	0	0	0
	M	0	0	0	0
Sexual Dissatisfaction (SEX)	F	7	7	5	2
	M	13	13	10	9
Role Orientation (ROR)	F	10	10	10	10
	M	10	10	10	10
Family History of Distress (FAM)	F	1	1	1	1
	M	4	4	5	5
Dissatisfaction With Children (DSC)	F	0	0	0	0
	M	0	0	0	0
Conflict Over Child Rearing (CCR)	F	0	0	0	0
	M	0	0	0	0

TABLE 6.2 GARF Scores and Subscore Monitoring per Conjoint Session (CS)

Subscale/global	CS-1	CS-2	CS-3	CS-4	CS-5	CS-6	CS-7	CS-8	CS-9
Interactional	46	46	62	66	70	71	78	80	83
Organizational	56	56	62	65	65	75	78	81	86
Emotional Climate	42	45	51	55	60	60	65	70	80
Global therapist GARF	52	52	58	63	68	70	75	80	83

healthy and functional couple facing a major stressor (i.e., job loss and its relational sequalae) and the couple appeared to have some relational skill deficits, skill-focused couples therapy seemed indicated. It is also noteworthy that this couple brought some important strengths to therapy: a relatively conflict-free 7-year marriage; their positive experience as parents; and Nancy's early secure attachment style, which implies that she possesses considerable emotional resilience. Accordingly, the goals of treatment were to increase communication and foster emotional intimacy and effective problem resolution and decision making (Step 4).

The first and second sessions initiated this emphasis on communication by focusing on increasing listening skills and learning to use the language of affect. Little change was noticed on GARF subscales after session 2, or on GDS, AFC, and PSC scores of the MSI-R. Accordingly, the treatment focus shifted in subsequent sessions to assertive communication and conflict resolution. For the next four sessions, the couple worked in sessions and between sessions on skill learning and practice in these two areas. Not surprisingly, Interactional, Organizational, and Emotional Climate subscales of the GARF improved (see Table 6.2), as did the AFC and PSC subscales of the MSI-R when they were assessed at the sixth session. Because overall marital distress and dissatisfaction with this couple seemed to be linked intimately to affective communication and problem-solving communication, the GDS was significantly lowered by the sixth session (see Table 6.1). Subsequent sessions—sixth through the ninth—focused even more emotional intimacy as well as problem solving involving specific issues such as jobs and careers. Relationally, things had improved considerably,so treatment would terminate with the ninth session.

In session eight Jack announced he had just been offered the position of comptroller for a mid-size service corporation. Although this was the next step in a senior accountant's career path, it was a step that Jack had avoided for the past few years, even though others had noted that he possessed the requisite skills and experience. Although he admitted to some feelings of uncertainty about whether he could handle the kinds of responsibilities associated with that position, he felt that with the recent upsurge in Nancy's support and encouragement, he would succeed (Step 5).

Pre–post treatment outcomes reflected the significant degree of change and growth in this marital relationship. On the MSI-R, major pre–posttreatment changes were noted on the three subscales directly related to the couple's main concerns. On the GDS, the change was from a 13 to a 2 for Nancy and a 12 and 3 for Jack; with AFC: changes from 12 to 2 for Nancy and 13 to 0 for Jack; and PSC: changes from 13 to 3 for Nancy and 1 to 2 for Jack. On these subscales, changes went from the highest or most problematic to the lowest or least problematic range (see Table 6.1). On the GARF, a noticeable shift from relational functioning was occasionally unsatisfactory to highly satisfactory. More specifically, the following subscale changes were noted: Interactional subscale from 46 to 83; Organizational subscale from 56 to 86; Emotional Climate subscale from 42 to 80; and overall GARF from 52 to 83. In other words, now a greater degree of shared understanding and agreement about roles, tasks, and decision making; better problem-solving communication and negotiation; and a general atmosphere of warmth, caring, and sharing were present (Step 6; see Table 6.2).

TABLE 6.3 Reference Guide to Clinical Outcomes Assessment Instruments With Families and Couples

Assessment instrument	Type/Use	Cultural/ Language	Administration: time and items	Computerized: a = scoring; b = report	Reliability (R); validity (V)	Availability
Global Assessment of Relationship Functioning (GARF)	Therapist rating/ couples and families		5–10 min for inquiry/scoring	None		Appendix B of DSM-IV-TR
Self-Report Family Inventory (SFI)	Self-report/ families	Spanish; Chinese	Easy to administer, 5–15 min; 36 items	None	R = test–retest .30–.87; V = criterion related	Journal article
Systematic Assessment of Family Environment (SAFE)	Self-report/ families	Spanish	21 items	a = yes	V = .74 and .82	Yingling et al. (1998)
Marital Satisfaction Inventory—Revised (MSI-R)	Self-report/ couples	Spanish	25 min to administer and score; 150 items	a = yes; b = interpretive report	Factor analysis	Western Psychological Services, Inc.
Dyadic Adjustment Scale (DAS)	Self-report/ couples	French; Chinese	5–10 min; 34 items (also 14-item version)	a = yes	R = .86–.96; V = .86–.88	Journal article; Multi-Health Systems, Inc.

CONCLUDING COMMENT

Because the concepts covered in this chapter have only recently become a part of the conversation of assessment with couples and families, they are seldom discussed in texts on family therapy, much less books on family and couple assessment. Nevertheless, the paradigm shift in accountability in clinical practice has propelled clinical outcomes assessment to center stage. This chapter highlighted five inventories or scales that have been shown to have some clinical utility in measuring and monitoring outcomes in couples and family therapy. Presumably, other instruments exist that research and clinical practice will show have similar value (see Table 6.3). As this text was going to press, Pinsof et al. (2004) have just completed the development Systemic Therapist Inventory of Change (STIC) which is purported to track changes in individuals, couples, and families from session to session.

REFERENCES

Adams, D., & Gingras, M. (1982). Short- and long-term effects of a marriage enrichment program upon couple functioning. *Journal of Sex and Marital Therapy, 8,* 97–118.

American Psychiatric Association (2000). *Diagnostic and statistical manual of mental disorders: fourth edition—text revision* DSM-IV-TR. Washington, D.C.: Author.

Atkisson, C., & Zwick, R. (1982). The clients' satisfaction questionnaire: Psychometric properties and correlations with service utilization. *Evaluation and Program Planning, 5,* 233–237.

Beavers, W. R., & Hampson, R. B. (1990). *Successful families: Assessment and intervention.* New York: W. W. Norton.

Brock, G., & Joanning, H. (1983). A comparison of the relationship enhancement program and the Minnesota couples communication program. *Journal of Marital and Family Therapy. 9,* 295–305.

Frank, B., Dixon, D., & Grosz, H. (1993). Conjoint monitoring of symptoms of premenstrual syndrome: Impact on marital satisfaction. *Journal of Counseling Psychology, 40,* 109–114.

Hampson, R., & Beavers, W. (1996a). Family therapy and outcome: Relationships between therapist and family styles. *Contemporary Family Therapy, 13*(3), 345–370.

Hampson, R., & Beavers, W. (1996b). Measuring family therapy outcome in a clinical setting: Families that do better or do worse in therapy. *Family Process, 35,* 347–361.

Hampson, R., Henny, S., & Beavers, W. (1996). *Relational diagnosis and assessment in family therapy.* Manuscript submitted for publication. Cited in Yingling, L., Miller, W., McDonald, A., & Galwaler, S. (1998). *GARF assessment sourcebook: Using the DSM-IV Global Assessment of Relational Functioning* (p. 32). Washington, D.C.: Brunner/Mazelet.

Hampson, R., Prince, C., & Beavers, W. (1999). Marital therapy: Qualities of couples who fare better or worse in treatment. *Journal of Marital and Family Therapy, 25*(4), 411–424.

Iverson, A., & Baucom, D. (1988). Behavioral marital therapy outcomes: Alternative interpretation of the data. *Behavior Therapy, 21,* 129–138.

Jacobson, N. (1984). A component analysis of behavioral marital therapy: The relative effectiveness of behavior exchange and communication/problem-solving training. *Journal of Consulting and Clinical Psychology, 52,* 295–305.

Jacobson, N., & Follette, W. (1985). Clinical significance of improvement resulting from two behavioral marital therapy components. *Behavior Therapy, 16,* 249–264.

Latham, J. (1990). Family-of-origin intervention: An intergenerational approach to enhancing marital adjustment. *Journal of Contemporary Psychotherapy, 20,* 211–222.

Prouty, H., Markowski, E., & Barnes, H. (2000). Using the DAS in marital therapy: An exploratory study. *The Family Journal: Therapy for Couples and Families. 8*(3), 250–257.

Pinsof, W., Zinbarg, R., Mann, B., Lebow, G., Knoblock-Fedder, L., & Friedman, G. (2004). *The systematic therapy inventory of change.* Evanston, IL: The Family Institute of Northwestern University.

Ross, N., & Doherty, W. (2001). Validity of Global Assessment of Relational Functioning (GARF) when used by community-based therapists. *American Journal of Family Therapy, 29,* 239–253.

Snyder, D. (1981). *Marital satisfaction inventory (MSI) manual.* Los Angeles: Western Psychological Services.

Snyder, D. (1997). *Marital satisfaction inventory, revised (MSI-I) manual.* Los Angeles: Western Psychological Services.

Snyder, D., & Aikman, G. (1999). Marital satisfaction inventory—revised. In M. Maruish (Ed.), *Use of psychological testing for treatment planning and outcome assessment,* 2nd ed. (pp. 1173–1210). Hillsdale, NJ: Lawrence Erlbaum & Associates.

Snyder, D., & Berg, P. (1983). Predicting couples response to brief directive sex therapy. *Journal of Sex and Marital Therapy, 9,* 114–120.

Snyder, D., Mangrum, L. & Wills, R. (1993). Predicting couples' response to marital therapy: A comparison of short- and long-term predictors. *Journal of Consulting and Clinical Psychology, 61,* 61–69.

Snyder, D., Wills, R. & Grady-Fletcher, A. (1991). Long-term effectiveness of behavioral versus insight-oriented marital therapy. *Journal of Consulting and Clinical Psychology, 59,* 138–141.

Spanier, G. (1976). Measuring dyadic adjustment: New scales for assessing the quality of marriage and similar dyads. *Journal of Marriage and the Family, 38,* 15–28.

Spanier, G. (1979). The measurement of marital quality. *Journal of Sex and Marital Therapy, 5,* 288–300.

Sperry, L. (1997). Treatment outcomes: An overview. *Psychiatric Annals, 27*(2), 95–99.

Sperry, L., Brill, P., Howard, K., & Grissom, G. (1996). *Treatment outcomes in psychotherapy and psychiatric interventions.* New York: Brunner/Mazel.

Wynne, L. (1988). *The state of the art of family therapy research: Controversies and recommendations.* New York: Family Process Press.

Yingling, L. (1996). *A manual for the use of the Systematic Assessment of the Family Environment (SAFE): A self-report instrument for assessing multi-level family system functioning.* Rockwell, TX: J & L Human Systems Development.

Yingling, L., Miller, W., McDonald, A., & Galwaler, S. (1994a). Verifying outcome: Paradigm for the therapist-researcher. Paper presented at the meeting of the Texas Association for Marriage and Family Therapy, January, San Antonio, Texas.

Yingling, L., Miller, W., McDonald, A., & Galwaler, S. (1994b).Verifying outcome: Paradigm for the therapist-researcher. Paper presented at the meeting of the American Association for Marriage and Family Therapy, November, Chicago, Illinois.

Yingling, L., Miller, W., McDonald, A., & Galwaler, S. (1998). *GARF assessment sourcebook: Using the DSM-IV Global Assessment of Relational Functioning.* Washington, D.C.: Brunner/Mazel.

PART III

Specific Applications

CHAPTER 7

Couples Assessment
Strategies and Inventories

DENNIS A. BAGAROZZI AND LEN SPERRY

In an article entitled "Family Diagnostic Testing: A Neglected Area of Expertise," Bagarozzi (1989) contended that the systematic assessment of marital and family systems was the sine qua non condition for effective and accountable clinical practice. This premise remains valid today. Ideally, any test, instrument, or procedure selected for pretreatment assessment and posttreatment outcome evaluation should operationalize one or more key concepts or constructs derived from an internally consistent and logically coherent theory of marital/family functioning, conflict/problem development, and conflict/problem resolution. Any intervention procedure employed by the therapist to help a couple or family resolve conflicts and/or solve the presenting problem should follow logically from the theory's basic tenets concerning problem development and problem resolution. How a therapist goes about implementing theoretically derived treatments is a matter of personal style. This is the artistry of therapy.

L'Abate and Bagarozzi (1992) identified a number of issues to be considered before selecting an instrument or battery of tests for use with a particular couple/family system. The first consideration is whether the instrument/procedure offers the therapist an "insider's" (family member's) perspective or whether the assessment is done from an "outsider's" (therapist's) perspective (Cromwell, Olson, & Fournier, 1976).

The second issue is scale/instrument construction. Several factors must be addressed:

- extent to which theory was used as a conceptual guide for instrument construction and development
- theoretical relevance and clinical utility of the concept/construct measured

- adequacy of sampling procedures used for items selected for inclusion and populations represented
- comprehensiveness of domains sampled when more than one concept/construct is measured
- quality and appropriateness of the methodological and statistical procedures used to establish reliability and validity

The third issue concerns the more practical aspects of testing and measurement: financial costs; time required for administration, scoring, and interpretation; applicability to various age, ethnic, and racial groups, and social classes; and clinical experience, specialized training, or expertise required for administration, scoring, and interpretation, and so forth.

This chapter describes 11 of the most commonly used self-report (insider) measures of marital quality and couple relationships (see Table 7.1). In addition, a protocol for selecting a self-report instrument useful in working with couples is provided. This protocol and several of the instruments described in this chapter are illustrated with a case example.

COMMON SELF-REPORT MEASURES FOR COUPLES

Locke–Wallace Marital Adjustment Test

Type of instrument. The Locke–Wallace Marital Adjustment Test was developed in 1959 to provide a reliable and valid measure of marital adjustment. Using selected, nonduplicated, and statistically significant items from a variety of previously developed measures with high item discrimination, Harvey Locke and Karl Wallace (1959) composed a 15-item marital adjustment scale. Marital adjustment is defined by Locke and Wallace as an accommodation of partners to each other at a given time.

Use–target audience. The purpose of this brief instrument is to assess relational adjustment. The Locke–Wallace Marital Adjustment Test is used with married or cohabitating couples clinical and in research settings.

Multicultural. This instrument is available only in an English version.

Ease and time of administration. The Locke–Wallace Marital Adjustment Test is a self-report instrument that it is easy to administer and takes approximately 5 minutes to complete. It is available only in a paper-and-pencil format,

Scoring procedure. This instrument can be hand scored in 5 minutes or less. No automated score system or computer generated report is available.

Reliability. Reliability studies were initially conducted by Locke and Wallace (1959). Internal consistency was estimated by the Spearman Brown formula and found to be a respectable .90 (Cross & Sharpley, 1981). Data on test–retest reliability are not available.

Validity. Known-groups validity of this instrument is high, with scores discriminating between adjusted and maladjusted couples. Hunt (1978) found the correlations between the Locke–Wallace Marital Adjustment Test and the Dyadic Adjustment Scale to $r = .93$ for husbands and for wives. Discrimination, item, and factor analyses have been conducted by Cross and Sharpley (1981).

Availability and source. The scale is available in the original journal article (Locke & Wallace, 1959).

Comment. The Locke–Wallace Marital Adjustment Test has been used extensively since it first appeared in 1959. Because of its history and widespread use, it is used as a benchmark standard for assessing the degree of adjustment in marriage. When it was first introduced, it was one of the first short measures of marital adjustment, and it remains that today. Because the instrument is a global measure, it may not be useful in planning treatment when behavioral specificity is indicated.

Dyadic Adjustment Scale

Type of instrument. Like the Locke–Wallace Marital Adjustment Test, the Dyadic Adjustment Scale (DAS) had its origin in family sociology. Developed by Graham Spanier, the Dyadic Adjustment Scale is a 32-item questionnaire that utilizes a Liker-type format. Because 11 of these items were taken directly from the Locke–Wallace Marital Adjustment Test, it is not surprising to find that the Dyadic Adjustment Scale correlates $r = .86$ with the Locke–Wallace Marital Adjustment Test. Four factors make up this scale: Dyadic Consensus, Dyadic Satisfaction, Dyadic Cohesion, and Affectional Expression (Spanier, 1976).

Use–target audience. This instrument is designed to assess relational quality as perceived by couples. It can be used as a general measure of marital satisfaction by using total scores, or its subscales can be utilized to measure cohesion, consensus, or expression of affect. The instrument has also been adapted for interviewing couples.

Multicultural. In addition to an English language version, French–Canadian and Chinese versions are available.

Ease and time of administration. This 34-item self-report instrument can be completed in 5 to 10 minutes. In addition, a briefer, 14-item version is available.

Scoring procedure. The instrument can be hand scored in 5 minutes or less. A Quik-Score™ form and DOS-based computing scoring are also available. Total scores are sum of all items, which range from 0 to 151.

Reliability. The Cronbach's alpha for the overall scale is reported to be .96. For the Dyadic Consensus, Dyadic Satisfaction, Dyadic Cohesion, and Affectional Expression scales, the Cronbach's alpha scores are .90, .94, .86, and .73, respectively (Spanier & Thompson, 1982).

Validity. Criterion-related validity was established by comparing the responses of married and divorced individuals for each of the 32 items. The divorced sample differed significantly from the married sample at the $p < .001$ level for each item. *T* tests were used for making these comparisons. The mean total score for married individuals was 114.8; the mean score for divorced individuals was 70.7. Concurrent validity is evidenced by high correlations ($r = .86$) with the Locke–Wallace Marital Adjustment Scale (Wackowiak & Bragg, 1980).

Availability and source. The scale is available in the original journal article (Spanier, 1976). It is also available from Multi-Health Systems, Inc., (800) 456-3003, including the Quik-Score form and DOS-based computing scoring.

Comment. The DAS is one of the oldest and most extensively used relational instruments in clinical practice today. Besides its value in clinical practice, the Dyadic Adjustment Scale continues to be used by researchers throughout the world. Because of its favorable psychometrics and ease of administration, it is commonly utilized in thesis and dissertation research.

Spousal Inventory of Desired Changes and Relationship Barriers: SIDCARB

Type of instrument. Although the Locke–Wallace Marital Adjustment Scale and the Dyadic Adjustment Scale have been used to represent marital satisfaction, neither actually asks respondents to rate their satisfaction with their spouse and/or their marriage. Essentially, adjustment has been equated with satisfaction. However, stable marriages are not necessarily satisfying marriages, and spouses dissatisfied with their mates may simply have "adjusted" to their conjugal situation and lot in life. To assess the dynamics of marital satisfaction and its relationship to marital stability, Bagarozzi (1983) developed Spousal Inventory of Desired Changes and Relationship Barriers (SIDCARB), based upon the three major principles of social exchange theory as applied to marriage: (a) satisfaction with the exchange process; (b) availability of more satisfying alternative relationships; and (c) absence of prohibitive barriers to separation and divorce.

Use–target audience. This instrument is useful in assessing marital satisfaction and stability in couples undergoing couples therapy and in couples workshops.

Multicultural. This instrument is currently available in an English version only.

Ease and time of administration. SIDCARB is a 29-item self-report questionnaire that takes approximately 5 minutes to complete. Currently, it is in a paper version only.

Scoring procedure. The questionnaire is hand scored, and it takes approximately 10 minutes to score each partner's questionnaire. No computer scoring or computer-generated report is available.

Reliability. Cronbach's alpha of reliability was computed for each subscale; the reliabilities for each were found to be .86, .74, and .80 for Factors I, II, and III, respectively.

Validity. Factor analysis revealed significant loadings on three factors: I = Dissatisfaction and Desire for Change in Spouse's Behavior; II = Willingness to

Separate and Divorce, and Internal Psychological Barriers to Relationship Termination; and III = External Circumstantial Barriers to Relationship Termination (Bagarozzi & Pollane, 1983).

Availability and source. SIDCARB and scoring guidelines are reprinted in Appendix A of Bagarozzi (2001).

Comment. When the Locke–Wallace Marital Adjustment Test, Dyadic Adjustment Scale, and Spousal Inventory of Desired Changes and Relationship Barriers are used in concert, the therapist can gain a better understanding of the interplay among several factors that will have a bearing upon therapeutic outcome, for example, Satisfaction; Adjustment; Stability; Level of Commitment; and Barriers to Separation and Divorce. Another important dimension to consider in marital assessment is the degree of emotional attachment that exists between the spouses. The presence of a positive emotional attachment (feelings of love, caring, closeness, and affection) between the partners often portends a successful therapeutic outcome. Conversely, the more distant, removed, estranged, and apathetic the spouses are, the less successful the therapy is likely to be. Therefore, this measure of positive emotional attachment can be a very helpful diagnostic tool.

Marital Disaffection Scale

Type of instrument. In 1993, Karen Kayser published the Marital Disaffection Scale (Kayser, 1993). She defined *disaffection* as the gradual loss of positive emotions—love, caring, affection, and closeness—that occurs between spouses over time as dissatisfactions accumulate. Disaffection does not necessarily lead to relationship dissolution because a number of internal and external barriers may cause a couple to remain together in what appears to be a stable marriage, even when the emotional relationship is dead. The theoretical model of the disaffection process is based upon the work of Snyder and Regts (1982) and Duck (1982).

Use–target audience. This instrument is a measure of the level of disaffection or loss of positive emotions toward one's spouse. Although it was designed primarily for use in couples therapy, it has been used in research studies in couples in clinical and nonclinical settings.

Multicultural. This instrument is currently available in an English version only.

Ease and time of administration. The Marital Disaffection Scale is a 21-item self-report inventory that takes approximately 3 to 5 minutes to complete. Currently, this inventory is available in a paper version only.

Scoring procedure. The range of scores for the Marital Disaffection Scale is 21 to 84. This instrument can be hand scored in 3 to 5 minutes. No automated scoring or computer-generated report is currently available.

Reliability. Using Cronbach's alpha, internal consistency of the instrument is reported as .93 (Kayser, 1993). Kayser (1996) also presents data on interitem reliability.

Validity. To determine construct validity, factor analysis was performed. Although three factors—Attachment, Emotional Estrangement, and Emotional Support—could be discerned, many of the items were found to cross load so that clear and distinct independent factors did not emerge. Therefore, Kayser (1993) considers the Marital Disaffection Scale to be unidimensional, suggesting that only the total, full scale score be used when measuring disaffection. Kayser's (1993) criterion-referenced study offered additional support for the scale's validity study. A comparison of recently divorced individuals with a random sample of married individuals from the general population showed means for these two groups were 70.8 and 33.7, respectively. Kayser (1996) presented additional data on criterion-related validity and discriminant validity

Availability and source. The instrument and scoring instructions are included in *When Love Dies: The Process of Marital Disaffection* (Kayser, 1993).

Comment. Interestingly, scores on the Marital Disaffection Scale showed significant positive relationships ($r = .36$) with a spouse's problem drinking behavior and ($r = .48$) with workaholic behavior of a spouse. These results support the use of the Marital Disaffection Scale as a measure of emotional estrangement in marriage (Flowers, Robinson, & Carroll, 2000). Besides possessing good psychometric properties, this scale has been demonstrated to be easy to use for assessing spouses' feelings of affection—disaffection toward their partner and for planning appropriate interventions in conjoint therapy.

Conflict Tactics Scales

Type of instrument. The Conflict Tactics Scales 2 (CTS2) was developed by Murray Straus, Ph.D., of the Family Research Laboratory at the University of New Hampshire. The original instrument, Conflict Tactics Scales (CT), consisted of 15 items to measure three tactics in resolving conflict: reasoning, verbal aggression, and violence in family relationships (Straus, 1979). CT is considered the most widely used measure of interpersonal violence in couples. Three forms of the instrument are: Conflict with Brother or Sister, Conflict with Parents, and Mother–Father Conflict. Its revision, CTS2, is a 78- item questionnaire designed to assess individual responses to conflictual couple and family situations. The original three scales have been replaced by six scales: Physical Assault, with subscales of minor and severe; Psychological Aggression, with subscales of minor and severe; Negotiation; Injury; Sexual Coercion; and Total Score. Clients are asked to report the frequency of conflictual situations that have occurred in the previous 12 months (Straus, 1995).

Use–target audience. The CT and CTS2 Conflict Tactics Scales are for assessing relational conflict, specifically verbal and physical violence in close, intimate relationships. Although the scale has been used primarily as a research instrument, it may have clinical value in the assessment of interpersonal violence in divorce and custody cases as well as a tool in couples therapy to process inappropriate aggression.

Multicultural. This instrument is currently available in an English version only.

Ease and time of administration. This 78-item instrument takes approximately 15 to 20 minutes to complete. Currently, the inventory is available only in a paper version.

Scoring procedure. The Conflict Tactics Scales (CTS2) can be hand scored in approximately 5 minutes. No automated scoring or computer-generated reports are currently available.

Reliability. The psychometric properties of CT regarding reliability were considered somewhat weak, with alpha coefficients ranging from .42 to .88, which raised concerns about the reliability of the instrument. However, alpha coefficients of the CTS2 are in the range of .79 to .86 (Straus, 1995).

Validity. Similarly, the psychometric properties of CT involving validity were somewhat weak, ranging from .19 to .80 (Straus, 1995). Recent factor analytic studies have suggested five discrete factors: Minor Psychological Aggression; Severe Psychological Aggression; Negotiation; Severe Physical Aggression; and Minor Physical Aggression.

Availability and source. The instrument is available in the *Manual for the Conflict Tactics Scales* (Straus, 1995).

Comment. The revision of this widely used research instrument appears to have considerable value in clinical settings in divorce and child custody evaluations and in couples therapy.

Areas of Change Questionnaire

Type of instrument. In the course of conducting research into marital conflict and behavioral marital therapy at the Oregon Research Institute, The Areas of Change Questionnaire was developed by Robert Weiss and colleagues (Weiss, Hops, & Patterson, 1973). The questionnaire has two parts: Part I includes the behaviors that the client would like the partner to do more, less, or not change; while Part II addresses what each thinks the partner would like more of, less of, or not change. Thus, this inventory lends itself to the calculation of a number of scores: desired change; perceived change; perceptual accuracy; and total change. Another version of this instrument, the Comprehensive Areas of Change Questionnaire, is briefly described in the "comments" section.

Use–target audience. The Areas of Change Questionnaire is a 34-item self-report inventory designed to assess the amount of change a couple desires for their relationship. Communication, Separation of Duties, and Sexual Activity are three areas.

Multicultural. This instrument is currently available in an English version only.

Ease and time of administration. The Area of Change Questionnaire consists of 34 items with a seven-point Likert Scale format. This inventory is available in a paper version as well as an MS-DOS computer version. It takes between 10 and 20 minutes to complete the inventory.

Scoring procedure. Hand scoring of this inventory is initially quite cumbersome because the responses of both partners—on two separate scoring sheets—must be compared at the same time. The amount of scoring time depends on the number of items scored and the scorer's facility with the scoring process. Fortunately, a computerized scoring system is available.

Reliability. Split half reliability has been found to be .80; Cronbach's alpha is between .84 and .89; and test–retest reliabilities for husbands and wives are reported to be .96 and .74 respectively (Mead & Vatcher, 1985).

Validity. Discriminant validity has been demonstrated between distressed and nondistressed couples (Birchler & Webb, 1977). Pre- and posttreatment sensitivity to change has also been reported (Baucom, 1982).

Availability and source. The Areas of Change Questionnaire is available from Multi-Health Systems, Inc., (800) 456-3003, which distributes the computer version and scoring system.

Comment. Although the Areas of Change Questionnaire provided a global indexing of marital complaints, Mead and Vatcher (1985) found that only 45% (13 of 29 categories developed by a national sample of therapists) was accounted for by the inventory. Therefore, Mead and Vatcher set out to develop a questionnaire that would truly canvas the 29 areas of change; this required increasing the number of items that the questionnaire now comprises, including 24 of the original items from the Areas of Change Questionnaire. Scoring procedures and categories from the original scale were retained. Psychometric properties of the new instrument equal or exceed the reliability and validity indices of the Areas of Change Questionnaire (Roberts, 1988; Vatcher, 1988).

Marital Satisfaction Inventory—Revised (MSI-R)

Type of instrument. The Marital Satisfaction Inventory (MSI) was developed and first published by Douglas Snyder, Ph.D., in 1979. The MSI (Snyder, 1981) included 280 true/false questions that assessed nine content areas of a couple's relationship as well as a Global Distress scale and two validity scales (Conventionalization and Inconsistency). In 1997, a revised version called the Marital Satisfaction Inventory—Revised (MSI-R) became available (Snyder, 1997). The revised version contains 150 true/false questions and has 13 scales:

- Global Distress
- Affective Communication
- Problem-Solving Communication
- Aggression
- Time Together
- Disagreement About Finances
- Sexual Dissatisfaction
- Role Orientation
- Family History of Distress
- Dissatisfaction With Children

- Conflict Over Child Rearing
- Inconsistency (validity scale)
- Conventionalization (validity scale)

Use–target audience. The MSI-R provides a rather comprehensive profile of a couple's problems, skills, and overall relational functioning. Commonly used as an initial screening tool in couples therapy, this inventory can also be used to monitor treatment as well as evaluate overall treatment outcomes.

Multicultural. The MSI-R is currently available in English and Spanish versions; it has been standardized on a sample following the U.S. Census with regard to ethnic categories, age, educational levels, occupations, and regional representation. Although a *T* score difference of 7 between African–Americans and Caucasians was reported on the MSI, the MSI-R manual indicates that score differences due to ethnicity or education should still be regarded as indicators of relational distress that bear further investigation by the therapist.

Ease and time of administration. While the MSI-R has 130 items fewer than the MSI, it still takes approximately 25 minutes to complete the inventory. Couples report that the true/false format makes taking the inventory more tolerable.

Scoring. The MSI-R can be hand scored, which can take 10 to 15 minutes or more, in part because the therapist must convert raw scores to *T* scores. Fortunately, computer scoring is available. Computer scoring options include mail or fax or the therapist can utilize convenient computer-scoring software. A clinician-friendly computer-generated interpretive report including both partners' scores is also available. Like standardized personality tests, the guidelines for clinical interpretation of the MSI-R are based on individual scale scores, commonly observed test patterns, and the match of individual profiles to group profiles.

Reliability. The MSI-R possesses high levels of internal consistency (Cronbach's alpha of .70 to .93) and temporal stability, that is, test–retest reliability of .74 to .88. Standard error of difference based on test–retest correlations average 6 *T*-score points (Snyder, 1997).

Validity. Three sources of validity are reported. Correlations between the MSI and the MSI-R range from .94 to .98. Over 20 studies examining the discriminant validity of the MSI and the MSI-R show that the inventory does discriminate between groups who are expected to differ on a conceptual or a theoretical basis. Convergent validity has been established based on high correlations with the Locke–Wallace Marital Adjustment Test and the Dyadic Adjustment Scale (Snyder, 1997).

Availability and source. The MSI-R is available only from Western Psychological Services, Inc., 800-648-8857.

Comment. The earlier version, MSI (Snyder, 1981), was well regarded and one of the most often used relational inventories in research and clinical practice. The MSI-R is useful as a diagnostic and a therapeutic tool, as well as a screening instrument. Detailed guidelines for interpreting each subscale are presented by Snyder (1997) along with clinical implications and case examples. A considerable amount of clinical expertise is required to interpret the MSI-R findings and to translate these findings into viable treatment goals. Chapter 6 describes the use of the MSI-R to monitor progress in couples therapy and as a clinical outcomes measure.

PREPARE, PREPARE–MC, PREPARE–CC, and MATE

Type of instrument. PREPARE is an acronym for The Premarital Personal and Relationship Evaluation Program, which was developed by David Olson, Ph.D., at the University of Minnesota in 1976 (Olson & Norem, 1976). The Premarital Personal and Relationship Evaluation Scale was developed as an assessment device to evaluate the program's effectiveness. Since it initially appeared, this scale has undergone several revisions, the latest in 2000. The original scale had 125 items. In 1981, the Premarital Personal and Relationship Evaluation-MC (marriage with children) was developed in order to address the special concerns of couples who were planning to marry but already had children. Of the 125 PREPARE items used in producing the PREPARE-MC scale, 90 were retained and 25 were revised or reworded. PREPARE-CC (cohabiting couples) was developed in 2001. This scale was also based upon the PREPARE and PREPARE-MC inventories, but includes 54 different or revised items and a new category called "cohabitation issues" (Olson, 2002).

In 1995 the Mature Age Transition Evaluation (MATE) Scale was developed to meet the needs of a growing number of couples over the age of 50 who were planning to marry but who found the PREPARE scale to be inappropriate for their needs and concerns. MATE contains three new areas that directly address the concerns of older couples: Life Transitions, Intergenerational Issues, and Health Issues.

The PREPARE, PREPARE-MC, PREPARE-CC and MATE Scales and the attending premarital programs developed by Olson and his colleagues are designed to be used by couples contemplating marriage. Each program is tailored to meet the specific needs of the particular client group. All programs can be considered educational and preventive rather than therapeutic or remedial. Each of the four instrument contains 165 items.

Use–target audience. PREPARE is designed to be used by couples contemplating marriage. It is considered an educational and preventive rather than therapeutic or remedial intervention. The goals of PREPARE are to help couples become aware of their areas of strength and potential growth; to evaluate their levels of idealism; to explore important topics that they might otherwise avoid; and to acquire communication and conflict resolution skills.

Multicultural. These four instruments are currently available in an English version only.

Ease and time of administration. All four instruments contain 165 items each. It takes approximately 20 to 30 minutes for couples to complete the inventory.

Scoring procedure. These instruments can be scored by hand or computer. A 15-page computer-generated interpretive report for the therapist is also available.

Reliability. Internal consistency is in the range of .73 to .85 with Cronbach's alpha. Test–retest reliability is also high, in the range of .74 to .93 (Olson, 2002).

Validity. In terms of concurrent validity, PREPARE correlates highly with the Locke–Wallace Marital Adjustment Test. With regard to construct validity, factor analysis found 11 separate factors among the 12 assessed dimensions. In two studies, PREPARE inventories that were completed 3 to 4 months prior to marriage were able to distinguish, with 80 to 85% accuracy, premarital couples who separated, divorced, or were rated as unhappily married from those who were happily married after 2 or 3 years. These studies suggest PREPARE has high predictive validity (Olson, 2002).

Availability and source. The three versions of PREPARE and MATE are available from Life Innovations, Inc., (800) 331-1661.

Comment. These four instruments and accompanying programs are designed to assist therapists, as well as clergy and others involved in marital preparations programs, to work with premarital couples by focusing on critical relational issues. These inventories help to increase awareness of strengths and development areas and to discuss areas of potential conflict openly; they function as a preventive tool in addressing couple issues before they become major problems. Although therapists seldom work with couples before marriage, when such couples do seek consultation, PREPARE can be of inestimable value in the premarital counseling process.

ENRICH

Type of instrument. PREPARE was designed for premarital couples; ENRICH was designed for marital couples. ENRICH is an acronym for enriching relationship issues, communication, and happiness. This instrument and program were developed by David Olson, Ph.D., David Fournier, Ph.D., and Joan Druckman, Ph.D. (1982), for married couples. It is very similar to the PREPARE questionnaire/program format in that it provides couples with a framework for discussing important relationship issues; some differences, however, should be noted. For example, the Realistic Expectations area of PREPARE was replaced with a series of questions dealing with Marital Satisfaction. In addition, two new areas—Marital Adaptability and Marital Cohesion (taken from the circumplex model of marital and family systems)—were included. In the development of the ENRICH questionnaire, the items from the PREPARE were reviewed for relevancy to married couples. Of the original 125 items from PREPARE, 15 items were revised or reworded and 17 new items were added. In 2000, ENRICH and PREPARE were revised and updated. ENRICH is the only instrument in this group of instruments/programs that can be used for marital counseling.

Use–target audience. ENRICH is used with couples in therapy or in couples enrichment workshops. It provides the therapist with a fairly comprehensive relationship assessment that yields diagnostic information and can be used by a seasoned clinician for pre–posttreatment evaluations. Like many of the self-report inventories described in this chapter, ENRICH is designed to generate a meaningful dialogue between the therapist and the couple.

Multicultural. This instrument is currently available in an English version only.

Ease and time of administration. ENRICH contains 165 items and it takes approximately 20 to 30 minutes for couples to complete the inventory.

Scoring procedure. These instruments can be scored by hand or computer. A 15-page computer-generated interpretive report for the therapist is also available.

Reliability. Research studies dealing with the development, standardization, reliability, and validity of ENRICH have been conducted for over 25 years. Internal consistency is in the range of .75 to .90 with Cronbach's alpha. Test–retest reliability is also high, in the range of .77 to .92 (Olson, 2002).

Validity. Data on content, concurrent, construct, predictive, and discriminant validity have been reported for ENRICH (Olson, 2002). In terms of concurrent validity, it correlates highly with the Dyadic Adjustment Scale and the Locke–Wallace Marital Adjustment Test. With regard to construct validity, factor analysis found 11 separate factors among the 12 assessed dimensions. ENRICH discriminates between stressed and nonstressed couples with over 90% accuracy. It is noteworthy that the five types of married couples identified by Olson and his colleagues were also found to represent couple types in the African American community (Olson, 2002).

Availability and source. ENRICH is available from Life Innovations, Inc., (800) 331-1661.

Comment. Although the ENRICH inventory was developed for use with the ENRICH program, the inventory and feedback report can be used independently of the program and by all therapists regardless of their theoretical or clinical orientation. However, systemic therapists who are familiar with FACES III will find the couple map section of the report that deals with the spouses' perceptions of relationship cohesion (closeness) and adaptability (flexibility) to be very helpful in planning structural/strategic interventions.

Intimacy Needs Survey

Type of instrument. Bagarozzi (1990, 2001) developed the Intimacy Needs Survey to help couples conceptualize their need for interpersonal closeness in a way that would make sense to them. This survey is a clinical tool that allows spouses to explore whether their needs for intimacy are being met in nine specific areas: Emotional; Psychological; Intellectual; Sexual; Physical (Nonsexual); Spiritual; Aesthetic; Social; Recreational; and Temporal. Intimacy is conceptualized as a basic human need that has its origins in and develops out of the more fundamental survival need for attachment. Intimacy differs from individual to individual, and the nine components of this more general need also vary in strength from person to person.

Use–target audience. The Intimacy Needs Survey is designed to assess couples' perceptions of their need for and type of intimacy. It allows the therapist to assess whether each spouse's intimacy needs are met satisfactorily by his or her partner. In addition to use in couples therapy, it can be used in couples enrichment workshops.

Multicultural. This instrument is currently available in an English version only.

Ease and time of administration. Administration of the Intimacy Needs Survey is simple and straightforward. This 44-item self-report questionnaire takes no more than 10 minutes to complete. It is currently available in a paper version only.

Scoring procedure. This instrument is hand scored in approximately 15 minutes. For the first eight subcomponent needs, numerical scores are calculated. The ninth dimension, Time, is viewed qualitatively and is considered separately. Three scores are computed for each of the eight component needs examined in the questionnaire: component need strength; receptivity satisfaction; and reciprocity satisfaction. A total intimacy needs strength score is calculated simply by summing all eight component needs strength scores. No computer scoring or computer-generated report is currently available.

Reliability. The Intimacy Needs Survey is still in its experimental stages of development. Reliability has yet to be established.

Validity. The survey is still in its experimental stages of development. Validity has yet to be established. Nevertheless, four interrelated factors are evaluated by the Intimacy Needs Survey: Overall Intimacy Needs Strengths of Both Partners; the Strength of Each Component Need for Both Partners; Each Partner's Satisfaction With His or Her Spouse's Openness, Receptivity, Responsiveness, Willingness, and Ability to Meet and Satisfy Each Specific Component Need; and Each Partner's Satisfaction With His or Her Mate's Willingness and Ability to Reciprocate Similar-Depth Levels of Sharing, Openness, Self-Disclosure, Self-Revelation, and Personal Exchange.

Availability and source. The Intimacy Needs Survey is reprinted in Bagarozzi (2001).

Comment. This instrument assesses several components of intimacy that are not considered in other instruments. Among these are spiritual intimacy, aesthetic intimacy, and temporal intimacy. Because it is common for couples to complain that they have "intimacy problems," it is valuable to distinguish these various components to determine which areas are problematic.

Sexual Desire Inventory

Type of instrument. The Sexual Desire Inventory was initially developed by Spector (1992) and further refined by colleagues (Spector, Carey, & Steinberg, 1996).

TABLE 7.1 Self-Rating Scales for Couples

Assessment instrument	Specific couple applications	Cultural/ language	Administration: T = time to take; S = scoring time; I = items	Computerized: a = scoring; b = report	Reliability (R)/ validity (V)	Availability
Locke–Wallace Marital Adjustment Scale	Assesses relationship adjustment, conflict resolution, cohesion, communication	English	T = 3–5 min; S = 5 min; I = 15	a = no; b = no	R = .90; V = .63	Journal article
Dyadic Adjustment Scale	Assesses relationship adjustment and couples' satisfaction	English; French; Chinese	T = 5–15 min; S = 5 min; I = 34 (14 items)	a = yes; b = no	R = .86–96; V = .86–88	Journal article; Multi-Health Systems, Inc.
Marital Satisfaction Inventory—Revised	Assesses several dimension of satisfaction in a couple relationship	English; Spanish	T = 25 min; S = varies; I = 150	a = yes; b = yes	R = .70–93; V = factor analysis	Western Psychological Services, Inc.
PREPARE	Premaritally assesses strengths and potential problems in couples	English	T = 20–30 min; S = varies; I = 140	a = yes; b = yes	R = .73–85 V = 80–85% predictive v.	Life Innovations, Inc.
ENRICH	Assesses problems, skills, and satisfaction in married couples	English	T = 20–30 min; S = varies; I = 140	a = yes; b = yes	R = .75–90 V = .90% predictive v.	Life Innovations, Inc.
Areas of change questionnaire	Assesses the amount of change desired in relationship	English	T = 5 min; S = 5 min; I = 15	a = no; b = no	R = .90; V = .63	Multi-Health Systems, Inc.
Intimacy needs survey	Assesses couples' perceptions of type and need of intimacy	English	T = 10 min; S = 15 min; I = 44	a = no; b = no	R = no data; V = no data	In *Enhancing Intimacy in Marriage: A Clinicians Guide* (2001)

Marital Disaffection Scale	Assesses level of disaffection or loss of positive emotions toward spouse	English	T = 3–5 min; S = 3–5 min; I = 21	a = no; b = no	R = .93; V = discriminant and criterion related	In *When Love Dies: The Process of Marital Disaffection.* (1993)
SIDCARB	Assesses marital satisfaction and stability in couples	English	T = 5 min; S = 10 min; I = 26	a = no; b = no	R = .74–86; V = factor analysis	Appendix A of *Enhancing Intimacy in Marriage: A Clinicians Guide* (2001).
Conflict Tactics Scale (CTS2)	Assesses physical and psychological aggression in intimate relations	English	T = 15 min; S = 5 min; I = 78	a = no; b = no	R = .79–86; V = factor analysis	Family Research Lab, University of New Hampshire
Sexual Desire Inventory	Assesses sexual desire—dyadic and solitary—in couples	English	T = 5 min; S = 5 min; I = 14	a = no; b = no	R = .76–96; V = factor analysis	Journal article

Items included in the scale were selected based upon models of sexual desire and the researchers' clinical experience in assessing sexual desire disorders. The inventory consists of two factors: Dyadic Sexual Desire (interest in having sexual relations with a partner—not necessarily one's specific partner) and Solitary Sexual Desire (interest in behaving sexually by oneself).

Use–target audience. The Sexual Desire Inventory allows the therapist to assess whether each partner's sexual needs are being met satisfactorily by his or her partner. The primary use of this instrument is in sex therapy and in couples therapy.

Multicultural. This instrument is currently available in an English version only.

Ease and time of administration. This self-report instrument consists of 14 items and is easy to administer. It takes less then 5 minutes to complete.

Scoring procedure. The instrument is hand-scored in 5 minutes or less. No automated scoring system or computer-generated report is available.

Reliability. Samples used to assess psychometric properties of the scale include college students (N = 380); geriatric adults (N = 40); and couples (N = 40). Internal consistency using Cronbach's alpha coefficient was r = .86 for the Dyadic Sexual Desire subscale and r = .96 for the Solitary Sexual Desire subscale. Test–retest reliability is reported to be r = .76 over a 1-month period.

Validity. Factor validity as well as concurrent and discriminant validity is reported by Spector (1992). For females, Dyadic Sexual Desire was shown to be positively correlated with relationship adjustment as measured by the Dyadic Adjustment Scale (Spanier, 1976); with sexual satisfaction as measured by the Index of Sexual Satisfaction (Hudson, 1992); and with sexual arousal as measured by the Sexual Arousal Inventory (Hoon, Hoon, & Wincze, 1976). For males, only Dyadic Sexual Desire was found to correlate with sexual satisfaction. Gender differences in responding to this scale have also been found; males were found to have significantly higher levels of dyadic and solitary desire than do females.

Availability and source. See the journal article for the inventory (Spector, Carey, & Steinberg, 1996).

Comment. The Sexual Desire Inventory is a self-report instrument that is quick and easy to administer and score. In addition to having credible psychometric properties, it has remarkably clinical utility. More specifically, discussing the results of the inventory provides therapists and couples an occasion for discussing the matter of dyadic as well as personal sexual desire, which can be source of considerable embarrassment to many couples.

PROTOCOL FOR SELECTING ASSESSMENT INSTRUMENTS:

The following simple, four-step process for selecting assessment instruments with couples should be useful to therapists.

1. *Assess marital quality.* This process begins with the therapist selecting some tried and true, empirically tested measure of relationship quality in order to get a fairly accurate appraisal of the couple's level of distress and dissatisfaction. The instrument selected is administered again at the conclusion of treatment so that the success of therapy can be determined through pretreatment/posttreatment comparisons of global satisfaction/ dissatisfaction scores for each spouse.

    Although such measures target some of the most salient domains of marital/couple dynamics that frequently are the source of conflict (e.g., finances, sexual relations, in-laws, children, friendships, recreation, expression of love and affection, conventionality, conflict resolution), they do not sample the broad range and scope of potential relationship conflicts and issues of concern necessary for advancement to the second step in the procedure. To do so, more comprehensive measures are necessary.

2. *Perform a comprehensive assessment.* The goal at this juncture of pretreatment assessment is to canvas as many areas of potential relationship conflict and dissatisfaction as possible. A number of instruments can be used for this purpose; guidelines for determining which would be the best one to use with a given couple are discussed in the case example.

3. *Categorize areas of conflict and disagreement.* Once all areas of conflict, issues of disagreement, problems, and so on in the marriage/relationship have been identified, they are categorized so that they can be dealt with more effectively. Categorization can be done in a variety of ways. For example, acts of aggression may constitute one category (verbal aggression, physical aggression, hostility, passive–aggressive behavior, etc.); trust may constitute another category (e.g., lying, deception, reliability, fidelity). Categorization may also be done according to couples' unmet expectations in specific areas of their relationship (e.g., finances, sexual relations, marital roles and tasks, parenting). Another way to categorize issues of concern, problems, and conflicts is to assign them to theoretically meaningful categories—for example, couple cohesion, communication patterns, relationship structure, power, rules, hierarchies, and boundaries.

    Once categories have been determined, they are hierarchically ordered and ranked according to their importance, severity, urgency, and so on, depending upon the needs of a given couple and the nature of the presenting problem. The couple, in conjunction with the therapist, then agrees upon a sequence in which these categories will be addressed in therapy.

4. *Assess specific areas of concern in a given category.* The fourth and final step in this procedure is refinement. Specific instruments are selected that

can be used for in-depth analysis and exploration of the problems, conflicts, and concerns included in a particular category. Depending upon the breadth and scope of a given category, more than one measure may be required if coverage is to be adequate, if not comprehensive.

CASE EXAMPLE

Mr. and Mrs. Turner came in for their initial appointment with a presenting problem of poor communication. Mr. Turner was 46 and Mrs. Turner was 38; they had been married for 7 years and had two daughters, ages 5 and 3. The couple was asked to complete the Locke–Wallace Marital Adjustment Test (MAT); the Dyadic Adjustment Scale (DAS); the Spousal Inventory of Desired Changes and Relationship Barriers (SIDCARB); and the Marital Disaffection Scale (MDS). Scores were:

Instrument	Mr. Turner	Mrs. Turner
MAT	87	80
DAS	92	88
MDS	39	42

Although Mr. and Mrs. Turner had scores on the MAT and DAS that fell within the maladjusted range, neither spouse showed a high level of disaffection. Scores for the SIDCARB were:

Factor	Mr. Turner	Mrs. Turner
I	62	64
II	55	57
III	53	58

Note: $X = 50$; $SD = 10$.

For the first factor (Dissatisfaction With One's Spouse and Desire For Behavior Change), Mr. and Mrs. Turner score slightly more than one standard deviation above the mean. Scores of this magnitude indicate moderate levels of dissatisfaction and desire for change. Neither spouse perceives high barriers to separation and divorce for Factor II (Internal Psychological Barriers) or Factor III (External Circumstantial Barriers). Essentially, the Turners, although dissatisfied with the current state of their marriage, are positively emotionally connected to each other. They see very few barriers to relationship termination, so it is safe to say that their marriage is a voluntary one. The prognosis for treatment with couples who have this type of relationship profile is good.

The couple was then given the Comprehensive Areas of Change Questionnaire (Mead & Vatcher, 1985). This questionnaire was utilized because it canvasses 29 conflict categories as opposed to the 13 assessed by Snyder (1997) and the 14 assessed by Olson (2002). Mr. and Mrs. Turner were asked to complete the standard 82-item version of the Comprehensive Areas of Change Questionnaire. Of the 29 possible areas of change canvassed by the questionnaire, Mr. Turner identified three: leisure time, friends, and sexual relations. Mrs. Turner listed four areas of desired change: communication, affection, loving feelings, and religion.

Conceptualizing the problems presented by Mr. and Mrs. Turner was a simple process because all the content areas could be grouped into one major theoretical category—intimacy. Results from the Intimacy Needs Survey showed that sexual intimacy and social recreational intimacy (a refinement of leisure time, friends and sexual relations) were the two areas of intimacy in which Mr. Turner's needs were not being met satisfactorily by his wife. Results for Mrs. Turner showed that she felt unfulfilled in the following areas: physical–nonsexual intimacy, emotional intimacy, and psychological intimacy (a refinement of affection and loving feelings). Religion, as an area of concern identified by Mrs. Turner on the questionnaire, did not present as problematic in terms of spiritual intimacy.

As part of the treatment process, couples are asked to rank order the problem areas they have identified in terms of an agreed-upon sequence in which they would like to address each issue in therapy. Functional communication skills are routinely taught to every couple entering treatment (Bagarozzi, 2001), so Mr. and Mrs. Turner were asked to sequence only the five areas of intimacy identified as problematic on the Intimacy Needs Survey, and religion as identified by Mrs. Turner on the Comprehensive Areas of Change Questionnaire. The Turners agreed that the order in which they would like to deal with these issues was:

- emotional intimacy
- psychological intimacy
- sexual intimacy
- physical intimacy
- social recreational intimacy
- religion

Religion, as an area of concern, was differentiated from spiritual intimacy by Mrs. Turner. Her concerns had more to do with the couple's participation in organized religion and religious practices than her husband's spirituality. Mr. and Mrs. Turner agreed that once they had successfully resolved their intimacy concerns, they would begin to concentrate upon the religious aspects of their relationship.

Individual interviews with Mr. and Mrs. Turner suggested that a sexual desire discrepancy might have existed in their relationship. Mr. Turner's desire to engage in sexual intercourse with his wife was much higher than Mrs. Turner's desire for sexual relations with her husband. For Mr. Turner, two or three times a week was preferable. For Mrs. Turner, on the other hand, twice a month was thought to be sufficient. When sexual desire discrepancies are identified in a relationship, it is important to determine whether these differences have always existed between the partners or whether one partner's desire for sexual intimacy has decreased significantly or been lost. Another important factor to consider when examining desire discrepancies is to determine whether the person whose sexual desire has diminished has lost his or her sexual interest in general or whether the loss or decrease in sexual desire is specific to his or her partner and their relationship.

The Sexual Desire Inventory (Spector, Carey, & Steinberg, 1996) was selected for Mr. and Mrs. Turner because of its ability to discriminate between global and specific sexual desires. This scoring procedure can be used to measure the extent of desire discrepancy in a relationship and its sensitivity to the more complex nature of female sexuality and sexual responsiveness. Findings from this inventory revealed that Mrs. Turner was experiencing a reduction in sexual desire that was relationship specific—she had lost her desire to engage in sexual relations with her husband, but she still engaged in solitary sexual behavior and was still sexually attracted to other men. Clearly, Mrs. Turner's loss of sexual desire for her husband was symptomatic of difficulties in their relationship.

For some women, sexual desire and sexual responsiveness to their partner's sexual overtures are affected by the emotional climate of the relationship. For such women, unresolved issues, conflicts, and resentments in other areas of the relationship can negatively affect them, causing a decrease or loss of sexual desire. However, once these conflicts have been satisfactorily resolved, sexual desire and interest return to preconflict levels. This was the case for Mrs. Turner. Resolving her feelings of alienation and disconnection from her husband because of unfulfilled intimacy needs (emotional and psychological) allowed her to regain her sexual interest and responsiveness once these issues were dealt with in therapy. The couple was then able to address the other problematic concerns, that is, social recreational intimacy and religion.

ADDENDUM: ADULT ATTACHMENT INTERVIEW

This chapter's purpose is to review and illustrate some self-report assessment instruments commonly used with couples. Obviously, other assessment modes besides self-report can be utilized with couples as noted in chapter 3and chapter 5. A semistructured interview method called the Adult

Attachment Interview (AAI) bears specific mention in this chapter although it is covered in more detail in chapter 3.

The effects of failed or problematic infant–mother attachment on personality development, identity formation, and ability to form and sustain intimate interpersonal relationships as an adult have been receiving much attention recently (Cassidy & Shaver, 1999). Assessing the type of attachment an individual is capable of forming is important to take into consideration when a therapist is attempting to treat marital struggles that revolve around issues of intimacy and interpersonal closeness and separateness. The AAI (George, Kaplan, & Main, 1996) is a clinical procedure that may be used by therapists to help individuals and couples identify their unique attachment patterns and dynamics that may be causing difficulties in forming committed, long-term intimate relationships.

The AAI allows the trained interviewer to identify four types of adult attachment patterns that have been shown to correspond to the four types of infant–mother attachment patterns identified by Ainsworth, Blehar, Waters, and Wall (1978): secure/autonomous (secure); dismissing (avoidant); preoccupied (resistant or ambivalent); and unresolved/disorganized (disorganized/disoriented). The interview is a semistructured, 1-hour protocol consisting of 18 open-ended questions. The entire interview is recorded verbatim. A scoring and classification system is then used to type individual attachment styles.

The interviewee is asked to give a general description of relationships with parents during childhood and then to give five adjectives or descriptive phrases that best describe the relationship with each parent. He is also asked to recall specific memories that can be used to illustrate and support why each descriptor was chosen; he is also asked to describe how his parents responded to unsettling events in his life such as being emotionally upset, physically hurt, or ill. Significant losses, separations, rejections, threats regarding discipline, incidents of abuse, or any other negative experiences that might have affected the interviewee's development are also investigated.

The central task of the interviewer is to determine whether the interviewee can recall and reflect upon memories related to attachment while simultaneously maintaining coherent conceptualizations and a consistent and collaborative discourse with the interviewer. Based upon this interview, the interviewee's state of mind is determined. From the interviewer's determination of this state, attachment style is inferred and categorized. Scales have been devised for each category; for example, two scales—coherence of transcript and metacognitive monitoring—make up the secure/autonomous category. Idealization of the speaker's primary attachment figures; insistence on lack of memory for childhood; and active and derogating dismissal of attachment-related experiences and/or relationships are associated with dismissing adult attachments. Anger-involved attachment to a primary attachment figure and passivity or vagueness in discourse are scales associated with preoccupied adult attachments.

Empirical work regarding the Adult Attachment Interview is substantial and cannot be reviewed adequately in this addendum. For a detailed discussion of AAI research findings, the reader should consult Hesse (1999). Research on the AAI can be broken down into four categories: psychometric properties; predictive validity studies; comparison group studies showing discriminant validity; and longitudinal studies. Rigorous training is required before one can become proficient in this highly sophisticated interviewing, scoring, and classification system. Only a handful of individuals are certified to conduct the special 2-week training institutes offered.

REFERENCES

Ainsworth, M. D. S., Blehar, M. C., Waters, E., & Wall, S. (1978). *Patterns of attachment: A psychological study of the strange situation.* Hillsdale, N.J.: Erlbaum.

Bagarozzi, D. A. (1983). Methodological developments in measuring social exchange perceptions in marital dyads (SIDCARB): A new tool for clinical intervention. In D. A. Bagarozzi, A. P. Jurich, & R. W. Jackson (Eds.), *New perspectives in marital and family therapy: Issues in theory, research and practice* (pp. 79–104). New York: Human Sciences Press.

Bagarozzi, D. A. (1989). Family diagnostic testing: A neglected area of expertise for the family psychologist. *The American Journal of Family Therapy, 17,* 261–274.

Bagarozzi, D. A. (1990). *Intimacy needs questionnaire.* Unpublished Instrument, Human Resources Consultants: Atlanta.

Bagarozzi, D. A. (2001). *Enhancing intimacy: A clinician's guide.* New York: Brunner–Routledge.

Bagarozzi, D. A., & Pollane, L. (1983). A replication and validation of the Spousal Inventory of Desired Changes and Relationship Barriers (SIDCARB): Elaborations on diagnostic and clinical utilization. *Journal of Sex and Marital Therapy, 9,* 303–315.

Baucom, D. H. (1982). A comparison of behavioral contracting and problem solving/communications training in behavioral marital therapy. *Behavior Therapy, 13,* 162–174.

Birchler, G. R., & Webb, L. J. (1977). Discriminating interaction behaviors in happy and unhappy marriages. *Journal of Consulting and Clinical Psychology, 45,* 494–495.

Cassidy, J., & Shaver, P. R. (Eds.). (1999). *Handbook of attachment: Theory, research and clinical applications.* New York: Guilford.

Cromwell, R. E., Olson, D. H., & Fournier, D. G. (1976). Diagnosis and evaluation in marital and family counseling. In D. H. Olson (Ed.), *Treating relationships.* Lake Mills, Iowa: Graphic Publishing.

Cross, D. G., & Sharpley, C. F. (1981). The Locke–Wallace Marital Adjustment Test reconsidered: Some psychometric findings as regards its reliability and factorial validity. *Educational and Psychological Measurement, 41,* 1303–1306.

Duck, S. (1982). A topography of relationship disengagement and dissolution. In S. Duck (Ed.), *Personal relationships IV: Dissolving personal relationships* (pp. 1–30). London: Academic Press.

Flowers, C., Robinson, B., & Carroll, J. (2000). Criterion-related validity of the marital disaffection scale as a measure of marital estrangement. *Psychological Reports, 86,* 1101–1104.

George, C., Kaplan, J., & Main, M. (1996). *Adult attachment interview protocol,* 3rd ed. Unpublished manuscript, University of California at Berkeley.

Haynes, S. N., Fallingstad, D. R., & Sullivan, J. C. (1979). Assessment of marital satisfaction and interaction. *Journal of Consulting and Clinical Psychology, 47,* 789–791.

Hesse, E. (1999). The adult attachment interview: Historical and current perspectives. In J. Cassidy & P. R. Shaver (Eds.), *Handbook of attachment: Theory, research and clinical applications*. New York: Guilford.

Hoon, E. F., Hoon, P. W., & Wincze (1976). The SAI: An inventory for the measurement of female sexual arousability. *Archives of Sexual Behavior, 5,* 291–300.

Hudson, W. (1992) *The WALMYR assessment scales scoring manual*. Tempe, AZ: WALMYR Publishers.

Hunt, R. A. (1978). The effects of item weighting on the Locke–Wallace Marital Adjustment Scale. *Journal of Marriage and the Family, 43,* 651–661.

Kayser, K. (1993). *When love dies: The process of marital disaffection*. New York: Guilford.

Kayser, K. (1996). The marital disaffection scale: An inventory for assessing emotional estrangement in marriage. *The American Journal of Family Therapy, 24,* 83–86.

Locke, H. J., & Wallace, K. M. (1959). Short marital adjustment and prediction test: Their reliability and validity. *Marriage and Family Living, 21,* 251–255.

L'Abate, L., & Bagarozzi, D. A. (1992). *Sourcebook of marriage and family evaluation*. New York: Brunner/Mazel.

Mead, D. E., & Vatcher, G. (1985). An empirical study of the range of marital complaints found in the Areas of Change Questionnaire. *Journal of Marital and Family Therapy, 11,* 421–422.

Olson, D. H. (2002). *PREPARE/ENRICH counselor's manual*. Minneapolis: Life Innovations, Inc.

Olson, D. H., & Norem, R. (1976). *Evaluation of five pre-marital programs*. Unpublished manuscript, Department of Family Social Science, University of Minnesota.

Olson, D. H., Fournier, D. G., & Druckman, J. M. (1982). *Counselor's manual for PREPARE/ENRICH* (Doctoral dissertation). *Dissertation Abstracts International, 40,* 2385–2386B.

Roberts, S. (1988). *Test–retest reliability of the Comprehensive Areas of Change Questionnaire*. Unpublished master's thesis, Family Sciences Department, Brigham Young University, Provo, UT.

Spanier, G. (1976) Measuring dyadic adjustment: New scales for assessing the quality of marriage and similar dyads. *Journal of Marriage and the Family, 38,* 15–30.

Spanier, G. B., & Thompson, L. (1982). A confirmatory analysis of the Dyadic Adjustment Scale. *Journal of Marriage and the Family, 44,* 731–738.

Snyder, D. K. (1979). *Marital Satisfaction Inventory*. Los Angeles: Western Psychological Services.

Snyder, D. K. (1981). *Manual for the Marital Satisfaction Inventory*. Los Angeles: Western Psychological Services.

Snyder, D. K. (1997). *Marital Satisfaction Inventory–revised*. Los Angeles: Western Psychological Services.

Snyder, D. K., & Regts, J. M. (1982). Factor scales for assessing marital disharmony and disaffection. *Journal of Consulting and Clinical Psychology, 50,* 736–743.

Spector, I. P. (1992). *Development and psychometric evaluation of a measure of sexual desire*. Unpublished doctoral dissertation, Syracuse University, New York.

Spector, I., Carey, M., & Steinberg, L. (1996). The Sexual Desire Inventory: Development, factor structure, and evidence of reliability. *Journal of Sex and Marital Therapy, 22,* 175–190

Straus, M. (1979). Measuring intrafamily conflict and violence: The conflict tactics (CT) scales. *Journal of Marriage and the Family, 41,* 75–88.

Straus, M. (1995). *Manual for the Conflict Tactics Scales*. Durham, NH: Family Research Laboratory, University of New Hampshire.

Touliatos, J., Perlmutter, B. F., & Straus, M. A. (Eds.). (2001). *Handbook of family measurement techniques: Vol. III*. Thousand Oaks, CA: Sage.

Vatcher, G. (1988). *An empirical study of the Comprehensive Areas of Change Questionnaire*. Unpublished doctoral dissertation, Family Sciences Department, Brigham Young University, Provo, UT.

Weiss, R. L., Hops, H., & Patterson, G. R. (1973). A framework for conceptualizing marital conflict, a technology for altering it, some data for evaluating it. In F. W. Clark & L. A. Hamerlynck (Eds.), *Critical issues in research and practice: Proceedings of the 4th Banff International Conference on Behavior Modification.* Champaign, IL: Research Press.

CHAPTER 8

Child and Family Assessment
Strategies and Inventories

LYNELLE C. YINGLING

Just as efficient manufacturing requires managers to analyze system process assessment data (Deming, 1993), effective family therapy requires the therapist to analyze family system functioning assessment data (Satir, 1972). Team assessment and team decision making work well in industry; collaborative family assessment and collaborative goal setting work well in family therapy. The foundation for both environments is a systemic perspective.

Perhaps systemic assessment can be explained effectively using a metaphor. When a horse trainer assesses the ability of a horse to run a fast race, he does not use a linear assessment technique of simply looking at the horse's feet. He uses a systemic or holistic assessment approach of looking at the horse's feet, muscle tone, joints, bone density, confirmation, lung capacity, heart rate, and so forth, along with the horse's will to run. Most important, he systemically examines how all of these attributes work together or work against each other to produce the overall assessment. Even then, a Seabiscuit can be overlooked if the assessor is not tuned in to the heart.

Family systems assessment requires a shift in paradigm to a unique multidimensional dynamic perspective. Functioning congruently in this new paradigm requires letting go of old linear assumptions and trusting one's ability to remain upright while "skating on the ice without holding on to the rail." Thus, the first challenge of family assessment is to "let go of the rail" and experience a new dimension of balance.

ISSUES AND CHALLENGES OF ASSESSING FAMILY FUNCTIONING

Once the mindset has changed to seeing the overall system as the client, the family therapist faces several challenges for effective family functioning assessment. Assessment data come from self-report of family members or observational report of an outside professional (therapist or researcher). Self-report data have several limitations:

- Each family member reports his unique individualized perspective, which will differ from other members' perspectives. How to blend the perspectives effectively into a valid whole becomes the challenge to the therapist/researcher.
- Putting honest beliefs about family relationships on paper is threatening to some family members' sense of safety in the family. In a family system trying to hide a serious problem, courage to report the truth is very difficult. Consequently, distortion of the family functioning can occur in self-reports, especially the family systems that most need accurate assessment.
- The victim of an abusive family system may be too young to express verbally and believably what is happening. Metaphorical expression through stories and drawings is open to misinterpretation and yet is often the only information available for courts to use in protecting children.

Observational data from the therapist or research observer is also subject to contamination in the following ways:

- Training is always limited by the personal biases of the instructors. If the instructor has not made the paradigm shift, the systemic thinking process will not be clear to the trainee. The therapist will then be vulnerable to focusing on linear solutions and overlooking the contribution of the system to perpetuating the problem.
- Working with families challenges the therapist's ability to keep clear boundaries by separating the client family's issues from the therapist's own family-of-origin issues. Family functioning biases from the therapist's childhood are difficult to keep filtered out of the client family assessment process.
- New ideas in the professional field often cloud the thinking of the family therapist. The current trend in the psychiatric community to diagnose everyone (even children) as bipolar tends to shape the assessment process as chemically driven. Because psychiatrists have more prestige than family therapists, the latter are likely to succumb to the pressure of the psychiatrist

to define the problem as chemically driven rather than as perpetuated by family functioning.

Even if the family therapist can accept the limitations of self-report and observational data, the *who*, *what*, and *how* of collecting data are still a challenge. One dilemma consists of deciding which subsystem data represent the "true" family system functioning and whether the information is valid if all subsystem data are not available. Another dilemma in measuring family functioning is determining which variables of family functioning to measure because various theoretical models use different variables. The Global Assessment of Relational Functioning (GARF) in the DSM-IV Appendix (American Psychiatric Association, 1994, pp 758–759) was developed as a collaborative effort of the primary family assessment researchers of the time (Group for the Advancement of Psychiatry, 1996). The three global variables agreed upon were (a) Problem Solving, (b) Organization, and (c) Emotional Climate.

Also, many pragmatic challenges to collecting data exist: Should family members complete forms at the office before an appointment (privacy is necessary for honest answers and sufficient time for all members to complete) or should it be mailed out to clients in advance; should data be collected before the first session and following the last (difficult to achieve consistently); and so forth.

After collecting self-report data, interpreting it also has challenges:

- Who is included in the family member's definition of family and how clear is that on the self-report questionnaire?
- How does the therapist/researcher interpret differing scores of family members? How can one come up with a single global score without averaging everyone's scores? Does averaging the scores from various family members' perspectives distort the results?
- At what age can the therapist expect children to read and cognitively understand the questions so that the responses are reliable?
- How does the therapist overcome language barriers to ensure reliable results?

With all the limitations of family assessment data, these data are still important to the family therapist in making intervention decisions. The following sections of this chapter will describe several family systems instruments/models available now for collecting data and describe a research-based clinical protocol for using these instruments (also see Table 8.1). A case example will illustrate the protocol.

FAMILY SELF-REPORT FOR MEMBERS AGE 10 AND OVER

Systemic Assessment of the Family Environment (SAFE)

Instrument name. The Systemic Assessment of the Family Environment is
referred to as the SAFE. It was developed by Yingling while teaching,
directing a clinic, and supervising dissertation research in a doctoral
program. The need for a brief inventory to assess three generational
subsystems of the family system using a single instrument for clinical and
research purposes prompted the development of the SAFE. The instrument
was utilized in two clinic settings and research projects before its publication in 1998 in the *GARF Assessment Sourcebook* (Yingling, Miller,
McDonald, & Galewaler, 1998).

Type of instrument. The SAFE is a self-report paper-and-pencil instrument for
all family members ages 10 and up.

Variables measured. Organizational structure and interactional processes are
measured. These variables were identified as global constructs in family
systems theory, which was generally included in other family assessment
instruments. At the same time that the SAFE was defined, the GARF
(American Psychiatric Association, 1994) was defined by Lyman Wynne's
DSM taskforce as an observational tool using very similar constructs. The
two models were then used simultaneously in a doctoral clinic and later in
a free-standing family therapy institute by Yingling.

Use–target audience. Scoring flexibility permits the SAFE to be used for families with or without children by separating the completion and scoring of
relationship dynamics by family subsystems: A = parent/spouse/partner to
parent/spouse/partner; B = parent to child; and C = parent/spouse/partner
to grandparent/former parent. Directions are clear for couples who have
not been married and for stepfamilies. The wording of items is adapted for
each of three respondent formats: child, parent, and grandparent. Dr. Dudley
Chewning has also developed a version of the SAFE for use with organizational team functioning assessment (see www.SystemsMediation.com).

Multicultural. All three formats (child, parent, and grandparent) have been
translated into Spanish by linguist Todd Smith. The constructs are global
enough to be useful in various cultural settings.

Ease and time of administration. The 21-item semantic differential one-page
paper-and-pencil instrument requires approximately 5 minutes for most
clients to complete, making it very user friendly as a clinic intake tool.
Directions are self explanatory, even for most children.

Scoring procedure. Weighted scores for each blank on the semantic differential
line are provided on a separate sheet and can be copied onto a transparency
overlay for quick scoring. A paper-and-pencil scoring grid on a separate
page creates a plotted outcome for each of the three generational relationships (parent–parent, parent–child, and parent–grandparent), as well as the
overall averaged family system. Outcomes fall within one of four quadrants
based on the intersection of interactional and organizational scores:

competent, discordant, disoriented, or chaotic. Recommended interventions based on family therapy theory are implied by the quadrant results according to subsystem. Competent families may need only an opportunity to tell their story to manage an unusually heavy outside stressor; discordant families need communication skills training and disoriented families need structural interventions. Chaotic families may need strategic interventions to realign structure before learning to communicate so that they can sustain an effective structure and create a safe environment in which family members can grow.

Reliability. Clinical use of the SAFE indicates highly reliable results with moderate- to low-functioning families who have enough safety to be honest in reporting. Children in low-functioning families do not always have the necessary level of safety.

Validity. One dissertation study (Scoville, 1999) tested the construct validity using Pearson correlations of the SAFE subscales with other accepted subsystem instruments. The SAFE Parent–Child Nuclear Family subscale score had a negative correlation of $r = -.74$ when correlated with the Beavers SFI score (the SFI scoring has higher numbers for lower functioning). Correlation of the SAFE Marital subscale with the ENRICH Marital Satisfaction scores yielded a coefficient of .82. No correlation was evident between the SAFE Family-of-Origin scores and the PAFS. Research on the SAFE is limited, although a major grant project using the SAFE to measure functioning of high conflict divorce families is in process.

Availability and source. The instrument and instructions are published in the *GARF Assessment Sourcebook* (Yingling et al., 1998). A more recent development of the stepfamily version is available at www.SystemsMediation.com.

Comment. Through 10 years of use in private practice as well as in clinic settings, Yingling and several trainees have found the SAFE a very valuable and efficient assessment tool to use with all clients. Some family mediators have found it especially helpful as a screening tool for planning mediation strategy. Initial concern about the need to reverse random items to increase reliability has not been confirmed by clinical observation. Despite the positive items loaded on the left side of the semantic differential scale, persons completing the questionnaire tend to spread out answers appropriately. Marking all responses on the same extreme rating is an immediate indication of untrue responses; the reason for this is then explored in therapy. The completed instrument is extremely efficient because it creates an immediate profile of three levels of the family system when handed to the therapist. The therapist does not need to score the instrument to see implications for therapeutic intervention. Immediate indications of power struggles in the marriage and contamination from extended family are especially helpful in determining effective therapeutic interventions.

GARF Self-Assessment for Families

Instrument name. The GARF Self-Assessment for Families was developed by Yingling based on the descriptors included in the Global Assessment of

Relational Functioning clinical rating observational scale in the DSM-IV Appendix (American Psychiatric Association, 1994; Group for the Advancement of Psychiatry Committee on the Family, 1996; Kaslow, 1996; Yingling et al., 1998). The GARF clinical rating scale was developed by a DSM-IV taskforce under the leadership of Dr. Lyman Wynne. A collaborative effort of family assessment researchers in the field produced the GARF, with possible results of calming the "range war" engaged in by the second generation of family therapists.

Type of instrument. This one-page, paper-and-pencil instrument lists all the descriptors included in the observational model of the GARF in the DSM-IV with a requested rating of 1 to 10 for each descriptor. The descriptors are grouped under the three variables with an "other" blank to allow family members to contribute their own thoughts to the family functioning concept. Self-scoring instructions are included on the single page.

Variables measured. The three variables measured by the GARF Self-Assessment are (a) problem solving/interactional skills for making this family work well; (b) the way in which this family is organized and structured; and (c) how members of this family feel about being a part of the family.

Use–target audience. All family members with basic reading and simple math skills (generally age 10 and above) can complete and score the instrument. It can be completed by any family subsystem members available, although more perspectives provide a more accurate picture of the family system. A primary use has been to train therapists in understanding and using the GARF clinical rating model. Dr. Dudley Chewning has developed a version of the GARF for assessing organizational team functioning (see www.SystemsMediation.com).

Multicultural. The instrument is available only in English at this time.

Ease and time of administration. Completing and scoring the instrument generally requires approximately 5 minutes. Therapist plotting of family scores on the profile chart generally requires less than 5 minutes.

Scoring procedure. Simple scoring procedures are included on the one-page instrument. Points under the three variables are totaled and averaged by the family member or the therapist/researcher. A GARF Profile Chart is included on a second page that plots the averaged scores of each variable for each family member in a comparison chart. This chart is quickly completed by the therapist and shared with family members to evoke discussion of how various members perceive the strengths and weaknesses of family functioning.

Reliability. No published or reported reliability testing is available for the self-report instrument. For data on the GARF clinical rating model, see chapter 5 of this book; Dausch, Miklowitz, and Richards (1996); and Yingling et al. (1998).

Validity. No published or reported validity testing is available for the self-report instrument. Personal use indicates moderate to high clinical utility and validity. For data on the GARF clinical rating model, see chapter 5 of this book; Dausch et al. (1996); and Yingling et al. (1998).

Availability and source. This is available at www.SystemsMediation.com.

Comment. This instrument works well for periodic assessment of family functioning by all family members to help set and measure change goals. Parenting coordinators/court-ordered family therapists find this instrument useful for assessing change in functioning. An unexpected use of the instrument has been to train therapists to become familiar with the GARF clinical rating model.

Family Adaptability and Cohesion Evaluation Scales (FACES-III)

Instrument name. The instrument was originally developed in 1978 through the dissertation work of Portner and Bell under the supervision of David Olson at the University of Minnesota. Several revisions have occurred as the instrument has been widely used in family functioning research. FACES II is recommended by the authors as most useful for research purposes and FACES III for clinical use until FACES IV has been fully tested and released in final format.

Type of instrument. The FACES III is a standardized 20-item, single-page self-report instrument with current linear scoring based on the revised 3-D circumplex model of marital and family systems. Family members are asked to rate each item with a five-point Likert scale with 1 (*almost never*), 2 (once in a while), 3 (sometimes), 4 (frequently), and 5 (*almost always*).

Variables measured. Family Cohesion and Adaptability are the two measured variables. Cohesion is scaled in four linear categories: disengaged, separated, connected, and very connected. Adaptability is similarly scaled: *rigid*, structured, flexible, and *very flexible*.

Use–target audience. This one-page instrument can be completed by all members of the family aged approximately 12 (seventh-grade reading level) and up.

Multicultural. The instrument is available only in English. Questions have been raised about the cultural bias interpretations of the cohesion scale, although research supports use with Mexican–American families (Olson, Russell, & Sprenkle, 1989).

Ease and time of administration. Family member completion requires approximately 5 minutes; linear scoring requires less than 5 minutes.

Scoring procedure. Research has led to changing the scoring from curvilinear (using negative numbers for the extremes) to linear scoring because higher scores mean better family functioning on the Cohesion and Adaptability scales (Olson, 1991). Cohesion and Adaptability raw scores from the instrument are converted to eight scaled points on a separate scoring sheet. The two scaled scores are averaged to equate to one of four family types: extreme, mid-range, moderately balanced, or balanced.

Reliability. Internal consistency is reported as $r = .84$ for the Cohesion scale and .79 for the Adaptability scale. Test–retest coefficients are reported as .83 for Cohesion and .80 for Adaptability (Kaslow, 1996).

Validity. Face validity and discriminate validity have been reported as very good in early reports (Olson, 1986). Later research challenges to construct validity (Green, Harris, Forte, & Robinson, 1991) led to a change in scoring of the FACES III from curvilinear to linear and the development and testing of FACES IV (Franklin, Streeter, & Springer, 2001).

Availability and source. Available from University of Minnesota, Family Social Science, 290 McNeal Hall, 1985 Buford Ave., St. Paul, MN, 55108, (612) 625-5289; or dolson@lifeinnovations.com, (651) 635-0511.

Comment. Research challenging the long-standing FACES III validity in the early 1990s and a decade of testing FACES IV highlight the difficulty in creating a self-report instrument that accurately captures the dynamics of a family system. One possible outcome is for family therapists to focus on the basics of family functioning, reassessing original assumptions (Green et al., 1991). This challenge to thinking that the journey is complete will hopefully keep therapists looking for constant improvement to the family functioning assessment process.

Beavers Self-Report Family Inventory (SFI)

Instrument name. The Self-Report Family Inventory (SFI) was developed by Robert Beavers and Robert Hampson following extensive research with the Beavers systems model clinical rating scale upon which it is based (Beavers & Hampson, 1990). Intent was to allow clinical constructs to drive the self-report instrument development.

Type of instrument. The 36-item self-report questionnaire uses a Likert scale response from 1 (*yes: fits our family very well*) to 5 (*no: does not fit our family*). Items 35 and 36 are global ratings of Competence and Style.

Variables measured. The two major constructs of the clinical model are Health/Competence and Style. Attempts at measuring style reliably in self-report format have not been very successful; the Cohesion scale is used as an estimate of style. Primary factors measured in the SFI are Health/Competence as a global score and Conflict, Leadership, and Emotional Expressiveness as subscores.

Use–target audience. All family members age 11 and older complete the questionnaire.

Multicultural. Research using the clinical rating scale with Caucasian, African–American, and Mexican–American families indicates some style differences but no significant differences based on ethnicity (Hampson, Beavers, & Hulgus, 1990). The SFI is available only in English.

Ease and time of administration. Instructions are straightforward and require approximately 10 to 15 minutes to complete. An inexperienced rater will likely require 10 to 15 minutes for scoring each instrument.

Scoring procedure. Scoring is rather complex, with reversed numbers using mathematical formulas to obtain individualized item scores. A scoring grid is provided, along with a chart for equating the self-report score to the observational score. The score for Competence can then be plotted with the Style score on the "pair of pants" graph, which divides competence into a 10-point continuum with five categories: *severely dysfunctional*, borderline, midrange, adequate, and *optimal*.

Reliability. Reported Cronbach's alphas are between .84 and .93, with test–retest reliabilities of .85 or better.

Validity. Validity is supported by canonical correlations of .62 or better on the SFI and clinical rating of Competence (Hampson et al., 1999), as well as high correlations of .77 to .92 with factors in the FAD and FACES III instruments.

Availability and source. The SFI is published in the book *Successful Families: Assessment and Intervention* (Beavers & Hampson, 1990) and is printed in Walsh (2003). The SFI manual and scales are available for $15.00 from the Family Studies Center, 6517 Hillcrest, Suite 401, Dallas, TX, 75205 or from www.familystudiescenter.org.

Comment. The clinically based foundation for the SFI has the advantage of leading directly to clinical interventions for the highly trained and experienced family therapist. However, the scoring and theoretical interpretations are challenging for inexperienced clinicians and require specialized training.

McMaster Family Assessment Device (FAD)

Instrument name. The FAD developed from ongoing work on the clinical McMaster model of family functioning (Epstein, Bishop, & Levin, 1978), and was first published in its current form in 1983 (Epstein, Baldwin, & Bishop, 1983). Development of the model continued at McGill University for a decade before moving to McMaster University in the late 1970s; in the 1980s, it moved to the Brown University Family Research Program. Beginning with an all-inclusive approach to item development with elimination of what did not support psychometric properties, the lack of theoretical foundation and supporting research have been criticized (L'Abate & Bagarozzi, 1993). A 1990 updated research report (Kabacoff, Miller, Bishop, Epstein, & Keitner, 1990) addressed some of the criticisms with a comprehensive report of data. For more recent challenges to the validity of the instrument in measuring proposed constructs with the current scoring, see Ridenour, Daley, & Reich (1999); Miller, Ryan, Keitner, Bishop, & Epstein (2000); and Ridenour, Daley, & Reich (2000).

Type of instrument. The 60-item paper-and-pencil questionnaire is to be completed by all family members age 12 and above. Responses are on a four-point Likert scale from *strongly agree*, agree, and disagree to *strongly disagree*.

Variables measured. The FAD includes a general functioning scale for Overall Health Pathology and six dimensional scales: Problem Solving, Communication, Roles, Affective Responsiveness, Affective Involvement, and Behavior Control. The scales are detailed in Walsh (2003). Ridenour and colleagues' (2000) construct validity challenge proposes that the FAD actually measures two constructs: Collaboration and Commitment. These two constructs appear to be similar to the SAFE and GARF constructs of Interactional Processes and Organizational Structure.

Use–target audience. The FAD was designed as a clinical screening tool for family functioning. The intent was "to identify problem areas in the most simple and efficient fashion possible" (Epstein et al., 1983, p. 171).

Multicultural. The FAD has been used in many countries and has versions in at least 16 different languages, including Afrikaans, Chinese, Croatian, Danish, Dutch, French, Greek, Hebrew, Hungarian, Italian, Japanese, Portuguese, Russian, Swedish, and Spanish.

Ease and time of administration. The questionnaire takes approximately 15 to 20 minutes to complete. Scoring for each questionnaire requires approximately 15 minutes.

Scoring procedure. A separate two-page scoring sheet that converts negative items and groups responses into the seven scales is provided. Scales are first summed and then divided by the number of completed answers in that scale to obtain an averaged score for each scale. Computerized scoring is available.

Reliability. Six of the seven scales have reported internal reliability correlations above .70. The Roles scale has a reported alpha of .69 in psychiatric and medical samples but a lower .57 correlation in nonclinical samples. Consequently, use of the Roles scale in nonclinical samples is questionable (Kabacoff et al., 1990).

Validity. Factor analyses results seem comparable to other similar instruments in accounting for variance. The General Functioning scale was reported as highly correlated with other items, supporting it as a single index of family functioning (Kabacoff et al., 1990).

Availability and source. A detailed description of the model is published in Walsh (2003). Information on continuing work is available from Dr. Christine Ryan, Potter 3, Rhode Island Hospital, 593 Eddy Street, Providence, RI, 02903. A manual is currently in publication process with Brunner–Routledge (Ryan, Epstein, Keitner, Bishop, & Miller, in press).

Comment. The McMaster model authors (Walsh, 2003) contend that two basic findings from the original 1969 study are still valid: (a) family functioning variables (organizational, structural, and transactional patterns) are more powerful than intrapsychic variables in determining family member behavior; and (b) emotional health of a child is closely related to the emotional relationship between parents. Keeping these two principles in mind will be helpful as family therapy professionals continue to evolve the self-report family assessment process into clinically useful resources, as well as reliable research instruments.

FAMILY SELF-REPORT FOR MEMBERS UNDER AGE 10

Self-report family assessment instruments provide family members a way to communicate how the family system is working for them when they may not be able to conceptualize and verbally communicate that information directly and quickly to the family therapist. Developing reliable and valid instruments is quite a challenge, as indicated from the development of the preceding instruments. However, those described instruments are designed for children approximately age 10 and above. How does a therapist hear the voice of the child younger than age 10? The younger the child is, the more the child functions on an intuitive metaphorical level. Consequently, instruments for children must be based on their communication styles.

SAFE Cartoons

Instrument name. The SAFE Cartoons instrument was adapted from the Systemic Assessment of the Family Environment (SAFE) described earlier.

Type of instrument. This single-page set of four cartoons is flexibly used with verbal instructions to children.

Variables measured. The assessment tool uses four cartoon drawings of family interactions involving parents and children but omitting grandparents: (a) father, mother, brother, and sister all holding hands and smiling with the children connected between the parents; (b) father and mother fighting with brother and sister watching helplessly; (c) mother, father, sister, and brother smiling (sister and brother are much larger in size than mother and father); and (d) mother and father watching helplessly as brother and sister fight while standing in front of the parents. These four pictures equate to the competent, discordant, disoriented, and chaotic quadrants in the scoring grid of the SAFE instrument.

Use–target audience. The SAFE Cartoons were developed for use with children age 10 and under to elicit communication about stressors in family functioning that are affecting the child.

Multicultural. The cartoons used are generic as to skin color, although specific racial characteristics have not been developed to relate to various cultures. Conversation with the child can be adjusted to account for cultural factors.

Ease and time of administration. This can be less than 5 minutes or expanded to the extent to which the child will continue to describe family functioning.

Scoring procedure. Children are handed a copy of the cartoon page and asked to tell the therapist which picture reminds them most of their family and why. If only one cartoon is selected, the therapist may ask if the family ever looks like any other of the cartoons and, if so, when. Comments from the child are recorded on the sheet by the therapist for the case file.

Reliability. This is not available.

Validity. This is not available.

Availability and source. The cartoon drawings are available in the *GARF Assessment Sourcebook* (Yingling et al., 1998) and www.SystemsMediation.com.

Comment. This tool has proven valuable in eliciting information about family functioning. Children will often comment that children are/are not bigger than the parents in this family (disoriented family). They will also talk about the parents fighting and how helpless they feel (discordant family). Insisting that the family is always the competent cartoon is a clue that something may be hidden in this family, resulting in the children feeling unsafe to be truthful.

GARF Self-Report for Families

Instrument Name. The GARF Self-Report for Families was developed by Dr. Alice McDonald.

Type of instrument. Selection of the most representative fairy tale provides a "quantitative" global rating similar to the GARF. However, the instrument is used primarily to elicit discussion about stressors and strengths in the family from the child's perspective.

Variables measured. Five brief descriptions of somewhat modified but familiar fairy tales are printed: (a) The Three Bears; (b) Little Red Riding Hood; (c) Cinderella; (d) Hansel and Gretel; and (e) The Ugly Duckling. Descriptions are written to parallel the descriptors of the five levels of the GARF.

Use–target audience. Children ages 8 to 12 make up the targeted group, depending on reading level.

Multicultural. The fairy tales used are rather universal, although the language available at this time is limited to English.

Ease and time of administration. Depending on the reading level, the child will likely take 10 to15 minutes to read through the fairy tales. Discussion time with the therapist varies.

Scoring procedure. Directions are for children to read through each story and decide which fairy tale is most like the family they live in right now; the selected story equates to one of the five quintiles in the GARF. If children are too young to read, the story can be read to them. To gain more specific information from older children who read well, the therapist can ask children to underline any descriptors in any of the five stories that remind them of their family.

Reliability. This is not available.

Validity. This is not available.

Availability and source. The instrument is available in the *GARF Assessment Sourcebook* (Yingling et al., 1998) and at www.SystemsMediation.com.

Comment. The underlined characteristics provide a great opportunity to discuss with the therapist their family problems on a metaphorical fairy tale level which feels safer for the child.

Kinetic Family Drawing Test

Instrument name. The Kinetic Family Drawing Test (KFD).

Type of instrument. This is a projective drawing measure of family functioning.

Use–target audience. This instrument is used primarily with children and adolescents, although all family members can participate.

Multicultural. The KFD has no cultural limits.

Ease and time of administration. Completion of the drawing generally requires less than 20 minutes.

Scoring procedure. The projective technique has very subjective interpretations and is perhaps more useful as a clinical tool to talk about feelings in the picture.

Reliability. Interscorer agreement is reported as .87 to .95.

Validity. Low and variable reports exist.

Availability and source. This instrument is distributed by Western Psychological Services, Inc.

Comment. The KFD (see chapter 4 for a full description) has been used to provide the greatest control of the child in communicating family functioning, although interpretation is subjectively controlled by the therapist/researcher.

SUBJECTIVE METHODS OF FAMILY ASSESSMENT

The preceding family assessment methods for adolescents and adults attempt to provide objective data that can be scientifically defended for research and court testimony purposes. For clinical purposes, subjective methods of family assessment should not be overlooked. Clinical observation is invaluable in understanding family functioning. Family organization indicators include: who schedules the appointment and for what reason; how family members enter the room and where they sit; and nonverbal eye signals encouraging or discouraging speaking. The trained family therapist can understand family interactional process indicators by observing how clearly each member can express his or her needs and how well other family members listen to those needs, along with their ability to problem solve effectively when given a task to discuss. Spontaneous connectedness through communication flow or physical contact can reveal the emotional climate of safety and support described by Satir (1972) as on a continuum of a nurturing or troubled family.

Family Genogram

Instrument name. Bowen's model of transgenerational family therapy gave rise to the use of the genogram. McGoldrick developed functional guidelines for using the genogram and Gerson developed the computerized software for drawing and labeling (McGoldrick & Gerson, 1985). DeMaria, Weeks, and Hof (1999) have expanded specific techniques.

Type of instrument. This is a graphic resource for collecting and interpreting three-generational family functioning information.

Variables measured. Basic family structure information is recorded for at least three generations: birth dates, marriages, divorces, children born/adopted, deaths, close/distant/conflictual/cut-off relationships, addictive and abusive patterns, and educational/career expectations. Asking individual family members with whom among those listed on the genogram they talk identifies resources to help solve problems, as well as communication barriers within the nuclear family.

Use–target audience. The genogram can be flexibly used to assess historically any issue identified as a focus for therapy.

Multicultural. Cultural themes are especially well suited to explore with the genogram.

TABLE 8.1 Matrix: Child and Family Assessment Strategies and Inventories

Assessment instrument	Specific couple and family applications	Cultural/ language	Instructions/use: T = time to take; S = time to score; I = items	Computerized: a = scoring; b = report	Reliability (R)/ validity (V)	Availability
Systemic Assessment of the Family Environment (SAFE)	All family members ages 10 and up; provides four typologies of systemic functioning: Competent, Discordant, Disoriented, Chaotic	English; Spanish	T = 5 min; S = 5 min or less; I = 21	NA	R = NA; V = .74 and .82	Yingling et al. (1998), GARF Assessment Sourcebook; www.SystemsMediation.com
GARF Self-Assessment for Families	All family members ages 10 and up; provides scores in three variables: Organizational Structure, Interactional Processes, and Emotional Climate	English	T = 5 min; S = 5 min; I = 16	NA	R = NA; V = NA	www.SystemsMediation.com
Family Adaptability and Cohesion Evaluation Scales (FACES-III)	All family members ages 12 and up; provides scores in two variables: Cohesion and Adaptability	English	T = 5 min; S = 5 min or less; I = 20	NA	R = .84 and .79 internal consistency; .83 and .93 test–retest; V = questioned	University of Minnesota, Family Social Science, 290 McNeal Hall, 1985 Buford Ave., St. Paul, MN, 55108, (612) 625–7250 or www.lifeinnovations.com
Beavers Self-Report Family Inventory (SFI)	All family members ages 11 and up; provides scores in two variables: Health/Competence and Style	English	T = 10–15 min; S = 10–15 min; I = 36	NA	R = .84 and .93 internal consistency; .85 test–retest; V = .62	Family Studies Center, 6517 Hillcrest, STE 401, Dallas, TX, 75205 or www.familystudiescenter.org

Instrument	Description	Language	Administration	Scoring	Reliability/Validity	Source
McMaster Family Assessment Device (FAD)	All family members ages 12 and up; provides scores in seven variables: General Functioning, Problem Solving, Communication, Roles, Affective Responsiveness, Affective Involvement, and Behavior Control	English; 15 other languages; others in process	T = 15–20 min; S = 15 min; I = 60	a = scoring available; b = printout of scores with subscales	R = .57–.70 internal consistency; V = NA	Dr. Christine Ryan, Potter 3, Rhode Island Hospital, 593 Eddy St., Providence, RI, 02903; manual currently in publication process with Brunner–Routledge
GARF Self-Report for Families	Children ages 8–12; if adequate reading level, provides a global rating in one of five functioning quintiles	English	T = 10–15 min; S = NA; I = 5	NA	NA	Yingling et al. (1998), GARF Assessment Sourcebook; www.SystemsMediation. com
SAFE Cartoons	Children ages 10 and under; provides a global rating in one of four typologies	Administer in any language	T = 5 min or less; S = NA; I = 4	NA	NA	Yingling et al. (1998), GARF Assessment Sourcebook; www.SystemsMediation. com
Family Genogram	All members; structural and interactional data	Administer in any language	T = 10–30 min; S = NA; I = NA	NA	NA	McGoldrick & Gerson (1985), Genograms in Family Assessment; DeMaria, Weeks, & Hof (1999), Focused Genograms
Kinetic Family Drawing (KFD)	Self-report/children; also adolescents and parents; to assess family relationships and interaction	Administer in any language	T = 20 min; S = variable time to score/interpret; I = NA	NA	R = .87–.95 interscorer agreement; V = not reported	Journal article; Western Psychological Services

Note: NA = not available.

Ease and time of administration. Time varies, depending on number and extent of themes explored.

Scoring procedure. This author always writes the genogram on an easel so that family members see the data and can collaboratively define healthy or unhealthy patterns. The genogram page is stored in the client file and put in sight for each following therapy session.

Reliability. This is not available.

Validity. This is not available.

Availability and source. Guidelines are available in McGoldrick & Gerson (1985) and DeMaria, Weeks, & Hoff (1999).

Comment. The genogram visually helps assure family connection and objectify data, providing a safer environment to talk about problems or recognition of the need for change in the system. Genogram expansion can also be used as an assignment outside therapy for exploring patterns of interaction and identifying resources for problem solving.

STRATEGY FOR UTILIZING ASSESSMENT RESULTS

Clarifying Theory Basis Desired in Selecting Methods of Assessment

Psychotherapy incorporates a broad spectrum of theories from which to choose. Effective family assessment requires a full commitment to family systems theory and, even within this theory, many different viewpoints abound. Because theory is the continuing thread from assessment, hypothesis formulation, and revising intervention planning–implementation, a clear understanding of one's theoretical foundation is critical for good results. Instruments discussed in this chapter are based on family systems theories that generally include assumptions about functional family structure (parental hierarchy, egalitarian marital relationships, and differentiated adult–adult family-of-origin relationships); effective communication (honest and open disclosure, listening and understanding, and effective problem solving); and a general environment of safety and support, which nurtures individual development within family members.

Working Out Logistics of Collecting Information

The setting for therapy defines some parameters for family assessment. Operating in a clinic with plenty of waiting room and administrative staff allows for incorporating a wider array of assessment strategies; family members need private space in order to answer paper-and-pencil questionnaires honestly. Having a therapy team behind the mirror also expands opportunities for using clinical rating scales, perhaps reducing the number of self-report instruments needed. Working in a training facility is a "resort" setting that includes clinic space and administration, therapy teams, live and group supervision, and a research focus. Family assessment is and should be a major component of family therapy training facilities. The budget for operating a facility can limit the use of purchased instruments. However, all instruments discussed in this chapter are available at minimal or no cost except for duplication of materials and purchase of books or manuals to use in interpretation. Creating a computerized record-keeping system with research analysis of family assessment data is a great asset in improving services. However, a solo practitioner can benefit from incorporating at least some of the instruments and strategies discussed in this chapter as part of the intake process.

Confidentiality Complications for Release of Information

When working with families involved in the court process, a therapist's clinical files sometimes become the target of subpoena. Without a release of information signed by all adult family members, the therapist must have a court order, statutory authorization, or threat of safety in compliance with state laws to release family information in the file. Protection of children's records is more unclear. Divorced parents have access to therapy records of their children unless prohibited by court order. Therapists can resist release of records, based on threat of harm, but the process is legally complicated.

Collaborative work between family therapy and family law professional organizations is needed to clarify and protect family therapy files legally (including family assessment documents) while allowing disclosure when a threat of family (including spousal) violence exists. Greater understanding of HIPPA regulations will help clarify which documents are included in therapy records versus notes and which confidentiality procedures apply.

PROTOCOL FOR FAMILY ASSESSMENT

Requesting clients to complete assessment instruments without a clear use in therapy or specifically authorized research is unethical. Consequently, assessment instruments must be brief and clinically useful. In a training facility, assessment data are especially useful in supervision to connect the theoretical base in assessment and intervention. In independent practice, assessment data should be utilized in creating treatment plans and shared with family members.

A suggested protocol for utilizing family assessment in the course of therapy includes these steps:

1. The family therapist should plan an intake procedure that includes some standardized method of self-report family functioning (this author uses

the SAFE) and an assessment of family violence (a brief violence scale/clinical observations).

2. When clients come into the office, they must first sign a written informed consent.
3. Clients then complete any written family functioning assessments.
4. Assessment continues throughout therapy, with regular documentation of family functioning in the GARF completed by the therapist.
5. Dynamic assessment guides the therapy process throughout by using clinical observations, the family genogram, and children's instruments to plan interventions and share data for goal setting with the client family.

CASE EXAMPLE

The following family story illustrates how family assessment tools can guide the process of therapy to a successful improvement in family functioning.

Family Chaos

This family was referred to the author's office to help resolve parental access conflicts blocking the finalization of divorce, which had been ongoing for 2 years; this was the second time the parents had separated and filed for divorce. The mother was now requesting supervised access for the father to the 6-year-old son, with accusations of family violence. (This was investigated and found to be unfounded during the second divorce filing; the father had no attorney on the first filing charges and the mother did obtain a protective order against him. She had set him up to violate this and then charged him with violation, resulting in his being on probation.)

During the first attempt at divorce, a social study had been conducted that recommended joint managing conservatorship (custody), with the father establishing primary residence because of the mother's history of psychological disturbance. The mother had revealed to the father that she was molested by her father, but had never been in therapy to resolve the trauma. She was completing her Master's degree in counseling when ordered into the program. The father admitted that he had historically had a problem with alcohol and was currently living with his parents because of financial difficulties resulting from the alcohol problems. The social study on the second divorce filing was almost finished when they came into therapy.

Family Assessment Process

The consent forms (Step 2), SAFE (Step 3), and a family violence abbreviated questionnaire based on the Conflict Tactics Scale (Step 3) were completed at the office before the first therapy session. During the first session, the SAFE cartoons (Step 5) were discussed with the son in a private interview. The genogram (Step 5) was used during the first session with all three family members present. In addition to structural information, family-of-origin rules about divorce and conflict management were identified on the genogram. The son added his own family drawings on the bottom of the easel page, including parents, grandparents, and two of his mother's children from a prior marriage who did not have primary residence with her. At the conclusion of the session, the therapist assigned the GARF score on the GARF Profile Chart (Step 4). Observational data were revealed during the session and by outside faxes.

Assessment Results and Utility

Because of the history of domestic violence charges, screening for family violence was the first goal of assessment (Step 1). The family violence questionnaire showed very consistent reporting from both parents: significant physical conflict had occurred during their living together, with each accusing the other of being the primary perpetrator; however, the physical assaults had stopped since the separation 2 years ago. The SAFE final item under the marital relationship assessment provided more confidence in safety (Step 5). The father reported extreme control and submission in the relationship, but the mother reported a neutral response. If the accused abuser had reported "both work together equally" and the supposed victim had reported "one controls and the other submits," the therapist would have been more inclined to investigate safety further.

Surprisingly, the mother scored the marital relationship mid-range on all items of the semantic differential. The father scored the marital relationship on the low side with one exception to the lowest score. Both scored the relationship between themselves and the son as somewhat positive but not perfect, although the mother indicated more power struggles than did the father. The father scored his relationship with his own parents as generally good; the mother scored her relationship with her parents as generally bad. It appeared that the mother perceived the relationship with the father as better than the relationship with her parents, despite how bad the marriage was. The son's first response to the SAFE cartoon was to select the competent family as his family. Later he reported that his parents did sometimes fight like the discordant family.

The genogram (Step 5) revealed that the mother had a prior marriage in which two children had chosen to live with their father and see her infrequently. Although molestation was not revealed in the joint session, the mother did indicate that conflict was handled by her mother submitting to her father's controlling behavior. The father's family-of-origin family resolved conflicts by talking things through, although his father traveled extensively and his mother, the primary caretaker, did not work outside the home.

Clinical observation (Step 5) was very revealing in this family. The mother had said that she could not be in the same room with the father, but attorneys did not back that up. She seemed quite comfortable in the same room, but did insist that she leave the office first and be given at least 5 minutes before the father left. This action appeared to be more of an attempt to convince the therapist of safety fears than actual fears for safety. Outside the sessions, the mother repeatedly faxed accusations of the father physically abusing the son and her calling CPS (i.e., the son had a bruise on his knee after spending the weekend with his father or the son said he bumped the end of the bed when getting up to go to the bathroom, assuring his mother that his father was neglectful). The son's reaction with both parents in the room was obvious anxiety and no talking at all. After his private interview with the therapist, he was able to share openly with his parents that he needed for them to stop fighting, be best friends, give him sweet dreams, and not let him watch scary movies.

At the conclusion of each of the six sessions with this family, the therapist recorded the GARF scores (Step 4). Scores progressed as follows:

- Interactional changed from 20 at the first session and 25 at the third session a month later to 30 at the final session 6 weeks later.
- Organizational changed from 30 at the first session and 35 at the third session to 40 at the final session.
- Emotional Climate changed from 10 at the first session and 30 at the third session to 35 at the final session.
- The son's openness with the parents seemed to have a big impact on them. Although many contaminations kept the functioning level low, the emotional climate did seem to level out with the organization and interaction functioning.

Outcome for the Family

Although family functioning remained low, the parents were able to reach significant agreements in the later sessions, which relieved some of mother's anxiety regarding an abusive father. Guidelines for assuring no drinking or illegal drugs when either parent was with the child were agreed to. Parenting guidelines regarding bedtime, parental exchange, and mutual support of the son's activities helped structure this family for more effective divorced coparenting. Parents worked out a plan for the father to take possession of his personal property, which had been stored in the mother's house for 2 years and had possibly been stolen during a burglary. This concrete action seemed to free them up to move forward with the divorce. Further litigation was avoided and both parents believed that their son could have "sweet dreams."

CONCLUSIONS

Formalized self-report family assessment has developed over the past generation. The current "young adult" phase seems focused on proving or disproving theory—challenging the parent generation's knowledge and needing to contribute something new. The challenge will hopefully lead toward greater understanding in the long run. However, the challenge to the FACES instrument has taken over a decade to be somewhat resolved. Similar challenges are now facing the FAD. Hopefully this debate will not take so long to find the good in the challenge. (See Franklin, Cody, & Jordan, 2003, for an excellent review of family assessment instrument research issues.) Perhaps the real benefit of using self-report family assessment instruments is in reframing the family members' thinking from linear to systemic before therapy begins.

Chewning (2001) suggests that effectively researching systemic change in family therapy may require a change in research procedures. Traditional statistical techniques need to be enhanced by using statistical process control (SPC) techniques used in industry (Wheeler & Chambers, 1992). Control charts are used to determine whether a system is stable before a measurement of change can be valid based on the normal variation range of the system. How much chaos can a family system experience—and how often—in order to continue to be a successful people making-operation? The principles of systemic assessment are the same in any setting. Perhaps future research in family assessment can incorporate what industry statisticians have learned to improve: the process.

REFERENCES

American Psychiatric Association. (1994). *Diagnostic and statistical manual of mental disorders* (4th ed.). Washington, DC: Author.

Beavers, W. R., & Hampson, R. B. (1990). *Successful families: Assessment and intervention.* New York: W. W. Norton.

Chewning, D. G. (2001). Using data to illustrate systemic improvement. *Journal of the Texas Association for Marriage and Family Therapy, 6,* 57–66.

Dausch, B. M., Miklowitz, D. J., & Richards, J. A. (1996). Global Assessment of Relational Functioning Scale: II. Reliability and validity in a sample of families of bipolar patients. *Family Process, 35,* 175–189.

DeMaria, R., Weeks, G., & Hof, L. (1999). *Focused genograms: Intergenerational assessment of individuals, couples, and families.* Pennsylvania, PA: Brunner/Mazel.

Deming, W. E. (1993). *The new economics for industry, government, education.* Cambridge, MA: Massachusetts Institute of Technology Center for Advanced Engineering Study.

Epstein, N. B., Baldwin, L. M., & Bishop. (1983). The McMaster family assessment device. *Journal of Marital and Family Therapy, 9*(2), 171–180.

Epstein, N. B., Bishop, D. S., & Levin, S. (1978). The McMaster model of family functioning. *Journal of Marriage and Family Counseling, 4,* 19–31.

Franklin, C., Cody, P. A., & Jordan, C. (2003). Validity and reliability in family assessment. In A. Roberts & K. Yeager (Eds.), *Desk reference of evidence-based research in health care and human services.* New York: Oxford University Press.

Franklin, C., Streeter, C. L., & Springer, D. W. (2001). Validity of the FACES IV family assessment measure. *Research on Social Work Practice, 11*(5), 576–596.

Group for the Advancement of Psychiatry Committee on the Family. (1996). Global assessment of relational functioning scale (GARF): I. Background and rationale. *Family Process, 35,* 155–172.

Green, R. G., Harris, R. N., Jr., Forte, J. A., & Robinson, M. (1991). The wives data and FACES IV: Making things appear simple. *Family Process, 30,* 79–83.

Hampson, R. B., & Beavers, W. R. (1996). Measuring family therapy outcome in a clinical setting: Families that do better or do worse in therapy. *Family Process, 35,* 347–361.

Hampson, R. B., Beavers, W. R., & Hulgus, Y. (1990). Cross-ethnic family differences: Interactional assessment of white, black, and Mexican–American families. *Journal of Marital and Family Therapy, 16*(3), 307–319.

Hampson, R. B., Prince, C. C., & Beavers, W. R. (1999). Marital therapy: Qualities of couples who fare better or worse in treatment. *Journal of Marital and Family Therapy, 25*(4), 411–424.

Kabacoff, R. I., Miller, I. W., Bishop, D. S., Epstein, N. B., & Keitner, G. I. (1990). A psychometric study of the McMaster Family Assessment Device in psychiatric, medical, and nonclinical samples. *Journal of Family Psychology, 3,* 431–439.

Kaslow, F. W. (Ed.). (1996). *Handbook of relational diagnosis and dysfunctional family patterns.* New York: Wiley.

L'Abate, L., & Bagarozzi, D. A. (1993). *Sourcebook of marriage and family evaluation.* New York: Brunner/Mazel.

McGoldrick, M., & Gerson, R. (1985). *Genograms in family assessment.* New York: W. W. Norton & Company.

Miller, I. W., Ryan, C. E., Keitner, G. I., Bishop, D. S., & Epstein, N. A. (2000). Commentary: Factor analyses of the Family Assessment Device by Ridenour, Daley, & Reich. *Family Process, 39,* 141–144.

Olson, D. H. (1986). Circumplex model VII: Validation studies and FACES III. *Family Process, 25,* 337–351.

Olson, D. H. (1991). Commentary: Three-dimensional (3-D) circumplex model and revised scoring of FACES III. *Family Process, 30,* 74–79.

Olson, D., & Tiesel, J. (1991). *FACES III: Linear scoring & interpretation.* St. Paul: University of Minnesota Press.

Olson, D. H., Russell, C. S., & Sprenkle, D. H. (Eds.). (1989). *Circumplex model: Systemic assessment and treatment of families.* New York: Haworth Press.

Ridenour, R. A., Daley, J. G., & Reich, W. (1999). Factor analysis of the Family Assessment Device. *Family Process, 38,* 497–510.

Ridenour, R. A., Daley, J. G., & Reich, W. (2000). Further evidence that the Family Assessment Device should be reorganized: Response to Miller and colleagues. *Family Process, 39,* 375–380.

Ryan, C. D., Epstein, N. B., Keitner, G. I., Bishop, D. S., & Miller, I. W. (in press). *McMaster model of family functioning: A comprehensive method for evaluation and treatment of families.* Philadelphia: Brunner–Routledge.

Satir, V. (1972). *Peoplemaking.* Palo Alto, CA: Science and Behavior Books, Inc.

Scoville, A. F. (1999). *Obesity and family functioning patterns of the marital, nuclear, and extended family systems.* Unpublished doctoral dissertation, Texas A & M University, Commerce.

Walsh, F. (2003). *Normal family processes* (3rd ed.). New York: Guilford Press.

Wheeler, D. J., & Chambers, D. S. (1992). *Understanding statistical process control* (2nd ed.). Knoxville, TN: SPC Press, Inc.

Yingling, L. C., Miller, W. E., Jr., McDonald, A. L., & Galewaler, S. T. (1998). GARF *assessment sourcebook: Using the DSM-IV Global Assessment of Relational Functioning*. New York: Brunner–Routledge.

CHAPTER 9

Child Custody and Divorce Assessment
Strategies and Inventories

M. SYLVIA FERNANDEZ AND SLOANE E. VESHINSKI

With the rising rates of divorce, trial and family courts are frequently called upon to set guidelines for custody and child visitation in these cases. Research suggests that high levels of parental conflict, diminished parental competence in child management behaviors, and decreased parental effectiveness, increase stress in children as well as predict maladjustment (Famularo, Fenton, & Kinscherff, 1993; Jaffe, Wolfe, & Wilson, 1990; McGill, Deutsch, & Zibbell, 1999). Mental health clinicians are often asked to assist the courts in making appropriate decisions. To this end, clinicians conduct assessments of the family, including administration of psychological tests; gather data about parent and child strengths and weaknesses and areas of conflict; and identify family support systems. In making recommendations, the well-being of the child or children is the priority. Clinicians seek to ensure that the child will be placed in an environment in which he or she is and feels safe in the care of the parents while preserving the positive aspects of the parent–child relationship (Garrity & Barris, 1994).

This chapter will focus on assessing the postdivorce parental relationship, the child's or children's relationship with each parent, and overall family functioning postdivorce. The outcome of testing and assessment will be to make recommendations for child custody and visitation, as well as, to determine the parents' ability to work together in the best interest of the child or children. The following assessment instruments are best used in combination and not as stand-alone instruments due to the limitations of what each is designed to measure. Multiple qualitative and quantitative data sources provide the best information to make appropriate recommendations.

ISSUES AND CHALLENGES OF ASSESSING CHILD CUSTODY AND DIVORCE

When a couple with a child or children decides to divorce, subsequent decisions and arrangements have to be made with regard to custody and visitation. In the event of a need to adjudicate these arrangements, psychological tests and assessments are typically administered to determine each parent's mental and emotional health as well as those of the child or children involved. Multiple issues must be considered while attending to the presenting challenges when administering tests and conducting assessments to facilitate custody and visitation recommendations and decisions.

The multiple issues to be considered comprise the family context, family relationships, and family culture. The family context includes family demographics (i.e. the current ages of the children involved), socioeconomic status, and living conditions such as each parent's ability to provide for the child or children. Also, safe and appropriate living arrangements, educational level of parents, and family of origin issues such as the involvement of grandparents in the child's or children's lives and available family support systems, need to be considered. Identifying family relationships refers to family status (i.e., blended family, single parent-led family, gay/lesbian parental dyad, or grandparents functioning as parents). Delineating the family culture aids in ascertaining several features, such as individual members' perceptions of the family, identified parental systems (matriarchal or patriarchal), parental and gender roles, parenting styles (authoritative, authoritarian, permissive), and parenting skills.

Presenting challenges to testing and assessment may include

- presence of domestic violence, whether physical, emotional, sexual, or economic, and who the perpetrator(s) and victim(s) might be
- presence and type of substance abuse, whether "recreational," daily, binge, or in recovery, and the type of substance abused, such as alcohol or other CNS depressants, stimulants, hallucinogens, or designer drugs
- presence of any active court actions, such as restraining orders, dependency actions, or misdemeanor/felony charges
- motivational issues, that is, who is requesting the testing/assessment, or the effects of assessment outcome on the family constellation, and the win–lose mentality toward the assessment process
- Parental Alienation Syndrome (PAS) or other diagnosed pathologies of either or both parents and/or child or children

Issues for the clinician performing the testing and assessment consist of adherence to the professional code of ethics with regard to custody evaluations. The American Association for Marriage and Family Therapy states in its Code of Ethics (7/1/01), Section 3.14,

> To avoid conflicts of interest, marriage and family therapists who treat minors or adults involved in custody or visitation actions may not also perform forensic evaluations for custody, residence, or visitation of the minor. The marriage and family therapist who treats the minor may provide the court or mental health professional performing the evaluation with information about the minor from the marriage and family therapist's perspective as a treating marriage and family therapist, so long as the marriage and family therapist does not violate confidentiality.

The American Counseling Association states in its Code of Ethics (1995), Section A.8,

> When counselors agree to provide counseling services to two or more persons who have a relationship (such as husband and wife, or parents and children), counselors clarify at the onset which person or persons are clients and the nature of the relationships they will have with each involved person. If it becomes apparent that counselors may be called upon to perform potentially conflicting roles, they clarify, adjust, or withdraw from roles appropriately.

Besides keeping distinct the role and function of therapist and of the assessor/evaluator who makes the recommendation regarding custody and visitation, the psychological tests administered must also be used within the guidelines for the test and the assessor/evaluator must have the requisite training and skills to administer the test and interpret the results. Some of the instruments discussed in this chapter can be administered by a nonclinician; however, most require scoring and/or interpretation of the resulting scores by a trained Master's-level clinician. It is incumbent upon the assessor/evaluator to practice ethically. If an assessment is required of a family in which physical, emotional, or sexual abuse may be present, compounded by substance abuse or mental illness, a general clinician is well advised to refer the family to someone who specializes in this area for this assessment.

INSTRUMENTS

Parent Awareness Skills Survey (PASS)

Instrument name. The Parent Awareness Skills Survey (PASS) developed by Barry Bricklin, Ph.D., in 1990 measures the understanding and effectiveness with which a parent responds to typical childcare situations.

Type of instrument. The PASS is a semistructured interview that presents parents with 18 childcare problems or dilemmas in six categories and asks how they would respond to each situation. The instrument reflects parent awareness skills of effective parenting regardless of the age of the children and specifics of their particular situation.

Use–target audience. This survey for parents of children aged 2 through 15 assesses parental awareness of their communication methods with their child and how attuned they are to the unique manner in which their child is able to respond and profit from that communication. The PASS is used for conducting custody evaluations.

Multicultural. The survey is easily understood by parents of diverse educational and cultural status.

Ease and time of administration. Individually and orally administered to each parent, it may take between 30 to 60 minutes depending on the experience of the clinician with the PASS. The parent is presented with 18 different situations and asked to tell what he or she would do in each situation. After responses are recorded, probing questions are asked to determine the issues the parents believe they should think about before and after their choice of response.

Scoring procedure. Scores reflect parents' responses at three levels: (a) spontaneous level is the unprompted and uninterrupted initial response; (b) Probe Level I asks two gentle, nonleading questions; and (c) Probe Level II asks two direct questions. Each level allows respondents to improve their score. PASS responses are scored with a 0 for no awareness, a 1 for minimal awareness, or a 2 for pronounced awareness in each of the six areas at each of the three levels. The scoring is subjective to the clinician's skill and knowledge in psychology and child development (Mental Measurements Yearbook, 2003).

Reliability. Statistics are not provided.

Validity. Statistics are not provided

Availability and source. The PASS Comprehensive Starting Kit is available from Village Publishing.

Comment—using with families. The PASS provides information on the parents' awareness of child-related critical issues and adequate solutions or interventions to theses issues. The PASS also provides information about the level of parents' awareness of their communications to their child in understandable terms to them, the importance of acknowledging their child's feelings, the relevance of the child's past history, and the need to attend to the child's feedback to the parents' response. The derived data are used to determine relative strengths and weaknesses of each parent, their conscious efforts in employing good parenting, and the influence of parental behavior on the child to facilitate custody decision making. The basic assumption of the instrument is that parenting effectiveness is a function of parents' awareness of the appropriate skills. The PASS is a good screening tool and is best used in combination with other instruments.

Parent Stress Index (PSI)

Instrument name. The Parent Stress Index (PSI), a 101-item instrument developed by Richard Abidin, Ph.D., is in its third edition (1998).

Type of instrument. The Parenting Stress Index (PSI), 3rd edition, is designed to identify stressful parent–child systems in order to provide interventions directed at reducing the stress. A screening tool for stress in the parent–child relationship, the PSI identifies dysfunctional parenting and predicts potential for parental behavior problems and child adjustment difficulties within the family system. It is used for early identification and prevention of family problems and helpful in planning intervention and treatment, assessing child abuse, and in evaluations for child custody.

Use–target audience. Although intended primarily for parents of the preschool child, the PSI can also be used with parents whose children are12 years old or younger.

Multicultural. The PSI has been validated in cross-cultural research with individuals of Chinese, Italian, Portuguese, Latin American Hispanic, and French–Canadian decent.

Ease and time of administration. Parents take about 20 to 25 minutes to complete the PSI, which is written at the fifth-grade reading level. A 36-item Short Form, which takes 10 to 15 minutes to complete, is also available.

Scoring procedure. A total stress score and two scale scores, Child Characteristics and Parent Characteristics, each of which identifies sources of stress within the family, are available for the standard form. The Short Form only provides a total stress score. Scoring time for this tool varies based on whether it is hand scored or if the PSI software is utilized.

Reliability. Reliability is reported to be adequate.

Validity. Validity is reported to be adequate.

Availability and source. Both forms can be administered in pencil-and-paper format or online using the PSI Software System, which automatically scores item responses and generates a report. This instrument is available from Psychological Assessment Resources.

Comment—using with families. The PSI identifies three major sources of stress: child characteristics, parent characteristics, and situational/demographic life stress. Child variables include: Distractibility/Hyperactivity; Adaptability; Reinforces Parent; Demandingness; Mood; and Acceptability. Parent variables include: Competence; Isolation; Attachment; Health; Role Restriction; Depression; and Spouse. Life stress factors include: Interrupted Infantile Apnea; Spina Bifida; Craniofacial Birth Defects; Insulin-Dependent Diabetes; Divorce; Marriage; Pregnancy; Income Increased; Debt; Moves; Promotions; Alcohol or Drug Problem; Death of Close Family Friend; New Job; School; Legal Problems; and others. The identification of the sources of conflict and parents' ability to cope with these will facilitate assessing placement of the child in the least stressful environment and with the more appropriate parent while making recommendations for therapy or stress management education.

Child Behavior Checklist (CBCL)

Instrument name. The Child Behavior Checklist (CBCL), authored by Thomas M. Achenbach and most recently published in 2001, is an instrument with 140 Likert-scale items. It is designed to record, in a standardized format, children's competencies and problems as reported by their parents and/or parent surrogates.

Type of instrument. The items are divided into two sections. Section 1 consists of 20 competency items regarding the child's participation in a variety of activities, peer interaction, and school functioning. Section 2 consists of 120 items on behavior or emotional problems during the preceding 6 months. The CBCL measures aggression, hyperactivity, bullying, conduct problems, defiance, and violence. Teacher Report Forms, Youth Self-Reports, and Direct Observation Forms are also available (Achenbach & Brown, 1991; Violence Institute, 2002).

Use–target audience. The CBCL is a tool used by parents or parent surrogates to rate problem behaviors and competencies of children between the ages of 2 and 18. It can also be used to measure a child's change in behavior over time or following a treatment.

Multicultural. The instrument was normed on 1,753 children, including those of African–American, Euro–American, and Hispanic ethnic descent, from 40 states and across socioeconomic levels. The CBCL is also available in Spanish.

Ease and time of administration. This instrument can be self-administered or administered through an interview with parents individually or in a group and takes about 15 minutes to complete. The responses are based on the child's current behavior or the behavior within the preceding 6 months.

Scoring procedure. The 140 items yield subtests and scores that can be obtained through manual or computer scoring. There are three competence scales (Activities, Social, and School); a Total Competence scale score; eight Syndrome scales (Aggressive Behavior, Attention Problems, Delinquent Behaviors, Social Problems, Somatic Complaints, Thought Problems, Anxious–Depressed, and Withdrawn); an Internalizing Problem scale score; an Externalizing Problem scale score; and a Total Problem scale score.

Reliability. The reported range of the test–retest reliability is between .95 and 1.00. The reported range of the inter-rater reliability is between .93 and .96, and the reported range of internal consistency is between .78 and .97 (Achenbach, 1991a).

Validity. Criterion validity was assessed and found to be acceptable.

Availability and source. The instrument is available from the Achenbach System of Empirically Based Assessment, which grants permission for use by Master's-level clinicians. This instrument has two versions: one for ages 18 months to 5 years and the other for 6 to 18 years old.

Comment—using with families. Instrument completer's responses provide comprehensive descriptions of the child's behavior that clinicians can use to distinguish between typical and disturbed behaviors. Description of the child's emotional and behavioral functioning at home and school postdivorce allows for assessing differences in and level of functioning of the child's coping ability when he or she is with either parent. These data could additionally lead to a referral for therapeutic intervention.

Behavior Assessment System for Children (BASC)

Instrument name. Behavior Assessment System for Children (BASC) was developed by Cecil R. Reynolds and Randy W. Kamphaus in 1992 and updated in 1998.

Type of instrument. BASC is a coordinated system of instruments designed to assess and identify children and adolescents with emotional disturbances and behavioral disorders. The BASC consists of five subtests intended to gather information about children or adolescents from a variety of sources, such as Teacher Rating Scale (TRS), Parent Rating Scale (PRS), Student Observation System (SOS), Self-Report of Personality (SRP), and Structured Developmental History (SDH; Hamilton Fish Institute, 2003).

Use–target audience. Those completing the instrument are asked to read each statement on the questionnaire and mark the response that best describes how the child has acted over the previous 6 months. This instrument is used to assess children between the ages of 2 and 18.

Multicultural. The norming sample included African–American, Asian–American, Euro–American, Hispanic, and Native American children from across the United States. The parent version is also available in Spanish.

Ease and time of administration. The BASC's five subtests may be used singly or in any combination. The instrument can be administered individually or in a group and takes about 15 to 35 minutes to complete.

Scoring procedure. The questionnaire has a built-in scoring system; the score is computed by summing up the number of circled items in each row. The total for each scale is found by summing the numbers in each column. The scales are Externalizing Problems; Internalizing Problems; School Problems; Atypical, Withdrawal and Adaptive Skills; Clinical Maladjustment; School Maladjustment; Sensed Inadequacy; Personal Adjustment; Behavioral Symptoms Index; Emotional Symptoms Index; and Sensation Seeking. Computer scoring is also available. Although no specialized training is required for administration, individuals need to have at least a Master's degree to interpret the results of the questionnaire (Mental Measurements Yearbook, 2003).

Reliability. Reynolds and Kamphaus (1992) reported the range of internal consistency to be between .62 and .95 and that it rises with age. Test–retest reliability ranges from .70 to 0.91. Inter-rater reliability ranges from .46 to .83. These range reports are inclusive of all eight versions.

Validity. Criterion validity was assessed and found to be acceptable.

Availability and source. American Guidance Service offers eight versions of the instruments, each of which is age specific.

Comment—using with families. The BASC provides a multidimensional view of the child or adolescent from multiple informants using multiple methods. This instrument is most effective with children and adolescents when used as part of an assessment battery with preschool children. The derived information of personality and behavior can lead to educational and therapeutic interventions to facilitate coping with the divorce and/or for working with problems that have arisen as a result of the divorce.

Millon Adolescent Clinical Inventory (MACI)

Instrument name. The 160-item Millon Adolescent Clinical Inventory (MACI), developed by Theodore Millon, Carrie Millon, and Roger Davis, is a self-report personality inventory designed specifically to assess adolescent personality characteristics and clinical syndromes.

Type of instrument. The MACI is used as an initial evaluation of troubled adolescents to confirm diagnostic hypotheses, in planning individualized treatment programs, and in measuring treatment progress.

Use–target audience. The MACI is used for assessment specifically with "disturbed" adolescents, 13 to 19 years of age, in outpatient, inpatient, or residential treatment settings.

Multicultural. The minority representation in the normative samples ranged from 16 to 28%. The audiocassette version of the MACI is also available in Spanish.

Ease and time of administration. Through a series of questions, the clinician assesses an adolescent's personality along with self-reported concerns. The true/false items are written at the sixth-grade level; it takes approximately 20 to 30 minutes to complete and can be administered individually or in a group.

Scoring procedure. Four options available for scoring are MICROTEST Q Assessment System software, mail-in scoring, hand scoring, and optical scan scoring. The MACI has 27 content scales and four response bias scales. The Content scales are: 12 Personality Patterns scales (Introversive, Inhibited, Doleful, Submissive, Dramatizing, Egotistic, Unruly, Forceful, Conforming, Oppositional, Self-Demeaning, and Borderline Tendency), 8 Expressed Concerns scales (Identity Diffusion, Self-Devaluation, Body Disapproval, Sexual Discomfort, Peer Insecurity, Social Insensitivity, Family Discord, and Childhood Abuse), and 7 Clinical Syndromes scales (Eating Dysfunctions, Substance Abuse Proneness, Delinquent Predisposition, Impulsive Propensity, Anxious Feelings, Depressive Affect, and Suicidal Tendency). The Response Bias scales are four modifying indices (Reliability, Disclosure, Desirability, and Debasement) (Mental Measurements Yearbook, 2003).

Reliability. Cronbach's alpha reliabilities range from .73 to .91, with most of the internal consistencies in the 0.80s (Retzlaff, Sheehan, & Lorr, 1990). Test–retest reliabilities range from .57 to .92.

Validity. Responses to the MACI were favorably intercorrelated with the Beck Depression Inventory, Beck Anxiety Inventory, and Eating Disorder Inventory.

Availability and source. The MACI is available in paper-and-pencil format, audiocassette, or online from NCS Assessments.

Comment—using with families. The MACI is most effective with adolescents experiencing a level of significant problems or concerns so as to determine treatment options and measuring treatment progress. The mental health needs of a troubled adolescent in the family raise coparenting issues, contradictory hidden parental messages, issues of loyalty in the family system, and the "role" the troubled adolescent plays in the functioning, or lack thereof, of the family.

State–Trait Anger Expression Inventory (STAXI)

Instrument name. The State–Trait Anger Expression Inventory (STAXI) developed by Spielberger is a 44-item self-report that measures the experience and expression of anger.

Type of instrument. The experience of anger is understood in the context of state (subjective feelings) and trait (predisposition); the expression of anger may be focused outward or directed inward and includes degree of anger control.

Use–target audience. The STAXI is designed for individuals aged 13 years and older.

Multicultural. This has not been reported.

Ease and time of administration. Written at the fifth-grade reading level, it can be self-administered and scored with little training; however, it should only be interpreted by clinicians with formal assessment training. Although this is not a timed test, it is typically completed in 15 minutes.

Scoring procedure. The 44 items of STAXI are distributed across five scales: State Anger (10 items), Trait Anger (10 items) with Angry Temperament (4 items), and Angry Reaction (4 items) subscales; Anger Expression includes Anger-In (8 items), Anger-Out (8 items), and Anger Control (8 items). All items are rated on a four-point scale assessing frequency and intensity of angry feelings. STAXI is hand scored with subscale totals entered on a grid. Raw score totals are converted to percentile ranks and T scores using normative tables specific to gender in three categories: adolescents, college students, and adults.

Reliability. The reliability ranges across categories are .87 to .93 for State Anger; .82 to .84 for Trait Anger; .85 to .89 for Trait Anger Temperament; .65 to .71 for Trait Anger Reaction; .73 to .86 for Anger Expression Inward; .73 to .78 for Anger Expression Outward; and .81 to .85 for Anger Expression Control.

Validity. Validity of the STAXI scales is based on convergent and divergent validity. Correlations were computed using the Eysenck Personality Questionnaire subscales, State–Trait Personality Inventory subscales, Buss–Durkee Hostility Inventory, MMPI Hostility Scale, and MMPI Overt Hostility Scale (Spielberger, 1988).

Availability and source. STAXI is available from Sigma Assessment Systems, Inc.; a qualification form for interpretation is required.

Comment—using with families. When used as a component of a battery of tests, the State–Trait Anger Expression Inventory (STAXI) has been effective with couples experiencing marital difficulties, planning or in the process of divorce, or working to resolve issues in a conflictual marital situation. The STAXI "provides an initial assessment of the key features of the direction of anger, useful when there are concerns for normal and abnormal expressions of anger" (Nurse, 1999, p. 169). The STAXI is also useful in determining how parents' anger at each other may affect their ability to deal with issues related to coparenting and decision making in the best interests of the child or children. When it is administered to teenage children, their anger toward their parents for the divorce provides a context for their input with regard to custody and visitation.

Parent–Child Relationship Inventory (PCRI)

Instrument name. The Parent–Child Relationship Inventory (PCRI) provides a qualitative evaluation of parent–child interactions.

Type of instrument. The PCRI is a self-report questionnaire that measures parenting dispositions and behaviors using a Likert scale. Content scales include: Parental Support, Satisfaction with Parenting, Involvement, Communication, Limit Setting, Autonomy, and Role Orientation.

Use–target audience. The PCRI is used in evaluating parents and their children (ages 3 to 15). Separate norms are provided for mothers and fathers.

Multicultural. This has not been reported.

Ease and time of administration. The PCRI, written at the fourth-grade level, can be administered individually or in a group.

Scoring procedure. The PCRI may be hand scored or scored through a mail-in service provided by Western Psychological Services, as well as by fax and microcomputer disk service.

Reliability. This has not been reported.

Validity. This has not been reported.

Availability and source. The PCRI is available from Western Psychological Services.

Comment—using with families. Gerard (1994) indicated that the PCRI was developed to assess parents' attitudes toward parenting as well as toward their children. The evaluation of parental attitudes and skills, family interaction, and presence of abuse provides information about conscious parenting and competence, and the quality of the familial relationship.

Burks' Behavior Rating Scale (BBRS)

Instrument name. Burks' Behavior Rating Scale (BBRS), developed by Harold F. Burks and published in 1977, is designed to identify problem behavior patterns in children.

Type of instrument. The BBRS can be used as an aid to differential diagnosis. The first of two versions of this scale consists of 110 items designed for children in grades 1 through 9; the second version is 105 items designed for children in preschool and kindergarten.

Use–target audience. A parent or teacher rates on a five-point Likert scale how often a behavior is seen in the child.

Multicultural. The standardization sample included elementary and middle school-aged children of different physical and mental abilities equally distributed by gender. It included Mexican–American and Euro–American children from three counties in California.

Ease and time of administration. The instrument is completed individually by raters who have daily contact with the child and is based on observation for at least 2 weeks; it takes 15 to 20 minutes to complete. It is recommended that interpretations be made by or with a Master's-level clinician.

Scoring procedure. The manually scored instrument yields 19 subtests and scores:, Excessive Self-Blame, Excessive Anxiety, Excessive Withdrawal, Excessive Dependency, Poor Ego Strength, Poor Physical Strength, Poor Coordination, Poor Intellectuality, Poor Academics, Poor Attention, Poor Impulse Control, Poor Reality Contact, Poor Sense Of Identity, Excessive Suffering, Poor Anger Control, Excessive Sense Of Persecution, Excessive Aggressiveness, Excessive Resistance, and Poor Social Conformity. The Poor Academics subtest is eliminated in the preschool version. Raw scores in each category are summed and plotted on a profile sheet partitioned in ranges labeled not significant, significant, and very significant (Mental Measurements Yearbook, 2003).

Reliability. The only type of reliability assessed is internal consistency, which ranges from .64 to .91 (Burks, 1996).

Validity. The claim of validity is supported by anecdotal rather than empirical data.

Availability and source. Both versions of the BBRS are available from Western Psychological Services, which grants permission to use the instrument.

Comment—using with families. The BBRS is a useful screening tool for rating behaviors and is age and developmentally specific. This instrument delineates problem behaviors and indicates special needs a child may have at home and/or school that, in turn, provide information for determining appropriate placement with parents(s) who can best meet the child-rearing demands.

Child Rearing Practices Report (CRPR)

Instrument name. The 91-item Child Rearing Practices Report (CRPR) developed by J. H. Block is designed to identify child-rearing attitudes and values (Block, 1972).

Type of instrument. The CRPR consists of two forms. The first is for parents to rate the phrases that describe their child-rearing practices. The second form is for adolescents and young adults to rate phrases that describe their parent(s).

Use–target audience. The report may be completed by the parent to describe his or her child-rearing behavior or by the adolescent/young adult child to describe the child-rearing orientations of his or her parents.

Multicultural. This test has been normed for use in Russian, Hungarian, Chinese, and French languages.

Ease and time of administration. The instrument employs a Q-sort technique. The time of completion is approximately 30 to 40 minutes.

Scoring procedure. This 91-item self-report instrument measures a number of constructs, including: Control, Control by Anxiety, Control by Guilt, Inconsistency, Investment in the Child, Protectiveness, Supervision, and Enjoyment of the Child.

Reliability. Test–retest reliability scores range from .61 to .71.

Validity. This has not been reported.

Availability and source. Both forms are available from Block.

Comment—using with families. Information gained from the results of this tool can be used to assist families in discussing parenting and child-rearing practices, from the parents' as well as the children's perspectives. Because this test is geared for adolescents and young adult children, testing results can assist parents in re-establishing patterns of parenting as children move into different developmental levels. It can assist adolescents in addressing levels of maturity, independence, and collaboration with their parents with regard to issues such as discipline. For custody and visitation assessment, the CRPR identifies the differences and similarities between parents in their child-rearing attitudes and behavior. The differences become areas for negotiations and/or change in parenting patterns as a result of the alterations in living arrangements and custody. Additionally, recommendations for therapy may also be made based on the information obtained.

Teacher Report Form (TRF)

Instrument name. The 118-item Teacher Report Form (TRF) was developed by Thomas M. Achenbach in 1991 to obtain teachers' reports of children's academic performance, adaptive functioning, and behavioral/emotional problems.

Type of instrument. On a three-point scale, teachers rate children's academic performance in each academic subject on a five-point Likert scale. Teachers use a seven-point Likert scale to rate adaptive functioning in order to compare the child to typical students with regard to how hard he is working, how appropriately he is behaving, how much he is learning, and how happy he appears to be.

Use–target audience. The TRF was designed for use with children ranging from 6 to 18 years old.

Multicultural. The norming group included children of African–American, Euro–American, and Hispanic ethnic descent across socioeconomic levels from around the United States.

Ease and time of administration. Administered individually by a Master's-level clinician, this instrument takes about 15 to 20 minutes to complete.

Scoring procedure. This instrument yields 17 subscales and scores and can be scored manually or by computer. The scoring system includes *T* scores and raw scores for two broad-band dimensions of child problem behavior:

Externalizing and Internalizing. In addition, the scoring method includes *T* scores and raw scores for several narrow-band scales describing: Delinquency and Aggression, Attention Problems, Withdrawal, Anxiety/ Depression, Somatic Complaints, Social Problems, Thought Problems and Sex Problems.

Reliability. Achenbach (1991b) reported the test–retest reliability to be .62 to .96, the inter-rater reliability to be .60, and the range of internal consistency to be .72 to .95

Validity. Criterion validity was assessed and found to be acceptable.

Availability and source. This instrument can be obtained by permission from Achenbach System of Empirically Based Assessment.

Comment—using with families. Child academic achievement is a main area of concern for parents. This tool can assist parents and teachers in identifying areas of strength and weakness in a child's ability to learn. The TRF identifies children's academic performance, adaptive functioning, and behavioral/ emotional problems that may be related to adjustment to changes necessitated by divorce.

Relationship Conflict Inventory (RCI)

Instrument name. The 120-item Relationship Conflict Inventory (RCI) developed in 1989 by Arthur M. Bodin is designed to evaluate relationship conflict and to measure progress and outcome of relationship therapy. The instrument was revised in 1996; the 2002 version has 121 items with an additional process item on metacommunication (Bodin, 2003).

Type of instrument. The RCI has 35 process items, which address "how" something is being discussed; 27 are on verbal conflict and 8 on physical conflict, and 85 content items address what is being discussed in terms of frequency, distress level, and causal attribution. This tool identifies process and content of relationship conflict.

Use–target audience. The instrument was designed for use with couples seeking a divorce and in conflict due to problematic communication (Bodin, 1996).

Multicultural. This has not been reported.

Ease and time of administration. The RCI, written at the sixth-grade reading level, typically takes 20 to 30 minutes to complete. A shortened version eliminates the content section, reducing it to 35 items with completion time of 15 to 20 minutes.

Scoring procedure. The subscales of the instrument report on Process Conflict and Content Conflict. Process Conflict focuses on Verbal Conflict (Communication Difficulties, Arguments, Painful/Deteriorating Relationship, Distancing, Intimidation, and Separation) and Physical Conflict (Physical Coercion/Intimidation, Indirect Aggression, three levels of Physical Abuse, and Use of Weapons). Content Conflict is channeled into nine clusters: Activities, Change, Characteristics, Communication, Habits, Preferences, Relationships, Responsibilities, and Values.

Reliability. This is currently being assessed.

Validity. This is currently being assessed.

Availability and source. The RCI is available from Bodin.

Comment—using with families. The RCI can be used with couples to assist them in identifying the content and process of conflict and adjusting styles of communication that lead to physical and verbal conflict. Results will assist couples in creating interventions that allow them to communicate in a more effective manner; identify areas of verbal and physical escalation, prior to their occurring; and increase positive communication to decrease and/or eliminate incidents of verbal and/or physical escalation. The focused overview of the relationship conflict provides information regarding parents' ability to acknowledge their differences, how they account for these differences in areas such as childrearing, and if they choose to argue about or seek accommodation for these differences. This information sets the stage for calm negotiations and mutual understanding and agreement regarding child custody and visitation in the best interest of the child.

Parental Nurturance Scale (PNS)

Instrument name. The 24-item Parental Nurturance Scale (PNS) developed by John R. Buri is designed to measure parental approval, acceptance, and affirmation of the child from the perspective of the child.

Type of instrument. This instrument has 24 statements to which the child responds on a five-point scale on how the statement applies to him/her and the gender-specific parent.

Use–target audience. The PNS can be used with a child of any age.

Multicultural. This has not been reported.

Ease and time of administration. Identical forms are used for mothers and fathers with only gender references changed.

Scoring procedure. Individual scores from each item are summed and half the items are reverse scored.

Reliability. Reported internal consistency has alphas of .95 for mothers and .93 for fathers. Test–retest reliabilities of .92 for mothers and .94 for fathers have been reported (Buri, 1989).

Validity. The PNS has good concurrent validity, with significant positive correlations with self-esteem for mother's and father's PNS (Fisher & Corcoran, 1994).

Availability and source. The PNS is available from Sage Publications.

Comment—using with families. The PNS is a valuable tool in that it provides the child's perception of parental nurturance, acceptance, and affirmation. The child's ability to verbalize this is seen as a positive factor when considering self-esteem and feelings of being loved and appreciated by each parent for assessment of the parent–child relationship in determining custody and visitation. The child's input about preferences for living with and/or visiting parents is tempered by this perception.

Parental Bonding Instrument (PBI)

Instrument name. The 25-item Parental Bonding Instrument (PBI) developed by Gordon Parker, Hilary Tupling, and L. B. Brown measures parent–child relationships as perceived by the child.

Type of instrument. The instrument is retrospective, meaning the individual completes the instrument based on how he remembers his parents during his development until about no more than age 16. The measurement uses two scales: Care (12 items) and Overprotection (13 items). The adult responds to the items on a four-point scale (Parker, Tupling, & Brown, 1979).

Use–target audience. Although targeted at children over 16 years old, preteens may also complete the instrument for how they remember their biological parents during their childhood up to the first 16 years.

Multicultural. Not reported.

Ease and time of administration. The instrument is completed for mothers and fathers separately and may take 2 to 5 minutes each.

Scoring procedure. The PBI is scored on a Likert scale with several items reverse scored; scoring takes approximately 5 to 7 minutes.

Reliability. The PBI is reported to have good internal consistency with split-half reliability coefficients of .88 for care and .74 for overprotection, and test–retest reliability correlations of .76 for care and .63 for overprotection.

Validity. The PBI is reported to have satisfactory construct and convergent validity.

Availability and source. The PBI is not copyrighted and can be freely used by clinicians and researchers.

Comment—using with families. The PBI can be useful in working with families to measure parental attitudes and behaviors as perceived by the child of any age. In child custody evaluations, the information gained from the PBI identifies the parent who the child perceives cares about him, who sets boundaries, who fosters his/her growth and development, and toward whom he feels most connected.

STRATEGY FOR UTILIZING ASSESSMENT RESULTS

When assessments/evaluations are conducted, systematic orientation and procedure are important to ensure consistent, comprehensive, and accurate data gathering. The following steps identify the essential information needed and from whom, the qualitative and quantitative data desired and data gathering methods, and how and when this assessment plan will be operationalized. The subsequent case example illustrates the use of the identified procedure.

TABLE 9.1 Matrix: Child Custody and Divorce Assessment Strategies and Inventories

Assessment instrument	Specific couple and family applications	Cultural/ language	Instructions/use: T = time to take; S = time to score; I = items	Computerized: a = scoring; b = report	Reliability (R); validity (V)	Availability
Parent Awareness Skills Survey (PASS)	Parents; reflects parents' awareness of effective parenting	English	T = 30–60 min including questioning; S = 30–60 min; I = 18 situations with 5 specific questions for each	a = no; b = no	R = not reported; V = not reported	Village Publishing
Parent Stress Index (PSI)	Parents; identifies stressful parent–child systems	English	T = 20–25 min (long form); 10–15 min (short form); S = varies; I = 101 (long form); 36 (short form)	a = yes; b = yes	R = adequate; V = adequate	Psychological Assessment Resources
Child Behavior Checklist (CBCL)	Parents and parent surrogates; records children's competencies and problems	English; Spanish	T = 15 min; S = 15 min; I = 140	a = yes; b = yes	R = .95–1.00 test-retest; .93–.96 inter-rater; .78–97 internal consistency; V = criterion validity acceptable	Achenbach System of Empirically Based Assessment
Behavior Assessment System to Children (BASC)	Children, parents and parent surrogates; assesses and identifies children and adolescents with emotional disturbances and behavioral disorders	English; Spanish (parent version)	T = 15–35 min; S = 15–35 min manually; I = 5 separate subtests, each with varying number of items	a = yes; b = yes	R = .62–95 internal consistency; 70–91 test–retest; .46–.83 inter-rater; V = criterion validity acceptable	American Guidance Service

Instrument	Description	Language	Administration	a/b	Reliability/Validity	Publisher
Millon Adolescent Clinical Inventory (MACI)	Disturbed adolescents; self-report personality inventory designed specifically to assess adolescent personality characteristics and clinical syndromes	English; Spanish (audiocassette version)	T = 20–30 min; S = 20–30 min manually; I = 160	a = yes; b = yes	R = .73–.91 internal consistency; .57–.92 test–retest; V = favorably intercorrelated with Beck Depression Inventory, Anxiety Inventory, and Eating Disorder Inventory	NCS Assessments
State–Trait Anger Expression Inventory (STAXI)	Individuals 13 and older; measures the experience and expression of anger	English	T = 15 min; S = 15 min; I = 44	a = no; b = no	R = .87–.93 (state anger); .82–.84 (trait anger); .85–.89 (trait anger temperament); .65–.71 (trait anger reaction); .73–.86 (anger expression inward); .73–.78 (anger expression outward); .81–.85 (anger expression control); V = convergent and divergent validity with subscales from variety of instruments	Sigma Assessment Systems, Inc
Parent–Child Relationship Inventory (PCRI)	Parents; provides a qualitative evaluation of parent–child interactions	English	T = 15 min; S = differs based on method (hand, fax, mail-in); I = 78	a = yes; b = yes	R = not available; V = not available	Western Psychological Services
Burk's Behavior Rating Scale	Parents and teachers; identifies problem behavior patterns in children	English	T = 15–20 min; S = 15–20 min; I = 105 (preschool and kindergarten); 110 (grades 1–9)	a = no; b = no	R = .64–.91 internal consistency; V = not available	Western Psychological Services

TABLE 9.1 (Continued). Matrix: Child Custody and Divorce Assessment Strategies and Inventories

Assessment instrument	Specific couple and family applications	Cultural/language	Instructions/use: T = time to take; S = time to score; I = items	Computerized: a = scoring; b = report	Reliability (R); validity (V)	Availability
Child Rearing Practices Report (CRPR)	Parents and child; identifies child rearing attitudes and values	English	T = 30–40 min; S = not available; I = 91	a = not available; b = not available	R = test–retest reliability scores at .61–.71; V = not available	J. H. Block (author)
Teacher Report Form (TRF)	Teacher; reports of children's academic performance, adaptive functioning, and behavioral/emotional problems	English	T = 15–20 min; S = 15–20 min; I = 118	a = yes; b = yes	R = .62–.96 test–retest; .60 inter-rater; .72–.95 internal consistency; V = criterion validity acceptable	Achenbach System of Empirically Based Assessment
Relationship Conflict Inventory (RCI)	Couples seeking a divorce; evaluates relationship conflict and measures progress and outcome of relationship therapy	English	T = 20–30 min (long form; 15–20 min (short form); S = not reported; I = 121 (long form; 35 (short form)	a = no; b = no	R – not available V– not available	Arthur M. Bodin (author)
Parental Nurturance Scale (PNS)	Any age child; measures parental approval, acceptance, and affirmation of the children from the perspective of child	English	T = 5–10 min; S = 5 min; I = 24	a = no; b = no	R – alphas of .95 for mothers and .93 for fathers V – good concurrent validity	Sage Publications
Parental Bonding Instrument (PBI)	Any age child; measures parent–child relationships as perceived by child	English	T = 10–15 min; S = 10 min; I = 25	a = no; b = no	R – good internal consistency V – good	Not copyrighted

1. Collect biopsychosocial data that include client's perception of current legal situation; educational, medical (physical and emotional), criminal, and employment history; past and present substance use and/or abuse; family constellation; support systems; and religious/spiritual orientation.
2. Review collateral data, such as divorce agreement, court orders, school records, and/or mediation agreements.
3. Collect and/or review clinical data to include prior and current individual, couples, and family therapy.
4. Interview the whole family and individual members.
5. Administer selected inventory/testing tools.
6. Interpret the results of the inventory.
7. Identify recommendations and interventions.
8. Provide feedback to the couple and/or family as appropriate.
9. Submit report and/or recommendations to court.

CASE EXAMPLE

Background Information and Reason for Testing

John and Jane had been married for 16 years when John was transferred by his employer to another state across the country. John and Jane mutually agreed that Jane would stay where they presently were because their children, John, Jr. (age 13), Madison (age 11), and Ryan (age 6), were well established in their respective schools and it would be less disruptive to them. Six months after John relocated, he contacted Jane to ask for a divorce because he had met someone else; during this same period he had only returned once to see his family. He also asked that the children be allowed to visit him during the summer and Christmas holidays. Jane, angry about the divorce, was denying John's request for visitation. As a result of their inability to come to an agreement about custody and visitation, the Family Court judge requested a child custody evaluation.

Individual and Testing Summary

In the initial interview and collection of biopsychosocial data for John, he verbalized understanding the reason for the interview was to determine custody and visitation privileges for him and his former spouse. He further indicated that he wanted a quick and fair resolution so that the children were not adversely affected by the divorce. John reported that he held an MBA in finance, was in good health, had no substance abuse or criminal history, and had worked for the same corporation for 15 years. His job relocation had resulted in his living less than 5 miles from his parents and allowed him to attend church with them weekly (Step 1). At the onset of this interview, John produced copies of the recently finalized divorce agreement and court motions that led up to this evaluation. Mediation was found to be unsuccessful due to John's and Jane's inability to come to an agreement. In this clinical interview, John verbalized that his experience in mediation with Jane was a negative one because she would not accept any recommendation he made with regard to the custody and visitation of the children. As a result of this conflict, neither party was able to come to an agreement about custody and visitation, which necessitated a referral by the Court for evaluation (Step 2).

John indicated no current or past history of individual, couples, or family therapy. When this was questioned, John indicated that their relationship was strong at the time he relocated, and it was only after the relocation that the issues between him and Jane surfaced. He was unable to fly home to take part in couples/family counseling, and he reported that Jane was opposed to counseling of any kind. (Step 3). Furthermore, John indicated that, although he would like to have primary custody of his children, he understood that they had attachments in their present home and school; he wanted to spend time with his children, while not overly disrupting their lives. John also indicated that he had been timely with child support and was not currently in arrears (Step 4). John was administered the Parent–Child Relationship Inventory (PCRI) and the State–Trait Anger Expression Inventory (STAXI). He completed the instruments within the time guidelines and in full. On the PCRI, John's strengths were his positive satisfaction with parenting and adequate support with his parenting. It appeared that he had some discomfort with allowing his daughter autonomy appropriate to her age. On the STAXI, all of his scores appeared to fall within the norm with the exception of one scale that suggested angry feelings and beliefs about being treated unfairly, while not expressing that anger (Step 6 and Step 7).

In the initial interview and collection of biopsychosocial data for Jane, she acknowledged that the interview was to determine custody and visitation for her and John. Jane had 2 years of college education, was in good health, and reported no substance abuse or criminal history. She had held clerical jobs up through the first 3 years of her marriage until her oldest son was born; since then she had been a stay-at-home mother (Step 1). Jane provided copies of the divorce agreement and court motions that led up to the order for this evaluation, which was a consequence of her and John's inability to come to an agreement (Step 2). Jane indicated no current or past experience with therapy of any kind (Step 3). During the clinical interview, she indicated that she needed to retain primary custody of her children because she has always been there for them and provided stability in their lives (Step 4). Jane was administered the Parent–Child Relationship Inventory (PCRI) and the State–Trait Anger Expression Inventory (STAXI). She completed the instruments in full within the time guidelines. On the PCRI, Jane's scores indicated an emphasis on discipline and setting limits, which appeared to be major characteristics. She also felt supported in her parenting. Her discipline and limit setting may have indicated a punishment orientation attitude. On the STAXI, most of the scores were moderate, with one very high score indicating frequent experiences with and aggressive expressions of anger (Step 6 and Step 7).

In the initial interview and collection of biopsychosocial data for the three children, John Jr., Madison, and Ryan indicated a level of sadness over their parents' separation. All of the children indicated that they attended school regularly and received good grades and denied use of drugs and alcohol and arrest history. John Jr. added that he missed his father particularly because his father had attended all of his softball games. Madison said that even though she loved her father, she felt more comfortable living with her mother but did want to visit her father. Ryan stated that he loved both his parents the same. All three children were administered the Parental Nurturance Scale (PNS) and John Jr. and Madison were administered the Parental Bonding Instrument (PBI).

John Jr.'s scores on the PNS indicated that he felt more nurturance and acceptance from his father than his mother. Scores were different by 18 points. Madison's scores indicated that she felt more acceptance and nurturance from her mother, although only 10 points separated the scores, which was significant in this case. Ryan's scores indicated an equal feeling of nurturance and acceptance by both of his parents, although his level of understanding of the testing instrument is unclear due to his young age. John Jr.'s results on the PBI indicated that he felt cared for by both of his parents and not as overprotected as his sister had indicated (maybe due to his age and opportunities to explore different levels of freedom from his parents). Madison's scores indicated that she felt highly cared for and a high level of overprotection. Again, the ages of these children and the developmental milestones they were approaching appropriate to their genders may have played a role in these results.

The outcomes of the structured and unstructured assessments pointed toward a family in which both parents had focused on and loved their children, in spite of their own inability to make a decision about the children's best interests with regard to custody and visitation. John Jr. had expressed a strong desire to spend time with his father, as well as wanting to complete school in his current neighborhood middle school. Madison clearly indicated a desire to live with her mother and visit her father; Ryan appeared to be too young to make a clear decision about each parent, although his statement about loving both parents equally demonstrated that good parenting had taken place in the home, with no issues of alienation on the part of either parent. Based on the test results and clinical interviews, it appeared that both parents took an active interest in the care and well-being of their children, but with different styles of parenting. This implied that neither parent was better than the other; they were simply different in their styles of discipline, communication, and boundary setting. In spite of the parents' interpersonal issues, which led to the divorce, and Jane's apparent anger over the situation, a clear plan of custody and visitation appeared to be one with which both parents could be happy.

Treatment and Custody Recommendations

To help John with his daughter, formal or informal education about child development and parenting approaches around the issue of independence of his child would be helpful (Step 7). It was recommended that Jane get individual therapy to manage her anger and deal with the loss she felt. It was also recommended that Jane arrange for family therapy for her and the children to discuss and process the changes in the home as a result of the divorce. All of the children presented as well adjusted to the situation and did not appear to be in need of individual therapy at the time.

With regard to custody recommendations, shared parental responsibility was the most desired and appropriate course to take. The three children should remain in the family home with their mother for the remainder of their education. Because the father lived on the opposite coast, it was recommended that John Jr. spend the Christmas holiday and entire summer with his father. It was recommended that Madison and Ryan spend the Christmas holiday (alternate years) and 3 weeks in the summer with their father. Spring break for all three children would be spent with the father (on alternate years), with the father having the first year's visit. Due to their ages, it was also recommended that this visitation schedule be revisited in 3 years. Telephone contact was highly recommended for all children, and John and Jane should continue to communicate openly with each other in regard to the physical, educational, and overall needs of their children.

Feedback of Results

The clinician met with John and Jane individually to discuss the results of the assessments (Step 8). Then the clinician met with them together to allow John and Jane an opportunity to share any information and for the clinician to identify to the parents the issues specific to each child individually and the parenting needs of the children collectively. Recommendations to be made to the Family Court judge were shared with both parents.

CONCLUDING COMMENTS

This chapter has described the use of psychological assessment methods to evaluate the postdivorce parental relationship, the child's or children's relationship with each parent, and overall family functioning postdivorce, as well as to determine the parents' ability to work together in the best interest of the child or children with the purpose of making recommendations for child custody and visitation. In this chapter, 13 instruments were discussed and a protocol for using these instruments in clinical practice was provided and illustrated by a case example. Finally, a matrix summarizing the key attributes of these tools and their use with families has been provided (see Table 9.1).

REFERENCES

Abidin, R. (1998). *Parenting stress index (PSI)* (3rd ed.) Odessa, FL: Psychological Assessment Resources.

Achenbach, T. M. (1991a). *Integrative guide to the 1991 CBCL/4-18, YSR, and TRF profiles.* Burlington, VT: University of Vermont, Department of Psychology.

Achenbach, T. M. (1991b). *Manual of the Teacher's Report Form and 1991 Profile.* Burlington, VT: University of Vermont, Department of Psychiatry.

Achenbach, T. M., & Brown, J. S. (1991). *Bibliography of published studies using the Child Behavior Checklist and related materials: 1991 edition.* Burlington, VT: University of Vermont, Department of Psychiatry.

American Association for Marriage and Family Therapy. (7/1/01). *Code of Ethics.* Retrieved 02/04/2002 from http://www.aamft.org/resources/lrmplan/ethics/ethicscode2001.htm.

American Counseling Association. (1995). Code of ethics. Retrieved 02/04/2002 from http://www.counseling.org/site/PageServer?pagename=resources_ethics.

Block, J. (1972). Generational continuity and discontinuity in the understanding of societal rejection. *Journal of Personality and Social Psychology, 22,* 333–345.

Bodin, A. M. (1996). Relationship conflict—verbal and physical: Conceptualizing an inventory for assessing process and content, In F. W. Kaslow (Ed.), *Handbook of relational diagnosis and dysfunctional family patterns.* New York: John Wiley & Sons, Inc.

Bodin, A. M. (2003). Relationship Conflict Inventory. Retrieved 7/6/2003 from http://mri.org/rcipossiblebenefits.html.

Bricklin, B. (1990). *Parent awareness skills survey.* Doylestown, PA: Village.

Buri, J. R. (1989). Self-esteem and appraisals of parental behavior. *Journal of Adolescent Behavior, 4,* 33–49.

Burks, H. F. (1996). *Burks' Behavior Rating Scales: Manual.* Los Angeles, CA: Western Psychological Services.

Famularo, R., Fenton, R., & Kinscherff, R. (1993). Child maltreatment and the development of posttraumatic stress disorder. *AJDC, 147,* 755–760.

Fischer, J., & Corcoran, K. (1994). *Measures for clinical practice—2nd edition.* New York: The Free Press.

Garrity, C., & Barris, M. (1994). *Caught in the middle: Protecting the children of high conflict divorce.* New York: Lexington Books.

Gerard, A. (1994). *Parent–child relational inventory (PCRI).* Los Angeles: Western Psychological Services.

Hamilton Fish Institute. (2003). Behavior assessment system for children. Retrieved 7/6/2003 from http://www.hamfish.org/measures/b/instruments/11.

Jaffe, P., Wolfe, D., & Wilson, S. (1990). *Children of battered women.* Newbury Park, CA: Sage.

McGill, J. C., Deutsch, R. M., & Zibbell, R. A. (1999). Visitation and domestic violence: A clinical model of family assessment and access planning. *Family and Conciliation Courts Review, 37*(3), 315–334.

Mental Measurements Yearbook. (2003). Retrieved 7/20/2003 from http://0-web5.silverplatter.com.novacat.nova.edu.

Nurse, A. R. (1999). *Family assessment.* New York: John Wiley & Sons, Inc.

Parker, G., Tupling, H., & Brown, L. B. (1979). A parental bonding instrument. *British Journal of Medical Psychology, 52,* 1–10.

Retzlaff, P., Sheehan, E., & Lorr, M. (1990). MCMI-II scoring: Weighted and unweighted algorithms. *Journal of Personality Assessment, 55,* 219–223.

Reynolds, C. R., & Kamphaus, R. W. (1992). *Behavior assessment system for children: manual.* Circle Pines, MN: American Guidance.

Spielberger, C. (1988). *State–Trait Anger Expression Inventory, research edition. Professional manual.* Odessa, FL: Psychological Assessment Resources.

Violence Institute. (2002). Child Behavior Checklist. Retrieved 7/6/2003 from http://vinst.umdnj.edu/VAID/TestReport.asp?Code=CBCA.

CHAPTER 10

Child Abuse and Family Assessment
Strategies and Inventories

WILLIAM N. FRIEDRICH, ERNA OLAFSON, AND LISA
CONNELLY

PURPOSE OF ASSESSMENT

The assessment question will be determined in part by whether the psychological testing is for diagnosis and treatment, or whether testing forms part of a forensic assessment for civil, domestic relations, juvenile, or criminal court. Patient privilege will also differ markedly between clinical and forensic evaluations. Informed consent, confidentiality, and privilege must be clarified in writing at the outset before interviewing or testing begins, with informed patient or caretaker consent documented in standardized forms that include client signatures. Psychological assessments for forensic purposes should be clearly distinguished from those for treatment purposes.

When child abuse or domestic violence has been alleged, in many circumstances, clinical psychological assessments performed as part of treatment may end up in court. Parents may separate during or after treatment, sue for custody and visitation, and subpoena prior treatment and psychological testing records. Criminal or juvenile court actions may also ensue. In cases in which extrafamilial child abuse is alleged, families or victims may subsequently sue for damages.

For these reasons, all treatment and psychological testing records should be created and maintained as if they will be scrutinized in a court of law.

Unforeseen legal involvements are more likely when domestic violence and child abuse are at issue than when psychologists test youngsters for attention deficit hyperactivity disorder, separation anxiety, or other childhood problems.

ASSESSMENT COMPLEXITIES

Acts Versus Diagnoses

The terms *domestic violence, child sexual abuse*, and *child physical abuse* cover a very wide range of interpersonal behaviors. These aggressions are acts, not diagnoses (Olafson & Boat, 2000). Indeed, victims and perpetrators may show few or no symptoms when assessed. The symptom patterns of victims are determined by many factors, including the severity and duration of the insult or trauma, the degree of subsequent interpersonal support, and the age of the victim (Kolko & Swenson, 2002; Putnam, 2003; Trickett, Noll, Reiffman, & Putnam, 2001). Many child sexual abusers and batterers appear to be psychologically normal when interviewed and tested (Kolko & Swenson, 2002; Olafson, 1999; Salter, 2003).

Symptom Discontinuity

In addition, symptom patterns change as children develop (Friedrich & Reams, 1986; Olafson & Boat, 2000). Following abuse or trauma, a child who appears to be asymptomatic at Time A may have a constellation of symptoms at Time B (Putnam, 2003). Psychologists who conduct assessments should be alert to this "sleeper effect" because at least one study has shown that sexually abused children who had the fewest initial symptoms evidenced the most marked deterioration over time (Gomez–Schwartz, Horowitz, & Cardarelli, 1990).

Developmentally Appropriate Criteria

Traumatized children are not Vietnam veterans. The posttraumatic stress disorder (PTSD) diagnosis was constructed a generation ago based on the symptom patterns observed in combat veterans returning from Vietnam. Other categories of trauma survivors—battered women, abused children, rape victims, and others—were then shoehorned into this construct (American Psychiatric Association, 1980, 1994; American Academy of Child and Adolescent Psychiatry, 1998). This shoehorning may be more suitable for survivors of adult traumas such as rape than it is for children.

The American Psychiatric Association's diagnostic manual, the DSM IV (APA, 1994), has added notations about some ways in which children's posttraumatic symptom pattern differ from adult responses. However, the symptom categories first arrived at with combat veterans are still generally applied to children (APA, 1994, pp. 423–429). Many instruments developed to assess PTSD in children attempt to be consistent with the DSM IV construct for PTSD and simply adapt the language of their questions slightly for children's reading level. This adult-based lens may well lead to distortions and omissions when researchers study traumatized children. Instruments that look freshly at children's responses to abuse and trauma instead of applying the lens of the adult PTSD construct have only recently been developed, for example, the Pediatric Emotional Distress Scale or the Trauma Symptom Checklist for Children reviewed in this chapter.

Single Versus Multiple Traumas in Adults and Children

Type I (single event) traumas are associated with different symptom patterns than Type II (multiple event) traumas are. Posttraumatic stress disorder as described in the DSM IV applies most clearly to Type I traumas. The efforts to include a category for complex posttraumatic stress disorder, the symptom constellation associated with chronic, severe trauma and maltreatment, have been so far unsuccessful (Pelcovitz et al., 1997). A national committee within the federally funded National Child Traumatic Stress Network (NCTSN) is revisiting the diagnosis of complex PTSD in children, attempting to integrate developmental and neurobiological components into the construct in order to assess children accurately.

How are traumatized children different from traumatized adults? Judith Herman wrote that "repeated trauma in adult life erodes the structure of the personality already formed, but repeated trauma in childhood forms and deforms the personality" (Herman, 1992/1997, p. 96). Since Herman first wrote these words, researchers have convincingly demonstrated that repeated trauma in early childhood forms and deforms the body as well as the mind (De Bellis et al., 1999; Putnam, 2003). Trauma and abuse exert more powerful effects on the developing brains and bodies of children than on adults.

Childhood maltreatment occurs during sensitive developmental periods for children, such as during the experience-dependent maturation of the central nervous system, so that chronically traumatized children have smaller brains and lower IQs by the time they start school than do nonabused comparison groups (DeBellis et al., 1999). A recent study has shown that children exposed to severe domestic violence have eight fewer IQ points than unexposed children, a suppression greater than that found in children chronically exposed to lead (Koenen, Moffitt, Caspi, Taylor, & Purcell, 2003). Abuse and trauma in childhood also affect fundamental developmental processes such as attachment, socialization with others, emotional regulation, impulse control, and the integration of the self (Putnam, 2003). Chronic trauma and maltreatment have the most powerful impact on these psychobiological developmental processes in children aged 7 and younger.

Misdiagnoses

Because understanding of children's posttraumatic responses is relatively recent and still very incomplete, many clinicians misdiagnose posttraumatic symptom patterns. Taking a complete history of trauma and maltreatment must be part of every psychological assessment, especially when bipolar disorder or attention deficit hyperactivity disorder (ADHD) form part of the differential diagnosis. Putnam and Trickett's longitudinal study of sexually abused girls and matched controls found rates of apparent ADHD in the sexually abused girls of over 30%, whereas the mean for the nonabused controls was less than 10% (Putnam & Trickett, 1997). Treating a traumatized child for an attention deficit disorder from which the child does not suffer, while missing the child's trauma history and symptoms, is not good clinical practice. The recent "epidemic" of childhood bipolar disorder diagnoses has erupted with only minimal attention paid to the frequent occurrence of bipolar-like symptoms in traumatized children. Children whose alleged manic symptoms include, for example, symptoms known to follow trauma and maltreatment, such as emotional dysregulation, impulse control disorders, or hypersexuality, should be questioned about maltreatment histories before they are subjected to powerful medication regimens (Friedrich, 2002). Ritalin and Depakote are not the drugs of choice for symptomatic child maltreatment victims.

Lack of Instrumentation

No instruments are available to assess some of the most damaging sequelae of childhood maltreatment. Attachment is studied formally in laboratory settings using the Strange Situation, but less formally in clinical settings; observations comprise the most useful data points (Friedrich, 2002). Other sequelae, such as impulse control difficulties or emotional dysregulation, are covered in child self-report and parent or teacher report measures, although all such measures have inherent limitations.

Many psychological batteries depend heavily on patient self-report inventories that contain validity scales to assess reporting attitudes. Individual, ethnic, cultural, developmental, and gendered reporting styles influence parent and child reports. When abuse and trauma are at issue, validity is especially challenging to assess. For example, children, especially those whose posttraumatic symptoms include numbing and avoidance, are poor reporters of their own internal states and symptoms (Friedrich, 2002; Olafson, 1999). Even nontraumatized children minimize undesirable response patterns such as anger. Traumatized adults who have PTSD or dissociative symptoms may appear to be "faking bad" on standard measures, or their test results may erroneously indicate that they suffer from thought disorders (Briere, 1997; Carlson, 1997). Secondary motives may also affect reporting accuracy, such as when clients are suing for damages or when custody and visitation are at stake.

Comorbidity

Much childhood maltreatment does not produce posttraumatic symptoms, but predisposes victims to depression, anxiety, conduct disorders, substance abuse, or somatic symptoms such as gastric disturbances, gynecological concerns, and headaches (Putnam, 2003). Depression in adults and children is 2 to 3 times more likely when a history of child abuse and neglect is present than when it is absent. For adult women, a history of child abuse is the single best predictor for drug and alcohol abuse. More than half of all abused children have significant school problems, and child abuse and neglect victims are more than twice as likely to be unemployed as adults than nonvictims are (Putnam, 2003).

The emotional health of parents and their capacity for supportive caretaking following trauma are crucial protective factors for children following abuse and trauma. Mothers have been studied more than fathers have, and it has been found that maternal support is the single factor most predictive of good outcomes for child victims (Friedrich, 2002; Reece, 2000). Parental maltreatment and trauma histories and assessment of their current functioning are a necessary part of the psychological testing of maltreated and traumatized children.

ASSESSMENT LIMITATIONS

This chapter does not address the neuropsychological symptoms suffered by many child maltreatment victims. If a batterer has beaten a pregnant woman's abdomen, shaken her or her child, or beaten mother or child on the face or head, a complete neuropsychological assessment referral for these victims is recommended (Valera & Barenbaum, 2003). In many cases, impulsive and aggressive males and females would benefit from neuropsychological assessments to determine if targeted psychopharmacological interventions might be of assistance to counter the effects of possible brain damage from child abuse or adult affrays.

Adaptations of standard psychological inventories for adults that include the MMPI-2, MCMI-III, Rorschach (Exner System), WISC III, and WAIS III are not addressed in this chapter. Instruments that assess adult posttraumatic symptoms, such as the Trauma Symptom Inventory (TSI) are also not included, although evaluation of parents may be essential for treatment success (see Briere, 1997; Friedrich, 2002; Olafson, 1999; Wilson & Keane, 1997). Although many psychological instruments were created before posttraumatic symptoms formed a routine part of differential psychological diagnosis, they are often the only instruments given in psychological batteries, even when abuse and trauma are known to have been part of patient histories. Every competent evaluator should become aware of the limitations and the distorted diagnostic picture that may emerge when only standard instruments are applied to trauma survivors such as Vietnam veterans, battered women, and child sexual assault survivors.

SELECTION OF INSTRUMENTS

The instruments reviewed in this chapter (see Table 10.1) were chosen because they have shown validity or promise in the assessment of children and caretakers when trauma or maltreatment are at issue. Parent and caregiver measures allow the examiner to assess the child's current functioning with particular focus on problems with dysregulation (e.g., dissociation, PTSD, sexual behavior problems, and quality of the parent's relationship with the child). Child-completed measures primarily assess problems with dysregulation and affective instability.

INSTRUMENTS

Parent, Caregiver, and Teacher Report Measures

- Child Behavior Checklist (CBCL)
- Child Sexual Behavior Inventory (CSBI)
- Child Dissociative Checklist (CDC)
- Pediatric Emotional Distress Scale (PEDS)
- Abidin Parenting Stress Index (PSI)
- Milner Child Abuse Potential Inventory (CAPI)
- Parent–Child Conflict Tactics Scale (PCCTS)

Child Self-Report Measures

- Trauma Symptom Checklist for Children (TSCC)
- Children's PTSD Reaction Index (CPTS-RI)
- Children's Impact of Traumatic Events Scale Revised (CITES-R)
- Impact of Events Scale (IES)
- Children's Reaction to Traumatic Events Scale (CRTES)
- Beck Depression Inventory (BDI)

- Kovac's Children's Depression Inventory
- Multidimensional Anxiety Scale for Children (MASC)
- Adolescent Dissociative Experiences Scale (A-DES)

Parent, Caregiver, and Teacher Report Measures

Child Behavior Checklist (CBCL) and Related Measures

Instrument name. The Child Behavior Checklists (CBCL 6–18; CBCL 1½–5), the Teacher Report Form (TRF), and the Youth Self-Report (YSR) were developed by Thomas Achenbach (1991a, b, c, 2001; Achenbach & Rescorla, 2000) and are part of the Achenbach System of Empirically Based Assessment (ASEBA). These scales have been widely used throughout the world and translated into a number of languages. The measures have been used in a very large number of epidemiological and clinical studies of disturbed and nondisturbed children and will be used to collect data from traumatized youth treated through the federally funded National Child Traumatic Stress Network sites in 35 locations throughout the United States. The original CBCL was for children aged 4 to 18 with a companion version for children 2 to 3 years old. The scales were revised to specify different age ranges in 2000 and 2001 but with very few changes in the questions.

Type of instrument. The CBCL for 6 to 18 year olds is a 118-item measure completed by the parent that assesses behaviors observed over the previous 6 months. A shorter, 100-item version of the CBCL has been developed for children 18 months to 5 years old. The TRF is a companion measure that correlates at a reasonable level with the CBCL and also contains 118 items. The YSR (Youth Self-Report) was developed for children ages 11 through 18 and has 112 items. All items are answered on a three-point format: not true, somewhat true, and very true. Training is required for administration and scoring, and computerized scoring is available. An advantage of computer scoring is that it can calculate the degree of concordance among CBCL, TRF, and YSR.

Use–target audience. The CBCLs are intended for children living in the home, ages 18 months to 18 years, to assess a broad range of internalizing and externalizing symptoms. The TRF is geared toward school-aged children and the YSR, very appropriately, is administered to children who have some capacity for self-report and are at least 11 years of age.

Multicultural. The CBCLs, TRF, and YSR have been translated into over 30 languages, including several versions of Spanish, and are used throughout the world. Dr. Achenbach and his laboratory colleagues at the Center for Children, Youth, and Families at the University of Vermont maintain a Web site that appraises researchers and clinicians of current research and enables access to hundreds of previous research studies.

Ease and time of administration. The two versions of the CBCL typically require from 10 to 17 minutes to complete; parents should have the opportunity for clarification of items.

Scoring procedure. These scales can be hand or computer scored and, in addition to the Social Competence subscales, they provide broad-band scale scores related to Internalizing, Externalizing, and Total Behavior Problems. Included in internalizing are Withdrawal, Anxious/Depressed, and Somatic Complaints. Externalizing subscales include Delinquent Behavior and Aggressive Behavior. The syndrome scales were derived with principal components factor analysis. The Assessment Data Manager (ADM) Windows Software allows the evaluation to enter, score, compare, and save data from all ASEBA forms quickly.

Reliability and validity. Because the scales were derived using factor analytic techniques, their internal consistency scores are redundant. However, the CBCL scales as well as those of the TRF and YSR have very adequate reliability and validity; in fact, these scales are the most widely used screening devices for child behavior problems and research is added weekly.

Availability and source. The measure, manuals, and scoring information are available from Dr. Achenbach at the Center for Children, Youth, and Families at the University of Vermont in Burlington, 05401, or via the Web site at www.aseba.org.

Comment. The family of CBCL-related instruments has been widely used in studies of traumatized and maltreated children. Two attempts have been made to develop PTSD-related subscales from the CBCL (Wolfe, Gentile, Michienzi, Sas, & Wolfe, 1991; Sim et al., in press) and these have met with some success at identifying children who also have PTSD diagnoses. Other research has focused on developing CBCL subscales that more closely adhere to diagnostic nosologies (Lengua, Sadowski, Friedrich, & Fisher, 2001) and are thus more clinically relevant than the empirically derived subscales of the CBCL, TRF, and YSR. Parental rejection of the child will be reflected in CBCL results. For example, elevated CBCL scores by parents relative to those of teachers are closely related to parental endorsement of such items as "my child knows how to bug me" and "I will feel better when this child is out of the room" (Friedrich et al., under editorial review).

Child Sexual Behavior Inventory (CSBI)

Instrument name. The Child Sexual Behavior Inventory (CSBI) was developed by William N. Friedrich, with the assistance of numerous colleagues (Friedrich, 1997). It is commercially available in English, although translations in several versions of U.S. Spanish are available from the author as well as German, French, and Dutch translations. This measure has been used in an increasing number of studies examining normative and disturbed sexual behavior in children.

Type of instrument. The CSBI is a 38-item measure developed for use with 2-to12-year-old children. Either parent can complete it, although the norms are based on maternal report. An additional four items designed to assess more aggressive and intrusive sexual behavior have been developed and are described elsewhere (Friedrich, 2002). Clinical use with teachers, daycare providers, and other relatives has also been reported in the literature. Training is required for administration and scoring, which is done by hand.

Use–target audience. CSBI is intended for children living in a home setting, ages 2 to 12 years. It assesses a variety of sexual behaviors exhibited over the preceding 6 months falling into such face-valid factors as boundary problems, self-stimulation, gender-related behaviors, sexual intrusiveness, and sexual knowledge.

Multicultural. The CSBI has been translated into several Western European languages and has also been used in an epidemiological study of sexual behavior in several Eastern European studies, including Latvia, Moldova, Macedonia, and Lithuania (Sebre et al., in press).

East and time of administration. The CSBI typically requires from 5 to 10 minutes to complete; parents should have the opportunity for clarification of individual items.

Scoring procedure. CSBI is hand scored and provides three summary scores, including total sexual behavior, developmentally related sexual behavior, and sexual abuse-specific items. Developmentally related sexual behaviors are those reported by at least 20% of the normative sample for that age and gender. Sexual abuse-specific items are behaviors that significantly discriminated abused from nonabused children for specific age and gender subgroups after controlling for age, gender, maternal education, and family income. A number of very unusual behaviors, typically exhibited primarily by sexually abused children, are not included in the SASI because of their rarity, but when present certainly raise concern.

Reliability and validity. The CSBI has very adequate test–retest reliability, and parents typically correlate with each other. It has demonstrated utility in identifying sexually abused children. Studies of normative sexual behavior in Sweden, the Netherlands, and the United States show considerable similarities among the more unusual behaviors.

Availability, and source. The CSBI is available from Psychological Assessment Resources, Odessa, Florida. It can be obtained by calling (800) 331-TEST or from the company's Web site, www.parinc.com.

Comment. The CSBI is the only normed, validated, and published measure of sexual behavior in children. A companion measure, the Adolescent Sexual Behavior Inventory (Friedrich, Lysne, Sim, & Shames, under editorial review), has been developed so that researchers can be in a better position to follow up samples long term and for those who want a more age-appropriate measure to use with teen samples. Parents of sexually abused children tend to minimize or maximize their child's sexual behavior more than do parents of nonabused children, and reviewing each behavior with parents can be useful to determine the validity of their reports. High scores do not necessarily indicate an increased probability of sexual abuse, but may reflect response bias, exposure to pornography, or overt family sexuality, or some mixture of externalizing behavior problems with sexual provocativeness.

Child Dissociative Checklist (CDC)

Instrument name. The Child Dissociative Checklist (CDC) was developed by
Frank Putnam, MD, and his associates in the 1980s (Putnam, Helmers, &
Trickettt, 1993; Putnam & Peterson, 1994). Over the course of its development, the CDC has progressed through three major versions. The current
version (V3.0-2/90) is a 20-item instrument designed to be a clinical
screening tool and a research tool for dissociative disorders; however, it is
not intended for use as a diagnostic instrument.

Type of instrument. The Child Dissociative Checklist is a 20 item parent/adult
report measure using a three-point scale response format (i.e., 2 = "very
true," 1 = "somewhat or sometimes true," and 0 = "not true"). The CDC
lists behaviors that describe children and reporters are asked to circle the
corresponding number (i.e., 2, 1, or 0) for each item that describes the
child "now" or "within the past 12 months." However, clinicians are free to
specify another time frame, for example, when the instrument is administered periodically to assess treatment progress.

Use–target audience. The CDC is designed for children ages 5 to 14. The CDC
should be completed by a parent, caretaker, teacher, therapist, or inpatient
staff member who is very familiar with the child's behavior and is in
frequent contact with the child.

Multicultural. The CDC is available in Spanish and many other languages.
Putnam reports, "We know less about the effects of gender and culture on
CDC scores. I am certain that these factors influence reported scores in
some cases, and probably more so for children than for adults" (Putnam,
1997, p. 252).

Ease and time of administration. The CDC is a brief, 20-item observer report
measure that takes about 5 to 10 minutes to administer and score.

Scoring procedure. The CDC score is the sum of all of the item scores and can
range from 0 to 40 on Version 3.0. Developmental, cultural, and individual
variables must be taken into account when interpreting a score. CDC
scores tend to decrease with age, suggesting that young children experience
slightly more dissociation than do older children. However, in the most
extreme cases of dissociation, maturation does not affect scores. Generally,
a score of 12 or higher is considered an indication of pathological dissociation warranting further evaluation. Children who do not have a trauma or
maltreatment history generally have very low scores on the CDC, just
above a score of 2. Maltreated children have higher scores, a mean of 6.0.
The mean for children with dissociative disorders is over 3 times the mean
score for maltreated children, at 20 and above. Normative data are available.

Reliability. The CDC has been shown to be a reliable instrument in several
studies. The CDC shows moderate to good 1-year test–retest stability
($r = .65$) and internal consistency (Cronbach's alpha = .86).

Validity. The validity of the CDC has primarily been assessed on its ability to
discriminate among groups. Several studies to date have found that sexually abused children score significantly higher on the CDC than nonabused
comparison children; the CDC is generally able to discriminate between

children with pathological dissociation and those without. In one study of four test samples, the CDC discriminated among normal control girls, sexually abused girls, children with dissociative disorder NOS, and children with multiple personality disorder (now named dissociative identity disorder; Putnam et al., 1993). Good convergent and discriminant validity have been indicated. The CDC appears to be sensitive to dose–exposure relationships; the more serious the abuse history is (e.g., combined physical and sexual abuse, multiple perpetrators), the higher the CDC score (Putnam, Helmers, Horowitz, & Trickett, 1994).

Availability and source. The CDC is a public domain document freely available for reproduction, distribution, and use. Readers who wish to make changes to it are asked to change the name to reduce confusion. The complete 20-item CDC is available in the appendices of Putnam (1997).

Comment. The complex disorders associated with severe and prolonged childhood trauma and maltreatment include pathological dissociation; indeed, dissociative disorders are rarely seen among those who have no victimization histories (Putnam, 1997). This easily administered, freely available, valid, and reliable instrument fills a need for screening children as young as 5 years old for the presence of pathological dissociation. High scores alert clinicians and evaluators to undertake structured clinical interviews for formal diagnosis. Many CDC items can be confounded with attention deficit disorders, so interviews with parents are necessary to determine if endorsed items are suggestive of dissociation or related to ADHD (Friedrich, 2002). The two diagnoses are not mutually exclusive; it is possible for children to have both. The CDC's sensitivity to dose–exposure adds to its usefulness with children. Because this instrument is freely available and easily administered, it is widely used in clinical and research settings.

Pediatric Emotional Distress Scale (PEDS)

Instrument name. The Pediatric Emotional Distress Scale (PEDS) was published in 1999 by Saylor and colleagues. It is not a measure of posttraumatic stress disorder as defined in the DSM IV—a diagnosis derived from work with traumatized adults and then adapted for use with children. Instead, the items on this scale were chosen based on behaviors identified as occurring in young children who have experienced or are experiencing trauma.

Type of instrument. The PEDS consists of 21 items (17 general behavior and 4 event specific) rated by the parent or guardian to measure the behavioral problems of children 2 to 10 years old after trauma. The scale consists of three subscales: Anxious/Withdrawn, Fearful, and Acting Out. In addition, some items ask about posttraumatic behaviors by children such as games, stories, and play about the trauma.

Use–target audience. The target audience comprises 2- to 10-year-old children who have been traumatized by homelessness, sexual abuse, natural disasters, and other negative experiences.

Multicultural. The PEDS is among the few instruments in which psychometric properties have been examined for homeless children. As a recently developed instrument, the PEDS has not been tested widely among diverse cultural groups. This instrument is not intended for use alone as a diagnostic or forensic instrument, but as a screening measure that forms part of a more complete assessment.

Ease and time of administration. The PEDS takes 5 to 10 minutes to administer and score. It appears to be a sensitive measure of stress in children, and its brevity provides an advantage in assessments during high-stress situations.

Scoring procedure. The higher the scores are, the greater the child's distress.

Reliability. The overall alpha coefficient for the first 17 items was .85. Test–retest reliability at 6 weeks ranged from .55 to .61. Inter-rater reliability between fathers and mothers ranged from .65 for the PEDS total and ranged from .47 to .64 for subscales.

Validity. Parental evaluations correlated with total scores. Further work on discriminant validity is needed. The scale shows good sensitivity and specificity for traumatized children compared with nonclinical samples of nontraumatized children and good sensitivity to the stressors experienced by homeless children. Although the PEDS assesses behavior problems common among traumatized children, many of these behaviors also occur among clinical samples of children who have not been traumatized, so further studies are needed to assess the discriminant validity of this measure on traumatized versus nontraumatized clinical samples (Ohan, Myers, & Collett, 2002). Years of education affected maternal scores, with less educated mothers endorsing fewer items at a high level.

Availability and source. A copy of this brief scale is printed in Saylor, Swenson, Reynolds, & Taylor (1999). Before using the scale, contact Conway Saylor for consent and further clinical information.

Comment. This brief and promising instrument fills a need by screening the responses of preschool children to trauma; however, it is still in the early stages of development and validation, and further work on discriminant validity is expected. This instrument has the advantage of not trying to fit stressed and traumatized children's symptom patterns into diagnostic categories developed during research with adults. The scale was constructed in consultation with investigators who had studied the effects of disasters on children and then reviewed by doctoral level clinical psychologists for appropriateness. Because the symptoms of fearfulness, anxiety, withdrawal, and acting out observed in traumatized children are also commonly seen in nontraumatized clinical samples, discriminant validity studies may not usefully separate these two populations. Nevertheless, anxiety or acting out associated with abuse and trauma histories in children will require different treatment approaches than nontrauma-based anxiety or acting out in children will. Complete abuse and trauma histories should always be obtained as part of differential diagnostic work for presenting symptoms of anxiety and acting out in young children.

Parenting Stress Index (PSI)

Instrument name. The Parenting Stress Index (PSI) and the Parenting Stress Index—Short Form (PSI-SF) were developed by Richard Abidin and were designed to assess stressful parent–child interactions. Parental stress is very important in the young child's emotional and behavioral development; child characteristics, parent characteristics, family contacts, and life stress are some of the facets of this parent–child relationship that have been determined to be important.

Type of measure. The PSI is a 120-item measure completed by the parent, which asks the parent to answer each question about the "child you are most concerned about." A five-point format is utilized: strongly agree, agree, not sure, disagree, and strongly disagree. The PSI-SF is a 36-item measure that follows the same point format.

Use-target audience. The PSI and the PSI-SF are intended for parents of children presenting for treatment because of behavioral and emotional disorders. It allows the user to identify systems characterized by behavior problems in the child as well as other important dimensions of parenting.

Multicultural. The PSI has been validated in a variety of U.S. samples, but also in transcultural research involving populations as diverse as Chinese, Italian, Portuguese, Latin American, Hispanic, and French–Canadian. This suggests that the PSI is a robust diagnostic measure that maintains its validity with diverse non English-speaking cultures.

Ease and time of administration. The PSI typically requires approximately 20 minutes to complete. The PSI-SF requires approximately 5 minutes to complete.

Scoring procedures. The PSI and the PSI-SF can be hand scored or computer scored. The PSI has six subscales in the Child domain and seven subscales in the Parent domain, as well as the total stress score. The Child domain subscales include Adaptability, Acceptability, Demandingness, Mood, Distractibility/Hyperactivity, and Reinforces Parent. The subscales from the Parent domain include Depression, Attachment, Role Restriction, Competence, Isolation, Spouse, and Health. The total stress score includes the majority of the PSI items. The PSI-SF has a total stress score derived from all 36 items, as well as three subscales of equal length: Parental Distress, Parent–Child Dysfunctional Interaction, and Difficult Child.

Reliability and validity. The PSI and the PSI-SF have been the focus of a considerable volume of research, although the PSI has a longer history of research. Relevant to child maltreatment is the fact that the PSI has been studied with maltreating parents. In fact, PSI profiles have been developed for physical abusers who are honest or who are good at faking, as well as parents at risk for child abuse.

Availability, and source. The measure, manuals, and scoring information are available from Psychological Assessment Resources, Odessa, Florida. The company can be reached at (800) 331-TEST or www.parinc.com.

Comment. The brevity of the PSI-SF makes it a nice complement to the CBCL and can provide a very well-rounded view of the parent and his or her perceptions of the child. The Difficult Child subscale from the PSI-SF focuses on some of the basic behavioral characteristics of children that make them easy or difficult to manage. These behaviors may include learned patterns of defiant, noncompliant, and demanding behavior. When parents deny their own distress but report a very troubled child, this clearly indicates parents who need professional assistance designed, in part, to help them with their negative perceptions of their child.

Child Abuse Potential Inventory (CAPI)

Instrument name. The Child Abuse Potential Inventory (CAPI) was developed by Joel Milner (Milner, 1986).

Type of instrument. The CAPI was developed with the goal that it could be employed by protective services workers to screen for physical child abuse. Because of its use in the field, another goal was that it be relatively simple. The initial item pool represented the existing empirical and theoretical literature on maltreatment.

Use–target audience. The CAPI is intended to be used primarily as a screening tool for the detection of physical child abuse. Although specifically designed to be employed by protective services workers, it is also used as a psychological test.

Multicultural. The CAPI has norms not only for the United States, but also for Spain. It has been translated into a number of other languages and research in other cultures has indicated that the underlying constructs of the CAPI are present in other cultures. However, this is an under-researched area of the CAPI.

Ease and time of administration. There is no time limit for completing the test and, given the circumstances of its use, some parents approach this task in a very deliberate manner. Typically, it takes from 12 to 20 minutes to complete.

Scoring procedures. These scales can be hand or computer scored. The primary clinical scale is a 77-item Physical Child Abuse scale that can be divided into six factor scales: Distress, Rigidity, Unhappiness, Problems With Child and Self, Problems With Family, and Problems From Others. In addition, the CAPI contains three validity scales: the Lie Scale, Random Response Scale, and Inconsistency Scale. The validity scales are used in various combinations to produce three response distortion indices: Faking Good Index, Faking Bad Index, and Random Response Index.

Reliability and validity. The CAPI manual (Milner, 1986) reports an impressive body of research supporting the internal consistency and temporal stability of the CAPI. In addition, the instrument correlates with the Parenting Stress Index ($r = .62$), as well as relevant personality factors derived from the Edwards Personal Preference Schedule, the 16 personality-factors questionnaire, and the MMPI. CAPI abuse classification rates in the literature are typically in the 80 to 90% of referred cases arena when severe-abuse parents are compared to nonabusing parents.

Availability and source. The measure, manual, and scoring information are available from PSYTEC, Inc., PO Box 564, DeKalb, Illinois, 60115.

Comment. It is impossible to argue for the PSI or for the CAPI because both of them assess very relevant and similar dimensions of the parent–child relationship. The advantage to the CAPI is that it also assesses for physical abuse potential. Consequently, if physical abuse is ever an issue, it is preferable to administer the CAPI rather than the PSI. Otherwise, for treatment purposes, the PSI-SF is usually sufficient to determine the degree to which parents are in need of support and how accurately they view their child. Because of its general nature, the CAPI cannot be used to differentiate between neglect and abuse.

Parent–Child Conflict Tactic Scale (CTSPC)

Instrument name. The Parent–Child Conflict Tactic Scale (CTSPC) was developed by Murray Straus and colleagues (1998), many of whom were at the Family Research Laboratory at the University of New Hampshire. This scale is one of several Conflict Tactic scales (CTS) developed by Straus and colleagues.

Type of instrument. The CTSPC is a brief measure that is practical for epidemiological research on child maltreatment and for clinical screening by professionals. It contains 22 items that assess nonviolent discipline, psychological aggression, and physical assault. In addition, five neglect items can also be included as well as supplemental questions regarding weekly discipline and sexual maltreatment experienced by the parent.

Use–target audience. The CTSPC is intended for the parents of children living in the home, typically ages 6 to 17, although the authors report that the prevalence and chronicity of corporal punishment decline rapidly from about the age of 5 on. Consequently, using it with younger children is appropriate.

Multicultural. The CTSPC research reveals no clear differences between Euro–American and African–American or Hispanic–American parents, although research on severe assaults has typically found higher rates for the two minority groups.

Ease and time of administration. The CTSPC requires 6 to 8 minutes to complete, and parents should have the opportunity for clarification of items.

Scoring procedure. The three core CTSPC scales contain 22 items. Fourteen supplemental questions that assess neglect, weekly discipline, and sexual maltreatment of the parent and the child can be added to the CTSPC core scales. The standard instructions for the CTSPC ask the parent to describe what happened in the previous year, although this period can be altered depending upon the individual. The parent is asked to describe practices with a specific child and can rate the frequency of discipline strategies on a six-point scale, with additional information on whether the parent has used this strategy, has used it in the past but not in the past year, or whether it has never happened. The CTSPC subscales include Nonviolent Discipline, Psychological Aggression, Minor Assault (corporal punishment), Severe Assault (physical maltreatment), and Very Severe Assault (severe physical maltreatment).

Reliability, validity, availability, and source. The internal consistency of the CTSPC varies widely depending upon the frequency of item endorsement, with very low coefficients for Neglect and Severe Physical Assault but acceptable coefficients for the other subscales. Because it was developed recently, research is only now occurring regarding this instrument's discriminant and construct validity. A measure is available from the Family Research Laboratory, University of New Hampshire. The CTSPC is a nice companion to the PSI-SF or the CAPI in that it allows the parent to indicate discipline strategies more specifically. Parents presenting to a clinical program vary in terms of their defensiveness on all self-report measures, and because of the face validity of the items, outright denial is certainly likely. However, when used in the context of a clinical interview, or as part of an ongoing therapy process, the openness of the parent is usually appropriate and can help make him or her aware of the need for changes.

Comment. Children and adolescents experience high rates of trauma. Adolescents are 2 to 3 times more likely to be criminally victimized than adults are (Hamby & Finkelhor, 2001). Because interest in juvenile trauma is a recent and evolving field, most trauma-related scales for children are relatively new and do not have the research base older instruments possess. Nevertheless, the CTSPC, which was developed by a highly respected authority in the violence assessment field, shows promise in filling this gap in the literature.

Child Self Report Measures

Trauma Symptom Checklist for Children (TSCC)

Instrument name. The Trauma Symptom Checklist for Children (TSCC) was developed by John Briere (1996) and has been used extensively and translated into Spanish. This instrument has been used in a growing body of clinical research of disturbed and nondisturbed children.

Type of instrument. The TSCC was designed to be used for 8- to 16-year-old children. It contains 54 items that are answered on a four-point response format: never, sometimes, lots of times, and almost all of the time. The TSCC can be used with the full version and with an abbreviated version that does not include the sexual concern items. No specific training in clinical psychology or related fields is required for administration and scoring of this measure, but it should be interpreted by professionals with training in psychometrics.

Use–target audience. The TSCC is intended for children ages 8 to 16 and assesses a broad range of trauma-related symptoms including anxiety, depression, anger, posttraumatic symptoms, dissociation, and sexual concerns. Dissociation and sexual concerns include two subscales: Dissociation—Obvious and Dissociation—Fantasy, and Sexual Concerns—Preoccupation and Sexual Concerns—Distress, respectively.

Multicultural. The TSCC has been used in numerous countries and has been translated into a large number of languages, although the English and Spanish versions are the only official ones available from the publisher.

Ease and time of administration. The TSCC typically takes about 15 to 20 minutes to complete. The administrator should be available to clarify items, particularly those included in the Sexual Concerns subscale.

Scoring procedure. The TSCC can be hand or computer scored; in addition to the clinical scales mentioned earlier, it also includes two validity scales pertaining to under-response and hyper-response.

Reliability and validity. The TSCC has very adequate test–retest reliability and its validity continues to be demonstrated in a number of studies.

Availability and source. This instrument is available from Psychological Assessment Resources, Odessa, Florida, at (800) 331-TEST, or www.parinc.com.

Comment. The TSCC is the only self-report measure available for this age range of children that includes PTSD-related symptoms and also sexual concerns. In combination, these are among the most relevant dimensions to assess sexually abused children (Kendall–Tackett, Williams, and Finkelhor, 1993). Unlike many other posttrauma measures, the TSCC also assesses levels of anxiety, depression, and anger, all of which are very common posttraumatic reactions. However, other anxiety and depression measures such as the BDI, the CDI, and the MASC appear to provide a finer grained assessment of these dimensions (Friedrich, 2002). The utility of the TSCC can be maximized if, after administration of the test, the evaluator reinterviews the child by anchoring endorsed PTS items to specific events (Friedrich, 2002). One disadvantage of the TSCC, or any self-report measure, is that the child fills it out, and traumatized as well as nontraumatized children may be poor reporters of their internal states. Poor reporting may be partly because young children and children from certain cultures lack the language to express feelings accurately. In addition, traumatized children often minimize and deny their distress. For this reason, the CITES-R, which offers a semistructured interview format that may be more effective in helping children disclose internal states, should be considered as a supplement for traumatized children who produce flat-line TSCC profiles (Friedrich, 2002). The CITES-R is stronger than the TSCC in assessing the avoidant aspects of children's PTSD; the TSCC is stronger than the CITES-R on most other scales (Crouch, Smith, Ezzell, & Saunders, 1999). Neither scale thoroughly assesses the sexually avoidant pattern known to occur in many sexual assault victims (Friedrich, 2002).

Children's PTSD-Reaction Index (CPTS-RI)

Instrument name. The Children's PTSD-Reaction Index (CPTS-RI) was developed by Robert Pynoos and his associates at UCLA in 1987 and has been widely used in the United States, Europe, and Asia. It has been selected as one of the instruments by which the federally funded NCTSN collects data on traumatized youth among its 54 centers.

Type of instrument. The CPTS-RI is a clinician-administered scale, but it can also be used as a self-report measure. Training is required for administration and scoring.

Use–target audience. This instrument is intended for children aged 7 to 18 to assess symptoms following exposure to trauma. The child version is worded for ages 7 to 12 and the parent version mirrors the child version for ages 7 to 12. The adolescent version, designed for youth aged 13 to 18, contains minor changes in wording from the child version.

Multicultural. The PTSD-Reaction Index has been translated into several languages and has been used in Armenia, Kuwait, Cambodia, and the United States.

Ease and time of administration. All three instruments are designed as self-report measures, which makes them easier to administer than other children's PTSD measures such as the Children's PTSD Inventory, the CPTSDI (Saigh, 2002), the Clinician-Administered PTSD Scale for Children, the CAPS-C (Nader et al., 2002). All three versions of the CPTS-RI contain 27 questions in the traumatic exposure section. For PTSD symptoms, the child version contains 20 questions, the parent version contains 21, and the adolescent version contains 22. The instruments can also be administered verbally to individuals or groups.

Scoring procedure. Scores are hand tallied. Scores of 12 to 24 = mild PTSD; 25 to 39 = moderate; 40 to 59 = severe; and higher than 60 = very severe PTSD.

Reliability. Internal consistency for the child version is .69 to .80; inter-rater reliability for the adolescent version is .88; and test–retest reliability is excellent over the short term.

Validity. Children with greater exposure to traumas had higher scores (Thaber & Vostanis, 1999). Sensitivity and specificity for PTSD diagnosis are moderate or good. The CPTS-RI factors overlap with but do not exactly measure PTSD symptoms as constructed in the DSM-IV. However, because PTSD in children may differ somewhat from the DSM-IV's largely adult-based construct (AACAP, 1998).

Availability and source. The CPTS-RI is not commercially available, but it may be obtained from Robert Pynoos, MD, at UCLA or Kathleen Nader, DSW, in Cedar Park, Texas. A recently released administration and scoring CD for use by NCTSN sites and others (2003) is available through Robert Pynoos, MD, Trauma Psychiatry Service, UCLA, 300 UCLA Medical Plaza, Los Angeles, California, 90024-6968.

Comment. Among the new instruments designed to measure PTSD symptoms in children, the CPTS-RI has several advantages. More extensively researched than some of the other new child instruments, it does not require clinician administration. It has been shown to be suitable for children with different kinds of trauma, of different ages, and from varied cultures. It is among the best studied of contemporary instruments for posttraumatic stress disorder as defined in the DSM-IV. As the 54 regional centers of the National Child Traumatic Stress Network apply this instrument to collect their data on a variety of traumatized youth, from domestically violent homes to homeless shelters to residential treatment homes, its utility may increase. One disadvantage is that this instrument is not designed to measure complex posttraumatic stress disorder—that is, the pervasive effects of long-term exposure to severe trauma and abuse that many children experience in their homes, schools, and neighborhoods (Herman, 1992; Pelcovitz et al., 1997). In addition, like other PTSD child measures, the CPTS-RI assesses traumatized children using a construct first identified in adults and then adapted for children, rather than building the construct afresh by studying traumatized children (AACAP, 1998).

The Children's Impact of Traumatic Events Scale-Revised (CITES-R)

Instrument name. The Children's Impact of Traumatic Events Scale-Revised was published in 1991 by Vicky Veitch Wolfe, Carole Gentile, and others, and is a 78-item questionnaire to which child sexual abuse victims answer *very true, somewhat true,* or *not true* with respect to their thoughts and feelings about the abuse (Wolfe et al., 1991). Although the CITES-R is designed as a clinician-administered structured interview, older children with good reading ability may complete it as a self-report measure. It is most useful as a semistructured interview, however, and may serve as a useful transition from assessment into treatment (Friedrich, 2002). It is designed to assess PTS symptoms, eroticism, perceptions of support following disclosure, and abuse attributions such as blame. The CITES-R has 11 scales. It has no normative data. A reworded version of the scale is designed for youths who have witnessed domestic violence (CITES-FVF; Ohan et al., 2002). No manual is available.

Type of instrument. The CITES-R is a structured interview instrument, although it can be used with older children as a self-report measure.

Use–target audience. The CITES-R is for sexual abuse victims aged 8 to 16. It fills a gap by inquiring not only about trauma-related symptoms but also about factors that mediate the development of symptoms, such as abuse-related attributions by victims (blame, responsibility, power/control) and victims' perceptions of social reactions of others following disclosure (Crouch et al., 1999).

Multicultural. The CITES-R has been used with Caucasian and African–American U.S. populations but not widely elsewhere.

Ease and time of administration. The CITES-R takes 20 to 40 minutes to administer as a structured interview and 5 to 10 minutes to score. No normative data are available.

Scoring procedure. The scale is hand scored; no computerized version is available. There are four rationally derived scales: PTSD, Eroticism, Social Reactions, and Attributions. These scales are further subdivided so that a total of 11 subscales is available.

Reliability. Subscales range in internal consistency from .56 to .91. Dangerous World and Personal Vulnerability have poor internal consistency, and the others range from moderate to excellent.

Validity. Validity of subscales ranged from very poor to moderate. In general, the most robust scales are for Intrusive Thoughts, Avoidance,

Hyperarousal, and Sexual Anxiety. The scales entitled Dangerous World, Social Support, and Empowerment have been found to be less robust and should be interpreted with caution (Chaffin & Schultz, 2001). Three of the four scales have been found to show improvement in symptoms during treatment, but subscales in the Abuse Attributions scale did not change in the expected direction (Chaffin & Shultz, 2001).

Availability and source. The CITES-R and the CITES-FVF are available from Vicki Veitch Wolfe, Children's Hospital of Western Ontario, 800 Commissioners Road East, London, Ontario, Canada, N6A 5C2 or go to http://www.uwo.ca.

Comment. The CITES-R measures constructs not assessed by other scales, so clinicians should consider adding it to pretreatment assessments for sexually abused children or children who have witnessed domestic violence. Because it is best used as a semistructured interview, the CITES-R may enable clinicians to obtain responses from traumatized children that they will not provide on self-report measures such as the TSCC. However, the lack of a manual, normative data, and consistently good psychometrics across various scales and subscales limits the usefulness of this scale. Clinicians should be familiar with the major publications about this instrument, such as those by Chaffin and his colleagues (2001) and by Crouch and Schultz (1999) to assess test results in the light of their findings about the robustness of the CITES-R scales and subscales.

Impact of Events Scale (IES)

Instrument name. The Impact of Events Scale (IES), published in 1979 by Mardi Horowitz, Nancy Wilner, and William Alvarez, was designed to measure the psychological impact of a trauma or stressor on adults. It has since been used with adolescents and children as young as 8 years old. The IES was created prior to the inclusion of PTSD in the American Psychiatric Association's diagnostic manuals; PTSD first appeared in DSM-III in 1980.

Type of instrument. The IES is a 15-item self-report measure. Seven of the items measure intrusion and eight measure avoidance; when combined, they provide a total subjective stress score. Respondents are asked to rank each item on a four-point scale according to how often each has occurred in the past 7 days. The scale assesses the frequency with which experiences of intrusions, avoidance, and emotional numbing related to traumatic/stressful events were experienced in the last week.

Use–target audience. The scale can be used with adults and with children and adolescents 8 to18 years old. Because of its brevity, it can easily be administered in the immediate aftermath of mass catastrophes as well as for individual traumas. However, like many PTSD measures developed upon adults and adapted for children, the IES has not undergone adequate developmental modification. Questions are merely reworded rather than changed to reflect child-specific posttraumatic symptoms and behaviors.

Multicultural. The IES has been translated into many languages and has been applied to adolescents from various cultures, thus helping to demonstrate that reactions to trauma are consistent across cultures. It has discriminated between traumatized and nontraumatized youth in Britain and Cambodia, among refugee populations in Asia and in the West, and among French children exposed to disasters. It has been translated into many languages.

Ease and time of administration. The IES takes 10 minutes to administer and score.

Scoring procedure. A total score is calculated by summing all 15 responses.

Reliability. The Intrusion and Avoidance scales have displayed acceptable reliability (alpha of .79 and .82, respectively), and a split-half reliability for the whole scale of .86 (Horowitz, Wilner, & Alvarez, 1979). The factor structure is not clear, and one possible subscale, Numbing, has only two items. No normative base is available.

Validity. The IES has also displayed the ability to discriminate a variety of traumatized groups from nontraumatized groups (see Briere, 1997, for review), including groups in Britain, Cambodia, and the United States, and France. This instrument can be used for repeated measurement over time, and its sensitivity to change allows for monitoring clients' progress in therapy.

Availability and source. The IES can be found in Horowitz et al. (1979).

Comment. As one of the earliest trauma-specific measures developed, the IES has been useful, especially as a "quick and dirty" screening measure that can be administered even during the chaotic days following mass disasters. It has been very widely translated and used since its first appearance a generation ago; in its original form, it is better used as a screening device than as a full PTSD assessment tool. A recent revision, the IES-R (Weiss & Marmar, 1997; Weiss, 2002), has been developed for adults, but normative data for children are not yet available. The IES was developed as an instrument before PTSD had been constructed and does not reflect full PTSD criteria (Horowitz et al., 1979). Designed to measure the impact of a single trauma rather than the chronic severe trauma and maltreatment experienced by many children who are assessed, it has nevertheless been widely used with children and adults in the generation since its creation and widely translated. It has been moderately good at distinguishing traumatized from nontraumatized people in a variety of cultures. Lack of developmental adaptation limits its applicability to children and adolescents.

The Children's Reaction to Traumatic Events Scale (CRTES)

The Children's Reaction to Traumatic Events Scale (CRTES) was based on the IES and the DSM-III-R criteria for PTSD to achieve a more developmentally suitable assessment for children. The CRTES was designed for children approximately 8 to 12 years old. The CRTES retained and reworded six of the fifteen items from the IES and added nine new ones. It may be better used as a screening measure than as a full diagnostic instrument. Reliability and validity data are not yet available on this promising, brief new instrument (Devilly, 2001).

Depression Measures

Children and adults who have been victimized by abuse and violence are far more likely than nonvictims to suffer from major depression or dysthymia (Kolko & Swenson, 2002; Putnam, 2003). Women who were sexually abused as children are 3 to 5 times more likely to suffer from depression than are women without a CSA history. When one recent study controlled for a history of CSA, men and women had identical lifetime depression prevalence, rather than the 2:1 (female:male) gender differences so many other studies have found (Whiffen & Clark, 1997). A history of child physical or sexual abuse appears also to alter major depression's clinical presentation and be associated with earlier onset and less responsiveness to standard depression treatments (Putnam, 2003). When boys are sexually abused, their symptom presentation during childhood and into adulthood is more severe than the symptoms of sexually abused girls (Gold, Lucenko, Elhai, Swingle, & Sellers, 1999).

Beck Depression Inventory (BDI-II)

Instrument name: The Beck Depression Inventory-II (BDI-II) is the newest edition of the Beck Depression Inventory, the most widely used depression instrument with adolescents in the United States. It was developed by Aaron Beck in 1978, revised in 1996 (Beck, 1996) and has been extensively researched among adult and adolescent samples.

Type of instrument: The BDI-II is a 21-item self-report measure with a Likert scale assessing graded self-evaluations by respondents. Although suitable for teenagers, it does not contain references to school and has no teacher or parent report forms. It can be administered verbally by a trained administrator.

Use–target audience: The BDI-II is intended as a screening instrument for adolescents and adults, aged 13 to 80, to assess cognitive, behavioral, somatic, and affective symptoms; it is not a diagnostic interview. It effectively discriminates depressed from nondepressed adolescents and depressed from anxious adolescents; however, unlike the adult samples, it is not as effective in measuring degrees of adolescent depression (Myers & Winters, 2002b).

Multicultural: The BDI-II translated into many languages. It has demonstrated good concurrent validity for males, females, and people of different ethnicities and ages. However, nationality, ethnicity, and gender affect cut-off scores (Myers & Winters, 2002b).

Ease and time of administration. Because of its brevity and ease of administration (5 minutes), the BDI-II is very widely used in primary care.

Scoring procedure. The Beck is hand scored and produces a single score assessing the intensity of a depressive episode.

Reliability. The BDI-II has excellent reliability, ranging in various studies from .86 to .93.

Validity. The Beck has evident face validity, a potential disadvantage because of the ease with which subjects can deny, minimize, and distort. It has excellent content validity. Concurrent validity studies have ranged from .65 to .77.

Availability and source. The BDI-II is available from the Center for Cognitive Therapy.

Comment. Because of its brevity, ease of administration, and excellent validity and reliability over generations of use, the BDI-II can easily be added to most assessments. For traumatized adolescents prone to avoidance, minimization, or denial, however, the Beck Depression Inventory may be less useful than projective instruments or structured interviews. In addition, this is an adult measure changed slightly for youths, so it contains no references to youth experiences such as school.

Children's Depression Inventory (CDI)

Instrument name. The Children's Depression Inventory (CDI) was developed and revised in the 1970s by Maria Kovacs, Ph.D., and finalized in 1979. This instrument was developed to fulfill a need for standardized assessment tools to study depressive symptoms in juveniles.

Type of instrument. The Children's Depression Inventory is a 27-item, self-report, symptom-oriented scale. The respondent is instructed to select the one sentence for each item that best describes him or her for the preceding 2 weeks.

Use–target audience. Based on the Beck Depression Inventory-II (BDI-II) for adults, the CDI is intended for use with school-aged children and adolescents aged 6 to 17. The CDI is written at a first-grade reading level.

Multicultural. The CDI is available in English, French–Canadian, and Spanish.

Ease and time of administration. The CDI is administered individually in a variety of settings (e.g., clinical research settings, schools, psychiatric and medical pediatric settings, and other nonclinical settings); however, a number of studies report group dissemination of the CDI with no difficulties. Respondents are handed a copy of the scale to follow along as the administrator reads the CDI aloud. This assists children who may have reading or attention problems. Respondents silently mark down their answers for each item as the administrator reads aloud. A 10-item CDI Short Form provides an assessment of a child or adolescent's depressive symptoms that can be used when a quick screening device is needed or when the therapist's time with the child is limited. The CDI and the CDI Short Form generally give comparable results. Completion time is around 15 minutes for the long version and 10 minutes for the short one.

Scoring procedure. The CDI is hand scored and consists of three choices, keyed from 0 to 2 in the direction of increasing severity; total score ranges from 0 to 54. The Quikscore™ automatically transfers responses onto the scoring sheet to be easily plotted and totaled on the Profile Form. The CDI Profile presents a total score as well as five factors that have been normed according to gender and age (i.e., negative mood, interpersonal problems, ineffectiveness, anhedonia, and negative self-esteem). The CDI discriminates between those with a psychiatric diagnosis of major depressive or dysthymic disorder and those with none or other psychiatric conditions.

Reliability. The internal consistency coefficients range from .71 to .89 and the test–retest coefficients range from .74 to .83 (over an interval of 2 to 3 weeks).

Validity. Data on the CDI's validity are equivocal. Its factorial structure may differ depending on the population studied. Studies suggest that the CDI alone should not be used as a diagnostic tool. It can serve as an index of the severity of depression and as a measure of change.

Availability and source. The long and short forms of the CDI are available through Pearson Assessments. Order by phone (800) 627-7271 or by fax (800) 632-9011, or at www.pearsonassessments.com.

Comment. Like all youth self-report measures, the CDI may be more or less valid depending on the child's capacity and willingness to report internal emotional states. It is best used as a screening measure rather than as a full diagnostic assessment. Its brevity and ease of administration and scoring add to its usefulness.

Dissociation Measures

Adolescent Dissociative Experiences Scale (A-DES)

Instrument name. When compared to parents of younger children, parents of teenagers become less familiar with the details of their children's lives. Because of this, and because adolescents are better self-reporters of behavior than younger children, the utility of the CDC during adolescence is limited. The Adolescent Dissociative Experiences Scale (A-DES) was the product of a collaborative effort among a number of individuals organized by Judith Armstrong, Eve Bernstein Carlson, and Frank Putnam to develop a self-report scale to screen for pathological dissociation in teenagers (Armstrong, Putnam, Carlson, Libero, & Smith, 1997).

Type of instrument. The A-DES is a 30-item self-report screening tool for serious dissociative and posttraumatic disorders. Items are neutrally worded and generally in the present tense. The questions ask about different kinds of experiences that happen to people. The answer response format is a 0 to 10 scale, anchored at the ends with *never* (0) and *always* (10). Adolescents circle the corresponding number based on how often the experiences happen to them when they have not had drugs or alcohol.

Use–target audience. The A-DES is a self-report measure for adolescents ages 11 to 20.

Multicultural. This instrument has been translated into more than 15 European and Asian languages.

Ease and time of administration. The A-DES is a brief, 30-item adolescent self-report measure. It takes about 10 minutes to administer and score.

Scoring procedure. The A-DES is scored by summing item scores and dividing by 30 (number of items). The overall score ranges from 0 to 10. A mean score of 4 or above signifies pathological dissociation. As a rule of thumb, the A-DES score is approximately the Dissociative Experiences Scale (DES; an adult measure of dissociation; Putnam, 1997) score divided by 10.

Reliability. Psychometric data on the A-DES indicate excellent reliability (Cronbach's alpha = .93; split-half = .92).

Validity. The A-DES differentiated abused and nonabused psychiatric patients; dissociative adolescents diagnosed independently of the A-DES scored significantly higher on the A-DES than other inpatients did.

Availability and source. The A-DES is a public domain document freely available for reproduction, distribution, and use. (Readers who wish to make changes to it are asked to change the name to reduce confusion.) The complete 30-item A-DES is available in the appendix of Putnam (1997).

Comment. Because of its face validity, the A-DES depends upon the willingness of youth to report unusual feelings and internal states. It is not to be used for diagnosis but as a screening measure to be followed by a full clinical interview to assess the presence or absence of dissociation. In addition, because it is an adaptation of an adult interview, some of its components are not appropriate for adolescents. However, despite these caveats, the A-DES is a very useful instrument with adolescents, especially psychiatrically disturbed adolescents who have histories of child sexual abuse (Kisiel & Lyons, 2001).

Anxiety Measures

Multidimensional Anxiety Scale for Children (MASC)

Instrument name. The Multidimensional Anxiety Scale for Children (MASC) was developed by John March (March, 1997). The MASC was developed, in part, out of research designed to understand childhood-onset anxiety disorders. Although it is fairly new, its brevity and the range of symptoms assessed have added to its popularity.

Type of instrument. The MASC is a 39-item self-report measure designed for individuals ages 8 to 19 years. It uses a four-point format in which respondents are asked to rate each item with respect to their own experiences. These points include never true, rarely true, sometimes true, and often true. People with minimal training can utilize the MASC, although the interpretation requires some understanding of basic principles of psychological assessment. It can be computer or hand scored.

Use–target audience. The MASC is designed to be easy to administer and score. It capitalizes on the fact that most individuals completing this measure have some capacity for objective self-report.

Multicultural. The MASC has been translated into Spanish and French; however, no separate norms exist for minority children.

Ease and time of administration. The entire process of administration and scoring typically takes less than 30 minutes. The administrator is allowed to clarify instructions and questions.

Scoring procedure. The 39 items of the MASC are distributed across four basic scales. These include Physical Symptoms, Harm Avoidance, Social Anxiety, and Separation/Panic, three of which have subscales, a scale measuring total anxiety and two major indices, Anxiety Disorder and Inconsistency. A separate form, the MASC-10, is also available that can be used in special situations in which a brief assessment of general anxiety symptoms is needed. Subscales from Physical Symptoms include Tense Symptoms and Somatic Symptoms. Perfectionism and Anxious Coping are the subscales for Harm Avoidance; Humiliation Fears and Performance Fears are the subscales for social anxiety. The Inconsistency Index is useful in identifying random or careless responding, and the Anxiety Disorders Index is useful in identifying respondents who might benefit from a more detailed clinical assessment.

Reliability and validity. Various reliability indices are appropriate on the MASC including internal consistency and test–retest reliability. Confirmatory factor analysis has validated the MASC factor structure and discriminant validity has also been demonstrated. The MASC correlates well with another self-report anxiety measure.

Availability and source. The measure, manuals, and scoring information are available from MultiHealth Systems, Inc. in North Tonawanda, New York. The Web site is www.mhs.com.

Comment. The MASC is a very appropriate ancillary measure to the Trauma Symptom Checklist for Children that also assesses anxiety, although the anxiety scale from the TSCC is not as inclusive. Affective distress is common in maltreated children, and the MASC provides a much more detailed assessment of anxiety,

PROTOCOL FOR USING TESTS IN WHICH CHILD TRAUMA/ABUSE/MALTREATMENT ARE ISSUES

Because trauma, maltreatment, and abuse vary greatly in their content and their effects, no single protocol is recommended. This chapter has given information about 16 instruments without covering all that are available in this rapidly developing and exciting field of inquiry. The selection of tests will be determined by the assessment question—for example, is trauma suspected? If so, was the trauma a one-time event or repeated over time? Were there multiple traumas and stressors? Are there concerns about anxiety or depression? Was the child maltreated by a family member or by a stranger? Was there sexual assault, so that possible sexualized behaviors need to be assessed? The following are general guidelines that are then applied to a single case for illustrative purposes.

1. Select psychological tests appropriate to this child. Include self-report measures, if the child is old enough, and parent or caretaker report measures, as well as teacher report measures if possible and appropriate.
2. Depending on the circumstances for this evaluation, review confidentiality and privilege parameters with the child, the child's caretakers, and other interested parties if any.
3. Administer and score the tests.
4. Collect additional information on the child's history, circumstances, and family situation through interview, observation, clinical records, court or social service records if applicable, and collateral informants such as social workers or victim advocates if applicable.
5. Review and share the findings and your report with the child and with the child's caretakers.
6. Make recommendations for the family or other interested parties as indicated by your test findings and your interviews.

CASE EXAMPLE[1]

Background

Abby was a 10-year-old girl who was referred because she had sexually touched Calvin, a 4-year-old boy, in a daycare setting. In her 3 months in this daycare, she had inserted herself into a parental role and frequently helped out with serving snacks, getting children packed up when parents arrived, and helping two younger children with toileting. One of these was Calvin, the 4-year-old boy who had reported being sexually touched during toileting.

Abby was adopted at the age of 4. She lived with her adoptive parents and had a 17-year-old sister, the biological daughter of her parents. Her postadoption adjustment was characterized as uneventful, and she had never been identified as a behavior problem. For example, her grades in school were typically above average. Her preadoptive experiences included neglect and physical abuse; sexual abuse had never been confirmed although it was expected, given her rearing circumstances.

Betsy, the adoptive mother, was interviewed and reported that Abby had exhibited a 9- to 12-month history of greater sexual interest and genital touching after the adoption, but this had faded before she entered kindergarten. More recently, she had started talking about boyfriends, and Betsy felt that Abby had a longstanding problem of being overly friendly with adult males. However, this has never presented as a problem. She also wondered if the interest in boyfriends paralleled her 17-year-old daughter's having a boyfriend.

---

1. Case example from William N. Friedrich, Mayo Clinic.

Betsy also reported that she and her husband were in marital therapy and most likely would be separating. Her return to full-time employment was in response to this likelihood and was the reason Abby was now in after-school daycare. She agreed that Abby had a very helpful side to her and thought this varied directly with her anxiety.

Betsy wondered whether Abby was adversely affected by the upsurge in family tension over the previous 6 months. She also was concerned about Calvin, the 4-year-old boy, whom she knew from having observed him at the daycare. Betsy described a number of incidents suggesting that he was an aggressive and provocative child. It was her opinion that Abby was in a vulnerable position with him and regretted that the two had been together unsupervised in the bathroom.

At the end of this first meeting, Betsy completed the Child Behavior Checklist, the Parenting Stress Index-Short Form, the Child Sexual Behavior Inventory, and the Parent–Child Conflict Tactics Scale. These measures provided an overview of her generic and more specific behaviors as well as the family context (Step 1 and Step 3). She signed a release to have Abby's teacher complete a Teacher Report Form, which was modified to include three additional sexual items: Plays With Sex Parts in Public, Sex Play With Peers, and Sex Problems (describe) (Friedrich, 1997). Betsy also agreed to ask the daycare provider to complete a Child Behavior Checklist and CSBI on Abby (Step 4).

Abby was very subdued on the first meeting and exhibited some separation anxiety in the waiting area, which persisted into the first few minutes of the interview. She was informed of the purpose of the visit and was told that the interviewer would share "important stuff" with her mother (Step 2). She had little recollection of her preadoptive life, although she had been told that she was hospitalized once as a baby for not gaining weight. She liked school and wanted to be a teacher when she grew up. She identified her best friend as a 7-year-old girl in the neighborhood.

She was highly uncomfortable speaking about the incident with Calvin and flushed and squirmed in the chair during this portion of the interview. She agreed that she had touched Calvin's penis three times and volunteered that he had asked her to touch him the first time and that his penis "grew bigger when I touched it." He asked to see her "privates," but she only showed them to him "once." She felt "funny" when this happened, but was able to elaborate after looking over a feelings poster that she had felt "scared," "excited," "ashamed," and "anxious." She knew it was "wrong," and assured the interviewer that it would never happen again because "Calvin can use the bathroom himself." She completed the MASC, CDI, and TSCC after agreeing to the interviewer's request that she read each item carefully and answer "honestly" (Step 3).

Parent–Caregiver Reports

Betsy's responses to the Child Behavior Checklist suggested social competence scores within normal limits, including Social, a subscale measuring relationships with friends. Two clinical elevations were noted, one on Anxious/Depression ($T = 66$) and also on Withdrawal ($T = 65$). She endorsed such items as "cries," "nervous," "fearful," "guilty," and "self-conscious" for Anxious/Depressed and "secretive," "shy," and "withdrawn" for Withdrawal. She endorsed four items on the Child Sexual Behavior Inventory. These were "stands too close to others," "overly friendly with men they don't know well," "touches another child's sex parts," and "interested in the opposite sex." This translated into T scores of 67 on total sexual behavior, 71 on developmentally related sexual behavior, and 60 on sexual abuse-specific items. On the Parenting Stress Index—Short Form, she answered validly and nondefensively, with her defensive responding score at the 45th percentile. Scores ranged from 15% on Parental Distress, 51% on Parent–Child Dysfunctional Interaction, and 44% on Difficult Child, resulting in a total stress score at the 40th percentile. Finally, she reported primarily positive parenting strategies on the Conflict Tactic Scale, for example, use of time out and positive reinforcement, but also admitted to occasional shouting and slapping on the hand.

Further support for the accuracy of Betsy's perceptions of Abby comes from the Teacher Report Form completed by Abby's fifth-grade teacher. Adaptive Functioning scores were in the normal range. Clinical scales were also in the normal range with the exception of a mild elevation on Withdrawn ($T = 63$). The teacher did not endorse any of the three sexual behavior items.

The daycare provider had only known Abby for 3 months. Consequently, she was less sure of many items on Social Competence. However, she did not report any clinical problems. On the Child Sexual Behavior Inventory, she endorsed two of the four items that Betsy had endorsed: "stands too close to others" and "touches another child's sexual parts." This translated into a Total Sexual Behavior of $T = 52$, $T = 45$ for Developmentally Related Sexual Behavior, and $T = 45$ for Sexual Abuse-Specific Items. At the bottom of the measure, she wrote that if she had rated Calvin, she would have endorsed 15 to 20 items. This comment suggested that Calvin was far more sexually focused than was Abby.

Child Report

Abby did report a clinically significant elevation ($T = 67$) on Social Anxiety from the MASC, with a secondary elevation on Humiliation/Rejection, a subscale from that domain. A sample item from Humiliation/Rejection is "I'm afraid other people will think I'm stupid." However, she did not report significant levels of Physical Symptoms or Harm Avoidance, and her MASC total score was $T = 57$.

On the Child Depression Inventory, she was clinically elevated on Negative Self-Esteem ($T = 68$), for example, "I do not like myself," and Interpersonal Problems ($T = 67$), for example, "I am bad many times." On the Trauma Symptom Checklist for Children, she answered validly and most T scores were in the 52 to 58 range, with the exception of Sexual Concerns ($T = 72$) and the related subscale, Sexual Distress ($T = 87$).

Summary

The parents were informed at a follow-up session that their ratings of their daughter as well as other caregiver ratings of Abby's general behavior suggested a girl who felt less sure with peers and responded with some withdrawal (Step 5). She also tended to be more anxious and emotional than average. Some of her sexual behaviors were more specific to the incident with Calvin but others suggested a needy girl whose interpersonal boundaries needed shoring up. Her adoptive mother did not report Abby to be overly challenging to her parent; she described her in a generally positive tone, and she generally employed very appropriate discipline techniques.

It is not very common, but always heartening, to see overlap between parent and child reports. Abby reported a significant level of peer insecurity and feelings of badness. When questioned, the negative self-esteem items from the Child Depression Inventory were related to her behavior with Calvin and suggested some elevation in shame. In addition, her report of elevated sexual concerns was appropriate to the situation and reflected a girl who was not denying her vulnerability in this domain. The fact that other trauma-related scales from the TSCC were not elevated was also positive and in keeping with her report that she remembered very little of her life prior to her adoption.

Recommendations

These test data allowed the clinician to suggest to Abby's parents that Abby's preference for caretaking and befriending younger children put her in a vulnerable situation with a provocative and sexualized boy (Step 6). Her adoptive parents' potential separation and divorce most likely added to her behavioral reactivity. Treatment suggestions included a greater focus on developing peer relations via play dates (Frankel & Wetmore, 1996), helping Abby see herself more accurately and with less shame, and increasing overall positive parent–child interactions (Hembree–Kigin & McNeil, 1995). In addition, Betsy and her husband were requested to work even harder on providing reassurances to Abby about her continued well being despite their problems.

CONCLUSION AND RECOMMENDATIONS

The evaluation of traumatized or maltreated children is made complex by several factors:

- These evaluations often have forensic implications.
- The evaluation target can be very elusive, not only because of "sleeper effects," but also because no one psychological diagnosis or syndrome type is associated with maltreatment.
- Maltreated children who are evaluated are often quite guarded about what they reveal and frequently are less capable of accurately talking about their feelings than children from nonabusive households.
- Maltreatment often occurs in deleterious contexts that have their own pernicious effects on the developing child. For example, it is very difficult to sort out the effects of poverty versus the effects of physical abuse, and to attempt to do so is contraindicated. Rather, the evaluator needs to know the child's context and spell it out clearly as part of the evaluation.
- Psychologists trained in traditional assessment need to learn an entirely new set of assessment strategies for abused or traumatized children than are typically taught in graduate school and used in clinical practice.
- Evaluators need to know how PTSD may superficially overlap with many other diagnoses that can be less precise in describing the child's functioning, such as anxiety, disruptive behavior, and mood instability.

The assessment of the abused child should include objective measures that assess the more common symptoms associated with maltreatment. In addition, maltreatment occurs in a context, and the assessment of the parent's potential for further abuse (if the parent was the abuser) or parental perceptions of the child, are as important as the input parents provide on behavior rating scales. This chapter has compiled some of the most commonly used and valid tools in this area. It is also very important to remember that psychological assessment in abuse cases may be initiated as a clinical activity but that legal issues are also operative and the evaluator may need to testify, even when the case did not start out as a forensic case.

Use and Misuse of tests

Child Custody Evaluations

This is one arena in which maltreatment allegations are often raised. Psychologists asked to conduct these evaluations need to keep in mind that these evaluations can be profoundly difficult to accomplish. Any prejudices about the psychological features of parents involved in custody disputes need to be

TABLE 10.1 Matrix: Child Abuse and Family Assessment Strategies and Inventories

Assessment intrument	Specific applications	Cultural/ language	Instructions/use: T = time to take; S = time to score; I = items	Computerized: a = scoring; b = report	Reliability (R); validity (V)	Availability
Child Behavior Checklist (CBCL)	For children living in the home, ages 18 months to 18 years; to assess a broad range of internalizing and externalizing symptoms	Translated into over 30 languages, including several versions of Spanish; used throughout the world	T = 10–20 min; S = +1 min; I = 100 or 118	a = yes; b = yes	R = excellent test–retest = .75–97; good interparent agreement V = very good construct	Dr. Achenbach, Center for Children, Youth and Families, University of Vermont in Burlington, 05401 www.aseba.org
Child Sexual Behavior Inventory (CSBI)	For children 2–12; assesses sexual behaviors exhibited over preceding 6 months	Spanish; German; French; Dutch	T = 5–10 min; S = 5 min; I = 38	a = no; b = no	R = excellent test–retest = .85; Cronbach's alpha = .72–.92; V = good convergent and divergent	PAR, Odessa, FL: (800) 331-TEST or www.parinc.com
Child Dissociative Checklist (CDC)	A dissociation screening measure for children aged 5–14	Spanish and other languages	T = 5–10 min; S = 5–10 min; I = 20	a = no; b = no	R = moderate to good 1-year test–retest stability (r = .65); Cronbach's alpha = .86; V = good convergent and divergent	Public domain— freely available for reproducing, distribution, use; available in appendix Putnam (1997)
Pediatric Emotional Distress Scale (PEDS)	2–10 year olds traumatized by homelessness, sexual abuse, natural disasters, and other negative experiences	Has been examined for homeless children; not yet tested on wide variety of cultural groups	T = 5–10 min; S = 5–10 min; I = 21		R = IC: .85 total; IR: .65 total; TR: 56 total	Journal article

Instrument	Description	Norms/Usage	a/b	Administration	Reliability/Validity	Source
Abidin Parenting Stress Index (PSI)	Preteen children presenting for treatment because of behavioral and emotional disorders; to identify behavior problems in child and other dimensions of parenting	Validated in variety of U.S. samples; Chinese, Italian, Portuguese, Latin American, Hispanic, and French–Canadian.	a = yes; b = yes	T = 20–30 min; S = 10 min; I = 120	R = acceptable test–retest .63–.96; Cronbach's alpha = .70–.84; V = moderate to excellent validity across samples	Psychological Assessment Resources, Odessa, FL, (800) 331-TEST or www.parinc.com
Milner Child Abuse Potential Inventory (CAPI) (3rd ed.)	Intended to be used as a screening tool for detection of physical child abuse; also used as psychological test	Norms for U.S. and Spain; translated into other languages; research finds constructs present in other cultures	a = yes; b = no	T = 12–20 min; S = 20 min; I = 77	R = split half = .96; alpha = .93; test–retest = .71–.92; V = excellent divergent and construct	Available from PSYTEC, Inc., PO Box 564, DeKalb, IL, 60115
Parent Child Conflict Tactics Scale (PCCTS)	For parents of children living in the home, ages 6–17; assess nonviolent discipline, psychological aggression, and physical assault	Research reveals no clear differences between Euro–American and either African–American or Hispanic–American parents	a = no; b = no	T — 6–8 min; S = 8 min; I = 22–36	R = Cronbach's alpha = .58–.68; test–retest = .80; V = moderate to excellent construct validity	Family Research Laboratory, University of New Hampshire
Trauma Symptom Checklist for Children (TSCC)	Children ages 8–16; assesses broad range of trauma-related symptoms	Used in many countries and available in many languages; English and Spanish only versions available from publisher	a = yes; b = yes	T = 15–20 min; S = 10; I = 54	R = IC: .89 total; TR: N/R; V = conv: .75–.82 subscales; disc: sexually abused/nonabused	Psychological Assessment Resources, Odessa, FL, (800) 331-TEST or www.parinc.com

TABLE 10.1 (Continued). Matrix: Child Abuse and Family Assessment Strategies and Inventories

Assessment intrument	Specific applications	Cultural/ language	Instructions/use: T = time to take; S = time to score; I = items	Computerized: a = scoring; b = report	Reliability (R); validity (V)	Availability
Children's PTSD Reaction Index (CPTS-RI)	Children aged 7–18; to assess symptoms following exposure to trauma	Translated into several languages; has been used in Armenia, Kuwait, Cambodia, and U.S.	T = 20–45 min; S = 20–45 min; I = 27—traumatic exposure section: 20 (child); 21 (parent); 22 (adolescent); PTSD symptoms section	a = no; b = no	R = IC: .69–.80; IR: .88 total; TR: .93 over 1 week; V = conv: .29–.91	Not commercially available, but may be obtained from Trauma Psychiatry Service, UCLA
Children's Impact of Traumatic Events Scale Revised (CITES-R)	Sex abuse victims, 6–18; assesses PTS symptoms, eroticism, perceptions of support following disclosure, and abuse attributions	Caucasian and African American U.S. populations but not widely elsewhere	T = 20–40 min; S = 5–10 min; I = 78	a = no; b = no	R = IC: = .56–.91; V = poor to moderate	No manual; Vicki Veitch Wolfe, Children's Hospital of Western Ontario, 800 Commissioners Rd., E., London, Ontario, Canada, N6A 5C2 or http://www.uwo.ca
Impact of Events Scale (IES)	Adults, and children ages 8–18; can be used for immediate aftermath of mass catastrophes as well as individual traumas	Translated into many languages; has been applied to adolescents from various cultures	T = 10 min; S = 10 min; I = 15	a = no; b = no	R = alpha of .79 and .82; split-half reliability = .86; V = discriminates traumatized groups from nontraumatized groups	Journal article

Instrument	Description	Notes	Administration	Norms	Reliability/Validity	Source
Children's Reaction to Traumatic Events Scale (CRTES)	Ages 8–12		T = 5 min; S = 5 min; I = 15	a = no; b = no	Preliminary data are promising	http:// www.criminology.unimelb.edu.au/victims/resources/assessment/assessment.html Children's PTSD-Reaction Index
Beck Depression Inventory-II (BDI-II)	Adolescents; screening instrument to assess intensity of depressive episode	Nationality, ethnicity, and gender affect cut-off scores	T = 5; S = 5; I = 21	a = no; b = no	R = .86–.93; V = excellent content validity; concurrent validity studies: .65–.77	Center for Cognitive Therapy
Children's Depression Inventory	6–17 Years old; to study depressive symptoms in juveniles	English; French-Canadian; Spanish	T = 10–15 min; S = 5; I = 27 (10 short form)	a = no; b = no	R = IC: .71–.89; test-retest coefficients: .74 –.83 (2–3 weeks); V = equivocal	Pearson Assessments, (800) 627-7271, fax (800) 632-9011, or www.pearsonassessments.com
Multidimensional Anxiety Scale for Children (MASC)	8–19 years; MASC provides more detailed assessment of anxiety, if any indication of disorder based on CBCL or TSCC	Translated into Spanish and French	T = 15 min; S = 30 min; I = 39	a = no; b = no	Various reliability indices are appropriate on MASC, including internal consistency and test–retest reliability; confirmatory factor analysis validated MASC factor structure and discriminant validity also demonstrated	Multi-Health Systems, Inc., North Tonawanda, New York, www.mhs.com
Adolescent Dissociative Experiences Scale (A-DES)	Ages 11–20; screening tool for serious dissociative and posttraumatic disorders	Translated into more than 15 Asian and European languages	T = 10–15 min.; S = 5; I = 30	a = no; b = no	R = Cronbach's alpha = .93; split-half = .92; V = face validity	Journal article

set aside. The overwhelming majority (85 to 90%) of divorcing parents with minor children settle custody without a dispute that requires professional evaluation. Custody disputes indicate that something is wrong, and it is simplistic to reflexively believe that both parents have a character disorder and are simply using the children as bargaining chips.

There is research indication that when one parent fights for custody, that parent knows or suspects that something is wrong with the other parent—something that will put the children at risk if they spend time alone with this parent (Bancroft & Silverman, 2003; Joffe, Leman, & Poisson, 2003). Throughout the marriage, the divorcing parent, who may have buffered the children from intermittent psychotic episodes, drinking binges, battering, emotional abuse, or child physical or sexual abuse by the other parent, has now given up on the marriage, and then learns that the courts refuse to buffer the children as the parent once did. Parents have been known to return to abusive partners rather than to turn their children over to the mercies of the domestic court system. Psychologists who evaluate only one parent when custody issues are on the table are doing a disservice to the entire case. In addition, physical abuse, partner battering, and child sexual abuse are crimes to be investigated and adjudicated. They are not marital squabbles to be evaluated and mediated in domestic relations courts. Psychologists are not detectives; they must be aware of their roles and the limitations of their scope of practice when these issues arise.

Cautions Against Overly Simplistic Interpretation

Psychological tests cannot be used to definitively determine: (a) if a child has been abused; (b) if a parent will abuse again; (c) if abuse is the sole cause of the child's symptoms; and (d) if a parent is a batterer or a sexual perpetrator. Many abused children are asymptomatic; abuse is an act and not a diagnosis, and the impact can be extremely variable. Many batterers and sexual abusers appear psychologically normal when evaluated.

Group data are used to establish norms for the measures suggested in this chapter, but each case must be interpreted in the context of the child's history and culture. For example, an abused child who scores low on a test of sexual behavior may or may not have a sexual abuse history. The same is true if a child scores high on this same measure. In addition, the child who scores low may score low for a number of reasons. For example, the child: (a) may truly not have sexual behavior problems; (b) may have sexual behavior problems but have a parent who does not report them because this parent is protective of a spouse; (c) may have sexual behavior problems but have a parent who does not report them because this parent is a poor observer; or (d) may have more subtle sexual behavior problems that are likely to cause future problems but do not show up in terms of current overt behavior.

Similar problems occur with PTSD. Follow-up interviewing as well as an appreciation of the child's context is critical to determining if a child has PTSD after scoring low or high on a structured PTSD protocol. Some children deny some PTSD symptoms simply because they are so bothered by any reminders that they deny all symptoms related to the event in question.

Abuse cases are complex, and evaluators may respond to this complexity by seeking simplicity, for example, accepting as true the ancient prejudice that children routinely lie. All evaluators need to examine their attitudes and practices and look for evidence that they are objective and capable of recognizing abuse when it exists. If that is not possible, then they should practice in another assessment field.

Parent–Child Relationship

The parent–child relationship is critical to the child's short- and long-term adjustment. This assessment framework borrows from attachment theory but does not specifically assess attachment because no instruments or structured interview protocols currently evaluate attachment. However, the PCCTS and the PSI can be used to evaluate the strength and quality of a parent's relationship with a child, and thus indirectly speak to the security of attachment. Reports of overly harsh parenting, whether emotional or physical, certainly imply insecure attachment because attachment is compromised in over 95% of cases in which maltreatment is present (Cicchetti & Toth, 1995). It is likely that an elevated score on the Difficult Child subscale of the PSI will validate the PCCTS data. It is relatively safe to say that PCCTS reports of emotional and/or physical abuse, in combination with the Difficult Child elevation, are consistent with parental rejection and insecure attachment. Elevated scores by the parent on the Beck Depression Inventory suggest an acute reaction to the child's victimization, have another immediate source, or may reflect chronic depression. It is important to assess the degree to which parental depression interrupts the parent's ability to be supportive, but parental depression generally interferes with attachment security.

Assessment and Treatment Planning

Assessment results must be relevant to therapy to justify the use of screening measures and tests. The first step is to view assessment and treatment as seamlessly connected. Assessment measures should prepare the child for therapy by outlining which issues are important. These same measures can be transported into therapy and used as a basis for early sessions, at least with some children. For example, cognitive distortions expressed on the CITES-R can lead to CBT-based interventions.

Another example of the interplay between assessment and treatment is the conundrum of what the treatment targets identified are and how they should be addressed. For example, PCCTS data suggesting frequent parental threats to kick the child out of the house need to be addressed before the therapist can expect much success in the individual treatment of abuse-related distress.

Therapists can also benefit from input from the evaluator regarding the child's ability to be open and nondefensive. Severe abuse that is not accompanied by the child reporting distress on at least some of the TSCC subscales, for example, raises concerns about the child's perceptions of how safe it is to be open about his or her emotions. A child's lack of self-disclosure can be caused by other situations, such as cultural constraints or dissociation, but lack of permission to talk about the abuse is one strong possibility that needs to be clarified early in the treatment process.

Finally, the field of therapy for maltreated children moves forward if clinicians learn what works. Therapists are strongly encouraged to readminister some of the measures at intervals throughout therapy, at the conclusion of therapy, and after time has elapsed, in order to learn which children seem to get better and which do not and in this way inform their practices.

REFERENCES

Abidin, R. R. (1995). *Parenting Stress Index* (3rd ed.): *Professional manual*. Odessa, Florida: Psychological Assessment Resources.

Abidin, R. (1998). Parenting stress index (PSI) (3rd ed.). In *Catalogue*. Odessa, FL: Psychological Assessment Resources.

Achenbach, T. M. (1991a). *Manual for the Child Behavior Checklist/4-18 and 1991 Profile*. Burlington, VT: University of Vermont Department of Psychiatry.

Achenbach, T. M. (1991b). *Manual for the Teacher's Report Form and 1991 Profile*. Burlington, VT: University of Vermont Department of Psychiatry.

Achenbach, T. M. (1991c). *Manual for the Youth Self-Report and 1991 Profile*. Burlington, VT: University of Vermont Department of Psychiatry.

Achenbach, T. M. (2001). *Child Behavior Checklist for Ages 6–18*. Burlington, VT: University of Vermont Department of Psychiatry.

Achenbach, T. M., & Rescorla, L. (2000). *Child Behavior Checklist for Ages 1½ to 5*. Burlington, VT: University of Vermont Department of Psychiatry.

American Academy of Child and Adolescent Psychiatry. (1998). Practice parameters for the assessment of children and adolescents with posttraumatic stress disorder. *Journal of the American Academy of Child and Adolescent Psychiatry, 37* (Suppl. 10), 4–26.

American Psychiatric Association. (1980). *Diagnostic and statistical manual of mental disorders*, (3rd ed.). Washington, D.C.: American Psychiatric Association.

American Psychiatric Association. (1994). *Diagnostic and statistical manual of mental disorders*, (4th ed.). Washington, D.C.: American Psychiatric Association.

Armstrong, J. G., Putnam, F. W., Carlson, E. B., Libero, D. Z., & Smith, S. R. (1997). Development and validation of a measure of adolescent dissociation: The Adolescent Dissociative Experiences Scale. *Journal of Nervous Mental Disorders, 185*, 491–497.

Bancroft, L., & Silverman, J. G. (2003). *The batterer as parent: Addressing the impact of domestic violence on family dynamics*. Thousand Oaks, CA: Sage.

Beck, A. T. (1996). *Beck Depression Inventory-II*. San Antonio, TX: Psychological Corporation.

Briere, J. (1996). *Trauma Symptom Checklist for Children* (TSCC), *professional manual*. Odessa, FL: Psychological Assessment Resources.

Briere, J. (1997). *Psychological assessment of adult posttraumatic states*. Washington, D.C.: American Psychological Association.

Carlson, E. B. (1997). *Trauma assessments: A clinician's guide*. New York: The Guilford Press.

Chaffin, M., & Shultz, S. K. (2001). Psychometric evaluation of the children's impact of traumatic events scale-revised. *Child Abuse and Neglect, 25*(3), 401–412.

Cicchetti, D., & Toth, S. L. (1995). A developmental psychopathology perspective on child abuse and neglect. *Journal of the American Academy of Child and Adolescent Psychiatry, 34*, 541–565.

Crouch, J. L., Smith, D. W., Ezzell, C. E., & Saunders, B. E. (1999). Measuring reactions to sexual trauma among children: Comparing the Children's Impact of Traumatic Events Scale and the Trauma Symptom Checklist for Children. *Child Maltreatment, 4*, 255–263.

De Bellis, M. D., Keshavan, M. S., Clark, D. B., Giedd, J. N., Boring, A. M., Frustaci, K., & Ryan, N. D. (1999). Developmental traumatology, part II: Brain development. *Biological Psychiatry, 45*, 1259–1284.

Devilly, G. J. (2001). Assessment devices. Retrieved September, 2003, from The University of Melbourne, Forensic Psychology & Victim Services Web site: http://www.criminology.unimelb.edu.au/victims/resources/assessment/assessment.html. Children's PTSD-Reaction Index

Frankel, F. (1996). *Good friends are hard to find*. Los Angeles: Prespective Press.

Friedrich, W. N. (1997). *Child Sexual Behavior Inventory*. Odessa, FL: Psychological Assessment Resources.

Friedrich, W. N. (2002). *Psychological assessment of sexually abused children and their families*. Thousand Oaks, CA: Sage.

Friedrich, W. N., & Reams, R. A. (1986). *Parentification of Children Scale*. Unpublished manuscript. (Available: W. N. Friedrich, Mayo Clinic, Rochester, Minnesota, 55905).

Friedrich, W. N., Lysne, M., Sim, L., & Shames, S. (under review). Adolescent Sexual Behavior Inventory: Reliability and validity.

Gold, S., Lucenko, B., Elhai, J., Swingle, J., & Sellers, A. (1999). A comparison of psychological/ psychiatric symptomatology of women and men sexually abused as children. *Child Abuse and Neglect, 23*, 683–692.

Gomez–Schwartz, B., Horowitz, J. M., & Cardarelli, A. P. (1990). *Child sexual abuse: The initial effects*. Newbury Park, CA: Sage Publications.

Hamby, S. L., & Finkelhor, D. (March, 2001). Choosing and using victimization questionnaires. Bulletin. Washington, D.C.: U.S. Department of Justice, Office of Justice Programs, Office of Juvenile Justice and Delinquency Prevention.

Hembree–Kigin, T., & McNeil, C. B. (1995). *Parent–child interaction therapy*. New York: Plenum Publishers.

Herman, J. L. (1992). *Trauma and recovery: The aftermath of violence—From domestic violence to political terror*. New York: Basic Books.

Herman, J. L. (1997). *Trauma and recovery: The aftermath of violence—From domestic violence to political terror*. New York: Basic Books.

Horowitz, M. J., Wilner, N., & Alvarez, W. (1979). Impact of Event Scale: A measure of subjective stress. *Psychosomatic Medicine, 41*, 209–218.

Jaffe, P. G., Lemon, N. K. D., & Poisson, S. E. (2003). *Child custody and domestic violence*. Thousand Oaks, CA: Sage.

Kendall–Tackett, K. A., Williams, L. M., & Finkelhor, D. (1993). Impact of sexual abuse on children: A review and synthesis of recent empirical studies. *Psychological Bulletin, 113*, 164–180.

Kisiel, C. L., & Lyons, J. S. (2001). Dissociation as a mediator of psychopathology among sexually abused children and adolescents. *American Journal of Psychiatry; 158*:7, 1034–1039.

Koenen, K. C., Moffitt, T. E., Caspi, A., Taylor, A., & Purcell, S. (2003). Domestic violence is associated with environmental suppression of IQ in young children. *Development and Psychopathology, 15*, 297–311.

Kolko, D. J., & Swenson, C. C. (2002). *Assessing and treating physically abused children and their families: A cognitive–behavioral approach.* Thousand Oaks, CA: Sage.

Kovacs, M. (1992). *Children's Depression Inventory.* Minneapolis: National Computer Systems.

Lengua, L., Sadowski, C. M., Friedrich, W. N., & Fisher, J. (2001). Confirmatory factor analysis of the Child Behavior Checklist. *Journal of Consulting and Clinical Psychology, 69*, 683–698

March, J. (1997). *Multidimensional Anxiety Scale for Children: Technical manual.* North Tonawanda, NY: MultiHealth Systems, Inc.

Milner, J. S. (1986). *The Child Abuse Potential Inventory: Manual* (2nd ed.). DeKalb, IL: Psytec.

Myers, K. M., & Winters, N. C. (2002a). Ten-year review of rating scales, I: Overview of scale functioning, psychometric properties, and selection. *Journal of the American Academy of Child & Adolescent Psychiatry, 41*, 114–122.

Myers, K. M., & Winters, N. C. (2002b). Ten-year review of rating scales, II: Scale for internalizing disorders. *Journal of the American Academy of Child & Adolescent Psychiatry, 41*, 634–659.

Nader, K. O., Kriegler, J. A., Blake, D. D., Pynoos, R. S., Newman, E., & Weather, F. (2002). The Clinician-Administered PTSD Scale, Child and Adolescent Version (CAPS-C). Available from Kathleen Nader, DSW, 2809 Rathlin Drive, Suite 102, Cedar Park, TX 78613; or from National Center for PTSD, White River Junction, VT (www.ncptsd.org).

Ohan, J. L., Myers, K., & Collett, B. R. (2002). Ten-year review of rating scales IV: Scales assessing trauma and its effects. *Journal of the American Academy of Child and Adolescent Psychiatry, 41*(12), 1401–1422.

Olafson, E. (1999). Using testing when family violence and child abuse are issues. In A. R. Nurse (Ed.), *Psychological testing with families* (pp. 230–256). New York: John Wiley & Sons.

Olafson, E. & Boat, B. (2000). Long-term management of the sexually abused child: Considerations and challenges. In R. M. Reece (Ed.), *The treatment of child abuse* (pp. 14–35). Baltimore: Johns Hopkins University Press.

Pelcovitz, D., van der Kolk, B., Roth, S., Mandel, F., Kaplan, S., & Resick, P. (1997). Development of a criteria set and a structured interview for disorders of extreme stress (SIDESNOS). *Journal of Traumatic Stress, 10*, 3–16.

Putnam, F. W. (1997). *Dissociation in children and adolescents: A developmental perspective.* New York: Guilford.

Putnam, F. W. (2003). Ten-year research review update: Child sexual abuse. *Journal of the American Academy of Child and Adolescent Psychiatry, 42*(3), 269–278.

Putnam, F. W., & Peterson, G. (1994). Further validation of the Child Dissociative Checklist. *Dissociation, 7*, 204–211

Putnam, F., & Trickett, P. (1997). The psychological effects of sexual abuse: A longitudinal study. *Annals of New York Academy of Science, 821*, 150–159.

Putnam, F. W., Helmers, K., Horowitz, L.A., & Trickett, P.K. (1994). Hypnotizability and dissociativity in sexually abused girls. *Child Abuse and Neglect, 19*, 645–655.

Putnam, F. W., Helmers, K., & Trickett, P.K. (1993). Development, reliability and validity of a child dissociation scale. *Child Abuse & Neglect, 17*, 645–655.

Pynoos, R. S., Frederick, C., Nader, K. et al. (1987). Life threat and posttraumatic stress in school-age children. *Archives of General Psychiatry, 44*, 1057–1063.

Reece, R. M. (Ed) (2000). *Treatment of child abuse: Common ground for mental health, medical, and legal practitioners.* Baltimore, MD: Johns Hopkins University Press.

Saigh, P. A. (2002). *The Children's Post Traumatic Stress Disorder Inventory (CPTSD-I).* Available from Phillip A. Saigh, Ph.D., Department of Educational Psychology, Graduate Center, City University of New York, 365 Fifth Avenue, New York, NY, 10016.

Salter, A. C. (2003). *Pedophiles, rapists, and other sex offenders: Who they are, how they operate, and how we can protect ourselves and our children.* New York: Basic Books.

Saylor, C. F., Swenson, C. C., Reynolds, S. S., & Taylor, M. (1999). The Pediatric Emotional Distress Scale: A brief screening measure for young children exposed to traumatic events. *Journal of Clinical Child Psychology, 28,* 70–81.

Sebre, S., Sprugevica, I., Novotni, A., Bonevski, D., Pakalniskiene, V., Popesku, D., Turchina, T., Friedrich, W., & Lewis, O. (in press). Incidence of child-reported emotional and physical abuse: Cross-cultural comparisons of rates, risk factors, and psychosocial symptoms. *Child Abuse and Neglect.*

Sim, L., Friedrich, W. N.,, Lengua, L., Fisher, J., Davies, W. H., Pithers, W., & Trentham, B. (in press). Parent report of PTSD and Dissociation Symptoms: Normative, psychiatric, and sexual abuse comparisons. *Journal of Traumatic Stress.*

Straus, M. A., Hamby, S. L., Finkelhor, D., Moore, D. W., & Runyan, D. (1998). Identification of child maltreatment with the parent–child conflict scales: Development of psychometric data for a national sample of American parent. *Child Abuse and Neglect, 22,* 249–270.

Thaber, A. A. M., & Vostanis, P. (1999). Post-traumatic stress reactions in children of war. *Journal of Child Psychology & Psychiatry, 40,* 385–391.

Trickett, P., Noll, J., Reiffman, A., & Putnam, F. (2001). Variants of intrafamilial sexual abuse experiences: Implications for short- and long-term development. *Developmental Psychopathology, 13,* 1001–1019.

Valera, E. M., & Berenbaum, H. (2003). Brain injury in battered women. *Journal of Consulting and Clinical Psychology, 71,* 797–804.

Weiss, D. (2002). *The Impact of Events Scale-Revised.* Available from Daniel Weiss, PhD, Department of Psychiatry, University of California at San Francisco, CA, 94143-0984.

Weiss, D. S., & Marmar, C. R. (1997). The Impact of Event Scales-Revised. In J. P. Wilson & T. M. Keane (Eds.), *Assessing psychological trauma and PTSD* (pp. 399–411). New York: Guilford.

Wilson, J. P., & Keane, T. M. (Eds.). (1997). *Assessing psychological trauma and PTSD.* New York: The Guilford Press.

Whiffen, V. & Clark, S. (1997). Does victimization account for sex differences in depressive symptoms? *British Journal of Clinical Psychology, 36,* 185–193.

Wolfe, V. V., Gentile, C., Michienzi, T., Sas, L., & Wolfe, D. A. (1991). The Children's Impact of Traumatic Events Scale: A measure of post-sexual abuse PTSD symptoms. *Behavioral Assessment, 13*(4), 359–383.

Wolfe, V. V., Gentile, C., & Wolfe, D. A. (1989). The impact of sexual abuse on children: A PTSD formulation. *Behavior Therapy, 20,* 215–228.

PART IV

Postscript and Future Prospects

CHAPTER 11

Couple and Family Assessment
Current and Future Prospects

LUCIANO L'ABATE

INTRODUCTION

In many ways this is not a typical chapter that readers encounter in textbooks, handbooks, or reference books. This chapter offers a critical review of the previous chapters and then sketches some future prospects for assessment and evaluation of couples and families. The review is decidedly critical and, some might say, even iconoclastic—if not heretical—of the current assessment. The chapter author challenged the contributors of the previous chapters to respond to his observations and assertions. These replies and the author's response to them round out this discussion.

THE CURRENT STATE OF ASSESSMENT METHODS IN COUPLES AND FAMILIES

All the chapters in this book illustrate an incredibly vast, if not bewildering, array of well-documented approaches to assess and evaluate couples and families: qualitative strategies and structured interviews (chapter 3); individually oriented tests (chapter 4); observational methods and rating scales (chapter 5); outcome measures (chapter 6); and inventories for couples (chapter 7), families (chapter 8), or specific situations like child custody and divorce assessment (chapter 9) or child abuse and family violence (chapter 10). They represent the result of years of painstaking work by the constructors of these approaches and by those who have validated them in the clinic and in the laboratory.

In addition to their strong clinical and laboratory validations, these approaches share some common characteristics worth highlighting in view of this chapter's forthcoming thesis: (a) tenuous, if not nonexistent, connection with a theory or theoretical models; and (b) inadequate, if not nonexistent, links between results of assessment and evaluation (the two processes are not synonymous) and the type of intervention seemingly applied from those results. Let us take each characteristic and dismantle it.

INADEQUATE LINKS WITH THEORY OR THEORETICAL MODELS

Most, if not all, of these approaches are disconnected from theory. With the exception of chapter 4, chapter 5, chapter 7, and chapter 8, the skeptical reader may look back at the references in these chapters to verify whether this conclusion is warranted or valid. At best, these approaches may be related to some undefined theoretical model, but this commentator failed to find that.

Along with segments of chapter 4, chapter 6, and chapter 7, Hampson and Beavers (chapter 5) stand out as one of the three exceptions to the foregoing generalization by including model-derived or model-related instruments, that is, the MCMI-III is based on Millon's empirically derived personology theory. However, one model does not a theory make. If one were to conceive of a theory as a framework that includes a variety of models, then chapter 5 is a series of apparently independent but probably overlapping models. If that is the case, what are the correlations among all these disparate models? How can one select one model over the others? Are some underlying dimensions common to all these models?

Bagarozzi (chapter 7) indicates how separateness–connectedness may be such an underlying dimension, including attachment as the underlying theoretical basis for such a dimension. Yet, evaluative instruments based on attachment theory (Bartholomew & Perlman, 1994) that have been validated in over 1,000 studies around the globe with individuals and couples are singularly absent from the chapters in this book. This omission is unfortunate because those instruments are the best and most well-known demonstration of how self-report, paper-and-pencil tests can be used in the laboratory as well as in the clinic, with individuals as well as couples, to validate a particular model. Furthermore, one dimension from one model does not make a theory. As relevant as a dimension of separateness–connectedness may be, it takes more than one dimension to make a theory.

In addition, Bagarozzi's (chapter 7) introductory statement is worth repeating. It represents well the credo to which most couple and family evaluators, including this writer, should subscribe (L'Abate, 1994a, 2005a, b). This credo supports the previous generalization about the inadequacy or absence of theoretical backgrounds in many assessment tools for couples and families:

... the systematic assessment of marital and family systems was the sine qua non condition for effective and accountable clinical practice. This premise remains valid today. Ideally, any test, instrument, or procedure selected for pretreatment assessment and posttreatment outcome evaluation should operationalize one or more key concepts or constructs derived from an internally consistent and logically coherent theory of marital/family functioning, conflict/problem development, and conflict/problem resolution. Any intervention procedure employed by the therapist to help a couple or family resolve conflicts and/or solve the presenting problem should follow logically from the theory's basic tenets concerning problem development and problem resolution. How a therapist goes about implementing theoretically derived treatments is a matter of personal style. This is the artistry of therapy (Bagarozzi and Sperry, chap. 7, this text).

In addition, Bagarozzi suggested that a variety of issues need consideration in scale/instrument construction and development. It is worth repeating them here to stress their importance:

- extent to which theory was used as a conceptual guide
- theoretical relevance and clinical utility of measured dimensions
- adequacy of sampling procedures
- comprehensiveness of domains sampled
- quality and appropriateness of methodology and statistical procedures used

From this credo and previous considerations, it is possible to include at least three criteria for the relationship between an evaluative approach and a theory (Bartholomew & Perlman, 1994):

- *Theory independent*—conceptually similar but empirically and practically separate concepts or constructs underlie the construction of an evaluative instrument, for instance, measures of couple satisfaction derived from different theoretical or empirical grounds.
- *Theory related*—links between the construction of an instrument and a theory bear some undefined but still possibly empirical or conceptual connections with a theory or model.
- *Theory derived*—construction of an instrument or approach is based completely on a theory or on a model of a theory, as in the case of attachment-derived measures.

Given these three criteria of connections between theory and a particular evaluative approach, whatever its structure, one needs to evaluate all the approaches presented in this book accordingly. Whoever constructs, selects, or supports a given evaluative approach will need to show whether it meets the criteria set by Bagarozzi and where it fits into the three preceding criteria. If these criteria are valid, then apparently, only the instruments mentioned by Hampson and Beavers in chapter 5 meet the criterion of being model derived.

The instruments reviewed in chapter 4 are all extremely well validated, but individually oriented and, in spite of what the authors claim, of limited relevance to the evaluation of couples/families. Why should one select them when much more relevant instruments are available?

Furthermore, which theory could one select—systems, social learning, circumplex, or psychoanalytic ones? What is the status of these theories from an empirical viewpoint? Social learning, although well validated, is somewhat limited in its relationship to couples/families, as is its close cognitive–behavioral school. Systems theory is too encompassing in its perspective and impossible to evaluate because of its lack of specificity. Which approach can claim to derive directly from systems theory and can this claim be backed up by empirical evidence? Which among the plethora of approaches in this book can claim and support with empirical evidence a direct link with systems theory? A theory that claims to explain everything (verbally) ends up explaining nothing (empirically). Systems theory is a metatheory—but not a theory because it has not produced testable models, especially when many of its supporters deny the importance of empirical evidence to theory and practice. The circumplex is very appealing, especially in interpersonal implications, and certainly more relevant to couple/family evaluation than the individually oriented tests reviewed in chapter 4. Psychoanalysis has failed to produce any directly related evaluative instrument, as most chapters in this book attest. Where does this state of affairs leave us?

What are the implications of this characteristic, if warranted or valid? No matter how many clinical studies or applications these approaches are subjected to, they cannot be linked to theoretical statements or models, except on an ad hoc or a post hoc basis. This commentator would argue that lack of such links is producing and will continue to produce approaches that may well be empirically and clinically sound and useful. However, their inadequate links with theory and their bewildering number without background theory make one wonder whether their empirical bases are disconnected from each other. If the theory or model underlying an approach is weak or nonexistent, then the approach has been constructed on an ad hoc basis, adequate and even useful for the short haul, but eventually not contributing to theory or to practice.

If valid, this state of affairs replicates what is going on in the field of individual as well as multirelational psychotherapy: the demand for many empirically based treatments without sound connections to theory (Little, Santisteban, Levant, & Bray, 2002). All that the skeptical reader must do to verify this conclusion is to check on the many publications in this area. No relationships to theory are made.

How is one to choose among the approaches so well documented in this book? What are the criteria whereby one approach is selected over the others? One would submit that the criteria, in addition to psychometric robustness and soundness, would be on the basis of theory derivation, easy of administration and scoring, and relevance to couples and families.

INADEQUATE LINKS BETWEEN EVALUATION AND INTERVENTION

The second characteristic is even more crucial to clinical and preventive applications of these approaches. No matter how much their presenters and supporters tried, none of these evaluative approaches leads *directly* and concretely to verified or verifiable links with matching interventions. It may have been conjecturally, but no single approach in this book can claim such a direct, one-to-one link. There is no connection between the results of an assessment and the kind of intervention used. As Bagarozzi concluded, the ideal criterion of this connection is not found in most evaluative approaches, whether for individuals, couples, or families. What are the implications of this characteristic, if warranted and valid?

Could it be that the limited use of evaluative instruments not only among most couple/family therapists but also among individually oriented therapists is due to this inadequacy? This writer has argued repeatedly (L'Abate, 1999c, 2001a, 2002; L'Abate & De Giacomo, 2003) that such a connection cannot be made easily by therapists on Main Street as long as talk is the sole medium of communication and healing.

Consequently, the major implication of the foregoing characteristic lies in the very medium used in interventions: talk. As long as talk is the sole medium of intervention, it will be practically impossible to link evaluation with treatment. This may be regarded as another rash judgment on the part of this writer. However, he has argued (L'Abate, 1999c), and so far no one has disagreed with him, that talk is a questionable medium of intervention. It can be distorted, forgotten, or misused; it is uncontrollable and difficult to evaluate. Its study is limited to a handful of dedicated researchers who qualify for grants from funding institutions. Certainly, this level of analysis is beyond the competence and interests of therapists and evaluators on Main Street (as well as this commentator).

POSSIBLE SOLUTIONS FOR THE FOREGOING CHARACTERISTICS

How is one going to resolve these two major characteristics and clear shortcomings among the contributions of this book? The answer to this question is: slowly and carefully.

Connections Between Theory and Test Instruments

Throughout his career this writer has attempted to construct a developmentally relational and contextual theory of personality socialization in intimate relationships, the family, and other settings, with clear connections to preventive and clinical applications (L'Abate, 1976, 1986, 1990, 1994, 1997, 2001, 2002, 2003a, 2004b; L'Abate & De Giacomo, 2003). In constructing this theory, the author has coupled it continuously with evaluation of its instruments and approaches in the laboratory as well as in primary, secondary, and tertiary prevention (L'Abate, 2003a; Stevens & L'Abate, 1989). He was especially mindful of the relationship between theory building and test construction to evaluate models composing the theory. Evaluation, therefore, went *pari passu* with theory building.

In addition to self-report, paper-and-pencil questionnaires, and rating sheets, the models of this theory can be evaluated through 100% replicable enrichment programs in primary prevention (L'Abate & Weinstein, 1987; L'Abate & Young, 1987); self-help workbooks in secondary prevention (L'Abate, 1986, 1990, 1992, 1996, 2001, 2002, 2004a, 2004b; L'Abate & De Giacomo, 2003); and therapeutic tasks in tertiary prevention (L'Abate, 1999b, c, 2000). The reason for this replicability is simple: all evaluative instruments, all enrichment programs, all workbooks, and all therapeutic tasks in psychotherapy are written; therefore, they are reproducible by anyone who can read and write (Table 11.1).

The theory is composed of 16 models (Table 11.1) that derive from three metatheoretical assumptions, plus three assumptions specific to the theory, and nine models related to the theory proper. Very briefly, metatheoretical assumptions relate to past knowledge that cannot be ignored in theory construction and that belongs to a variety of theories, not just this one.

The first metatheoretical assumption relates to how relationships are viewed horizontally in their width, so to speak, according to an information processing, circular model composed of five resources necessary for living and relating: emotionality, rationality, activity, awareness, and context (ERAAwC). A self-report, paper-and-pencil test composed of 10 items for each resource, this model has been evaluated with the Relational Answers Questionnaire (RAQ). A more detailed background and statistical information about the validity of the RAQ is found in L' Abate and Cusinato (2003) and in Cusinato, Corsi, Maino, Franzaso, and L'Abate (2003).

The second metatheoretical assumption relates to how relationships are viewed in depth rather than in width. This model is composed of two major levels—descriptive and explanatory. The descriptive level is subdivided into presentational and phenotypical sublevels. The explanatory level is subdivided into genotypical and historical developmental levels. Even though some levels have been evaluated by others, they have not yet been evaluated by this writer or his collaborators.

TABLE 11.1 Summary of Strategies to Evaluate a Theory of Personality
Socialization in Intimate Relationships and Other Settings

Models	Tests	Enrichment	Workbooks	Tasks
Meta-theoretical Assumptions				
Horizontality				
ERAAWC[1]	RAQ*	Negotiation Potential	Negotiation	
Verticality				
Levels of Observation/ Interpretation2	To be evaluated			
Settings[3]	Time estimates			
Theoretical Assumptions				
Space:				
Ability to Love[4]	WATMTIAW?**			
Time				
Ability to Negotiate[5,6,7]	WATMTIAW?**	Negotiation Potential	Negotiation	
Modalities[8]			Assignment in Negotiation	
Theoretical Models				
Likeness: Model[9]	Likeness Scale Likeness Grid WATMTIAW?**		Who Am I?	
Styles in Relationships[10]	PIRS***	Negotiation Potential	Negotiation Assignment	f2f Interviews
Selfhood:[11]	SOPC+ PIRS*** DRT++		Self-Other Co-dependency	Drawing Lines
Priorities[12]	Grid, Inventory	Negotiation Potential	Negotiation Assignment	
Negotiation[13]		Helpfulness	Negotiation	
Intimacy[14]	SOHS+++	Intimacy		Sharing of Hurts, 3HC
Drama Triangle[15]			Depression Assignment	
Distance Regulation[16]			Depression Assignment	

TABLE 11.1 (Continued) Summary of Strategies to Evaluate a Theory of Personality Socialization in Intimate Relationships and Other Settings

Models	Tests	Enrichment	Workbooks	Tasks
Classification of Relationships[17]	Partially Evaluated			
Integration of Models[18]	Partially Evaluated			

Note: Superscript numbers represent model numbers.
Source: From L'Abate & De Giacomo, 2003. Reprinted with permission.

*Relational Answers Questionnaire (Cusinato, Corsi, Maino, Franzoso, & L'Abate, 2003).
** What Applies To Me that I Agree With? (L'Abate & De Giacomo, 2003).
***Self-Other Profile Chart (L'Abate, 1992, 1994, 2001, 2002, L'Abate & De Giacomo, 2003).
+Problems in Relationships Scale (L'Abate, 1992, 1996).
++Dyadic Relationships Test (Cusinato & L'Abate, 2003a, 2003b).
+++Sharing of Hurts Scale (Stevens & L'Abate, 1989).

The third metatheoretical assumption relates to how relationships occur in settings: home, school/work, leisure and surplus time activities. The latter are divided into transit (cars, planes, etc.) and transitory settings (barbershop, beauty saloon, grocery stores, etc.) necessary to survival and enjoyment. Objectively, these settings can be evaluated by the amount of time spent in each. Subjectively, the meaning of these settings can be evaluated with the semantic differential.

The three assumptions of the theory deal with

- ability to love, according to a dimension of distance (approach–avoidance)
- ability to negotiate according to a dimension of control (discharge–delay)
- modalities of exchange according to
  - presence (the ability to be emotionally available to self and intimate with others in committed, prolonged, and close relationships)
  - performance in services and information
  - production of money and goods

The models deriving from these assumptions as well as other models of the theory can be evaluated with the "what applies to me that I agree with?" instrument (L'Abate & De Giacomo, 2003). This is a 200-item questionnaire that has not been evaluated yet in its psychometric properties.

The remaining nine models have been evaluated or are in the process of being evaluated through additional instruments, most of which have exhibited satisfactory psychometric properties. The likeness continuum is a dialectical model consisting of six ranges that cover *symbiosis* through sameness, similarity, differentness, oppositeness, and *alienation*. This model has been evaluated through the Likeness Scale, the Likeness Grid (L'Abate,

1994a), and an instrument developed by Cusinato and his students (L'Abate & De Giacomo, 2003). It can be evaluated also through the "what applies to me that I agree with?" instrument. The styles in the relationships model, Abusive–Apathetic, Reactive–Repetitive, and Creative–Conductive, derive from the likeness continuum. Symbiosis is dialectically paired with alienation, sameness is paired with oppositeness, and similarity is paired with differentness. These styles are evaluated with the Problem in Relationships Scale (PIRS; L'Abate, 1992a; McMahan & L'Abate, 2001a), which will be described in greater detail in the next section.

The major model of the theory, self-hood (about how a sense of importance attributes to self and to intimate others), has been subjected to evaluation through a variety of different test instruments:

- Self–Other Profile Chart (SOPC; L'Abate, 1992a, 1994a, 1997, 2001, 2002, 2004a; L'Abate & De Giacomo, 2003)
- Dyadic Relations Test (DRT; Cusinato & L'Abate, 2003a, b)
- PIRS

The priorities model has been subjected to evaluation through the Priorities Grid and the Priorities Inventory (L'Abate, 1994a). The intimacy model—sharing of hurts and fears of being hurt—has been evaluated with the Sharing of Hurts Scale (Stevens & L'Abate, 1989). None of the remaining models, negotiation, the drama triangle, and distance regulation, have been evaluated through paper-and-pencil, self-report instruments. However, their clinical usefulness has only been evaluated anecdotally or through written enrichment programs, homework assignments, or therapeutic tasks.

Connections Between Test Instruments and Interventions

Because no concrete and clear connection can be made between evaluation and intervention as long as talk is the sole medium of intervention, this medium will need to be changed to writing, which is not the only change that needs to occur. In addition, couple/family therapists of the future will need to give up the expensive face-to-face personal contact in favor of more effective and perhaps even more effective distance approaches: telephones, computers, and the Internet (L'Abate & De Giacomo, 2003).

Writing is classified according to goals, structure, specificity, and structure; the latter can be (a) open ended (diaries, journals); (b) focused (autobiography, traumas); (c) guided (written questions answered in writing); and (d) extremely structured (programmed, as in workbooks). With this wide repertoire of selections available, completely new preventive and therapeutic possibilities are available to couple/family therapists as well as the individuals, couples, and families whom they try to help. Of special interest to this writer has been programmed writing that, in its systematic applications, is synonymous with self-help workbooks (L'Abate, 1996, 1990, 1992a, 2001a, 2002, 2004, 2005a; L'Abate & De Giacomo, 2003).

The number of such workbooks available on the marked has increased steadily in the last decade and there is no sign that such trend will abate (L'Abate, 2004, 2004b). They are cost effective (clearly 10% of what a face-to-face talk session will cost), versatile (for use as adjuncts or as sole interventions in primary, secondary, and tertiary prevention face to face or at a distance), and are mass-produced, making them available to wider populations than talk therapies are (L'Abate, 1999c, 2000, 2001a, 2001b). The first meta-analysis of workbooks found a medium estimated effect size of .44 (Smyth & L'Abate, 2001). Additional effect size analyses were conducted by L'Abate (2004b) on 10 studies conducted in his former Family Study Center approximately 25 years ago.

Workbooks can be classified according to:

- composition of respondents—individuals, children, adolescents, adults, couples, and families
- theoretical orientation—theory derived (behavioral, cognitive, humanistic, etc.) versus theory related versus theory independent (clinical practice, research, pop literature, etc.)
- format—fixed or nomothetic versus flexible and idiographic
- derivation—from referral question and/or from single test score or multidimensional test profile
- style—straightforward linear versus paradoxical, circular
- level and type of functionality–dysfunctionality
- specific content—addictions, affective disorders, couples, families, intimacy, and so forth

In view of their connections between evaluation and interventions, workbooks developed on the single test scores, like the Beck Depression Inventory, among many others, as well as multiple dimension scores like the MMPI-2, among many others, are worth stressing. Given an array of items from a test or from a factor analysis, it is a simple step to convert them into a workbook by asking respondents to define each item and to give two examples to describe it. Once this first task is completed, respondents are asked to rank order them according to how these items apply to them. This rank order determines how subsequent assignments will be administered. The item ranked first becomes the first assignment, the second item, the next assignment, until all items considered relevant by the respondent are completed. This format allows one to administer nomothetically the same number of assignments in case of research. However, because of the individualized nature of rank orders, these assignments are idiographic.

An example of a theory-independent, but prevention-related, prescriptive test is found in the Family Profile Form (Kochalka & L'Abate, 1997). This test is a specific instance of how an evaluative instrument can be linked with specific enrichment exercises. Another example of a theory-related, prescriptive test is the RAQ, which is coupled with a negotiation workbook (Table 11.1). Other examples of theory-derived workbooks are those based on the SOPC; one based on the sharing of hurts, Intimacy Scale, and so forth.

Thus, through the use of prescriptive tests such as those described here and specifically matching workbooks, the considerable gap that has existed between evaluation and treatment can be bridged. This gap will continue to exist as long as only talk is used as the sole medium of intervention.

Solutions and Domains

The solutions propounded here contain four major domains:

- *Media of intervention*—talking, writing, and nonverbal. Writing and nonverbal tasks, such as sharing hurts and hugging, holding, huddling, and cuddling (3HC; L'Abate, 2001b; L'Abate & De Giacomo, 2003) (Table 11.1) have major relevance to the theory and to ties between evaluation and interventions.
- *Function of evaluative instruments*—instruments (used here in a generic sense to include a wide variety of approaches) that are not only diagnostic and predictive, as in the past and most, if not all, approaches presented in this book, but also and especially prescriptive (L'Abate, 1990). Illustrations have been given of a new kind of prescriptive test, matching interventions with evaluation, provided interventions take place in writing, and especially through workbooks.
- *Theoretical derivation*—some instruments are theory independent but often derived from clinical practice or lore instead. Some are theory related, in the sense that some tenuous connections between the theory and its evaluative approach exist. Finally, some are theory- or model derived, as earlier examples showed, as well as in questionnaires developed from attachment theory (Bartholomew & Perlman, 1994).
- *Levels of prevention*—three levels necessary to view interventions according to a continuum rather than on an either–or view (L'Abate, 1990). Primary prevention includes universal approaches that deal with functional or semifunctional couples/families. Secondary approaches deal with targeted or at-risk populations such as adult children of alcoholics. Self-help workbooks can make their mark here because they can be administered. Tertiary prevention, such as psychotherapy, is an expensive enterprise that can be

reduced in costs if therapists relied more on written homework assignments such as workbooks.

CHAPTER AUTHORS' RESPONSES TO L'ABATE

Maureen Duffy and Ronald J. Chenail

L'Abate's critique of evaluation and, for that matter, the state of affairs in psychotherapy, because of weakness or absence of a connection to theory raises some important points and obscures others. His concern about the need for critical reflection on our practices of evaluation and intervention are concerns that we share and take seriously. The fairly recent and tragic case of the girl in Colorado who suffocated and died during a rebirthing/rebonding process purportedly based on attachment theory reminds us how real our theories and practices are. Theory development and attention to the relationship between theory and practice is not simply an academic pursuit; it is an ethical one, and we share L'Abate's position that we need to pay attention to theory and connect our practices of evaluation and therapy to it.

What is obscured is that L'Abate is situating his comments within the positivist paradigm, which is just as much a metatheory as the systems theory he critiques. Rigorous and systematic practices of evaluation (or counterevaluation) and therapy conducted within other paradigms (e.g., social constructionist) are validated qualitatively in ways congruent with the paradigm. Mixing paradigms is more problematic for us than mixing theories within a paradigm. The paradigm issue is not trivial because the views of reality and knowledge contained within it are fundamentally different.

We would argue with L'Abate that "systems theory has not produced testable models" and point again (see chapter 3) to the outstanding work of the research teams from the University of Miami (Liddle & Dakoff, 1995; Szapocznik & Coatsworth, 1999) who have been testing systemic approaches over long periods of time with the adolescent substance-abusing population and confirming meaningful positive treatment outcomes. Additionally, evidenced-based research on systemic family therapy is able to be translated into manualized formats similar to manualized medical protocols. (Pote, Stratton, Cottrell, Shapiro, & Boston, 2003)

Rather than fretting about how to select a particular theory to which to adhere (a difficult task in family therapy), looking at what is common across multiple models of therapy seems more promising. The social sciences suffer this lack of mid-range theory and practitioners and clients suffer as a result. The factors for which specific theories account may not in the end be curative. What the client brings to the table in terms of resources, the therapeutic relationship, and hope may have more to do with cure than practices derived from specific models (Hubble, Duncan, & Miller, 1999).

Talk is messy. Writing is no less messy and we fail to see how changing from the medium of talk to writing will solve the problem of a poor connection between evaluation and intervention. The anthropologist Alton Becker (1991) notes that writing is at once overstated and understated—it says too much and leaves too much out. Writing shares many of the same problems of signification as does talk. Qualitative approaches to assessment in family therapy avoid making a problem of any mode of communication (oral, written, gesticular, graphic, artistic, or performative) by embracing all modes as significations of the meanings of human experiences and as open to assessment from the expert and the collaborative standpoints.

L'Abate's Reply

I am delighted to disagree strongly with Duffy and Chenail. They are doing their best to distract me and the readers with the issues I have raised in my final chapter. Their dialectical anti-empirical position is contradicted by the construction of an objective test. This construction implies a logical positivism position—that is, performing operations (i.e., constructing and validating a paper-and-pencil test) not found in dialectical approaches. If they like those approaches, why not simply use the interview method with all its explicit dangers of subjective interpretation, and so forth? By producing and validating an instrument, they have embraced a logical positivistic position.

Another distracting point that avoids the basic issue about writing is to equate it with talk in its qualities, shortcomings, and defects. The bottom line of writing is reproducibility and replicability—qualities that are expensive in reproducing talk, audio-, or video tapes. Talk is subject to distortions, generalizations, or forgetting, which do not occur when writing is used as a medium of communication. If talk is so great, why did they construct a test based on writing? Progress in science, industry, law, government, medicine, and psychology is made on the basis of writing, not talk.

I wish Duffy and Chanail had stayed with the issues rather than going outside them. Nonetheless, I appreciate their looking at the larger picture and raising issues that, although tangential to my points, remain relevant to overall evaluation of couples as well as all our respondents—individuals and families.

Sylvia Fernandez and Sloane Veshinski

The identified need for tools to measure and assess, in a structured way, constructs deemed important in understanding the family- and system-specific issues and values led to the development of an array of instruments. The choice of instruments discussed in the chapter dealing with custody and divorce assessment is based on issues and theories regarding healthy and appropriate family functioning, such as the family context, family relationships, and family culture. The selected instruments have been or are in the process of being field tested and their psychometric properties being determined and/or reported (Nurse, 1999).

L'Abate's critique of inadequate links with theory or theoretical models with the selected instruments may not be disputed by many of the instrument developers. However, they may disagree with him regarding the appropriateness of the constructs measured and the functionality of the outcomes for determining interventions and making custody and visitation recommendations. L'Abate further observes inadequate links with results of assessment to the type of intervention. Anecdotal evidence suggests effectiveness of interventions (Fischer & Corcoran, 1994).

Assessment instruments are a diagnostic or screening tool that may substantiate already available data or provide a beginning point for treatment and interventions. The training and experience of the clinician is the moderating variable in how the assessment data are used in determining the appropriate treatment and intervention. The choice of instruments and interventions is a reflection of the clinician's knowledge, skills, and counseling/therapy orientation.

L'Abate's challenges regarding the adequacy of the links of the identified instruments to theory or theoretical models and that of the results of assessment to the type of intervention are on target and well taken. With the exception of three, the selected instruments had been developed since 1990 and still have a long way to go to be satisfactorily validated; as L'Abate acknowledged, this is a long and tedious process. Reviewers of the tests, discussed in chapter 9, cited in the Mental Measurements Yearbook (Plake, 2003) voiced similar concerns about the theoretical grounding and empirical reliability and validity of the tests and instruments. Thus, caution when using these tests and instruments is recommended.

L'Abate challenges the sole use of talk as a means of assessments and suggests that relying on programmed writing may be the direction to go. Solely relying on talk or writing potentially takes away the opportunity to seek clarification, to use multiple avenues for gathering information, and, possibly, to miss multicultural influences. L'Abate offers his model, which is currently in development and at a point at which he charges other test developers are: it is still empirically unsubstantiated. Qualitative and quantitative data provide the best range of data for making appropriate recommendations and interventions.

The assessment instruments discussed in chapter 9 are not recommended for use singly, but rather in combination to provide the best range of data to facilitate making a decision or recommendations, as illustrated in the case example. Using only one approach would be flawed and biased toward clinicians' knowledge, skills, and theoretical orientation. Interventions that depend solely on talk presuppose the verbal ability of the client and the cognitive level of functioning; those that depend solely on writing presuppose the client's literacy, that is, his ability to read, comprehend, and write.

The task of the authors of chapter 9 was to identify that which is currently available to meet the needs for child custody and divorce assessment strategies and inventories to assist clinicians in making appropriate recommendations. The authors' task was neither to critique the reported reliability and validity nor to deconstruct the selected instruments.

L'Abate's Reply

I agree with almost everything Fernandez and Vershinski say; however, I want to add a couple of references not contained in my original response, but relevant to the points made there. They may illustrate and reinforce my position: linking evaluation with workbooks, workbooks with face-to-face (f2f) or distance interventions, and using workbooks in education and prevention, rather than only in therapy. Through workbooks, I am trying to bridge the considerable gaps between evaluation and therapy, prevention and therapy, and theory with practice. In the work that I have already cited in this chapter (L'Abate, 2004b, 2005), I make workbooks instruments of model and theory testing, adding another dimension to their versatility.

Dennis Bagarozzi

Dr. L'Abate's remarks about chapter 7 deserve attention because they highlight important issues concerning marital/family assessment, that is, "insider–outsider" perspectives and the role of expertise in assessment. Clearly, Bartholomew and his colleagues have used the Relationship Questionnaire in their research concerning attachment styles for over a decade. This short, forced-choice, paper-and-pencil instrument offers a valuable insider's perspective. The AAI, on the other hand, offers an outsider's/expert's vantage point. In the best of all possible worlds, both perspectives would be considered. Dr. L'Abate's preference for paper-and-pencil self-report measures that do not rely upon face-to-face observations and therapist–patient interactions are consistent with his emphasis upon writing and distance approaches to intervention.

As a therapist, I am convinced that self-report measures, regardless of how they are obtained, only give a unidimensional insider's perspective that is subject to experimenter effects. Nothing can replace the therapist's critically trained eye as he observes the interactive dynamics of couples and family systems. I have reservations about any approach to behavior change that relies solely upon self-report. Knowing Dr. L'Abate, I am sure he does not intend to "throw the baby out with the bath water." I invite his observations about my comments.

L'Abate's Reply

I strongly, but amicably, disagree with Dennis on some of his responses to this chapter. One can get into respondents' (i.e., couples') perspectives as much as by what they write as what they talk. In 20 years of using writing in its various structures with couples and families, I received information through writing I would have never received through talk. Talk is deceptive (and so writing can be), uncontrollable, and subject to distortions, generalizations, and forgetting that explain why writing has been used for centuries as the basis for progress. Skyscrapers are built on talk, not on blueprints, and I view this position that observers' omnipotent but subjective observations are paramount with a jaundiced eye.

Recently, our (L'Abate, L'Abate, & Maino, 2005) review of clinical records accumulated over 25 years of part-time private practice failed to confirm my biases about the cost effectiveness of workbooks. During the first 10 years of our practice, individual, couples, and families were seen without homework assignments (i.e., workbooks). During the next 15-year phase of our practice, treatment was in some ways made contingent on respondents' completing written homework assignments. In all that I have written about workbooks, I claimed their cost effectiveness as their major advantage, but I was wrong. We found convincingly and statistically significantly that all our respondents (individuals, couples, and families) had a much greater number of f2f sessions than respondents without homework—so much for clinical judgment or, at least, my clinical judgment. Therapists have nothing to fear from administering written homework assignments!

Furthermore, keep in mind that thousands of relationships, many of them intimate, are established online. Over the last few years, I have established collaborative relationships with colleagues around the world. Thus, it is beneficial to use the power of the Internet to reach and help the many people (i.e., couples) who need help and not necessarily talk.

Lynelle C. Yingling

In his commentary, Dr. L'Abate makes some helpful comments. I agree that, in order to be valid, family assessment must have a connection with family systems theory and must have a clinical purpose based on family therapy technique models. Unfortunately, L'Abate overlooks the contributions made by Dr. Lyman Wynne in the GARF DSM-IV taskforce to bring together primary family assessment leaders to reach consensus on the overlapping variables from clinical and theoretical orientations. If there is any hope for family assessment to be accepted as helpful and necessary by clinicians and consumers (including managed care companies), we should probably continue on that path of consensus building. If we could agree on the basics, we could stylistically expand the details to fit personalities of various clinicians and to be implemented through the various media tailored to fit the functioning level of the family. Written instruments are helpful in reframing the attention of the client family members. However, I have few clients in my practice who can make change based on written workbook materials alone; talk is still essential in order to calm reactivity and enable a client to think clearly and experience change through clinical coaching. Perhaps some day our society will see the benefit of preventive enrichment activities, but that is not the world I see in my office today.

As we try to make progress in family assessment, I am reminded of a metaphor shared by a rancher husband of an attendee at a Groves Conference many years ago. At the banquet, I asked what he thought of the conference. He replied that it reminded him of an island where horses existed. Over time the horses became so inbred that they finally self-destructed. Are we on an island?

L'Abate's Reply

Of course I have heard about Wynne's taskforce. However, instead of talk, as most task forces do, I prefer to offer writings that deal with the issue (L'Abate, 2005, submitted for publication) or present relational models incorporating DSM-IV into a theory-derived, research-based framework. This framework allows integration of various psychiatric syndromes into one coherent, relational theory (L'Abate, 2005, submitted for publication; L'Abate, Lambert, & Schenk, (2001). In this theory, psychiatric categories are continuous and contiguous with each other, allowing a traditional categorical psychiatric list of syndromes to be integrated into a coherent whole. Perhaps, Dr. Yingling may want to read about what has been done in this area, rather than wait for future words from my friend from Rochester and his taskforce.

I fail to see how the rancher's metaphor applies to what I have written. Perhaps I do not share the same sense of humor as the rancher or Dr. Yingling. As a past presenter to the Groves Conference, I found it to be a very enlightened group of sociologists with a sprinkling of psychologists. Perhaps Dr. Yingling may explain how that metaphor applies to what I have written? Finally, I do not share Dr. Yingling's pessimism about the future of prevention.

Friedrich, Olafson, and Connelly

Luciano L'Abate wrote his comments before reading our completed chapter 10 and the full reference list, so he may wish to amend them after he has had a chance to review the final draft. What follow are our interim responses to his preliminary responses.

L'Abate notes that most of the book's chapters, ours included, were disconnected from theory. Evaluation, assessment, and treatment of childhood trauma and abuse are new, disparate, and rapidly changing fields. It would be premature to impose a unifying theory upon them. Indeed, research findings from this dynamic area of inquiry have challenged and even undermined existing theoretical models, especially those in family systems theory, but also psychoanalytic theory and that school of biological psychiatry that seeks the genetic basis for mental disorders. The disconnection from theory has been one of the strengths of this new area of inquiry; it can allow researchers to see afresh what is in front of them, rather than shoehorning their data into rigid schemata. To give just one example: children who have been chronically abused and traumatized do not present with symptomatologies similar to the adult combat veterans upon whom the classical PTSD diagnosis was formulated; however, theory-bound psychometricians continue to develop instruments to assess children using these adult male criteria. Only in 2003 did a major committee in the federally funded Network of Child Traumatic Stress centers look afresh at the Complex Posttraumatic Stress Disorder diagnosis in severely, chronically abused children in order to reconstitute a theoretical base upon which more adequate instruments could be developed. This will be done by gathering data without preconceptions from the DSM IV—Aristotle trumps Plato.

L'Abate's second criticism, that inadequate links exist between evaluation and intervention, criticizes chapter writers for what they did not set out to achieve. This is not a book about treatment. Many psychological assessments, especially when family violence, childhood trauma, and child abuse are at issue, are conducted for forensic, not treatment, purposes. Child trauma treatment is a new and very promising field, and certain instruments in chapter 10, such as the DES, the CBCL, and the TSCC, can be administered at 3-month intervals to assess treatment process. A number of studies not included in our reference list (because that was not our mandate) have used these instruments to assess treatment process. Readers interested in a survey of instruments and available child trauma treatments are referred to Saunders, Berliner, and Hanson, 2002.

L'Abate's Reply

I really do not have any reply to these authors. I think they have done a good defense job, even though the excuse of not writing for a treatment book is somewhat lame. Indeed, it proves the point that this book is concerned with evaluation but leaves the whole issue of relationships between evaluation and treatment completely unresolved. It also demonstrates my point that evaluation and treatment continue to be disconnected from each other. As long as this practice continues, the issue of relating treatment to evaluation will remain a murky one.

If evaluation is not linked to treatment, what is the good of evaluation? Decisions are made on the basis of evaluation about treatment and what kind of treatment. We can no longer think of "just psychotherapy" or, with children, "just play therapy," or, more to the point, "just couple therapy." The days of one treatment fits all are gone. Have we reached the stage that we wanted years ago — "What kind of treatment for what couple at what cost and by whom?" Just look up the recent publication of the *Handbook of Family Therapy* edited by Sexton, Weeks, and Robbins (L' Abate, 2003b) and see how many treatments are available. Yet, there is no way to define and know which treatment is good for which couple.

Why? Clinicians and couple therapists, as in the case of individual and family therapists, simply do not use objective tests. They are not required by third parties or by national professional organizations, nor is the use of objective tests included in many codes of ethics. Then why evaluate? If treatment is not differentiated to the point of "different strokes for different folks," the enterprise of evaluation is like a leaf in the wind—it goes nowhere until it falls to the ground. The only reason I see for evaluation is now taking place in what is called the *stepped-up care* movement. (Years ago, in 1990, I called this *increasing hurdles*.) Borrowing from the medical model (without any shame or doubt), one starts with the cheapest, most ubiquitous, and most expedient instrument—for example, the thermometer. Given the results, one institutes the cheapest treatment ("Take two aspirins and call me in the morning"). If that does not work, "Visit me" is the response. Each step is more expensive then the preceding one (e.g., more tests). Why all these tests? A diagnosis about the nature (type, severity, location, etc.) of the complaint needs to be reached. Why? A specific treatment matches the nature of the "disease." This may be a hit-or-miss proposition, as in the prescription of many antidepressant or antipsychotic medications, but eventually a "goodness of fit" is found. Is this process perfect? Of course not. However, evaluation is taking place to determine what specific treatment to apply.

I have argued, and will continue to argue, that as long as treatment is taking place verbally, it will be nearly impossible to obtain the match necessary to link treatment with evaluation. That means that our treatments will not be replicable from one therapist to another or from one clinic to another and thus no progression because the final arbiter of what treatment to apply is going to be the word of the therapist. I have shown, as mentioned in my reply to Dennis, how incorrect clinical judgment can be, especially my own. As long as we rely on words to treat people, no progress will take place (L' Abate, 2003a). To those who ask me to define progress, I answer, "When we do the most good for the most people with the least amount of expense." Psychotherapy with couples, individuals, and families is and will continue to be a small drop of water in a large bucket. We need to come up with new ways to help all the hurting, stressed, and distressed couples, individuals, and families who are not reached, and do not want to be reached, by talk. Writing and distance writing may be one answer; TV will be another.

Robert Hampson and Robert Beavers

Dr. L'Abate has made several important points regarding the relationships among family assessment, family models, and family theory. Our chapter apparently passed some degree of muster, while others did not link methods to models or theories. One possible explanation is that Dr. L'Abate's comments were based on his reactions to a first draft of each chapter; some authors were perhaps not as cued into theoretical tie-ins as they were to clinical practicality. Another may be that the connections among measurement, model, and theory were not made explicit. For example, the Self-Report Family Inventory (SFI), reported in chapter 8, is a direct offshoot of the Beavers systems model, firmly based in systems theory and clinical practice. A third explanation is the more troublesome possibility that most of these tools do not relate to theory or model.

One question raised about the observational measures in our chapter related to his observation that they may be measuring some fairly similar family behaviors. Therefore, what are the correlations among all these disparate models? A study we conducted several years ago utilized the observational and self-report measures of the McMaster, circumplex, and Beavers models, and their utility in discriminating clinic versus nonclinic families (Beavers & Hampson, 2000). The following correlations were obtained among the global observational scales across models for all 68 families in the study:

	McMaster	Circumplex	
	General functioning	Change	Cohesion
Beavers competence	+.76	+.36	+.44
McMaster general function		+.27	+.46
Circumplex change			+.15

Thus, some degree of overlap is present, particularly with the linear, directional Beavers and McMaster models. The circumplex scales are theoretically curvilinear, although the cohesion scale shares some strong linear trends.

Another issue raised had to do with how one would select one scale over the others. Discriminant function analyses with these same data classified families into clinic versus nonclinic status, in comparison with their actual status. Measures from the circumplex model (CRS, FACES) correctly classified 26 of 36 clinical families, as well as 26 of 32 nonclinic families (81%): Wilk's lambda = .725; chi-square (5) = 10.14; $p < .07$.

Measures from the McMaster model (FAD, CRS) correctly classified 29 of 36 clinic families, and 26 of 32 nonclinic families (90%): Wilk's lambda = .298; chi-square (8) = 44.85; $p < .01$. The instruments for the Beavers model (Observational Competence, SFI) correctly classified 30 of 36 clinic families, and 31 of 32 nonclinic families (91%): Wilk's lambda = .385; chi-square (7)

= 80.82; $p < .01$. Because the Beavers rating scale takes only 10 minutes, it appears to be an efficient and accurate measure. The McMaster scales were nearly as precise.

The fact that the Beavers and McMaster models derived from general systems theory *and* careful clinical observations probably increases their clinical validity. The circumplex model is firmly based on theory, but appears to have lower levels of clinical validity. This makes me think that the global assertion that an assessment model and tool must be soundly connected to theory may not be universally necessary. A nice blend of systems theory and clinical reality can do well.

The assertion that evaluation should be linked to intervention is directly on target. This was fairly explicit in our chapter for the Beavers and McMaster models. Our book, *Successful Families: Assessment and Intervention*, although not a cookbook, linked necessary tasks and stances of therapists, given the clinical typology of the family, based on the assessment. Several articles found that therapy works best when these guidelines are followed by therapists (Hampson & Beavers, 1996a, b). Epstein and his colleagues (1981) also identified family strength/weakness patterns and the recommended therapeutic interventions (problem-centered systems therapy of the family (PCSTF).

Finally, the challenge that therapy must be more than talk is also on target. Cognitive and straight talk or narrative approaches work well for certain types of families: those that respect words, negotiate fairly well, and are probably no worse off than midrange levels of competence. Families who cannot coordinate actions, distrust words, and are in chronic emotional pain that words cannot solve need something different from their therapists. These families are more disturbed, and often more centrifugal in style on the Beavers model.

Thanks to Dr. L'Abate for his insightful comments.

L'Abate's Reply

What can one say in response to compliments, except to express my admiration for these two contributors' work? If or when I grow up, I would like to be more like them!

CONCLUSION

This writer is grateful to the editor for inviting him to comment on the contributions in this book. The foregoing comments may have been harsh and iconoclastic; however, he congratulates all contributors for their work. It is sad and unfortunate that all these contributors' work is not receiving the attentions of a wider community of couple/family therapists. Unless professional associations and managed care companies require pre–post intervention evaluations unquestioningly as a standard operating procedure (as veterinarians do with pets), the field of couple/family evaluation will remain in the hands of a small section of dedicated professionals, such as those represented in this book. The majority could not care less because there are no consequences to current professional practices still based on the subjectivity of the professional, rather than on intersubjective and objective approaches above and beyond the personal opinion of the professional.

The prognosis for the field of couple/family evaluation is easy. As long as talk remains the sole medium of intervention, the status quo will prevail. By relying on writing as an additional or sole medium of intervention at a distance from respondents, drastic changes may occur, requiring changes that many couple/family therapists may be afraid to undertake—the devil we have is better than the devil we do not know.

REFERENCES

Bartholomew, K., & Perlman, D. (Eds.) (1994). *Attachment processes in adulthood.* London: Jessica Kingsley.

Beavers, W. R. & Hampson R. B. (2000). The Beavers systems model of family functioning. *Journal of Family Therapy, 22,* 128–143.

Becker, A. L. (1991). A short essay on languaging. In F. Steier (Ed.), *Research and reflexivity* (pp. 226-234). Newbury Park, CA: Sage.

Cusinato, M., & L'Abate, L. (1994). A spiral model of intimacy. In S. M. Johnson & L. Greenberg, (Eds.), *The heart of the matter: Perspectives on emotion in marital therapy,* (pp. 108–123). New York: Brunner/Mazel.

Cusinato, M., & L'Abate, L. (2003a). Evaluation of a structured psychoeducational intervention with couples: The Dyadic Relationships Test. *American Journal of Family Therapy, 31,* 79–89.

Cusinato, M., & L'Abate, L. (2003b). The Dyadic Relationships Test: Creation and validation of a model-derived, visual–verbal instrument to evaluate couple relationships (submitted for publication).

Esterling, B. A., L'Abate, L., Murray, E., & Pennebaker, J. M. (1999). Empirical foundations for writing in prevention and psychotherapy: Mental and physical outcomes. *Clinical Psychology Review, 19,* 79–96.

Fischer, J. & Corcoran, K. (1994). *Measures for clinical practice. 2nd Edition.* New York: Free Press.

Hubble, M. A., Duncan, B. L., & Miller, S. D. (1999). *The heart and soul of change: What works in therapy.* Washington, D.C.: American Psychological Association.

L'Abate, L. (1976). *Understanding and helping the individual in the family.* New York: Grune & Stratton.

L'Abate, L. (1986a). *Systematic family therapy.* New York: Brunner/Mazel.

L'Abate, L. (1986b). Prevention of marital and family problems. In B. A. Edelstein and L. Michelson. (Eds.), *Handbook of prevention,* (pp. 177–193). New York: Plenum.

L'Abate, L. (1990). *Building family competence: Primary and secondary prevention strategies.* Newbury Park, CA: Sage.

L'Abate, L. (1992a). *Programmed writing: A self-administered approach for interventions with individuals, couples and families.* Pacific Grove, CA: Brooks/Cole.

L'Abate, L. (1992b). Family psychology and family therapy: Comparisons and contrasts. *American Journal of Family Therapy, 20,* 3–12.

L'Abate, L. (1994a). *A theory of personality development.* New York: Wiley.

L'Abate, L. (1994b). *Family evaluation: A psychological interpretation.* Thousand Oaks, CA: Sage.

L'Abate, L. (1996). Workbooks for Better Living <www.mentalhealthhelp.com>

L'Abate, L. (1997). *The self in the family: A classification of personality, criminality, and psychopathology.* New York: Wiley

L'Abate, L. (1999a). Increasing intimacy in couples through distance writing and face-to-face approaches. In J. Carlson & L. Sperry (Eds.), *The intimate couple* (pp. 327–339). Bristol, PA: Brunner/Mazel.

L'Abate, L. (1999b). Structured enrichment and distance writing for couples. In R. Berger & T. Hannah, (Eds.), *Preventative approaches in couples therapy* (pp. 106–124). Philadelphia, PA: Taylor & Francis.

L'Abate, L. (1999c). Taking the bull by the horns: Beyond talk in psychological interventions. *The Family Journal: Therapy and Counseling for Couples and Families, 7,* 206–220.

L'Abate, L. (2000). Psychoeducational strategies. In J. Carlson & L. Sperry (Eds.), *Brief therapy strategies with individuals and couples* (pp. 396–346). Phoenix, AZ: Zeig/Tucker.

L'Abate, L. (Ed.) (2001a). *Distance writing and computer-assisted interventions in psychiatry and mental heath.* Westport, CT: Ablex.

L'Abate, L. (2001b). Hugging, holding, huddling, and cuddling (3HC): A task prescription in couples and family therapy. *The Journal of Clinical Activities, Assignments, and Handouts in Psychotherapy Practice, 1,* 5–18.

L'Abate, L. (2002) *Beyond psychotherapy: Programmed writing and structured computer-assisted interventions.* Westport, CT: Ablex.

L'Abate, L. (2003a). *Family psychology III: Theory building, theory testing, and psychological interventions.* Lanham, MD: University Press of America.

L'Abate, L. (2003b). Treatment through writing: A unique new direction. In T. L. Sexton, G. Weeks, & M. Robbins (Eds.), *The handbook of family therapy* (pp. 397–409). New York: Brunner–Routledge.

L'Abate, L. (2004a). *A guide to self-help workbooks for mental health clinicians and researchers.* Binghamton, NY: Haworth.

L'Abate, L. (Ed.) (2004b). *Workbooks in prevention, psychotherapy, and rehabilitation: A resource for clinicians and researchers.* Binghamton, NY: Haworth.

L'Abate, L. (2005). *Personality in intimate relationships: Socialization and psychpathology.* New York: Kluwer Academic.

L'Abate, L., & De Giacomo, P. (2003). *Intimate relationships and how to improve them: Integrating theory with preventive and psychotherapeutic interventions.* Westport, CT: Praeger.

L'Abate, L., & Kern, R. (2002). Workbooks: Tools for the expressive paradigm. In S. J. Lepore and J. M. Smyth (Eds.), *The writing cure: How expressive writing promotes health and well-being* (pp. 239–255). Washington, D.C.: American Psychological Association.

L'Abate, L., & Weinstein, S. E. (1987). *Structured enrichment programs for couples and families.* New York: Brunner/Mazel.

L'Abate, L., & Young, L. (1987) *Casebook of structured enrichment programs for couples and families.* New York: Brunner/Mazel.

L'Abate, L., De Giacomo, P., McCarty, F., De Giacomo, A., & Verrastro, G. (2000). Testing three models of intimate relationships. *Contemporary Family Therapy: An International Journal, 22,* 103–122.

L'Abate, L. (2005, submitted for publication). Summary of a relational theory for the DSM-IV.

L'Abate, L., L'Abate, B. L. & Maino, E. (2005). A review of 25 years of part time professional practice: Workbooks and length of psychotherapy. *American Journal of family therapy, 33,* 000-000.

L'Abate, L., Lambert, R. G., & Schenck, P. (2001). Testing a relational model of psychopathology with the MMPI-2. *American Journal of Family Therapy, 29,* 221–238.

Liddle, H. A., & Dakoff, G. A. (1995). Family-based treatment for adolescent drug use: State of the science. In E. Rahdert & D. Czechowicz (Eds.), *Adolescent drug abuse: Clinical assessment and therapeutic interventions* (pp. 218–254). National Institute on Drug Abuse Research monograph 156. NIH Pub. No. 95-3908. Rockville, MD: National Institute on Drug Abuse.

Little, H. A., Santisteban, D. A., Levant, R. F., & Bray, J. H. (Eds.) (2002). *Family psychology: Science-based interventions.* Washington, D.C.: American Psychological Association.

McMahan, O., & L'Abate, L. (2001). Programmed distance writing with seminarian couples. In L. L'Abate (Ed.), *Distance writing and computer-assisted interventions in psychiatry and mental heath* (pp. 137–156). Westport, CT: Ablex.

Nurse, A. R. (1999). *Family assessment.* New York: Wiley.

Plake, B. (Ed.). (2003). *Mental measurements yearbook. 15th edition.* New York: Buros Institute.

Pote, H., Stratton, P., Cottrell, D., Shapiro, D., & Boston, P. (2003). Systemic family therapy can be manualized: Research process and findings. *Journal of Family Therapy, 25*(3), 236–262.

Reed, R., McMahan, O., & L'Abate, L. (2001). Workbooks and psychotherapy with incarcerated felons. In L. L'Abate (Ed.), *Distance writing and computer-assisted interventions in psychiatry and mental heath* (pp. 157–167). Westport, CT: Ablex.

Saunders, B. E., Berliner, L., & Hanson, R. F. (Eds.) (2002) *Child physical and sexual abuse: Guidelines for treatment (Final Report: December 10, 2002).* Charleston, SC: Authors

Smyth, J., & L'Abate, L. (2001). A meta-analytic evaluation of workbook effectiveness in physical and mental health. In L. L'Abate (Ed.), *Distance writing and computer-assisted interventions in psychiatry and mental heath* (pp. 77–90). Westport, CT: Ablex.

Stevens, F. E., & L'Abate, L. (1989). Validity and reliability of a theory-derived measure of intimacy. *American Journal of Family Therapy, 17*, 359–368.

Szapocznik, J., & Coatsworth, J. D. (1999). An ecodevelopmental framework for organizing risk and protection for drug abuse: A developmental model of risk and protection. In M. Glantz & C. R. Hartel (Eds.), *Drug abuse: Origins and interventions* (pp. 331–366). Washington, D.C.: American Psychological Association.

INDEX

In this index, page numbers followed by the letter "t" designate tables.

V

W

Z